Industrial Districts
and economic regeneration

Industrial districts and local economic regeneration

Edited by F. Pyke and W. Sengenberger

International Institute for Labour Studies   Geneva

ISBN 92–9014–471–8

First published 1992

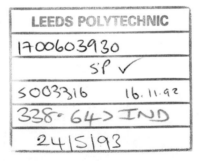

Preface

This volume contains a collection of papers that were presented at a conference organised by the International Institute for Labour Studies at the International Labour Office in Geneva in October 1990.[1] The conference, entitled "Industrial Districts and Local Economic Regeneration", was convened primarily to discuss the conclusions of a research programme carried out in the Institute on the subject of small firm industrial agglomerations or "industrial districts".

The research programme had started three years previously and focused in its first phase on the industrial district phenomenon in Italy, the country with which this model of economic organisation is most commonly associated. Research was commissioned to cover a range of historical, theoretical, empirical, political, and institutional aspects and the results were published under the title, *Industrial districts and inter-firm co-operation in Italy* [Pyke et al. (eds.), 1990].

In a second phase, it was decided to move further towards considering the more general significance of the industrial district phenomenon and the principles by which such local economies are organised. Accordingly, studies were commissioned focusing either on the relevance of industrial district principles in the economic development of a number of (mainly European) regions, or on some more specific policy issues of particular relevance to local governments, trade unions, and employers' organisations. These studies formed the basis of the presentations made at the above-mentioned conference.

This book is structured broadly in accordance with the themes of the commissioned studies. In Part I, Werner Sengenberger and Frank Pyke provide an introduction by setting out the key organisational principles of the industrial district form of development, discussing their significance in the context of industrial change occurring at a broad level and highlighting issues of particular research and policy concern.

Part II concentrates on the relevance of the principles of industrial organisation found in Italian districts to other areas of Europe. To begin with, Carlo Trigilia discusses the continuing presence of the industrial district phenomenon in Italy; then follows the presentation of three non-Italian cases: Lauren Benton considers Spain; Peer Kristensen discusses Denmark; and Hubert Schmitz looks at Germany.

---

1. Other papers presented at the Conference have been published in *Labour and Society*, Vol. 16, No. 1.

In Part III, the relevance of the organisational principles to other countries forms a sub-theme, with authors referring to experiences in regions in Canada, Cyprus and the United States of America. The main focus in this part, however, is on policy issues and the institutional mechanisms which can be implemented to help local economies regenerate. To this end, Sebastiano Brusco discusses the important policy value of real service centres; Robin Murray describes the practical attempt to introduce ideas similar to the industrial district principles in Cyprus; Paulo Brutti puts forward an Italian trade union point of view and calls for the recognition of industrial districts as a distinct form of development, requiring specific, targeted policies; Charles Sabel argues that a vital element for an effective policy initiative at the local level - "trust" - can, and should, be consciously created; and Pierre-André Julien underlines the importance of intervention by local and regional institutions for long-term promotion and co-ordination, emphasising in particular the role they can play in developing information networks.

Finally, in Part IV, Jonathan Zeitlin presents an overview and assessment of the contributions to the book, paying particular attention again to policy implications.

Frank Pyke
Werner Sengenberger

Contributors

Lauren Benton: Assistant Professor of International Studies, University of Washington, USA.

Sebastiano Brusco: Professor of Industrial Economics, University of Modena, Italy.

Paulo Brutti: General Manager, Confederazione Generale Italiana del Lavoro, Rome, Italy.

Pierre-André Julien: Directeur du Groupe de recherche en économie et gestion des PME, Université du Québec à Trois-Rivières, Quebec.

Peer Hull Kristensen: Associate Professor of Industrial Organisation, Copenhagen Business School, Denmark.

Robin Murray: Fellow of the Institute of Development Studies, University of Sussex, United Kingdom.

Frank Pyke: Research Officer, International Institute for Labour Studies, Geneva, Switzerland.

Charles Sabel: Professor of Political Science, Massachusetts Institute of Technology, Boston, USA.

Hubert Schmitz: Fellow of the Institute of Development Studies, University of Sussex, United Kingdom.

Werner Sengenberger: Head, New Industrial Organisation Programme, International Institute for Labour Studies, Geneva, Switzerland.

Carlo Trigilia: Associate Professor of Sociology, University of Palermo, Italy.

Jonathan Zeitlin: Lecturer in Modern Economic and Social History, Birkbeck College, University of London, United Kingdom.

Acknowledgements

In addition to the authors and conference participants, the editors would like to thank the following people:

Gerassimos Potamianos and John Morley of Directorate V, and Martin Harvey and Alan Mayhew of Directorate XXIII, of the European Commission in Brussels, who have actively helped to bring about a very successful collaboration between our two international agencies; as well as providing intellectual involvement, valuable financial support was given by Directorates V and XXIII towards the commissioning of papers for the conference on "Industrial Districts and Local Economic Regeneration", and towards the cost of organising the conference;

Gowrie Ponniah, Hilary Mueller, Hilary Wyatt, Hazel Cecconi, Marie-Claude Laforest-Schaer, and other staff of the Institute for organising the conference;

Hazel Cecconi for copy editing, formatting and proof reading this volume;

Christopher Woodall for translating from Italian into English the papers by Sebastiano Brusco, Carlo Trigilia and Paulo Brutti;

Ximena Subercaseaux for the design of the cover;

Michel Bagès for graphic work.

Table of contents

Part III: Policy perspectives (continued)

Part I: Introduction: Research and policy issues

1 Industrial districts and local economic regeneration: Research and policy issues

Werner Sengenberger and Frank Pyke

I. Industrial districts

The main impetus for the industrial district model has undoubtedly come out of Italy. A review we carried out of the industrial district phenomenon in Italy [Pyke et al., 1990], identified what we would consider, by traditional academic standards, a novel, dynamic approach to regional economic development. In our opinion, there are clearly principles of organisation which could very usefully be used in other contexts and countries, and we think these should be brought to people's attention. This is not to say that what is on offer is a perfect model that will magically solve all developmental problems at a stroke. Neither does it mean that we are totally happy with all aspects of what we have come to know about the districts that exist. Nevertheless, we feel that there are positive lessons to be learnt and that their implications should be discussed.

The Italian districts are concentrated in the North Central and North East parts of the country, with the heartland being the province of Emilia-Romagna with its capital, Bologna. It is quite clear that these districts differ in their characteristics and that it would be wrong to overgeneralise. Nevertheless, we can set out an ideal type characterisation to which some of the strongest districts, like the towns of Carpi and Prato, have at some time, or still do, resemble, and to which many other "quasi-districts" approximate.

1. Principles of organisation

The crucial characteristic of an industrial district is its *organisation*. That is to say that economic success for the industrial district has come not so much through advantageous access to low cost factors of production - cheap labour, land or capital - as from a particularly effective social and economic organisation based on small firms. This organisation may vary at the margins, but typically there are a number of key principles which help to "explain" or identify the most successful districts.

However, before going on to describe what industrial districts are, it is worth mentioning briefly what industrial districts are *not*. Industrial districts are not a "company group", defined simply as a concentration of firms within the same manufacturing sector and operating in a limited geographical area. Industrial districts are much more than this. They are also more than collections of disparate firms and services organised together on what the British call "industrial estates" and the French *zones industrielles*. What is specific and different is the way the firms are *organised together* according to certain principles discussed below.

Perhaps paramount amongst these is the existence of strong *networks* of (mainly) small firms which, through specialisation and subcontracting, divide amongst themselves the labour required for the manufacture of particular goods: specialisation induces efficiency, both individually and at the level of the district; specialisation combined with subcontracting promotes collective capability. Economies of both scale and scope are the result. It is the firm as part of, and depending on, a collective network, which perhaps more than anything else encapsulates the essence of the district's character. A small firm in an industrial district does not stand alone; a condition of its success is the success of the whole network of firms of which it is a part. An industrial district is not simply a conglomeration of essentially isolated, individually competitive firms that happen to be located together, with no linkages between them. Rather, the firms of a district are organised together according to definite principles. Thus, key questions are not in the vein of: "What makes an individual small firm succeed? What turns a firm into a winner or loser? How can we identify potential winners?" Rather, what must be posed are questions like: "What key principles serve to make the *community* of firms a success? What obstacles to or assistance for the development of the small firm *network* can we identify?" Thus, the success of development policies cannot be measured in terms of *individual* improvement - which is an assumption made in most small firm promotion. Rather, it is the growth of the district as a whole which should be evaluated.

The networks of an industrial district belong to the *same industrial sector*, in the sense of containing all the upstream and downstream processes and services going towards the manufacture of a family of products (such as ceramic goods or knitted clothes). In an industrial district these networks tend to be locally related; i.e. an industrial district is *geographically bounded*. Geographical proximity between firms, and between individuals, firms and local institutions, improves effectiveness: for the spread of ideas and technical innovation; for various kinds of collaboration, between firms and of a broader political kind; for social cohesion and a sense of collective consciousness; and for ease and speed of interfirm transactions.

A readiness amongst firms for *co-operation* is another important characteristic of industrial districts, a kind of co-operation that, far from implying a stifling of competition, in fact aids it. It is clear from our research that certain kinds of co-operation at certain levels, or in certain contexts, can promote competitive efficiency at other levels or in other contexts. Thus, for example, there can be a readiness to share information, such as ideas about new technologies or products, which help all firms in the district to become more efficient through better productivity, quality, design, etc. This sharing of information might be carried out informally at a personal level or more formally through specially established institutions. Such institutions might be associations of employers or workers, or service centres providing advice "over the counter". The collective provision of services and information makes affordable something which small firms otherwise could not hope to manage as isolated individual units. The existence of institutions, and perhaps ideologies, capable of sustaining collective co-operative relations would appear to be crucial.

A further feature is the pervasiveness of an *entrepreneurial dynamism*. This dynamism is itself a product of numerous conditions, which include: ease of formation of new firms (access to capital, premises, etc. and an advantageous legal framework); protection from domination and dependency upon large firms (permitting independent design capabilities and ease of access to final markets); knowledgeable individuals capable and confident enough to establish new firms; and access to the networks, ideas and services mentioned above.

The most successful districts *compete on a range of dimensions* and not just on price. At their best, they represent a type of industrial organisation that meets competitive challenges through differentiated high quality products, flexibility of adjustment, and the ability for innovation. The ability to offer quality, design flair, choice, flexibility, speed, and innovation is itself a product of a particular kind of organisation, based, as we have indicated, on a peculiar mixture of competition and co-operation. *Flexibility* is perhaps the characteristic which people most often associate with the industrial district's advantages over the large centralised corporation. Often people refer to the combination of flexibility and specialised production units typical of industrial districts as "flexible specialisation" and contrast it to Fordism, the inflexible organisation of production on mass market lines, employing dedicated machines and specialised, often unskilled or semi-skilled, workers [see Piore and Sabel, 1984].

Central to the organisation of the successful district is the role of *the workforce*. As mentioned, flexible response is one of the key competitive strategies that tends to mark out successful districts. A crucial component of this kind of response is the availability of a trained, adaptable workforce and, possibly, an adaptable social structure and environment. An adaptable workforce goes hand in hand with an innovative atmosphere, speed of reaction, and a co-operative attitude. Adaptability in the workplace is aided by the breaking down of rigid divisions between managers and workforce, and the pervasiveness of an atmosphere of trust.

Trust and co-operation, so crucial to the successful performance of the district, is helped by an attitude that seeks competitive success not by aggressive cutting of direct labour costs but by general organisational competence, standards and productivity. The maintenance of labour standards, including good wages, improves the performance of labour and the performance of the district. The establishment of good basic conditions, whether by collective bargaining with trade unions or by use of national or international law, is part of a social contract that lubricates flexibility.

2.   The appeal of industrial districts

The principles of organisation typical of industrial districts, described above, are not limited to the Third Italy. They can be found, individually or collectively, in other countries of Europe, North America and other parts of the world. In this volume, we present, together with the Italian case, three well researched cases of regional development: the region of West Jutland in Denmark; Baden-Württemburg in Germany; and several regions in Spain. They include a discussion of how far, and in what way, they may be called industrial districts. It is likely that there are other regional industrial structures in Europe and elsewhere which may resemble industrial districts, in part or in whole, but which have not been identified as such because they have not been subjects of research. To date, there does not exist anything approaching a systematic survey or an inventory of the spread of such forms of industrial organisation.

What has made industrial districts known internationally, and has captured the attention of researchers and politicians alike, is their remarkable economic success. They have penetrated international markets to an extent unprecedented for small enterprises. They have led regions to prosperity. They have propelled Emilia-Romagna, Tuscany, Veneto and other provinces in what is now called the "Third Italy" from the mediocre position which they held two or three decades ago to the top of the regional income ladder. Bologna, situated in the midst of dynamic industrial districts, was chosen in 1989 as the city where most Italians would like to live. Industrial districts have contributed to move Italy, as a nation, into the ranks of Europe's front-runners. Its gross national product - both aggregate and per capita - is now well ahead of Great Britain's, and the country ranks fifth in the group of the seven largest Western industrialised nations.

There are three reasons for discussing industrial districts in the context of local economic development and local economic regeneration in particular.

First, industrial districts are emblematic of the profound *industrial restructuring* which we have been able to observe in virtually all industrialised countries since 1975. The re-emergence of small units of production, the spread of subcontracting, and a geographical reorganisation of the economy have been essential ingredients of the transformation of industrial organisation.

Secondly, our theme touches on alternative ways of meeting the new *competitive challenges* posed to virtually all industrialised countries. We are interested in identifying strategies and forms of industrial restructuring and competition which do not infringe on labour standards but, on the contrary, are apt to improve and further develop these standards [see Sengenberger,

1990]. We are keen on identifying types of industrial organisation which combine economic targets, such as efficiency and flexibility, with social targets, such as good pay and good working conditions, participation and equity.

Thirdly, we consider it worthwhile looking more closely into industrial districts because they might tell us something about perspectives and ingredients for *development*. The promotion of "balanced and sustainable development" has come increasingly to the forefront of ILO concerns. It is a notion which goes far beyond the purely quantitative objective of attaining economic growth.

Industrial districts could stimulate the debate on development because they refocus attention on the critical role of "social organisation". They lead us to emphasise such things as non-hierarchical organisation, autonomy, co-operation, local and regional networks, competent entre-preneurship, and differentiated industrial structure. They thus set us on a track which is somewhat different from the standard development models which tend to see mainly financial resources and sophisticated technology as being the keys to economic and social advancement; these, in our view, are clearly not enough. We feel that what needs to be explained is the enormous variation in economic performance, and perhaps even its increasing disparity, in a world which appears to be increasingly equal in its access to advanced technology. That is to say, apparently technology alone does not do the trick. Nor, alone, does capital infusion. How much money has been poured into the revitalisation of the old smoke-stack industrial regions of Europe without yielding the expected take-off? While some have improved due to a successful restructuring of their economic bases, others seem bound to further decline.

II. The growth of small units of production

The past decade has been characterised by apparently contradictory tendencies in industrial organisation. One of them has concerned the size structure of business. On the one hand, there have been claims that most new employment is generated by the small firm sector; delegates from the employers' group to the annual International Labour Conference, for example, have stated repeatedly that the potential for employment growth is particularly strong in small and medium-sized enterprises (SMEs). It is also contended that small firms are more flexible, more efficient, and more capable of adapting to market requirements than large, cumbersome, bureaucratised enterprises. Repeatedly, international organisations have endorsed the idea that it would be worthwhile promoting small firms; and in 1990, an OECD conference, held in Trieste and addressed to Eastern European policy-makers, argued that small and medium-sized enterprises are the basis for a healthy economy. They were said to accomplish the renovation of industrial structure, innovation and the diffusion of technology.

On the other hand, you can read almost every day about a new marriage between two or more giant corporations. The number of mergers and takeovers in the industrialised world has occurred at an unprecedented pace in recent years. Transnational companies have extended their empires, and formed new holdings in Europe in anticipation of the advent of the single market.

How do these two developments fit together? In an attempt to shed some light on these issues, we have examined - with the help of an external research group - developments in the size structure of business [see Sengenberger et al., 1990]. We asked whether and why small firms create new employment and what this employment looks like. What we found was the following.

Since the mid-1970s there has indeed been a shift in the size composition of business. There has been an increase in the share of total employment in small enterprises and establishments that has occurred mainly at the expense of large units. While the magnitude of the shift varies from one country to the other, it can be found in nearly all industrialised market economy countries, as well as in many newly industrialising ones. It is most visible in industry, but in a number of countries it is also prevalent in the service sector. To quote the latest figures from just one country: in France, small enterprises (with fewer than 50 employees) increased their proportion of total employment from 43.3 per cent in 1976 to 52.5 per cent in 1988. In the same period, the employment share of large companies (with more than 500 employees) declined from 20.7 per cent to 14.6 per cent. The recomposition affected all economic sectors [*Le Monde*, 13 June 1990].

The shift is due, to varying degrees, to two different components: a decline of the average size of enterprises or establishments; and an increase in the number of (small) new enterprises created. While the mortality rate of enterprises - and especially that of newly-created enterprises - has also risen, the birth rate has exceeded the death rate, leading to overall positive employment effects in the small firm sector.

Countervailing trends towards larger businesses notwithstanding, the forces pushing towards smaller scale look sufficiently robust for one to be able to speak of the reversal in the past 15 years of a previously dominant pattern of centralisation, i.e. the trend towards larger enterprises and establishments.

What accounts for the shift to small units? There have been several factors at work, none of which can claim exclusive power of explanation. First, small firm creation and small firm expansion are a reaction to *economic slump*. The shortage of wage-employment opportunities in a period of mass unemployment induces, or even forces, workers to seek employment in the small firm sector, or to set up their own businesses, and use cheap secondhand machinery and equipment that becomes available from firms going bankrupt. In other words, small business plays the role of a "shock absorber" for the economic cycle. There is evidence from industrialised and developing countries that the share of self-employment is linked to the level of unemployment [see ILO, 1990, pp. 15 and 19].

A surge of small businesses, and a loss of employment in large firms, occurred during the Great Depression in the 1930s. It recurred in the 1970s and 1980s following the recession after the oil shocks. Yet, when the national economies expanded again more strongly during the 1980s, the trend to small firm employment continued, suggesting that small firm expansion is more than a transitory, cyclical phenomenon.

Secondly, some of the shift in size may be attributed to the *sectoral shift* of economic activities from industry to the service sector which has accelerated in the past 20 years. As the average scale of enterprises and establishments in services is smaller, sectoral change leads to smaller units. But again, this cannot be the whole story, because we find a sufficient number of instances of small unit growth within sectors.

A further explanation frequently used relates to lower costs and a *better business climate* in small firms. Moving production to small plants, and establishing new small firms, could be a vehicle for saving on labour costs and on taxes, escaping trade unions and difficult labour relations, or evading labour market regulation and "sticky" rules. In fact, there exist substantial differentials in wages and other elements of worker compensation according to size of establishment; small firms are often exempted from certain social provisions and legal or contractual protection; worker representation in small firms, either by trade unions or works councils, is weak.

The impact of these factors remains questionable, however. Why should these factors have mattered in the last 15 years, and not before? There are no clear statistical links between changes in size-related wages and the expansion of small firm employment. There are even cases of small firm growth in the face of a narrowing wage gap; moreover, where small firms pay much less than large firms they also tend to have lower productivity levels, so that unit labour costs in small firms are not necessarily lower. Incidentally, we have found that the claims that small firms are more efficient, or more profitable, cannot be generally substantiated.

Neither have we found evidence of superior technological standards in small firms. It is doubtful whether the attribution of innate economic superiority can be made to either large or small enterprises. If it were the small size of business as such that makes them perform better, why then should small firms decline at first and then later grow again? Also, and perhaps of even more importance, how can we account for the enormous variability in the economic viability and social standards exhibited by small firms by sector, region, and country? Why have small firms in the same industry excelled in some countries and failed in others? Why do we find highly flexible, efficient small firms, offering good pay, in some quarters and so-called sweat shops in others? Why do we observe, even after holding industry composition constant, enormous size differences in business organisation in different economies? Japan and Italy, for example, have a preponderance of comparatively small enterprises and establishments in their manufacturing sector, whereas units in the United Kingdom and United States are much more likely to be large.

In order to obtain satisfactory answers to these questions we need to get away from looking only at small firms. We must examine their status and role in the larger economic and institutional context, and see the expansion of small units as part and parcel of a profound and pervasive *industrial restructuring* which includes small and large firms in the analysis, and changing relations between large and small enterprises.

We will then see that large companies have altered their organisational complexion as well; and a good deal of the expansion of the small firm sector originates in the organisational reform of large companies. Much has resulted from decentralisation, devolvement and disintegration policies initiated in large companies during the 1970s. *Decentralisation* of production occurs when large enterprises, or plants, are broken up into smaller units, but retained under the same ownership, by a division into small establishments, or by the creation of new subsidiary companies. There is evidence that, compared to 15 years ago, large firms have on average more plants, but these plants are of a smaller scale. Furthermore, we find a surge of *devolvement* such as licensing and franchising practices, under which large companies cease to own smaller establishments directly, but retain revenue links with them. Finally, organisational *disintegration* indicates a fragmentation of large enterprises into separate units of ownership, or the increase of outsourcing of production and services. A variety of forms exist such as subcontracting, managements' and workers' buy-outs, and the splitting of enterprises into separate legal entities, such as "ownership" and "production" units.

The various types of fragmentation in the organisation of production enable us to explain why production and employment have shifted to smaller units. But does this imply that the large corporation must thereby fade away? Not at all: it would be difficult to argue that the large enterprises have lost power and influence; in fact studies using indicators of industrial concentration do not permit the conclusion that the power of large companies is vanishing. Rather, what seems to have happened has been the development of a new and possibly extended division of labour between various types of firms, and firms in different size brackets. Many large companies have broadened and diversified their activities; they have entered new industries and offer more and more products and product groups; but of each product they sell, they produce less themselves leaving that to other, mostly smaller, firms; whilst integrating horizontally, through diversification and partly through mergers and acquisitions, they are disintegrating vertically. This interpretation would be in line with the statistical observation that in large enterprises the rate of increase in the volume of sales is above average, while at the same time production and employment is declining; conversely, small firms are expanding their production and employment at a higher rate than the average, but have sub-average increases of sales and value added [see Bade, 1987]. All this would suggest that a substantial part of the restructuration that has taken place, including the expansion of the small business sector, has evolved under the control of larger firms, thus raising doubts about claims for the viability of independent, innovative and dynamic small entrepreneurs, whose rise is due to their superiority over large corporations.

However, while a good deal of the re-emergence of small units of production is linked to, and controlled by, large companies, there are instances of more independent small firm growth; or at least of small firms which, although they might owe their birth to large firm support, have managed increasingly to exist by themselves. The most interesting cases are those where small firms operate in the same markets as larger firms, and are capable of competing effectively. Where this is the case, there seems to be one over-riding critical organisational prerequisite, namely a *horizontal-type organisation or system of lateral linkage* among the small firms; small firm industrial districts are not the only, but the most conspicuous, type of such small firm communities.

III. Strategies and choice: The "high road" and the "low road" to industrial restructuring

The extremely varied performance of the small firm sector, that is, the co-existence of efficient, innovative small enterprises with those that survive only through "sweating" or self-exploitation, is a reflection of the diversity of choice and competitive strategy.

As emphasised earlier, "smallness" or "bigness" of a firm - though not irrelevant - is in the end not the decisive criterion for its performance. What is crucial is the organisational and institutional context in which small firms, as well as large firms, operate. Small firms can become "big" through collective organisation and concerted action. The main problem for small firms is not being small but being lonely. What this metaphor means is that small firms as individual entities, acting on their own, are in a poor position to compete. They lack the resources and the economies of scale and scope normally available to large companies; and they lack the political voice necessary for influencing their economic and political environment. In other words, they lack the facility for strategic action, that is being able to choose how they become and stay competitive. Particular areas of economic activities apart, they need to link up with resource pools of others, be it large firms or small firms, to gain strategic options. Thus, links and networks are paramount to small firm success.

Links to others, exchange, and the sharing of resources are today inescapable, even for the largest corporations. Toyota, General Motors, Volkswagen, Fiat, and the giants in the electronics industry have formed strategic alliances through which they seek to cover the sharp increases in the levels of cost of R & D, or the design of world brand products, and the increased share of these activities in the overall cost of business. Such development occurs against the background of shortened life cycles and faster turnover of many investment and consumer goods.

In view of the extended inter-firm division of labour, co-ordination across enterprises is increasingly assuming the role which co-ordination within firms and plants had in the 1960s and 1970s. Firms depend increasingly on specialised goods and services which need to be effectively co-ordinated to yield economic benefits. The relations between firms, between producers and suppliers, become of utmost significance. Do they enter an exchange as super- and sub-ordinates, or as partners on an equal footing? Is the flow of know-how between firms a one-way or a two-way street? Do firms share costs of investment and risks and uncertainties of volatile markets, or do they pass these on unilaterally to some units or sectors, thus creating dependency and "social pollution"? It will very much depend on the nature of these relations as to whether subcontracting, for example, leads to precarious employment or not; and whether dualism in the economic structure and segmentation in the labour market exists.

One may distinguish between two principal approaches by which enterprises, industries, or regions have tried to meet the challenges of international competition. The first may be termed the "low road" to restructuring. It consists of seeking competitiveness through low labour cost, and a deregulated labour market environment. It is believed that cost-cutting will boost productivity and profits, and create new employment. Institutions and rules aimed at regulating competition are seen as mere straightjackets, and should be kept to a minimum.

In a number of countries this approach has been recommended and actually practised for the promotion of small firms, e.g. when small firms have been relieved from an industry-wide agreement and become part of two-tiered wage structures, or been exempted from protective labour standards, or been subject to tax privileges.

The problem with this approach is that the improvement it yields for competitive performance, if there is one at all, is frequently short-lived. Mostly, in fact, it accentuates the *malaise*. Poor wages and terms of employment hinder the firm in acquiring and keeping the qualified labour required for efficiency and flexibility; and they rarely induce the firm to "invest" in its labour force to make it more productive. So, in the absence of better performance and alternative possibilities, further cost-cutting may become inevitable, resulting in a vicious, downward-spiralling cycle.

The principal alternative to such "destructive" competition is the "high road" of constructive competition, based on efficiency enhancement and innovation; that is, through economic gains that make wage gains and improvements in social conditions feasible, as well as safeguarding workers' rights and providing adequate standards of social protection.[1] The key to attaining this is better organisation and a better mobilisation and utilisation of productive labour, which then permits a better use of technology (rather than the other way around).

To make labour more productive, labour standards are required. They are needed to curb destructive downward-directed competition in wages and working conditions; and promote constructive competition through co-operation and its sub-processes of participation, joint resource utilisation, and joint conflict resolution. Co-operation is needed for exchanging information, and thereby reaching common efficiency. It cannot be sustained without trusting relationships between firms, and between employers and workforces; we know from studies that a mutual understanding, or agreement, not to undercut wages and violate laws, is often required to maintain trust.

Thus labour standards provide an opportunity to elicit constructive competition. They have often been unjustly criticised as pushing up costs, curbing efficiency, and stifling competition. We would argue, on the contrary, that labour standards are more likely to have the opposite effect and help to achieve lasting and comprehensive development.

Judging by what we know, we cannot say that industrial districts match the high road model in all cases and in every respect. In fact experience is mixed. As Brusco states in his contribution to this volume, it is best to think of districts as lying on a continuum between "better" and "worse", or "more advanced" and "less advanced", with districts like Carpi and Prato being closest to the sort of ideal model we have presented whilst other areas are less advanced. However, even though the presence of the elements needed for the "high road" kind of competition in practice varies, as does the form they take, nevertheless it is clear that the general experience of the Italian districts, and areas based on similar principles in Denmark, Spain, and elsewhere, have demonstrated the kinds of elements that need to be drawn upon.

IV. Industrial restructuring, industrial districts and development

A desirable objective is to achieve a type of economic and social *development* which could be regarded as *comprehensive, balanced and sustainable*. That is to say, a "comprehensiveness" of development that is not merely geared towards quantitative objectives, such as economic growth, or more jobs, but also to autonomy, job satisfaction, a good working environment, and other quality aspects; "balanced" means that development

---

1. This approach has been specifically demanded for SMEs in the conclusions of the High-Level Meeting on Employment and Structural Adjustment, ILO, 23-25 November 1987.

will not proceed at the expense of others, i.e. other workers, firms, regions, etc.; and "sustainability" of development implies that, as the Brundtland report put it: "It meets the goals of the present without compromising the ability of future generations to meet their own needs" [World Commission on Environment and Development, 1987, p. 43].

The experience of the industrial districts suggests lessons for development elsewhere. The key principles of organisation that appear to lie behind the success of the most advanced districts are summarised at the beginning of this article, but it is worthwhile elaborating upon some of them here, and placing them in a wider policy context.

1.   What sort of flexibility - active or passive?

If people had to choose a key word for industrial organisation in the 1980s, "flexibility" would be the most likely candidate. It is widely accepted that more flexibility is demanded, from enterprises as well as from workers. This need is usually linked to factors such as the intensification of international competition, a changing consumer demand in the direction of more differentiated products, and an increased desire for products of higher quality; these in turn evoke changes in the productive system, such as a capability for larger product variety, shorter product cycles, and accelerated innovation rates. To create this capability it is necessary to acquire the ability to respond to the new and changing production and market requirements.

Flexibility can take different forms and an important question is how this relates to the goal of development; it can take the form of "active versatility" or "passive pliability" [Semlinger, 1990]: that is, it can consist of the ability to exploit market niches and quickly respond to orders, based on a skilled and polyvalent labour force; or it can also mean simply to submit to outside pressures from customers, and to accept cutbacks, and to pass on the flexibility requirements of the market to the workforce in a coercive manner through expanding and retrenching production volume, forcing wage concessions, making "flexible" use of short-time and casual employment, etc.

Small firms run a high risk of indulging in the second form of flexibility, as they are often exempted from protective regulation; they often have no formalised industrial relations, no union representation, and no works councils;[2] employer-employee relations are frequently highly personalised and patriarchal.

Productive organisation on the basis of principles gleaned from the behaviour of industrial districts would seem to offer at least the possibility

---

2.   See, for example, the Bélier Report in France: *Rapport de M. Gilles Bélier*, Conseil Social au Ministre du Travail, de l'Emploi et de la Formation professionnelle, Paris, March 1990.

of an "active versatility" regime. One concept which helps to understand how this can happen is "collective efficiency" - an efficiency and flexibility derived from the advantages that clustering bestows upon individual small firms [see Schmitz, 1990].

2.   Collective efficiency through specialisation and co-ordination

In the ideal case, the industrial district comprises in one and the same local area all the various activities required for the development, manufacturing, and commercialisation of a product. These include the final assemblers, the producers of parts and components, or firms engaging in one of the successive vertical stages of production, producers of machinery and equipment, product designers, marketing firms, export specialists and banks. That is, the district provides all the activities and services up-stream and down-stream from the final product. If this vertical production process is well co-ordinated it can combine various benefits of specialisation, with the advantages of running a fully-fledged business operation in which all essential business functions are integrated; specialisation and integration boost efficiency and quality, whilst individual units maintain their independence. To achieve this, collective inter-firm organisation and co-ordination is called for.

It can hardly be envisaged that a single small firm could carry out by itself all the functions necessary for competitive efficiency that the collectivity as a whole could provide; it would have difficulty financing the necessary, ever-increasing research and development and design costs; or training the full range of skilled labour it might require; or indeed manufacturing all the components to go into a complicated product. Also, the small firm may lack the scale to operate expensive capital equipment effectively; costly numerically-controlled (NC) or computer numerically-controlled (CNC) machinery may, however, be profitably utilised in the small firm sector if the firm acquiring it provides special services for a number of customers rather than just occasionally for itself; at the same time the customers benefit from purchasing the product from the specialised producer at a lower cost than they could make it themselves.

Geographical proximity of the specialised firms helps to secure synergy effects, not only by reducing transport and other transaction costs, but by permitting and lubricating continuous communication between the producers. For instance, substantial synergy effects may be obtained from a close, door-to-door co-operation by the producers and the users of capital equipment. The producer of tools and machines can tell the user, let us say a weaving or knitting firm, how best to operate the equipment, how to deal with problems of machine standstill and other operational problems; conversely, the user can feed back information or deficiencies in the design of the machine, and perhaps even propose improvements; such information can then be used by the producer to build machines better adapted to the needs and abilities of the users in the district. Each specialist producer benefits from an increasing expertise in his chosen product area, whilst all the firms of the district benefit from being able to rely upon the expertise of others when needed.

It is not only in the sphere of production that individual firms can benefit from a division of specialisation; this is also the case in services, and in marketing. A good example of the benefits of specialisation would be the export firm or export agency in the district. Italian industrial districts have excelled in exporting their manufactures. Exporting today demands an enormous amount of technical knowledge and legal expertise; expensive know-how about the technical norms, licences, legal procedures, etc., in foreign countries is needed. An individual firm would be hopelessly overburdened if it attempted to keep up with that, and this might explain the reason why small firms have often failed to enter international markets.

The provision of co-ordinating agencies in the Italian districts, run by representatives of the firms or their associations, providing what Brusco, in his chapter in this book, calls "real services" - providing advice on exports, making bulk purchases at favourable prices, obtaining credit at lower interest rates, handling accounts, promoting products at trade fairs, etc. - highlights the strong role of co-operation.

3.   Competition and co-operation

The efficient co-ordination of the district's activities and the promotion of dynamic growth is not simply a product of the unfettered operation of classic competitive market principles; on the contrary, what is at work is a complex amalgam of both competitive *and* co-operative principles. Certainly, competition, in all its forms (price, quality, delivery, etc.) is a strong feature relating firms producing similar products or at the same stage of the productive process. Weavers compete with weavers, dyers with dyers, etc. And because in a well developed district there are many firms specialising in similar products, or providing similar services, competition is rife.

But, as we have seen, there is also co-operation, and co-operation is at least as important as competition for organising the district. Contributions to this book by Benton (on Spain) and Kristensen (on Denmark) point to the presence of various forms of co-operation in the most successful districts; and there have been studies in other countries, including, for example, France [Raveyre and Saglio, 1984; Courlet, 1990], Japan [Friedman, 1988], and Britain [Pyke, 1988], that have highlighted the importance of co-operative mechanisms for improving the competitive capacities of small firm communities and networks. But of course it is the classic cases of Italy that provide the most compelling evidence for the role of co-operation. Brusco, in this book, underlines its importance in Italian districts; so do recent articles by Becattini [1990] and Trigilia [1990].

The forms co-operation can take are several, and most have already been referred to: the subcontracting and dividing up of orders, allowing individual companies to accept orders beyond their normal manufacturing capacities (see the chapter by Kristensen in this book where he points out that this kind of co-operation allows individual manufacturers in Jutland to present collections or ranges that the *district as a whole* can produce); the collaboration between individual firms at different phases of the production cycle whereby "partners" develop together the most appropriate technical specifications and designs; collaboration to train labour for the district as a whole [see Hirst and Zeitlin, 1990]. Whereas in a competitive environment small firms, unable to afford to train their own labour, will compete strongly to take as much as they can from an ever-diminishing pool, in a regime of co-operation and trust the same firms will combine their resources to ensure a collective provision of skills, the collective provision of services already referred to, and the kind of co-operation that takes the form of "good neighbourliness" - lending of tools, helping out with spare parts, passing on of advice, assistance in emergencies, etc.

In summary, then, industrial districts can be an arrangement for the joint procurement, development, utilisation and financing of resources, thereby overcoming the "resource gap" problem and attaining better economies of scale and scope. In this, co-operation, as well as competition, plays a vital role.

4.   Endogenous regional development

Can industrial districts and small firm communities contribute to *endogenous regional development*, that is, regionally adapted technology and greater self-reliance through the mobilisation of existing resources and self-created local organisation? This would be an alternative to expecting impetus, know-how, and financial inputs to come from elsewhere, by attracting incoming activities through tax exemptions, subsidies, the promise of low wages, and other means of competitive bidding. In fact, regions and municipalities have often tried to attract new firms and new jobs, by outcompeting one another in their offers of low costs and the provision of a favourable business climate. One consequence is that the financial resources spent on giving incentives to firms are not available for investment in the regional or local infrastructure from which the economy as a whole could have benefited. Attracting business with the carrot of financial incentives has often failed to generate permanent and stable development. Firms have used the incentives to set up plants in boom periods, and close them down in times of recession, hence creating nothing more than "extended work-benches".

Endogenous regional development, in contrast, would attempt to commit enterprises to continuous local and regional development. It would create a regional identity, economically, politically and culturally; it would integrate key actors - firms, business associations, trade unions, the local and regional government, employment exchanges, banks - into regionally and locally based agencies, with all groups participating in efforts for regional development. It could lead to greater autonomy, and less external dependence; it could support new efforts to preserve and redevelop the physical environment.

It would, however, require a reorientation of existing structures and policies. Take the trade unions, for example: the principle of a territorial organisation of trade unions was predominant in the early, formative phase of trade unionism, but it increasingly gave way to trade union organisation and worker representation linked to employment, particularly in large enterprises. Today, as jobs in large enterprises have diminished, standard full-time regular employment has declined and, as there are more footloose workers employed on a temporary or casual basis, strengthening territorial organisation at the local or district level may again make sense for trade unions and employers alike. It could possibly help to overcome the organisational distance between trade unions and small firms which Wassermann [1991] identified as the main origin of low union density and the lack of social protection in that sector. Territorial organisation may also be an answer to the increasingly blurred boundaries between firms, and between industries.

Refocusing development at the local level, and creating new or strengthening existing local industries, should not be dismissed as "romanticism", or a retrogression to a traditional kind of economic organisation. The issue at stake is how regionalisation is undertaken and in what way employers' and workers' institutions could be involved in the process.

Of course, one must not overlook certain dangers involved in emphasising local and regional development. There is a risk of increasing regional disparity and regional inequalities which may spill over into wages, employment opportunities and labour standards. In part, such disparities may result from the ineffectiveness of conventional public policy attempts to balance regional development. This possibly follows from a failure to recognise that localism and regionalism works better if there is concurrently based economic, political, and cultural autonomy. These spheres go hand in hand, and support one another. At the same time, supra-regional policies geared to balancing regional opportunities may be necessary. In Europe, the Commission of the European Community is actively collecting information on the regions with the aim of interventions to reduce disparities, by facilitating financial resource transfer and the provision of collective services via such means as the European Fund for Regional Development.

New localism should not mean egoism and parochialism. In fact, Italian provinces such as Tuscany, developing strong business communities, benefited enormously from their "cosmopolitan" orientations and their old trade links. As Ghandi suggested: "Think globally and act locally"; in modifying this principle in relation to industrial districts one might have to say: "Think *and* act both locally *and* globally."

5.   Business community and social community

The organisation of economic relations in an industrial district tends to be intertwined with social relations; that is to say, the boundary between the spheres of business and community tends to blur. A consequence is that economic behaviour and standards are likely to be at least in part shaped by community norms and expectations, producing customary arrangements and ways of doing business.

The advanced forms of co-operation to be found in the districts are greatly sustained by a social community holding supportive sets of values. An orientation towards long run development as an objective, rather than a quest for short-term economic gains, would be a typical widely shared value. Others, such as a belief in strategies of innovation, pride in the district's products and name and a collective awareness, might also feature.

An important element in such a community would be the pervasive reliance on *trust* as a guiding principle in business relationships. Being able to act "on trust" introduces an essential dynamism to the economy by removing the paralysing inertia that can occur when firms are afraid to take action because they are not sure that others will refrain from acting opportunistically by taking advantage of temporary weakness. In other words, it removes the fear of taking risks; or rather, it removes the risk. It allows entrepreneurs to engage in heavy investment on the understanding that other community members will buy the products of the investment, rather than take their custom elsewhere. It allows people to exchange commercial information, pass on design ideas, knowledge of technical processes, etc., knowing that "partners" will not abuse the trust bestowed upon them by making selfish, unilateral use of the information to the detriment of the information giver, or fail to bestow useful information in return in the future. It means that an entrepreneur can be confident that he or she can rely on others to help him or her out in times of difficulty, just as he or she would help others. The entrepreneur in an economic community built on principles of co-operation and trust knows that other firms will help him/her to remain part of the community because it is in their interest that his/her expertise and capability remain part of the collective resource pool. Producers visit each others' firms and freely discuss their production problems with one another - that is, the shop itself is open (see, for an elaboration of this, Piore [1990]). Firms do not, contrary to textbook descriptions of the ideal competitive market, seek every opportunity to destroy their rivals. In the ideal industrial district model, the individual firm does not see survival and success in terms of a fight to the death with rivals; rather, the accent is on collective growth, where each individual unit benefits from the success of the whole.

As Sabel explains in this volume, acting according to principles of trust does not imply that people cease to act in self-interest; rather, it means a specific, broader understanding of self-interest which includes the welfare of others, and one's own welfare in the future. Trust does not come overnight: it successively evolves and grows as people learn through experience that social exchange can and does yield extensive gains.

Trust can be based on various catalytic institutions: kinship, ethnicity, political or religious affiliation, and collective agreement, be it informal or formalised. The frequently heard argument that the successful industrial districts cannot be reproduced elsewhere because they are rooted in specific cultures is both right and wrong at the same time. It is right to say that it takes time to develop trusting social relations; however, it is wrong in the sense that it denies even the slightest possibility of the development of common norms of conduct in certain spheres. From various studies we know that even fierce competitors can agree, sometimes formally, sometimes informally, not to contravene certain rules, such as the undercutting of wage standards.

6.   Competent entrepreneurship

Most people would agree that the competence of the entrepreneur, that is the person who owns and operates a firm, is a key variable in business success. Yet it is surprising how little attention is paid in the areas of research and policy formulation to the question of how competent entrepreneurship is actually achieved. Should this not be a priority concern, given the substantial increase in the number of business start-ups that have occurred in some countries (in the United States, for example, the annual number of start-ups has doubled since 1970), and also in view of the much increased number of enterprise casualties? A substantial proportion of the newly-established firms dies within a few years of start-up.

Several issues should be raised in relation to entrepreneurial competence: how are entrepreneurs chosen or "made"? What opportunities do they have to continuously enhance their abilities? What happens to them if they fail and go bankrupt? Again, these questions must be linked to the broader business context in which small firms operate; and entrepreneurial competence should also be seen in connection with worker competence.

Industrial districts in Italy and elsewhere provide valuable insights. As workers pursue their careers in small firms they not only accumulate knowledge about their own particular trades but also about how to run the businesses in which they work. In the Third Italy, persons setting up new firms frequently come from the ranks of experienced, senior employees, be it in small firms or in large enterprises. They are already familiar with the network of firms, and the spectrum of managerial tasks and functions, the more so the more such tasks had been delegated to them by the owner.

Thus, the sharing of managerial work between workers and entrepreneur creates the opportunity to learn how to run a business whilst "on the job".

An inducement to pick up entrepreneurial skills is provided by the existence of clear objective opportunities to establish new firms and the subjective perception of career paths towards self-employment. Social mobility between the status of dependent worker and manager or entrepreneur can be very high in the districts. The perception of such opportunities stimulates workers to participate and co-operate and this is of great importance to the dynamism and innovative capacity of the local economy. A local ideology or set of values promoting the idea of self-employment is a further inducement. Thus workers become "socialised" into a culture of small firm entrepreneurship. In Italy and Germany, early socialising into the role of businessman is to some extent undertaken in the artisan or the *Handwerk* sectors, where there is a career path from apprentice to journeyman and on to master or/and business owner. In Denmark, as Kristensen relates in this volume, entrepreneurs in Jutland are also produced in the atmosphere of a long-standing local ideology favouring self-employment, with expectations and opportunities further encouraged by the maintenance of a tradition of training workers in broad-based skills that can be flexibly adapted to rapidly changing market requirements.

In the context of an economic environment dominated by small firms, the desire and expectation of establishing one's own business is "normal" and culturally acceptable. In areas dominated by large firms, in contrast, such as in parts of Great Britain, the strong self-identity of "wage-worker" experienced by the mass of the community can militate against a possible self-image as employer or entrepreneur; this is all the more likely where working experience has been restricted to tightly defined manual roles in large hierarchical organisations, typified by remote managerial co-ordination. In the small firm industrial districts, distance between management and shop-floor is necessarily short, and sharply defined manual and mental distinctions tend to break down. It may not be by accident that economic dynamism in the recent past has been in areas and regions in Europe which were outside the traditional industrial heartlands.

The chance for success may be significantly improved if the setting up of a new firm is organically tied into the growth, and the extended division of labour, of a business community. This presents an alternative to becoming a firm owner "out of the blue", i.e. totally unrelated to existing firms. We know, for example, of the immense difficulties, and the high failure rates, of small businesses started by unemployed workers (who sometimes under existing public programmes use their capitalised unemployment benefits to start up on their own without being adequately prepared for this venture).

Another important question is what happens to the entrepreneur, and the workers he employs, if the firm goes bankrupt? Does this mean social disaster, or are there chances for a "softer landing" in the sense of not all qualifications and experiences accumulated in the firm being lost.

Information from Italy suggests that where bankruptcy occurs the reintegration of the workers and the owner into other firms in the district is likely to occur without the stigma of failure. Entry into and exit from business may be related. Entry may be less risky when the cost - individual and social, material and immaterial - of a business is limited. This implies that small firm promotion should be geared not only to removing entry barriers, but should be concerned with how to deal with the serious problem of failure.

7.   Labour

Our experience with industrial districts directs our attention to the crucial importance of labour as a dynamic factor of production. Too often economic analyses ignore the labour factor, or at best treat it almost as an afterthought - something that should be mentioned but not treated as integral to economic success. If labour is included, usually it is referred to in static terms, as a cost on a balance sheet - like the cost of land, or a bank loan - but not in active terms, as an input of varying quality and varying effectiveness.

By "labour" we mean at least the following two elements: the quality of the labour force, which is an essential prerequisite to dynamic efficiency and adaptation; and labour organisations as part of the industrial setting. In respect of the former, it can be said that in recent years, as economies in general have undergone enormous restructuring in the face of new types of competitive pressures and market demands, the quality and value of the labour force has come to the forefront of managerial thinking. The most sophisticated managers, epitomised, perhaps, by those in the giant car firms, have realised that survival has meant both the reorganising of relations with suppliers - on the lines of co-operation and trust - and the reorganising of relations within the factory. The essence of the shop-floor reorganisation and change in managerial philosophy has been the recognition of labour as a resource that can give different returns according to circumstance and organisation. In many quarters, the movement has been to release worker initiative and to increase worker involvement by breaking down old ways of working and inflexible divisions between jobs and between mental and manual labour.

A basic requirement in industrial districts is the presence of a pool of local labour and expertise versed in the various functions and processes associated with the main product of the community - be it shoes, furniture, machinery, or something else. The widespread expertise might be handed down "through the community", from father to son, mother to daughter, and from colleague to colleague, such that it forms part of a long-standing cultural heritage for the area. Alternatively, or additionally, the expertise might be provided by technical schools and craft colleges. Accounts by Capecchi in a recent publication on Emilia-Romagna [in Pyke et al., 1990], and Kristensen on Jutland in this volume emphasise the leading roles of such institutions. Other accounts from Italy have noted the part played in the past by large firms in introducing and disseminating new skills.

In the best cases of industrial districts a "high road" industrial strategy is the norm, that is a strategy aimed at continuous product improvement, fashion awareness, and innovation. Such a strategy places a high value on the quality of the labour force and the quality of relations between managers or entrepreneurs and employees. Continuous restructuring, with the introduction of new technology, necessarily involves continuous training, reskilling, and labour mobility. Workers need to be broadly trained in order to provide a flexible supply of labour that can adapt to changing market requirements.

By integrating all essential production stages, producer-related services, and commercial activities needed for producing a product or set or products within localised geographical boundaries, the industrial district is able to benefit from a broad range of activities and skills. In more complex cases, the range is further increased when the production networks are able to orient themselves to more than one product family, as when two initially separate industrial districts begin to merge into one another. This has happened to some extent in parts of the Third Italy where we find, as close neighbours in provinces like Emilia-Romagna, such diverse industrial districts as ones focusing on knitting, ceramics, sports car manufacture, agricultural machinery, and others. Such diversity produces a rich and less vulnerable labour market structure. More diversified demand for skills leads to a broader stock of inventory of available labour qualifications, which means in effect that firms have more options in the product market and in the selection of production processes.

The district's adaptability depends on a flexible labour force. Flexibility, as we have already mentioned, is something that is widely desired, not just in industrial districts, and the way it is implemented can vary. To be successful with a "high road" industrial strategy, labour flexibility must be achieved in such a way that all sides of industry benefit. As we indicated earlier, flexibility must be implemented in order to achieve "active versatility" rather than "passive pliability"; it must be implemented so as to achieve an economically efficient labour allocation, but not at the expense of security and loss of income and the undermining of worker confidence and motivation. Basically, there have to be mechanisms in operation that remove the age-old fear of unemployment without imposing sclerosis on the system. This is perhaps one of the greatest challenges that new patterns of industrial organisation are creating for workers' organisations and employers' organisations alike.

There is evidence that in many cases of industrial districts, the security has been provided, at least in part, by "family" mechanisms, such as the support given by extended families in times of need, and the presence of several family members capable of earning, and the availability of several alternative sources of employment or income (such as employment on the land). However, a stronger framework for security could also be provided in the labour market, involving institutions and conventions to "cover" workers' losses incurred through structural change. Only by providing such security and removing coercion can it be expected that trust, loyalty and active co-operation will prevail.

Our studies indicate that particular care must be taken to ensure that the "cost" of flexibility is not passed on to marginal groups so that certain individuals are coerced to work non-standard hours, or extended hours, against their wishes. In many Italian districts it would appear that much of the labour flexibility - particularly flexibility of working time - is provided by women. An important issue is the extent to which the required workplace flexibility, and labour flexibility, *complements* the organisation of household time and the pursuit of activities in other realms, including activities aimed at acquiring other sources of income. In other words, the terms on which the flexibility is provided are important.

It may be that, in order to achieve a regulated system that promotes both efficiency and equity, old practices, assumptions and institutions based on the dominant mass production, large firm model of the post-Second World War period might have to be jettisoned and new concepts put in their place. At the heart of a new organisation might be a social security system which effectively deals with a variety of non-standard working patterns [see Rodgers, 1989], encourages change by not penalising workers for (flexible) job loss, recognises that "work" takes place in the home as well as the factory and the office, and conceives of the worker as a crucial active input to the success of the business - the effectiveness of which will be recognised as likely to vary according to perceptions of long-term opportunity, security, and adequate labour standards.

A second key aspect of labour as a productive factor concerns co-operative relations between workers and employers and their respective collective organisations. Such co-operation can only be built on a process of mutual trust, with the consequence that the development of economies along district lines would be more difficult in regions with a history of hostile behaviour by one side or the other.

It is also no secret that trade unions have expressed reservations about policies aimed at promoting small firms given the relative weakness, if not absence, of their organisations in that sector. A basic problem is that the organising of the small firm sector, and the provision of trade union services in that sector, are far more costly, far more difficult, and far more complicated than is normally the case in large firms. There appears to be a general recognition, however, that this problem has to be faced and overcome. In respect of small firm industrial districts, the implication from Brutti's contribution to this volume is that Italian union attitudes have become increasingly positive. Similarly, we might note that within a German context, Wassermann [1991] is optimistic about the establishment of social dialogue regarding small and medium-sized firms in that country.

8.   A new role for local government and the State

Until recently, a common viewpoint was that industrialised countries had become overburdened by state intervention in the economic sphere. It was said that the state had become a shackle on free enterprise and, with supposed over-inflated bureaucracies and over-paid government officials, a very expensive one. A very influential movement developed to severely prune the state sector and its alleged constraints on competition, the working of free markets, efficiency, and economic growth.

More recently, however, the pendulum has swung slightly back the other way, as it has been realised that whatever past excesses might have existed, the state, both nationally and locally, does have a vital role to play in development and the regeneration of regional economies. This is being found to pertain as much in the industrialised countries as in the developing world.

At the regional level, the local authority is an agency that can intervene to try and upgrade regions or proto-districts towards ideal dynamic social and economic systems. Several of the writers in this volume touch on this or similar issues. Schmitz, comparing similar developments in the Third Italy and Baden-Württemberg, Germany, emphasises the role that government institutions can play to expand economic potentialities and to introduce innovation to already existing local agglomerations. Kristensen sees that certain areas in Denmark have taken on characteristics reminiscent of the Italian districts despite the absence of any planned conscious strategy; the opportunity is there, he says, for the intervention of conscious strategy. Benton makes a similar point regarding parts of Spain. Sabel suggests that with the growth of the need for, and in many cases the reality of, new kinds of co-operative networks capable of responding adequately to the latest competitive and productive requirements, the involvement of the state can take on a qualitatively new aspect as it becomes part of new kinds of social, economic and administrative structures and practices.

The experience with industrial districts suggests several points at which intervention by local government agencies could be particularly effective. For example, service and environmental infrastructures can be provided. These range from the creation of special industrial parks to the encouragement of the establishment of real service centres and the introduction of adequate financial and educational services.

The local authority can also play the role of social co-ordinator in the sense of bringing together different interest groups to discuss the problems of the region and to come to commonly-agreed programmes of action. In Spain, political and economic decentralisation, according to Benton has provided new opportunities for local alliances to come together to promote their regions. It is this political opportunity which she sees as the best hope that potential districts could be promoted into actual districts along desired lines. Sabel describes the vital role that state agencies are playing in Pennsylvania, USA, as they seek to create a new atmosphere of trust between various interest groups and become involved in the creation of new effective collaborative networks of firms and service institutions.

Such networking is an aspect that local authorities in general can encourage. The local authority can work with real service centres, or specialised economic analysis centres, to identify points of weakness in the economy. Individuals, institutions, and firms, can be encouraged to co-operate in various ways, whether in a direct production sense, or in the sense of providing collectively desired inputs like trained manpower, or in the sense of sharing vital information. For small firms in particular, not having their own specialised internal departments or staff, access to a range of information - on suppliers, markets, fashions, technology, laws, etc. - is especially important.

Intervention might also take the form of actively supporting efforts for an independent small firm employers' association that can establish a strong political voice of its own to promote its specific sectoral interests. In Italy, the importance of organisations representing small businesses, like the National Confederation of Artisans, is well known. Concerning Denmark, Kristensen argues that the industrial districts there - and the embryonic districts - would be better served if there were small firm associations that were not dominated by, or subordinated to, the interests of large firms.

It would seem that if a local economy based on small firms is to develop, it must do so on an autonomous basis. In the case of small firms, this could mean that they must be free from any strong subcontracting dependency relationship, only carrying out production orders issued by parent firms. This is said to have been a typical situation in the Third Italy in earlier times but it was a situation from which small firms managed to free themselves. Now industrial districts there are typified by a relatively high proportion of small firms with direct access to the market. One policy intervention, then, could be to aim to strengthen this autonomy by helping to create direct links with the end market through such means as trade fairs, joint marketing schemes, and common service centres.

Having said that, the necessity for an economy based on the principles of organisation outlined earlier to require the strong domination of small firms is disputed. Schmitz, for example, argues that small firms and large firms can co-exist in an organisational framework essentially similar to the small firm-dominated Italian industrial districts. However, Schmitz points out that where large firms are significant in the local economy, the fact that they have loyalties and obligations beyond the regional boundaries implies difficulties for regional interventionist policies, and certainly implies a need for different policies than those appropriate for a situation where small firms predominate.

Alongside the kinds of interventionist measures described above, the local government, providing it has sufficient powers, can also establish a legal and regulatory framework appropriate to the specific production or service organisation of the local economy. In the case of small firm industrial districts, this could mean laws, taxation rules, and investment incentives favouring the small firms in these economies. It could also mean encouraging trade unions and employers' associations to negotiate specifically suitable agreements.

An appropriate background or framework for effective intervention is a degree of harmony between the policies of the local government and the local institutions it supports, and the activities, regulations, and objectives of higher level political and institutional authorities, including supra-national ones such as the Commission of the European Community.

V. Conclusion

In our view, the experience with industrial districts in Italy, and similar phenomena in Denmark, Spain, Germany, Canada and elsewhere, has demonstrated the comparatively successful organisation of local economies according to the kinds of principles we have discussed in this article. We believe that these organisational principles could be borrowed for use in other places. Of course, it is not being suggested that somehow the total experience of one country such as Italy could be simply transferred to another one; rather, what is being suggested is that other countries could learn from what has happened in the Third Italy or Denmark or Germany, and consider how the sorts of principles that we have highlighted could be successfully applied to, or adapted to, local circumstances.

As Ricoveri et al. [1991] have pointed out, the starting point must be the current conditions existing in the area to be developed, from which point efforts should be made to steer the local economy in the direction of the industrial district model or something similar. This "directing", however, should be by consent and, as argued by Benton, Sabel, and others in this volume, it would necessarily involve close discussions with all the leading political and interest groups, including employers and trade union bodies. An objective would be to encourage political consensus and collaboration in an atmosphere of trust.

Although it is not our aim in this chapter to put forward specific policy proposals, we will, however, in this final concluding section, make a few remarks of policy relevance. Our experience in studying the industrial district phenomenon has led us to question some of the assumptions on which policy initiatives undertaken by national governments and international agencies are based. One assumption still made by many is that big is better and more efficient. Our findings indicate, however, that "it depends": small firms can compete when organised in the appropriate way. And this competition need not take place on the basis of inferior working and payment conditions; we have found small firm sweat shops operating alongside relatively high paying small firms using the latest technology.

Another assumption often made is that "traditional industries" cannot survive, and should not be promoted in advanced industrial economies and that they should be allowed to migrate to low paying developing countries. In fact, it is clear that diversity is possible. There is no compelling reason to engage in a global division of labour in accordance with variations in labour costs, as some would argue. Italian districts which have performed well in such areas as footwear, leather products, textiles, clothing and other traditionally labour-intensive industries, and Danish industries which have prospered in textiles and furniture, have demonstrated that these sectors are not necessarily deemed to disappear from high wage countries. Development in the North should not exclude the continuation of "old" industries, just as the South should not be precluded from a viable investment goods sector.

Related to the last assumption is one that says that developing countries, and perhaps countries in Eastern Europe, should rely on using their "natural advantage" of abundant cheap labour to attract outside capital and develop traditional industries. Our research indicates that the cheap labour, low labour standard, route to development (what we call in this chapter the "low road" strategy) is neither necessary nor desirable. Neither is it necessary to rely entirely on attracting outside "footloose" multinational companies; such companies could, of course, have a role to play, but we think regions should also consider promoting endogenous development from local resources and under basically local control.

References

Bade, F.-J. 1987. "Die wachstumspolitische Bedentung kleiner und mittlerer Unternehmen", in Fritsch, M.; Hull, C. (eds.): *Arbeitsplatzdynamik und Regionalentwicklung*, Berlin.

Becattini, G. 1990. "The Marshallian industrial district as a socio-economic notion", in Pyke, F. et al. (eds.): *Industrial districts and inter-firm co-operation in Italy*, Geneva, International Institute for Labour Studies.

Capecchi, V. 1990. "A history of flexible specialisation and industrial districts in Emilia-Romagna", in Pyke, F. et al. (eds.): *Industrial districts and inter-firm co-operation in Italy*, Geneva, International Institute for Labour Studies.

Courlet, C. 1990. "Industrialisation et territoire: Les systèmes productifs territorialisés", Paper presented to the Conference on Industrial Districts and Inter-Firm Co-operation: Lessons and Policies for the Future, Trois-Rivières, Quebec, April.

Friedman, D. 1988. *The misunderstood miracle: Industrial development and political change in Japan*, Cornell University Press.

Hirst, P.; Zeitlin, J. 1990. *Flexible specialisation vs. post-Fordism: Theory, evidence and policy implications*, Birkbeck Public Policy Centre Working Paper, May.

ILO. 1990. *The promotion of self-employment*, Report VII to the 77th Session of the International Labour Conference, 1990, Geneva, International Labour Office.

Piore, M.J. 1990. "Work, labour and action: Work experience in a system of flexible production", in Pyke, F. et al. (eds.): *Industrial districts and inter-firm co-operation in Italy*, Geneva, International Institute for Labour Studies.

Piore, M.J.; Sabel, C.F. 1984. *The second industrial divide: Possibilities for prosperity*, New York, Basic Books.

Pyke, F. 1988. "Co-operation among small and medium-sized establishments", in *Work, Employment and Society*, Vol. 2, No. 3, pp. 352-365, September.

Pyke, F. et al. (eds.) 1990. *Industrial districts and inter-firm co-operation in Italy*, Geneva, International Institute for Labour Studies.

Raveyre, M.F.; Saglio, J. 1984. "Les systèmes industriels localisés: Eléments pour une analyse sociologique des ensembles de PME industriels", in *Sociologie du Travail*, No. 2, pp. 157-176.

Ricoveri, G. et al., 1991. "Labour and social conditions in Italian industrial districts", in *Labour and Society*, Vol 16, No. 1.

Rodgers, G.; Rodgers, J. (eds.) 1989. *Precarious jobs in labour market regulation*, Geneva, International Institute for Labour Studies.

Schmitz, H. 1990. *Flexible specialisation in Third World industry: Prospects and research requirements*, New Industrial Organisation Programme Discussion Paper No. 18, Geneva, International Institute for Labour Studies.

Semlinger, K. 1990. "Small firms and outsourcing as flexibility reservoirs of large companies", Paper presented to a workshop on the Socio-Economics of Inter-Firm Co-operation, Berlin, Social Science Centre.

Sengenberger, W. 1990. *The role of labour standards in industrial restructuring: Participation, protection and promotion*, New Industrial Organisation Programme Discussion Paper No. 19, Geneva, International Institute for Labour Studies.

Sengenberger, W. et al. (eds.). 1990. *The re-emergence of small enterprises - Industrial restructuring in industrialised countries*, Geneva, International Institute for Labour Studies.

Trigilia, C. 1990. "Work and politics in the Third Italy's industrial districts", in Pyke, F. et al. (eds.): *Industrial districts and inter-firm co-operation in Italy*, Geneva, International Institute for Labour Studies.

Wassermann, W. 1991. "The importance of small and medium-sized enterprises in the Federal Republic of Germany", in *Labour and Society*, Vol. 16, No. 1.

World Commission on Environment and Development. 1987. *Our common future*, Oxford, Oxford University Press, xv + 383 pp.

Part II: European case studies

2 Italian industrial districts: Neither myth nor interlude

Carlo Trigilia

I. Introduction

Discussing the prospects for small-firm development, David Landes, a well-known historian of the Industrial Revolution, returned to the question: "Is small really beautiful?". This time, the answer was "no!". Landes concluded starkly that mass production based on large-scale industry remains *the* form of production best suited to the requirements and resources of the majority of consumers [Landes, 1987]. The view expressed by Landes reflects an assessment that has gained ground steadily in Italy, in response to the recent difficulties faced by small firms and to the success of large companies during the 1980s. There is a growing temptation to view small-firm development as an interlude that can now be seen for what it was. This is also reflected in current international literature on the subject. As Bennett Harrison has put it: "the big firms are coming out of the corner" [Harrison, 1989]. My view, however, is that greater caution is required.

The pitfall that now beckons is the very opposite of what it was a few years ago. In the early 1980s, there was a strong tendency to present small firm industrial districts as *the* emerging successful form of economic organisation, contrasting them with declining large companies. "Flexible specialisation" was identified at times too rigidly with small firms. Paradoxically, the risk today is the exact opposite of this. It is to write off the experience of industrial districts as a brief interlude and to make a distorted assessment of the recovery of the large firms. A less partisan and more evenly balanced approach is needed.

Italian experience suggests that the industrial district phenomenon should be seen as neither a myth nor an interlude. The notion, therefore, that the relations between large and small firm models are a kind of "zero-sum game", so that the success of one form can occur only at the expense of the other, should be rejected. Such an idea is not only mistaken in historical terms, it is also seriously misleading as a key to understanding more recent developments. There are at least two good reasons why this is so.

Firstly, in view of the profound transformations to the organisation of production that are continuing to assail the economies of the highly-industrialised countries, a categorical opposition between large and small industry, defined in isolation, makes less and less sense. Size, in terms of numbers of jobs or of employees directly involved in productive work, has lost much of its importance as a factor in economic success. In other words, to be beautiful it is not enough simply to be big or small. Rather, it is the ability to adapt to an environment that has become more uncertain and unstable, by combining internalised activities with activities founded on co-operative and/or market relations with other firms, that seems to exert a decisive influence on a company's success. Consequently, even if current changes are still very fluid and rule out the provision of clear definitions of interpretive models, there is a growing consensus that the creation of organisational synergies - the formation of networks - is assuming greater importance than the mere size of individual firms. These networks can take on different features. They may be centred on large traditional companies, concentrated in certain areas, caught in the throes of restructuring; or on a set of small firms that are seeking closer links. In either case, the organisational forms in question are far removed from the old-style vertical integration and function-internalisation occurring within a single company.

If one bears this phenomenon in mind, a better assessment may be reached regarding the second aspect that I wish to emphasise: it is becoming ever more difficult to lump small firms together in an all-purpose "small" category. There is, in fact, a wide range of different kinds of small firms systems. In my view, this is one of the most valuable lessons, especially as regards Italy, to be learnt from more than a decade of intense research and investigation into small business, involving economists, sociologists and other experts.

As Brusco [1986] has pointed out, at least three different types of small firm can be distinguished. The first type is the "traditional small firm" that produces directly for a market of non-standardised goods and that may - but does not necessarily - have to rely for its competitive position on low labour costs and weak labour protection. A second type is the small firm that acts as a "dependent sub-supplier". This kind of firm manufactures parts or components for one or a few larger companies. As a result, it is not only very dependent but, in order to retain a strong competitive position vis-à-vis similar firms, it relies above all on cheap labour and flimsy labour protection. This second type of firm mushroomed in Italy during the 1970s as a consequence of the decentralisation of manufacturing. Large companies, confronted at that time with considerable labour conflict and hefty wage increases, turned to decentralisation as a means to save on labour costs and enhance their flexibility. The "industrial district" is a quite different model. Here, the small firm forms part of a network of firms with a highly-specialised division of labour in typical manufacturing sectors and within a specific geographical area. As Becattini [1990] has stressed, the industrial district, rather than the isolated small firm, is the unit of analysis for this form of economic organisation. The district, therefore, is a sort of functional alternative to the large company. It has its own technological and productive dynamism, in addition to the ability to maintain high wage and employment levels. Over the last 20 years in Italy, there has been a marked growth of industrial districts, especially in the central and northern regions.

If one bears in mind the considerable range of circumstances within which small firms operate, two consequences become visible. Firstly, it is hard to assess the specific performance of industrial districts. Therefore, any aggregate statistical analysis, relying on size thresholds to distinguish between small and large firms in terms of employee numbers, should obviously only be used with great caution. To assert on such a basis that labour costs are lower in small firms (e.g. below the 100 employee mark), or that there is less investment in new technologies, may well be misleading. Data of this type reflect mean values behind which a host of different situations may be lurking. Secondly, there are a number of implications for industrial policy-making. It would clearly be a mistake to apply the same political and trade union policies to widely differing types of small business.

These observations suggest, therefore, a need for caution in assessing the performance and development of districts. What we need is the kind of disaggregate and specific analyses that are not often available. As regards Italy in particular, we know a great deal about how the districts emerged and how they function, but little about the transformations now occurring. This does not mean, however, that industrial districts do not run into problems. Indeed, there are signs from time to time that indicate quite considerable problems of adjustment. But one cannot, in principle, rule out the possibility that institutional interventions will be found to address the new constraints, or that the districts will continue to co-exist with other forms of productive organisation in which large companies play a more central role. There do not appear to be any rigid technological constraints on the reproduction of districts. The main problems are organisational. Indeed, the increased flexibility of the new technologies might be expected to enable the co-existence of a broader range of different organisational models than in the past. We may thus assume that productive organisation will tend to become increasingly polymorphous. The emergence of one model rather than another would therefore depend less on technological constraints than on the overall institutional context and past experiences. Of course, we do not yet know whether, or to what extent, the institutional interventions able to tackle the emergent problems in industrial districts will be pursued. But it seems essential that any such interventions should be properly focused on the specific needs of the kind of small business for which they are designed. A catch-all approach to small business leads to distortions in both interpretation and policy-making.

In the following, I shall refer to the Italian industrial districts. Section II provides a brief account of how the districts emerged and the ways in which they function. In Section III, I discuss the main problems that districts are now facing. For reasons that have already been clarified, the analysis of this aspect will by necessity be more tentative. I shall then turn to the analysis of several policy implications relating to the strengthening of industrial districts (Section IV), and, finally, to the development of similar forms in underdeveloped settings (Section V).

II.   Italian districts

It is well known that in the 1970s, market changes and the costs and rigidities associated with hierarchies created major difficulties almost everywhere for large mass production "Fordist" companies. Over the same period, new technologies able to cut the costs of flexible production were opening up fresh opportunities for small firms to adapt more rapidly to a market that was increasingly differentiated and unstable (especially in production lines influenced by fashion trends). The crisis affecting large firms was particularly acute in Italy where - for reasons that we cannot examine here - mass production had developed rapidly, but without adequate institutional adjustments in industrial relations and the welfare state.

Paradoxically, however, Italy offered a particularly favourable set of institutional resources which ensured that the new opportunities for small firm development were grasped more rapidly and in a more wholesale manner than in other countries. Such resources were in especially good supply in the central and north-eastern regions - the so-called *terza Italia* ("Third Italy") [Bagnasco, 1977]. It was in these areas that the development of small business took the form mainly of the industrial district (there are about 50 such districts). Some industrial districts have developed in the north-west and in the south, but in the north-west there is a very marked concentration of large firms and metropolitan areas, and in the south there are major outstanding problems relating to underdevelopment. Industrial districts tend to be specialised in traditional sectors - textiles, clothing, footwear, furniture - but there has also been a significant development in modern sectors, especially in mechanical engineering. Thus, for example, Prato has specialised in textiles, Poggibonsi in furniture, Sassuolo in ceramics, Montegranaro in footwear, Modena in machine tools and agricultural machinery, and so on. Industrial districts usually coincide with small urban areas and cover one or a handful of communes: the population of the district does not usually exceed 100,000.

Three institutional factors appear to have been of crucial importance in the growth of industrial districts [Trigilia, 1986, 1990; Bagnasco, 1988]. All three may be found in their typical - though not their only - forms in the small business areas of the centre and north-east of Italy:

1.   A network of small and medium-sized urban centres with strong craft and trading traditions. These centres have acted as the principal pools from which entrepreneurial skills and resources could be drawn.

2.   The spread of family-based agricultural smallholdings (sharecropping, peasant farms), helping to create the original flexible supply of an inexpensive workforce whose skills and motivations were well suited to the development of small business.

3. The presence of local political traditions and institutions linked in with a Catholic tradition and a socialist and communist movement. The influence of political life on the development of small business should not be misconstrued. This development was not decisively stimulated through direct political measures, or through the application of economic or industrial policies. Historically, political subcultures, albeit in a variety of different forms, have helped to preserve a specific socio-economic fabric, characterised by a peculiar mix of traditional and modern elements. Furthermore, these political subcultures have promoted the emancipation of politics from civil society. In contrast with what has happened, for example, in the south, politics have thus become more independent of family and private interests, and more strongly tied to the defence of collective interests. This has helped to institutionalise the market. On the one hand, it has focused the pursuit of personal success on the market rather than on politics or crime. On the other hand, it has promoted good industrial relations and locally-based policies, and hence the generation of "collective goods".

But the influence of the institutional context affects not only the origins of industrial districts; indeed, it extends to the specific ways in which this form of economic organisation operates. We have already drawn attention to one essential economic feature of the districts: the highly-developed division of labour between numerous small firms, only some of which have direct contact with the market. These small firms take on orders and produce the goods, while making use of a dense network of sub-suppliers specialised in particular stages of the production process. There are markets, therefore, for each stage of production and the small specialist firms are thus stimulated by competition to innovate. The possibility of working for several different customers reduces the dependence of sub-suppliers on single companies and enables them to put flexible machinery to full use. It is in this way that "flexible specialisation" [Piore and Sabel, 1984] is achieved, permitting districts to excel in the production of goods for which demand fluctuates greatly and whose production may be divided into decentralised stages.

We can now assess the way in which socio-cultural and political factors not only impinge from the outside but also intervene in the concrete functioning of the labour and sub-supply markets. The production of goods in the district obviously demands a high degree of co-operation between many entrepreneurs and between the said entrepreneurs and workers employed in many different production units. How is such co-operation achieved? In sub-supplying, for instance, there is certainly strong competition, but this is offset by mechanisms of co-operation with the result that neither the customer nor sub-supplier has much leverage when they find themselves in a favourable market position. That is to say, they do not maximise short-term profitability. This brings mutual advantages in the medium and long term, for example in terms of delivery times or - even more important - as regards innovation processes involving risks to both sides. These forms of co-operation, which supplement mechanisms of competition, are founded on a network of trust that is sustained by the cultural and community-based features outlined above.

As regards the labour market, too, various forms of co-operation come into play that limit short-term market rationality, especially as it affects sections of the workforce with more specific skills. Yet it can be shown that alongside these mechanisms, linked to the cultural and community fabric, a specific form of political regulation of the labour market has gradually developed, and with it a very particular model of industrial relations. This has occurred in particular where the institutional context referred to above has been strong. The existence of a local institutional context, with deep-rooted political and associative traditions, has promoted unionisation, and thereby supported the development of identity and organisation. Over time, these resources were deployed to launch a model of industrial relations quite different from that prevalent in large companies, which has attracted, and continues to attract, more attention.

In industrial districts there has developed, side by side with economic growth, a co-operative and locally-based model. The trade unions do not place constraints on the flexible use of labour - either within or between firms - although they do bargain over related wage levels and, more recently, over the forms taken by such flexibility. In exchange for their co-operation, they obtain often substantial increases in locally negotiated wages that apply even to the smallest firms; full employment at a local level; the delivery of social services by local governments, usually more efficient than those provided in large cities and in the south. In the bargaining process, local considerations are generally more important than company-specific ones, but in some areas union presence may be significant at the company level as well. This accounts for the fact that union membership levels are higher in the small business areas in the centre and north of Italy than in large companies. It also explains the growth in real wages, which in many areas are higher, or at least no lower, than those in large firms - even if in general working time is longer. Of course, as I have already pointed out, this trend cannot be observed merely by referring to aggregate statistical data that lump the various different kinds of small business together.

In conclusion, for a considerable proportion of small firms - those that display the greatest dynamism - it is not, as is often maintained, the lack of constraints placed on the market that has promoted development. Rather, it is the presence of constraints and socio-cultural and political rigidities that has sustained flexibility. Or, as Dore [1986] would say, it is the presence of "flexible rigidities". Where the institutional conditions that we have mentioned are most in evidence, there has been most success in grasping new opportunities for the development of more autonomous and dynamic small firms systems as well as for the modernisation of more backward forms (traditional decentralisation). This is not to say that all small firms have gone down this road, but many have been able to do so, especially in areas where there has been a favourable institutional context. This helps to explain not only the particular spread in Italy of small firms integrated according to a district-centred logic, but also the difficulties that this form of economic organisation has encountered, for example in the south, for fundamentally non-economic reasons. This has a number of obvious implications for any attempt to promote industrial districts in backward areas, a point to which I shall return later.

III. New challenges and the need for adjustment

After the success enjoyed by industrial districts in the 1970s and early 1980s, there followed a more uncertain phase. At a time when large Italian companies were leading a spectacular process of productive restructuring, many districts were running into trouble. Despite the lack of research into on-going processes, I shall attempt to focus on the problems posed by modernisation, and the constraints encountered by more sophisticated forms of productive, technological and organisational integration. Viewed from this angle, a number of general problems can be pinpointed that assume different manifestations according to the concrete features of the single district. These problems are in part a consequence of the process of development itself, as it relates for example to environmental or infrastructural concerns or to socio-cultural changes. But they are also linked to the basic organisational characteristics of the productive structure and to the resulting constraints on a process of innovation capable of meeting the challenges of the market.

As regards this last point, I should like to focus attention on an aspect of particular importance for the discussion. It can be argued that current trends make forms of organisational regulation increasingly important for the consolidation of development. That is to say that the actions of interest groups and local governments and, in particular, that of regional governments, can play an important role. I shall attempt to clarify this aspect below.

During the 1980s, a number of the exogenous variables that previously operated in the interests of small firms in Italy underwent change. Macro-economic policies pursued at national level were modified, with important repercussions on exchange rates and credit. In particular, Italy's entry into the European Monetary System (EMS) put an end to the policy of gradual lira devaluation that had propped up Italian exports throughout the 1970s. International competition grew tougher and there was no slackening of uncertainty and instability. The devaluation of the dollar had a very negative effect on exports. However, just as it would be blinkered to ascribe the dynamism of small business in the 1970s exclusively to favourable exogenous variables, it would be equally short-sighted to interpret the present situation as a mere reflection of exogenous changes. A close look must be taken at the organisational features of the productive structure and at its ability to respond to external constraints. Local and regional public operators and business and trades union organisations are in any case obliged to take this approach in order to frame their strategy.

From this vantage point, I would like to raise the following point: productive flexibility - the small firm's prime resource - now appears less able on its own to guarantee positive results. This can be better appreciated if one bears two facts in mind: (a) the marked increase in labour costs, and increasing competition from low-wage countries in the production of poor quality goods; (b) the increased competitiveness resulting from new technology, which tends to bring down the costs of flexibility for large firms as well.

Under the conditions now emerging, the stages of new product planning and design and of marketing and market relations are assuming greater importance. Productive flexibility itself entails a continual emphasis on innovation. The spread of mechanical expertise in small business areas has paved the way for important innovations in the productive process. The incremental "bottom-up" nature of this type of innovation has been clearly demonstrated - and its contribution to the continual upgrading of the potential and flexibility of machinery should not be underestimated. However, looking ahead, greater attention should be paid to new electronic technologies. But this is constrained by prevailing mechanical orientations, as well as by the expense that new technology often involves. Similar points may be made as regards marketing and market relations. These aspects are assuming increasing importance as a competitive resource, and large firms are now directing considerable efforts in this direction. Small businesses, however, tend to be oriented more towards the product than towards the market. Moreover, innovation in marketing is costly and difficult for small isolated firms to undertake.

Innovations are therefore required in technology, organisation, business and management training, and labour skills. Productive units, given their limited size, are not able effectively to internalise such resources and services, besides which they are often scarce in the districts where the firms are located. Problems in adapting productive structures can therefore be summed up in terms of an overall need for greater organisation. It has to be seen to what extent forms of co-operation between firms, that is, regulation mechanisms that operate between market and hierarchies, can be developed.

Indeed, in the new circumstances, the former combination of the market and of relations of trust limits the possibility of innovation by hindering the concentration of resources and the allocation of related risks. But traditional vertical integration can no longer be advocated, given the growing quantitative and qualitative variability in demand, and the need for organisational flexibility that this entails. It is no accident that large companies have themselves moved away from forms of rigid vertical integration, opening the door to collaboration with small, specialised firms, integrated in a more or less stable way within their organisational framework. If, therefore, as Sabel [1987], for example, has observed, the efficient operation of the network to which they belong is becoming increasingly important for both large and small firms, there remains one fundamental difference that I should like to emphasise. Large companies have at their disposal a unitary command system and a set of financial and organisational resources that allow them greater decision-making speed and autonomy when it comes to constructing their networks and shaping the architecture of their systems around a strategy that prioritises flexibility and quality. Under the new conditions of competition, it is more difficult for small firm networks, i.e. districts, to grasp and consolidate the opportunities opened up by the strategy of flexibility. Greater co-operation in the creation of "collective goods" is called for. Although it may not appear to be in each individual actor's immediate interest to contribute to the development of "collective goods", their creation is essential for the future welfare of each and every actor within the district. This is why it is vitally important that the local institutional context should be able to promote the creation of "collective goods" by fostering innovation and co-operation, professional training, environmental and infrastructural resource control, and conflict management. Of course, some steps in this direction have already been taken. In small business areas, a variety of new types of organisation are already springing up: consortia, business services centres, co-operatives, groups of companies, etc. In many areas, however, these trends seem unable to address the problems of adjustment.

IV. Policy problems

There is broad agreement about the need for more effective forms of organisation located between the market and the hierarchy. There does not, however, appear to be any corresponding consensus regarding two important consequences that I believe flow from this outlook. I shall therefore present them as hypotheses for discussion.

The first point is that innovation in small business now raises a problem of territorial scale. It underscores the relation with larger towns and cities as centres of services, and throws into relief the city as a place at which strategic functions are concentrated (research, finance - an aspect that has so far been neglected -, marketing, promotion, etc.).

The second hypothesis is that, given the constraints of scale that at present limit experimentation with broader organisational synergies, a regulatory dimension at the regional level might be more relevant for future development, covering both regional government and interest groups. The promotion of forms of co-operation and organisation among small firms, the easing of much-needed access to credit, the building of relations between industrial districts and those large centres better disposed towards innovation, would all be fostered by an "intermediate government" of development. This point needs to be clarified with reference both to policies and to actors.

As regards policies, the provision of strategic services for small firms and the difficulties encountered by districts in this area are of obvious importance. What is needed is analysis and imaginative initiatives on a variety of levels. It is often emphasised that innovation cannot easily be brought into small and medium-size business systems in a "top-down" way. Innovation must grow up from the bottom, involving the potential users and stimulating a demand that may otherwise not be there, and organising its encounter with supply. This makes it necessary for certain services to be decentralised and for them to be developed in close symbiosis with production. Other services - whose impact is less immediate if no less important - require an urban environment, synergies with available cultural and scientific institutions, and links to dimensions broader than the district. An example is provided by scientific parks, or forms of institutionalised collaboration between companies, universities and top-flight research centres.

In this perspective, policies should reveal a basic requirement: they should be organised through an "intermediate" government, a regional dimension not able to manage directly, of course, but to stimulate and co-ordinate both the differentiation and the integration of a range of public and private initiatives and actors, even if located in different areas. It is not a question of suppressing the forms of locally-based regulations that have been vital for the development of small business, but rather to integrate local elements in a regional dimension in order to help them overcome the worsening bottlenecks that are currently bedevilling them.

As for the actors, it is worth emphasising that this kind of outlook does not entail any straightforward reduction in the role of local actors - trade unions, business organisations, local governments - in favour of regional level bodies. It is a matter of developing a more efficient division of labour between the various levels. This, however, does demand a strengthening of regional government.

Perhaps this point can be clarified by an example. The problems of restructuring local systems and of bringing in new technology involve important processes of training and reskilling, of flexibility and labour mobility. There is reason to think that a greater involvement of trade unions at company level as well as locally in the handling of problems relating to job training, flexibility and mobility, might help to speed up and smooth processes of adjustment. A strengthening, therefore, of the regulatory role of local actors - trade unions, business organisations, councils - could represent a resource for the districts. However, this cannot be taken on trust given that resistance from individual firms and often from individual employees has to be overcome. At the same time, unless there is a means of directing and selecting forms of intervention at a level broader than the individual district, the creation of a "collective good" such as job training would be compromised. To be effective, job training requires, at the highest levels, a focusing of effort and an integration of technical and scientific infrastructures. Indeed, from a utilitarian standpoint, it may be rational for individual companies and for actors in individual districts not to contribute to the creation of this "collective good", the advantages of which none the less accrue to the entire regional economy. But the inadequate supply of a "collective good" such as job training in the end undermines the ability of individual districts to make the necessary adjustments. To avoid this and similar traps besetting the creation of "collective goods", the ability to pool interests needs to be strengthened at a regional level and particular attention needs to be paid to furthering co-operation between interest groups and regional development.

This need is also clearly highlighted by other factors concerning, for example, land use and local planning, energy supplies, environmental protection, refuse disposal, traffic, and the need to overhaul transport and communications networks. These are areas in which the limits of locally-based regulation can be readily appreciated. Obviously, the small business economy consumes an increasing amount of local environmental resources, while creating externalities that go far beyond the individual areas concerned. It is the public as a whole that has to foot the bill, but in the final analysis the costs have to be met by the companies, too.

In conclusion, the point to stress is that in small business areas in the past a relation between politics and the economy was generally created at a local level. It was mainly based on redistribution. A kind of division of labour between business, unions and local government developed. Business was free to respond flexibly to market opportunities. Union and local government bodies concentrated their energies on compensation for labour flexibility. The unions did so by focusing bargaining initiatives on economic aspects and wages, even if there were episodes of more specific negotiation on flexibility. Local government has above all pursued social policies and sought to make a number of fundamental infrastructural interventions. The regional governments joined this mechanism in the 1970s basically to provide backing for the redistributional action of the local authorities, and the local regulative framework.

This model now seems to have become weaker and less able to sustain development. On-going changes have made it necessary to redefine the relation between politics and the economy, shifting the emphasis away from redistribution and towards the active stimulation of economic and social conditions conducive to development. One essential implication of the foregoing remarks is that the various kinds of policies designed to support industrial districts must be primarily of the "supply policy" variety, tailored to strengthen the systemic capacities and horizontal integration of industrial districts. Such policies, however, if they are to operate efficiently must: (a) be context-sensitive, with a high degree of flexibility and differentiation over time and space; (b) possess a concentration of resources resulting from the co-ordination and integration of different policies; (c) avoid assuming traditional bureaucratic forms, and involve instead intense collaboration with the various interests in play, not only in the initial stages, but also in the process of implementation.

From this it follows that interventions of this type presuppose the existence of strong institutional interlocutors at the decentralised level: a regional dimension in development management. This, in its turn, seems to demand the integration of localism into a regional perspective, and thus the reinforcement of the ability to politically redefine the interests at this level and the co-operation between interest groups and regional government. Naturally, an answer of this type will not necessarily emerge. But the ability of interest groups and of local and regional governments to assume a new regulatory role will influence the development of small business in Italy to a greater extent than has been the case in the past.

V.   Districts and regional development

Are there any lessons to be learnt from the experiences of industrial districts that would be of relevance to the development of backward areas? This question usually elicits two contrasting responses. The first and more pessimistic response tends to view the success of districts as a contingent fact, stressing the specificity of the institutional context that encouraged the growth of districts in a number of regions. Accordingly, districts are not deemed a valid alternative for the development of backward areas. The second response, however, is more optimistic. The success of districts is considered to be more long-lasting. While recognising the influence of specific institutional factors in the origins of small firm development, this view argues that appropriate political interventions could provide substitutes for such factors.

In my opinion, the Italian experience should counsel caution in this respect also. Districts cannot be regarded as *the* strategy for endogenous development. But nor should it be ruled out that, *under certain circumstances*, such a strategy might prove effective. I shall attempt to show that the difficulties derive from the fact that it is not simply a matter of devising efficient economic policies: what is needed is a whole package of interventions designed to "create" the appropriate actors for such policies.

Above all, it should be recalled that Italian experience confirms the importance of non-economic factors in the growth of districts. It is no accident that, as we have seen, districts are concentrated in regions where the institutional context encourages co-operation and horizontal integration between firms. In southern Italy - especially on the Adriatic side - there are many small firms, but hardly any full-fledged districts. Mostly, one encounters small, isolated, traditional firms or dependent sub-suppliers working for northern firms. For situations of this type - which are probably widespread in other backward areas, especially in the Mediterranean countries - is it possible to conceive of a development strategy that takes its inspiration from industrial districts?

As regards policies for southern Italy, the first observation to make is that it is pointless - indeed it can often be counterproductive - to rely on financial incentives targeted on single firms. This form of intervention exerts an attraction above all on large firms from outside the area. These large firms thus obtain extra resources to finance costly restructuring processes. But, in general, they are concentrated in sectors of production that are not characterised by high labour intensity and that do not stimulate the growth of local small and medium-sized firms. As for the said small local firms, the existence of incentives tends to encourage initiatives of doubtful efficiency, based more on political protection than on hard-headed business calculation. Past experience of incentives to small firms has not therefore been positive, and the orientation adopted by the European Community to limit recourse to this instrument is well-motivated.

Having dispensed with direct and individual incentives, one might wish to focus attention on interventions designed to encourage the kind of horizontal integration between small companies that, in the case of industrial districts occurs spontaneously, owing to the historical features of the institutional context. Of course, a strategy of this type presupposes the existence of small, traditional firms or of dependent sub-suppliers. In such cases, it would be a matter of making use of those "supply policies" that we have mentioned in relation to districts' problems of consolidation. These "supply policies" ought to encourage the creation of "collective goods" in terms of economies external to the individual companies: the spread of technological know-how, trade promotion, business skills training, worker training, and so on. But while these resources may facilitate the adjustment process undertaken by already existing districts, it is doubtful that they would suffice for backward areas. For in backward areas one of the main constraints on growth is mutual distrust between operators, which does nothing to promote productive specialisation or economies of agglomeration. The spread of services external to the firms, in the field of technology, in marketing and in training, may help to build a climate of greater collaboration, but is probably not sufficient on its own. One might therefore think in terms of more complex interventions, for example of projects designed to encourage co-operation between local firms, while orienting them towards production lines of greater quality. To this end, specific and temporary services might be supplied, backed by public funding, but no direct incentives. It might also be useful to involve in these projects medium-sized and large firms from outside the area, in order to learn from their experience.

But who ought to manage such complex policies? As we have seen, in order to be effective, supply policies have to be flexible, inter-sectorial, non-bureaucratic, and managed in collaboration with those whose interests are at stake. Hence the need to enhance the role of local and regional government. But this raises a problem that the Italian experience has clearly highlighted. Generally speaking, in backward areas, local and regional authorities are weaker than elsewhere and less able to carry out effective economic policies.

In the case of Italy, we have seen the importance for the growth of districts of a solid local institutional context, a well-organised and autonomous civil society, and efficient local government. And these are precisely the weak points in southern areas. The pervasiveness of a kind of politics that functions as a regulator of social relations makes civil society dependent and disorganised. Both business and trade union associations are weak. Political relations of the client-patron type, between single individuals or between groups and members of the local political class, prevail. This renders local government institutions inefficient because there are no representative structures able to hold particular interests in check. The results are: the subservience of the bureaucracy, distributive policies that make it possible to share the spoils widely, and non-decisions on everything that is less easy to divide up.

Given this framework, it might be dangerous to rely too heavily on local government institutions. On the other hand, effective supply policies cannot be implemented from the centre. What, then, should be done? A convincing and consistent answer to this query still has to be tried out. All that we can do here is to suggest a number of directions in which it might be worth developing further discussion.

Looked at from this angle, it seems to me important to examine ways not only of strengthening local government institutions but also - at the same time - of enhancing the autonomy and organisation of civil society. It is not enough merely to provide local and regional governments with the skills and resources needed for local supply policies, nor is it enough to train the local bureaucracy, though in several countries, including Italy, even these aims are hard to reach. It is necessary also to stimulate the creation of strong interlocuters within civil society. Organisations representing different interests need to be reinforced by institutional means and their role in the design and implementation of new policies should be enhanced. Such organisations could, in fact, supply the information and the necessary consensus for effective policies and could help to limit pressures from the local political class in favour of inefficient distributive policies. The political construction of the interlocuters is an essential part of a development strategy because these organisations might eventually "internalise" the advantages deriving from the production of "collective goods" and might, as a result, develop a longer-term view of individual interests, inducing them to co-operate more effectively.

The attempt to apply lessons from the experience of industrial districts to economically backward areas is thus fraught with considerable difficulties. It is not merely a matter of finding and implementing the right economic policies. More complex interventions need to be devised to reinforce the autonomy of civil society vis-à-vis the local political system. Unless a more autonomous and better-organised civil society is created, and unless a more autonomous and better technically trained bureaucracy emerges, any new policy is liable to prove inefficient and to stimulate the growth of political entrepreneurship rather than economic development. It is not an easy job. But none of the alternatives so far tried is any more appealing.

References

Bagnasco, A. 1977. *Tre Italie. La problematica territoriale dello sviluppo italiano*, Bologna, Il Mulino.

---. 1988. *La costruzione sociale del mercato*, Bologna, Il Mulino.

Becattini, G. 1990. "The Marshallian industrial district as a socio-economic notion", in Pyke, F. et al. (eds.): *Industrial districts and inter-firm co-operation in Italy*, Geneva, International Institute for Labour Studies.

Brusco, S. 1986. "Small firms and industrial districts: The experience of Italy", in Keeble, D.; Wever, E. (eds.): *New firms and regional development in Europe*, London, Croom Helm.

Dore, R. 1986. *Flexible rigidities. Industrial policy and structural adjustment in the Japanese economy*, London, Athlone Press.

Harrison, B. 1989. *The big firms are coming out of the corner*, Paper prepared for the International Conference on Industrial Transformation and Regional Development, Nagoya, Japan, September.

Landes, D. 1987. "Piccolo è bello. Ma è bello davvero?", in Landes, D. (ed.): *A che servono i padroni? Le alternative storiche dell'industrializzazione*, Turin, Bollati-Boringhieri.

Piore, M.J.; Sabel, C.F. 1984. *The second industrial divide: Possibilities for prosperity*, New York, Basic Books.

Sabel, C. 1987. *The reemergence of regional economies: Changes in the scale of production*, Paper prepared for the SSRC Western European Committee.

Trigilia, C. 1986. *Grandi partiti e piccole imprese. Comunisti e democristiani nelle regioni a economia diffusa*, Bologna, Il Mulino.

---. 1990. "Work and politics in the Third Italy's industrial districts", in Pyke, F. et al. (eds.): *Industrial districts and inter-firm co-operation in Italy*, Geneva, International Institute for Labour Studies.

3 The emergence of industrial districts in Spain: Industrial restructuring and diverging regional responses[1]

Lauren Benton

I. Introduction

We now know enough about recent industrial restructuring processes to say that certain patterns of spatial and productive reorganisation tend to support one another. In particular, the spatial reconcentration of industry - the reappearance of strong local and regional economies - and the emergence of systems of "flexible specialisation" in the wake of widespread industrial restructuring are inter-related, and sometimes mutually reinforcing, trends.[2] Simple geographical concentration of industry, and particularly the concentration of small and medium-sized firms, appears to help promote the kinds of relationships among firms that are considered the hallmark of flexible production systems. The close proximity of businesses in the same or related sectors may facilitate communication among firms and so help to fuel a collective process of innovation; the overlap between residential and working communities may also strengthen social ties that help to minimise conflict and support alternatives to destructive forms of competition. Local and regional concentrations of industry may thus act as incubators for a style of industrial growth that is particularly responsive to the intensified international competition and fragmented markets of the 1990s.

Yet, the relationship between new spatial patterns in industry and dynamic growth is not always clear-cut. A close reading of the literature on flexible specialisation shows that the process through which flexible production systems evolve is necessarily open-ended. Dynamic growth and

1.   The author would like to thank María Teresa Costa Campi, Josep-Antoni Ybarra, and Frank Pyke (who are, of course, responsible for none of the paper's shortcomings) for their insightful comments on an earlier draft.

2.   Sabel [1982, 1987] gives the clearest explanations of both phenomena. See also Capecchi [1989, 1990] on the origins of flexible specialisation and its contrast to Fordist production; on industry's spatial reorganisation and the relationship of its process to flexible specialisation, see Scott [1988].

novel forms of industrial organisation emerge in some places in the wake of industrial restructuring, while elsewhere similar economic pressures have perpetuated the dominance of large firms or recreated a reliance in small firms on cheaper, unprotected labour in systems of subordinate sub-contracting.[3] A range of outcomes appears possible even in superficially similar settings. We must look beyond the spatial characteristics of industrial settings and analyse the character of these communities - the nature of relations among businesses, between workers and employers, and between the worlds of work and social life outside the workplace - if we are to understand how dynamic patterns of growth evolve in some places, and how they can be cultivated elsewhere.

Previous case studies of industrial restructuring teach us the utility of focusing our analysis on forms of co-operation inside concentrations identified as "industrial districts." These dynamic centres of industrial activity are characterised by, among other features, intricate relationships among firms of varying sizes and market orientation, often in the same sector or in closely related sectors; a high degree of innovation that supports success in national and international markets; and a fluid relationship between workplace activities and social life that has been described as "a 'thickening' of industrial and social interdependencies."[4] Earlier research reveals the importance of various forms of *co-operation* in and around industrial districts as a complement to competition. These sets of relationships have the potential to transform destructively competitive settings into fertile environments for the development of dynamic systems of flexible production.

Throughout this paper, I will make reference to three forms of co-operation in analysing Spanish industry. First, *inter-firm co-operation* emerges when independent firms begin to form relationships based on their ability to produce complementary products or carry out related but non-competing production processes. This situation contrasts with that in a subordinate subcontracting system, where relationships among firms can be represented as a downward-pointing branch, with firms at each level competing against each other to supply a narrower range of clients with similar products or services. In flexible systems, the lines connecting firms compose a complex web, as producers begin to attract clientele by offering specialised products

---

3. Although critics such as Amin and Robins [1990] often focus on the more ambitious claims of the literature that represent flexible specialisation as a model, or even a universal trend in industry, the open-endedness of the process of industrial restructuring is a central point in key writings on flexible specialisation; see especially Sabel and Zeitlin [1985]. The possibility for strikingly different outcomes of industrial reorganisation that feature off-the-books employment and subordinate subcontracting is explored by Portes et al. [1989]. See also Benton [1990].

4. The quote is from Becattini [1990a]. Helpful discussions of the key features of industrial districts, and the definition of the concept, include those by Becattini [1990b] and Piore [1990]. Brusco [1990] traces the origins of the concept in writings on Italian industrial development.

that offer direct competition to a much smaller group of peer firms.[5] One
type of inter-firm co-operation, then, exists between client firms and
subcontractors, as they work more closely together on technological change
and product design.

Another type involves the freer exchange of information among
many smaller firms that no longer compete directly for clients, as they begin
to share information about production techniques and markets. In some
cases, such co-operative relationships are formalised, as evidenced in some
industrial districts where firms in the same sector band together to perform
collectively certain critical functions that small enterprises generally find it
difficult to carry out alone: for example, co-operating to present products at
national and international trade fairs, combining resources to invest in
research and development, or even joining together to engage professional
accounting services. More broadly, inter-firm co-operation may be enhanced
simply where the flow of information among entrepreneurs is increased - thus
the importance of overlapping work and social relationships in the close-knit
communities of industrial districts.

A second kind of co-operation that is more often overlooked in case
studies, perhaps because it is more difficult to document, is that which takes
place *inside* firms. Early studies of flexible specialisation in central Italian
districts emphasised the marked departure in many smaller firms from the
hierarchical organisation of work inside the large factory. Especially for
skilled workers, production of short batches in close collaboration with clients
opened the opportunity for greater autonomy inside the firm. Routinised
work assignments gave way to a looser organisation in which more flexible
and variable tasks, often built around teamwork, predominated. Worker-
entrepreneurs, too, by participating in production, often found themselves
collaborating with workers rather than supervising them, a change that
opened the way for less conflictive relationships on the shop floor. Just as
inter-firm co-operation was supported by social ties that extended into the
community, *intra-firm co-operation* depended, too, on perceptions of work
that were moulded outside the workplace. In particular, workers' past
experiences with collective protest in Fordist factories often reinforced their
search for alternative ways of organising the production process.

A third key form of co-operation is represented in local-level
alliances among government, labour groups, political parties, and employer
associations. In the central Italian case, Communist Party affiliation often
crosses the boundaries of these groups and promotes perceptions of common
interest. Social ties in the community, or participation in local cultural
activities, may serve the same function. This *institutional co-operation* itself
appears to be crucial as a support for inter- and intra-firm co-operation. By
funding services to small firms (in the manner described by Brusco in this
volume), for example, municipal or regional governments may give vital

---

5.   Diagrams of both types of production systems are presented in Capecchi [1989].

sustenance to inter-firm associations. Relationships inside firms, at the same time, may be influenced by policies that promote such causes as worker training, the formation of co-operatives, and access to credit for skilled workers seeking to start new enterprises.

Where we find that some or all of these elements of co-operation are missing (or where co-operation takes different forms), the process of industrial restructuring is likely to take a different path. For some sectors and for some national industries, the direction that industrial restructuring takes is vitally important. In Spain, the case that is the subject of this chapter, the capacity of industry to move towards flexible production is widely considered to be crucial to the country's ability to compete internationally, without the benefit of the significant wage-cost advantage that underwrote an earlier phase of rapid industrialisation. Although many examples in the Spanish case would contradict claims about the generalisable success of industrial districts, taken together, the examples support the view that strong pressures to create industry that is more flexible are universally present, and that this situation at least creates the possibility for new areas of consensus and new forms of co-operation among industry, labour, and local communities. It is this *opportunity* for a new relationship between communities and industry that deserves our attention. By contrasting cases in which industrial districts work to enhance both competitiveness and community well-being with cases in which they are characterised more by internal conflict and short-term, exploitative growth strategies, we can begin to identify those sets of policies and local conditions that promote the former outcome over the latter.

This chapter discusses the ways in which different patterns of inter-firm relationships, the organisation of production, and the dynamics of local alliance-building have shaped diverging regional responses to industrial restructuring in Spain. I argue, in particular, that on-going efforts to promote growth in emerging industrial districts must begin with the analysis of such local co-operative relationships and must build policy interventions that respond specifically to their logic. The chapter begins with a look at the broad political and economic context shaping the emergence of industrial districts in Spain. It then presents an analysis of the industrial restructuring process and profiles cases representing two emerging patterns: the industrial district on the urban periphery and the mono-sectoral industrial district in rural surroundings. A final section considers past industrial policy and its effects on districts and suggests directions for future policy to support dynamic growth.

II. Industrial restructuring in Spain

Some conditions in Spain pose a striking contrast to the Italian case and suggest that the trajectory of industrial restructuring must necessarily be very different. Although the pressures, both economic and political, to restructure industry after the mid-1970s have been very strong, Spanish industry began this process from a very different baseline and, also, in the midst of a global economic downturn and internal political transformation. This timing has meant that many sectors have restructured more out of economic necessity and cost-cutting strategies "from above" than as a result of collective strategies "from below" to take advantage of new market opportunities, create alternatives to established forms of production, or build on artisanal traditions or movements for local autonomy. Not surprisingly, the first stages of restructuring saw the growth of a large informal sector of off-the-books employment in mainly under-capitalised, and not especially innovative, new small firms. A related phenomenon was the rapid growth of some new zones of industrial concentration, where firms attracted by low land and operating costs benefited from none of the advantages of "embeddedness" in supportive local communities.

The timing of the period of rapid restructuring has also meant that new patterns of industrial growth have evolved when virtually all of the local (and even national) institutions and corporate groups have been either in flux or forming anew. Business associations and unions were legally established only in the late 1970s (although one of the principal unions, and even some of the employer associations, were active underground during much of the authoritarian period). These organisations' roots among many constituencies, then, are still quite weak; particularly significant is that both unions and employer groups have very weak representation among small firms and in highly fragmented sectors and therefore have little influence over the restructuring process in these sectors. Both sets of organisations, moreover, have, since the middle of the transition period, concentrated on bolstering national bargaining positions, sometimes at the expense of sectoral and local interests. As a result, rapid restructuring in many sectors proceeded virtually in an institutional void, with firms scrambling to reduce costs by evading taxes and regulations, and workers being left to negotiate the terms and conditions of employment against the background, but without the active enforcement, of official contracts.   In national tripartite bargaining, the political environment of the transition also did not favour policy supports for flexible production or for the strengthening of industrial districts. While employer associations championed the cause of dismantling the costly provisions of a rigid labour code, the unions were caught in a defensive position, ironically rallying to protect privileges established under the paternalistic labour policies of the authoritarian regime. Where national-level bargaining focused on particular industries, it was mostly in negotiating the timing and extent of cut-backs in subsidies to heavy industry.

Government policy, too, has been focused on politically sensitive regions and sectors, and has moved only slowly away from a pattern of supporting large industry.   Autonomous regional governments are the creation of only the last decade, and though they have rapidly involved themselves with industrial policy, they are still new and largely inexperienced players. Municipal governments, virtually absent as important political forces during the Franco regime, are also in a phase of consolidation and are financially quite weak.

The combined effect of this institutional framework is that there is a significant absence of strong leadership from local institutions to form the kinds of alliances that would underpin the emergence of dynamic industrial districts. This weak alliance-building at the local level has meant that even where other conditions seem to favour inter- and intra-firm co-operation, these initiatives have sometimes lacked crucial policy supports. Exceptions, as we shall see, do exist, and they reflect the wide differences in the social and political make-up of Spain's regions. In some cases, of course, other local conditions pose barriers to co-operation. Worker experiences in past political protests have, in some sectors, fuelled apathy towards collective action, while tactics used by employers to cut costs - in particular, the expansion of the informal sector - have also acted to weaken labour unity. Immediate benefits from individual strategies have also discouraged many producers from forming co-operative arrangements with other firms. And some local communities, as we note above, lack (though perhaps only partially or temporarily) the peculiar brand of social cohesiveness that would foster such arrangements.

Despite the variability of experiences, in a broad sense the restructuring process has responded to a unique set of pressures and has centred on similar strategies. The decade-long recession that began in Spain in the mid-1970s had a strong adverse impact on industrial employment.[6] Job losses clearly took place in the context of significant reorganisations of production. Outside sectors of heavy industry, such as steel and shipbuilding, where state-sponsored cut-backs dictated employment loss, restructuring mainly took the form of productive decentralisation. To some degree this process is reflected in employment statistics. Even as salaried employment decreased steadily, self-employment outside of agriculture showed a marked increase.[7] As unemployment rose - from only 5 per cent in 1976 to a startling 22 per cent by 1984 - other indicators suggested that off-the-books employment in the informal sector was expanding rapidly. A 1985 government survey reported that one in five Spanish workers was employed

---

6. Between 1975 and 1983, salaried industrial jobs fell by 19.5 per cent. Regions with the greatest industrial concentration tended to show the most substantial declines in industrial employment: Catalonia lost 24.2 per cent of industrial jobs between 1973 and 1983; the Basque provinces showed a 27.8 per cent decline; and the Madrid economy, though buoyed by the strength of its services sector and local demand, registered a drop of 13.9 per cent during the same period. The Valencian region fared somewhat better, with a decrease of only 10.8 per cent in industrial employment, and other intermediate industrial areas such as Burgos and Pontevedra also registered more moderate declines [del Castillo and Rivas, 1988; Vázquez Barquero, 1988].

7. In construction, for example, self-employed workers increased by 25.5 per cent between 1980 and 1984, while salaried jobs declined by 30.9 per cent.

in unregulated activities, a dramatic contrast with the highly regulated labour market only a decade before.[8] The proportion of small firms in the economy was also rising. In Catalonia, for example, the average number of employees in new firms from 1972 to 1976 was 20; the average from the next five years fell to 17; and from 1982 to 1986, new firms averaged only 8 employees [Costa Campi, 1990].

We must look to case studies to understand the full scope of what Spanish industrialists themselves came to label "spontaneous reconversion." A surge in subcontracting across major industries essentially reshaped the profile of many sectors and created a new set of relationships among firms. For example, Estevan [1984, 1986] traced production trends in the professional electronics industry and found that the large, highly centralised firms began, in the late 1970s and early 1980s, to subcontract all of the main phases of the production process, and even portions of design and testing. At the same time, a new segment of smaller firms was being formed by professional ex-employees of the large firms, and these new businesses were streamlined from the start, with various phases of production being placed with the burgeoning sector of new micro-enterprises, in metalwork, painting, printed circuits, and other sub-sectors. In less than a decade, the profile of the industry was entirely transformed [see also Benton, 1989].

Productive decentralisation was more dramatic still in lighter, labour-intensive manufacturing sectors where firms were responding, at least initially, less to market shifts and more to declining demand and the steady rise in real wages. In a range of consumer goods industries in Catalonia and Valencia, a structure of medium-sized, fairly centralised firms dissolved in a short time and gave way to a new structure in which streamlined producers and commercial agents subcontracted production to a rapidly rising number of smaller firms, many of them operating entirely in the informal economy. This process began in the wake of a decline in exports in the late 1970s and accelerated in the early 1980s, when factory owners began *en masse* to take advantage of a loophole in Spanish business law that permitted them to declare false bankruptcies, thus wiping out their social security debts and obligations to employees and allowing them to start up streamlined or semi-informal enterprises using part or all of the same workforce. In some cases, factory owners assisted former employees in purchasing secondhand machinery and setting up subcontracting shops. The decentralising process also entailed an increase in the number of homeworkers in industry, and the appearance of speciality sweatshops employing former factory workers for piecework compensation. Estimates suggest that the informal sector

---

8.   A detailed analysis of the growth of the informal sector in industry is provided elsewhere by Benton [1990]. Findings from the national survey are reported in Muro et al. [1988]. Interesting case studies include those by Sanchís [1984]; Vázquez and Trigo [1982]; and Casals and Vidal [1985] for light manufacturing on the Mediterranean littoral; and studies by Celada et al. [1985]; Estevan [1984]; and Benton [1989] for informal sector growth as a by-product of productive decentralisation in Madrid.

accounted for as much as 40-50 per cent of production in some industries by the early 1980s [Miguélez Lobo, 1982; Casals and Vidal, 1985; Sanchís, 1984; Ybarra, 1982, 1990; Benton, 1990].

The possibility of moving away from subordinate systems of subcontracting based on informal labour and towards more dynamic systems of flexible specialisation became a vital issue as Spain's industry emerged from the recession with a changed mission: international competitiveness would have to rest not just on lower costs but on the ability to produce higher-quality, higher-fashion goods. Having based a rapid and impressive industrialisation drive in the 1960s and early 1970s on the country's ability to produce industrial goods of medium quality and relatively low cost for OECD markets, Spain in the 1990s must now compete in higher-priced, less standardised markets. Manufacturers are squeezed by lower-cost competition from countries such as Brazil and South Korea on one side, and, on the other side, by producers in Italy and in other European countries that have already adapted to the needs of more upscale markets and have clear advantages over Spain in design leadership and international reputation. Making Spanish industry more flexible, and more responsive to the opportunities in upscale or more specialised market niches, is crucial to continued competitiveness.

Despite existing institutional barriers, some internal political trends lend support for emerging flexible production systems. As we have already noted, the reappearance of regional governments in the 1980s has created a new arena for industrial policy that, for the first time, is sensitive to local and sectoral interests. Political decentralisation opens the opportunity for new sets of alliances to shape the regulatory context for geographically concentrated industry. Supporting this trend is the gradual weakening of the system of tripartite bargaining that lent stability to the transition period. The conciliatory posture of corporate-group leadership and their focus on a narrow range of issues have opened the door for the reappearance of strong grass-roots organisations with more specific objectives. Such a trend would help to shift the focus of bargaining away from provisions of the labour code and towards more substantive issues of concern in emerging industrial districts, such as opportunities for worker mobility, technological upgrading, and infrastructure improvements.

Still, most assessments of the impact of productive decentralisation on industry have concluded that the intent has been mainly to reduce costs (rather than to permit greater flexibility and innovation) and that the effect has been essentially to downgrade labour conditions and depress earnings (rather than to give workers more control over the production process).[9] As the crisis subsided in the mid-1980s and gave way to rapid growth, observers

---

9.   This assessment was provided in a number of monographs tracing the effects of productive decentralisation on particular sectors, regions, or groups of workers. See, for example, the studies by Celada et al. [1985]; Sanchís [1984]; and Ybarra [1982].

were tempted to take a more benign view of industrial restructuring, at least in a handful of sectors and sub-regional economies.[10] The opportunity for the emergence of flexible production systems, some of them based in dynamic industrial districts, clearly exists; the actual evolution of social relations inside nascent districts, and the political context surrounding them, sometimes leads in this direction, and sometimes does not.

As a result, it is possible to identify, in Spain, a wide variety of settings that approximate to quite different degrees the industrial districts of central Italy. Some of these cases I will refer to as "emerging industrial districts" because existing patterns of co-operation seem to support a familiar trajectory. Elsewhere the development of these relationships is less certain, and we can only note features of the industrial landscape that suggest the *potential* for industrial districts to form in the future.

We can identify, in addition, two geographical patterns of change that have given rise to potential sites for industrial districts. First, productive decentralisation has been associated with a movement of industry away from the core and inner ring of major metropolitan areas and the expansion of an outer ring made up of larger numbers of small firms. This trend is apparent in both leading industrial cities, Madrid and Barcelona, where the recession had a severe impact on traditional, large-scale industry, and spurred the growth of complex, multi-sectoral industrial zones on the metropolitan periphery. Second, many mono-sectoral rural- and town-based industrial concentrations - phenomena with a long history within Spain - have become consolidated.[11]   Although   productive   decentralisation   has   sometimes

---

10.   In fact, some sectors and regions performed better than average during the crisis, in part because decentralisation itself helped to create a segment of innovative firms. The Madrid electronics industry is an example of a sector in which the results of restructuring were clearly mixed; see the studies by Estevan [1984, 1986] and Benton [1989]. Costa Campi [1988, 1990] finds some positive effects from productive decentralisation in Catalonia, and Celada et al. [1990] conclude the same for Madrid; both these regional cases are discussed in detail in later sections of this chapter.

11.   Vázquez Barquero [1988] identifies 83 areas of "endogenous industrialisation" in Spain and argues that these zones have been historically more important to Spanish industrial growth than have urban industrial centres that depend more heavily on government investment or international capital. The study has some relevance for a discussion of industrial districts in Spain, since Vázquez Barquero also hypothesises that these areas are characterised by a high level of social cohesiveness, a strong entrepreneurial culture, and levels of growth and per capita income that are substantially higher than in surrounding regions. At best, though, we might view Vázquez Barquero's list as a partial set of potential sites for industrial districts. The author considers only municipalities of over 10,000 inhabitants that are located outside a range of 70 kilometres from Madrid and Barcelona and 25 kilometres from cities of 100,000 or more, a restriction that clearly omits some cases that would fall within the study's own definition of endogenous industrialisation and certainly leaves out some examples of emerging industrial districts near large urban centres. Further, although a handful of the areas is examined in greater depth, the analysis tells us very little about the internal dynamics of the zones.

favoured spatial diffusion (for example, through increased subcontracting of homework to more remote rural areas), key industry functions, such as commercial and financial services, auxiliary industry connections, or recruitment of highly skilled workers, remained centralised in these potential districts.[12]

The case studies presented in the following section document the development, within examples of each of these patterns, of relationships of co-operation in support of flexible production. As the profiles show, the social and political character of the districts, rather than merely their geographical setting or sectoral make-up, determine the direction of restructuring. Multi-sectoral districts on the periphery of Spain's two largest cities appear to be quite similar but reveal very different internal dynamics. And in Valencia's town-based mono-sectoral districts, class alliances and tensions promote sharply contrasting patterns of change. Finally, we will take a brief look at an interesting, although somewhat exceptional case, the striking success of the complex of co-operatives in the town of Mondragón in the Basque region.

III. Industrial districts on the urban periphery

Both Madrid and Barcelona were hard-hit by the decline in industry during the ten-year downturn, and particularly during the second half of that period. Areas of the cities with the largest industrial concentrations were especially affected: in Madrid, the southern periphery of the city, in and around Getafe, where the largest transport plants were located; and in Barcelona, traditional industrial zones of the city itself and the *comarca* Baix Llobregat to the south. In both Madrid and Barcelona, the decline prompted an exodus of firms toward the periphery in search of lower land costs, cheaper rents for industrial plants and, in the case of Madrid, cheaper wages for the generally poorer inhabitants of the city's peripheral zones. But this shift was also in part a symptom of the break-up of large firms and the proliferation of new, small enterprises that were responding to the rising demand for subcontracting, to new opportunities in the market, and to the needs of workers and worker-entrepreneurs who could no longer rely on the availability of jobs in established industry.

Despite many similarities in this process of restructuring, industrial growth on the periphery of the two cities was in many respects quite different, reflecting the differences in local politics, in the pre-existing

---

12.   Some Madrid firms have shifted piecework to rural areas as far away as La Mancha, and in Alicante, shoe producers increased the supply of homeworkers by recruiting women in agricultural communities outside the Vinalopó Valley. Ybarra [1982] found in 1982 that investment in semi-rural areas around the major shoe-producing towns had outpaced growth of investment within those municipalities.

conditions of industry in the regions, and in local traditions. Industrial growth in Madrid had been divided between very large-scale industrial plants that were financed by national and international capital - and that experienced the effects of the economic crisis with particular severity - and small-scale industry that served mainly the local market and that responded in varying ways to the downturn. Barcelona industry, in contrast, had a long-established tradition of commercial ties outside Spain and produced a wider mix of consumer and intermediate goods. Here a tradition of family-run, highly competitive business was also already in place, as was a tradition of associations of employers. Solidarity among industry participants in Barcelona might be based in part on a common regional identity. Madrid, in contrast, was a city that had been created and run under the direct, almost unfiltered influence of the central government; its industrial base was newer, and the tradition of employer associations of worker co-operatives was extremely weak.[13]

These differences come into sharp focus when we trace the evolution of new industrial concentrations on the periphery of these cities. In Madrid, the years of the recession, and particularly the period after 1978, saw rapid growth in the number of new, small firms settling in the "second ring" of municipalities around the city. As recently as the late 1960s these towns had been small agricultural centres, well outside the range of commuters and beyond the purview of urban investors. In the space of about a decade, these small settlements saw their populations expand drastically, and they simultaneously attracted thousands of industrial firms. A large proportion of the latter were located on land that was still zoned for agricultural uses and that often lacked even basic infrastructural improvements. In some cases, the transformation was dramatic. Paracuellos del Jarama, for example, was in the early 1970s a small agricultural town of a few thousand inhabitants on a high bluff not far from Madrid's airport; by the early 1980s, the town's population had grown to around 25,000, and more than 300 industrial firms were perched on the slope of the bluff and on the riverbank below. Many of the firms served larger enterprises in the nearby highway corridor where the region's electronics firms are concentrated; all of them were on agriculturally-zoned land and most were in makeshift industrial parks that lacked paved roads, postal service, and adequate water.[14]

In Barcelona, industry expanding to the periphery encountered a different environment, one that made for a different industrial "atmosphere." Many of the zones outside the city had an established industrial base, even a long history of industrial employers' associations. Spain's textile industry has been heavily concentrated in Catalonia since the eighteenth century.

13.   For an analysis of the failure of co-operativism in Madrid, see Benton [1990, Chapter 6].

14.   An excellent outline of the expansion of industry to peripheral towns in Madrid is provided by Celada et al. [1985].

About 85 per cent of textile production is concentrated here, with a handful of small towns outside Barcelona (most notably Sabadell and Terrassa) specialising in certain industry sub-sectors. This well-developed industrial region cradled a strong local bourgeoisie that has shown unusually high rates of participation in industry-based employer associations, even during the Franco regime, when such organisations were subsumed under the corporatist "vertical union." By one estimate, 90 per cent of employers belong at least to sub-sector organisations, which in turn are affiliated to an industry-wide association.[15] The long-established presence of the textile industry has also generated broad participation in industry and, at times, a cohesive workers' movement.[16] Finally, the industry has developed ties to other regional sectors, most notably the chemical industry because of the growth of synthetic fibre production. These factors together have helped to establish a wide zone in and around Barcelona that is characterised by a strong industrial tradition and pre-existing social and economic ties among industry participants.

In both Madrid and Barcelona, then, the industrial structure is evolving away from subordinate forms of subcontracting and towards a more complex structure of interdependencies among small firms located in specific districts on the periphery. But the process meets with very different structures of support. In Madrid, the change is taking place *despite* the nature of the surrounding communities, which are characterised by poor housing conditions, high unemployment, a dearth of services for both businesses and residents, and, until recently, a lack of support for local development by regional and local governments. In Barcelona, local industrial policy has also been lacking, but employer associations have functioned to support the trend toward inter-firm co-operation. Some peripheral communities have been among the region's leaders in industrial growth.

1. Fuenlabrada-Humanes: An emerging industrial district

The expansion of Madrid industry into the second ring of peripheral municipalities coincided rather neatly with the worst phase of the industrial recession. Many of the firms that appeared in peripheral areas during this period settled on land that was not zoned for development. A 1984 study conducted for the Madrid regional government estimated that there were

---

15. A detailed discussion of employers' associations in the textile industry is provided by Solé [1987].

16. On the development of the textile industry in comparison to other sectors, see Solé [1987] and Martín Rodriguez [1989]. The strength of the workers' movement in the industry has been undermined since the late 1970s by the growth of the informal economy, as documented in a study of Casals and Vidal [1985].

some 1,300 plants on improperly zoned land in satellite towns that were within the border of the Metropolitan Area. A sample of these firms revealed that over half the plants had been located after 1980 and that over three-quarters of them had less than 25 workers. The vast majority - over 70 per cent - were not branches of firms but single establishments, and nearly two-thirds of them were also first-generation plants. Clearly, then, the growth of these areas was not due to an exodus of established firms from Madrid's centre but signified an explosion of new, small firms that were responding to subcontracting opportunities and providing alternative employment strategies to many of the region's unemployed.

A monograph produced for the regional government in 1985 provided a more detailed profile of firms in two peripheral areas - Paracuellos to the north-east and Fuenlabrada to the south - and concluded that these concentrations represented a degraded substratum of the industrial structure [Celada et al., 1985]. Many of the firms, the study reported, were engaged in subcontracting for larger plants. A high percentage of the firms were metalworking and woodworking shops, with a diverse mix of other industries, especially printing, food processing, chemicals, and plastics. Of the nearly 300 firms surveyed, 44 per cent produced finished goods. Although the researchers emphasised the subordinate status of most of these firms in the industrial structure and their precarious placement in the market, some findings clearly pointed to the possibility for other outcomes, at least for a portion of the firms. Only 18 per cent of the firms worked exclusively from designs supplied by commercial agents or by other firms, while a slightly larger proportion arrived at the design through consultation with clients. Even among firms producing intermediate goods, nearly one-quarter (24 per cent) worked from their own designs, while another 17 per cent negotiated design specifications with their clients. Findings about marketing strategies also suggested that some firms were moving quickly beyond a subordinate status as subcontractors. Only 7 per cent of firms were dependent on a single client, and many firms marketed their goods directly through wholesale or retail outlets. Still, researchers found that many firms continued to rely on unregulated labour; their competitiveness as subcontractors often depended more on cost-cutting than an ability to produce high-quality products in a flexible manner.

This ambiguous character of the peripheral industrial zones was also evident in studies of productive decentralisation in the professional electronics industry. Madrid holds Spain's largest concentration of firms in professional electronics and accounts for around 80 per cent of production. Traditionally a large-firm sector, the industry underwent rapid restructuring in the late 1970s and early 1980s, and this process gave rise to both a new set of small and medium-sized producers targeting special market niches and a larger number of subcontractors that specialised in various parts of the production process. A 1985 study of 25 of these tiny subcontractors found that most of them were located in Madrid's industrial second ring. A small subset of the firms boasted a large clientele, owned numerical control machines or other equipment that allowed them to produce high-quality and precision goods, and were experimenting with innovative ways of organising the production process that allowed for greater flexibility. A slightly larger number of firms were highly dependent subcontractors that competed mainly on the basis of low costs. Most firms, however, could be placed in a middle category: having begun with rudimentary equipment and family or off-the-books labour, they were struggling to establish reputations as high-quality producers, to improve equipment, and to train or attract more skilled workers. For these firms in particular, the nature of the immediate environment - the dearth of local services, weak or tentative ties with other local firms, and little government support, particularly to obtain credit - seemed crucial obstacles to their progress and, by extension, to the continued expansion of the industry [Benton, 1989].

An in-depth study of one peripheral industrial zone tends to confirm these earlier findings. In 1987 a study conducted for the regional government profiles industrial development in Fuenlabrada and three nearby municipalities [Celada et. al., 1990]. For a number of reasons, this area seemed the most likely place to look for the emergence of a dynamic industrial district. Of the peripheral zones that have become centres for new, small industrial firms, this area is the largest, both in population and in its contribution to regional industry. In 1985, Fuenlabrada boasted, after Madrid, the largest number of industrial establishments in the region (1,764 industrial firms and an industrial workforce of 17,850). Humanes, a neighbouring town of still more recent industrial development, shows the highest industrial employment per 100 inhabitants in the region. Industrial growth in the zone is perhaps most impressive because it has been so rapid. In 1950, Fuenlabrada and the nearby towns of Parla, Humanes, and Torrejón de la Calzada were tiny, agricultural communities with a combined population of 4,253. A few industries were present in Fuenlabrada in 1968, but the surrounding communities remained largely rural. By the mid-1970s, the population was growing rapidly, but the towns had little industrial development. A high proportion of men were employed in construction (more than double the percentage for the workforce in the region), and the unemployment rate in Fuenlabrada and Parla was a mere 2.7 per cent.

Several trends coincided after 1975 to rapidly change the area's pattern of growth. First, a surge in migration occurred, particularly of young couples and families, from Madrid and its inner ring of municipalities. These families came in search of cheaper housing, and many of them were feeling the effects of the economic downturn (which at the same time became more pronounced in the Fuenlabrada zone itself with the steep decline of the construction industry). The search for affordable housing was accompanied by a search for jobs; employment creation in the second ring of peripheral towns during the first five years of the crisis was substantially greater than in the first ring of towns that were within 15-30 kilometres of Madrid. Nevertheless, the number of economically active males entering the district was very high, so that unemployment in the area increased steadily. By 1981, the zone had an unemployment rate of 19.38 per cent (compared to the rate of 16.2 per cent for the Madrid region as a whole), and by 1986 this figure had increased to 22.06 per cent (again, higher than the regional rate of 20.65 per cent).

Along with these changes came a surge in the number of industrial firms moving to or being founded in the area. By 1978, there were already 906 industrial establishments in the zone, with an average of 16.3 workers per firm. Mortality among these firms proved to be very high, and industrial employment actually decreased over the next several years. The mix of sectors represented in the district is quite varied. The largest proportion of firms are in metalworking (tool making, metal construction, mechanical parts, etc.), followed by wood shops (specialising in wood furniture), graphic arts, food processing, and plastics. Compared to rates of representation in the rest of the region, the Fuenlabrada zone has a strong specialisation in wood furniture, and is in fact the principal centre for production in the region, with a concentration in Fuenlabrada, Humanes, and La Moraleja of an estimated 30 per cent of establishments in the Madrid region and 47 per cent of employment [Castillo, 1989]. Metal and plastics firms are also over-represented, although firms dealing in the more skilled sub-sectors of metalworking are largely absent (Fuenlabrada is on the other side of the metropolitan area from most of Madrid's large electronics producers, major clients for more advanced metal subcontractors).

By 1987, the Fuenlabrada zone held 1,504 industrial firms. The very high mortality rate meant that only 295 of these had been founded before 1978. Significantly, around 80 per cent were founded during the worst phase of the economic crisis, between 1978 and 1985. A small proportion of businesses had closed to reopen again. In a re-examination in 1987 of 158 firms that had been studied in 1982, researchers found that although about one-third of the firms had closed, a significant percentage of these (29 per cent, or around 9 per cent of the total sample) had performed "false closures," that is, they had declared bankruptcy in order to wipe out social security and other tax debts and had set up new firms to continue the same economic activity [Celada et al., 1990].

Such figures indicate that the zone is very much the product of, and a participant in, the rapid industrial restructuring taking place in the wider Spanish economy during the crisis period. Here, as elsewhere, the pressures of the recession helped to generate the formation of new, small firms but also operated against the consolidation of stable industrial areas in which continuity of firms could support the development of networks of co-operation. Nevertheless, it is significant that out of this tumultuous environment a segment of highly innovative and successful firms has indeed emerged. Researchers found that among those firms in their sample that survived between 1982 and 1987, employment had increased and average investment in fixed capital was also up strongly. Although only 18 per cent of these firms were now exporting their products, the majority reached markets outside the Madrid region. More significantly, 60 per cent of the surviving firms reported owning general-purpose machinery, 20 per cent had special-purpose machinery, and another 20 per cent owned at least one numerical control machine. Over half reported owning a computer, and more than one-third of these firms said they used it in some production capacity [Celada et al., 1990].

It would seem, then, that the zone is in fact serving as a cradle for some new enterprises that are moving in the direction of more flexible production for widening markets. A recent study of woodworking firms in the area gave further evidence of this trend. Alongside more dependent subcontractors, a segment of firms in the sector - mainly wood furniture producers - markets products directly and displays generally higher skill levels among workers. Many of the firms adopt systems for organising production that emphasise flexible work assignments and production in short series. The wood furniture producers, moreover, show a higher rate of participation in employer associations and co-operate in the organisation of trade shows and fairs [Castillo, 1989].

Nevertheless, such experiences appear to exist in spite of, rather than because of, either the local entrepreneurial culture or the support of the local community. In general, entrepreneurs' attitudes towards employer associations are quite negative. In the 1987 survey described earlier, 58 per cent of owners report that they do not belong to any association. The lack of interest reflects the perception that associations serve only as instruments for collective bargaining and not to represent the interests of factory owners to the government or to foment inter-firm co-operation [Celada et al., 1990].

This sceptical attitude towards associations is symptomatic of a more general disdain for collective action. Interviews with local entrepreneurs show that they have highly individualistic goals and strategies [Castillo, 1989]. Most firm owners were in salaried work before becoming entrepreneurs - this was true of 72 per cent of firms in the 1987 survey - and this background seems to make them view employers' associations as fundamentally opposed to workers rather than positively in favour of small firm interests.

This perception is in part quite accurate. Employer associations *have* acted mainly to represent large firms and to take national political stands in opposition to the unions. Only rarely have employer associations in the post-transition period become activists on behalf of small and medium-sized firms or addressed serious sectoral or regional problems that affect such firms.[17] The unions, meanwhile, also opted for participation in national bargaining over local and sectoral militancy. For entrepreneurs who may have participated, as workers, in the strikes of the 1970s, disillusionment with collective action was a common, if not logical, response to that experience. Possibly as a result, co-operativism in the entire region has been very weak

17. For analyses of the character of employers' associations in the transition and post-transition periods, and the effects of the legacy of Francoism, see Linz [1981] and Solé [1987].

and has been followed mainly as a strategy for salvaging jobs when owners threaten closure.[18]

Conditions in the towns themselves may also contribute to the sense of disconnectedness from the surrounding community that some employers express. The social and political institutions of the towns have yet to adjust to the massive influx of new residents. Between 1981 and 1986, the population in the Fuenlabrada zone increased by 38 per cent, compared to a rate of only 2 per cent for the region as a whole. The influx created a population that is much younger than the average distribution for the region, that has a much lower education level on average, and that contains a much smaller proportion of professionals and technicians. The community has a substandard housing stock (mainly hastily constructed apartment blocks with few amenities), an overburdened school system (with a drop-out rate substantially higher than the regional average), and a dearth of services, both for local residents and for business.

The unemployment rate in the zone continues to be higher than in the region as a whole, and, more significantly, conditions for workers also appear to be worse on average. Only about two-thirds (67.6 per cent) of those who are employed have indefinite work contracts. Eleven per cent of workers are self-employed, and a large proportion is made up of *eventuales*, or temporary/intermittent workers. The proportion of *eventuales* is 16.2 per cent in Fuenlabrada and 19 per cent in Parla, compared to a regional average of 12.1 per cent. This last figure is significant because it is also clear that temporary work leads frequently to unemployment; nearly a third of the unemployed population in Fuenlabrada were formerly *eventuales*. The authors of the 1987 study conclude, based on these findings, that given "the low level of participation in schooling, the low level of skills in the population, and the presence of forms of labour that tend to be highly precarious, we can predict an unfavourable evolution of the labour market in this zone." [Celada et al., 1990, p. 54].

Clearly, the Fuenlabrada area has some of the features of a dynamic industrial district: a sector of innovative, small firms; growing complexity of interconnections among firms; and a clear, though slow, trend toward greater co-operation among firms in at least one sector, wood furniture manufacturing. But the history of the zone's development and the broader political climate in which that development has taken place have created a surrounding community that is still struggling with very fundamental problems - infrastructural, administrative, and social - and that supports as a result the continued existence of a larger, more marginal segment of firms and a labour force willing to accept poor conditions. Several current trends seem to favour the evolution of this zone more towards the classic profile of

---

18.   A more detailed discussion of the effects on workers' views of collective action of the strikes of the transition period is provided elsewhere by Benton [1990, Chapter 6]. That work also analyses other factors contributing to the weak co-operativist movement in the region.

an industrial district. For example, there is evidence of a growing overlap between patterns of residence and employment in the zone, a trend that will presumably strengthen industry-community ties.[19] Policy changes in the regional government, discussed in the last section of this report, also appear to be sensitive to the zone's potential to develop itself as a centre for innovative industrial growth. Conditions in the zone bear watching, certainly. At the moment, we might best characterise Fuenlabrada as an emerging industrial district whose future is still open to highly contrasting alternatives.

2. The Vallés Oriental in Catalonia: Inter-Firm co-operation and diversified growth

As Spain's leading industrial region, Catalonia was strongly affected by the economic crisis, with a loss of 24.2 per cent of industrial jobs in the region between 1973 and 1983. Much of this loss was concentrated in the seven *comarcas* that make up the Greater Metropolitan Area of Barcelona, where over 70 per cent of the region's industrial employment is concentrated. More specifically, the areas of large-scale industry inside the city and on its southern periphery showed especially steep declines, as did towns such as Sabadell that specialise in textiles and other traditional manufactures.[20]

Yet, Catalonia has emerged from the crisis period with its position as leading industrial region firmly in place. Industrial growth has recovered since 1986 and, more significantly, current data reveal a geographical redistribution of industrial growth during the last decade. This pattern features the relative rise of a group of intermediate *comarcas* that tend to benefit from their lower costs in land and labour, and their easy access to markets because of placement along major communication routes. This process of industrial diffusion has been accompanied by a strengthening of sub-regional specialisations, as indicated by the relative growth of industrial investments. Finally, the region as a whole shows a substantial decline in average firm size, as larger firms have been dismantled and replaced with streamlined enterprises that engage in wider networks of subcontracting.

---

19.   The study of Celada et al. [1990] shows that 16.7 per cent of employers live in the zone, compared to 9 per cent when their businesses were first founded. Thirty-four per cent live in other municipalities of the south-west periphery, and this figure has also shown a slight increase, from 31.5 per cent, since the firms were founded. Only one change in residential patterns suggests a reverse trend: in 1987, 7.8 per cent of employers were living in the more affluent municipalities to the north-west of Madrid, while only 1.1 per cent had done so when their businesses were founded. This trend suggests that as some entrepreneurs become successful, they opt for residence in better-endowed, higher-status communities. Such a trend can only harm the development of strong local community-business ties.

20.   On the geographical redistribution of industrial growth inside Catalonia, see the studies by Baiges et al. [1988], Capellades [1989], Cots Reguant [1988], Lleonart and Garola [1989], Parellada and Güell [1988], and Pedreño [1989].

These trends together suggest that a substantial restructuring of Catalonian industry is under way, in part in response to the crisis itself, in part in reaction to new market conditions.[21]

In and around Barcelona, the restructuring has had some predictable results. One of these is the initial decline of more centrally located industrial zones, and the relative expansion of more diversified peripheral areas. Although superficially similar to the process described for Madrid, productive decentralisation in Barcelona has some strikingly different features. The most important of these perhaps is that the peripheral zones of expansion around Barcelona did not begin this process as small and underdeveloped agricultural areas. On the contrary, the surrounding *comarcas* have a long tradition of industrial development dating from at least the last century. All were heavily industrial prior to the onset of the crisis. The outlying areas also contained intermediate towns that already offered an important concentration of services. In addition, in contrast to Madrid, the areas of greatest expansion were often more valued as residential zones than areas closer to the city centre. Indeed, part of their attraction to new investors was that the zones offered higher standards of living in close proximity to industrial concentrations.[22] These factors - an existing tradition of industrial development and entrepreneurship, established community institutions, high residential value, and fluid communications with other industrial zones in Barcelona - appear to offer an environment much more conducive to inter-firm co-operation among the burgeoning numbers of small industrial enterprises.

This, at least, is what is suggested by the few existing studies of inter-firm co-operation and subcontracting networks on the Barcelona periphery. The most extensive of these is the study by María Teresa Costa Campi of the *comarca* of Vallés Oriental [Costa Campi, 1988]. This area has experienced many of the trends described above, including the proliferation of small firms, an influx of residents from Barcelona, and a relative strengthening of its industry specialisation in plastics and wood products, particularly furniture. However, the *comarca* is exceptional in several important ways. It has a greater diversity of industrial sectors than most other *comarcas* in the region, and it has shown exceptional dynamism in recent years, even during the worst phase of the economic crisis. In contrast to trends in the rest of both Catalonia and Spain, the number of industrial jobs in Vallés Oriental actually increased by 28.85 per cent between 1970 and 1981. Finally, compared to peripheral areas of Madrid, networks of subcontracting and relationships of co-operation among firms appear to be highly developed, even if they have

---

21.   See Costa Campi [1990] for an analysis of productive decentralisation in the Catalonian case.

22.   Thus we find a shift in population out towards peripheral *comarcas* since the mid-1970s. See Capellades [1989].

not reached the level of complexity and resiliency of such relationships in the key industrial districts of central and northern Italy.

The vast majority of the firms in Vallés Oriental are small and medium enterprises; 95.9 per cent have fewer than 100 workers and account for 55.2 per cent of employment in the *comarca*, while two-thirds of firms are micro-enterprises with only one to nine workers. The predominance of small and medium firms holds true across sectors. Compared to other *comarcas*, the area has a particularly strong concentration of firms in chemicals (mainly plastics) and wood furniture production, but also has significant production in metalworking (including mechanical parts), food processing, and textiles. These five sectors account for 78.7 per cent of firms in the *comarca* and absorb 81.6 per cent of industrial labour.

Costa Campi [1988] has traced production networks in the leading sectors of the district and finds that particularly in chemicals, metal, and woodworking, a complex web of relationships exists that comprises both vertical subcontracting and, less frequently, horizontal links among producers. The vertical subcontracting chains, though perhaps more extensive, do not appear to be vastly different from subcontracting links documented in Madrid industry: strong pressures to externalise risks and costs lead metal and plastics producers to put out parts of production to smaller firms, some of which become relatively independent of their clients and some of which remain low-cost, subordinate producers, occasionally relying on informal labour or irregular hiring practices to cut costs. At the same time, however, there is evidence of other, quite different sorts of relationships evolving among firms, as in the case of metalwork firms that subcontract horizontally, not to increase production but to enable them to diversify product lines while maintaining narrow specialisations in their own firms.

The most interesting case is that of the wood furniture industry. This sector is characterised by very small firms, with an average of only eight workers per firm. Within the zone, firms are grouped according to product specialisation, with a full range of speciality firms serving each product mini-region. Classic forms of vertical subcontracting are common, with firms that specialise in design and assembly subcontracting various phases of production to smaller speciality workshops. But horizontal subcontracting is also common, since firms need to diversify types of product within a particular style. Significantly, producers have organised a commercial association to market the district's products, both wholesale and through a large retail outlet run and managed as a joint venture.

The level of inter-firm co-operation is certainly not as great as that found in classic industrial districts such as Prato. But entrepreneurs clearly value the opportunity they have in an area such as the Vallés Oriental to work closely with both clients and suppliers. A small representative sample of firms in the greater Barcelona area, including the Vallés Oriental, revealed that employers consider inter-firm relationships carefully in evaluating locations for their firms. Reporting the reasons for choosing their current locations, factory owners cited most often their desire to live and work in the same zone; the benefits of being close to suppliers and clients; and the concentration of industry in the same sector in the zone.[23]

It is important to add that the dynamism displayed in Vallés Oriental and in other fast-growing *comarcas* in the last several years is owed at least in part to conjunctural factors. Particularly with Spain's entry into the EEC, foreign investment has increased considerably. Indeed, foreign investment in a core group of industries - food processing, transport equipment, computers, other metal sectors, and chemicals - has accounted for the largest part of new investments in Catalonia. Foreign-financed firms may themselves take advantage of the dense network of small suppliers and subcontractors. But a more complete evaluation of the impact of this phenomenon on the industrial structure - both in Barcelona and Madrid - remains a task for the future.

To summarise, the Vallés Oriental displays many of the characteristics of an industrial district: a complex structure of relationships among firms, growing inter-firm co-operation, and diversity and dynamism even during the worst years of the industrial recession. In contrast to the Fuenlabrada-Humanes region outside Madrid, this consolidating district builds upon a strong local tradition of industrial development and entrepreneurship, and draws strength from its status as a fairly high-level residential area within the larger metropolitan region. Having noted these crucial differences, we must also emphasise that the *comarca* benefited from the same economic forces present in Madrid. Growth in both places in the last decade resulted from a more general pattern of productive decentralisation that drew investment away from metropolitan core areas and from a first ring of industrial centres and towards a second, less developed ring. This process, at the same time, favoured the development of small and medium-sized firms to allow for diversified, flexible production.

IV. Diffuse industrialisation and the emergence of the mono-sectoral industrial district

The second broad pattern of industrialisation in Spain that has given rise to new industrial districts is diffuse, rural-based industrial growth. Often begun in the last century but reinforced during the boom of the 1960s, industrial growth in previously agricultural zones has tended to favour the development of communities or groups of towns devoted to production in a

---

23.   These findings are reported by Parellada and Güell [1988]. Contrast these results with the findings of a survey of owners of firms established on improperly zoned land on the Madrid periphery; rather than alluding to the positive benefits of the chosen location, most owners cited the problems they were having in previous locations (excessive cost, insufficient space or infrastructure, zoning problems) as reasons for relocating [*Oficina de Planeamiento Territorial*, 1985].

single sector, or in very closely related sectors. These zones have fared differently both during and in the wake of the economic crisis, as the cases we profile in the next section will illustrate.

The degree to which these experiences vary is interesting to the wider debate about industrial districts because it shows that the closeness between community and workplace ties is not a sufficient condition for economic dynamism and continued competitiveness. Indeed, the effects of both conflicts at work and class tensions in the community may be magnified by the intimate setting of industry. As Becattini suggests [1989], the impact of such conflicts may not be fatal for industry. They can hinder, however, the development of the high-trust atmosphere that favours innovation in the organisation of production and informal information-sharing among firms. Clearly, much more is needed than geographical concentration and a strong regional or local identity to sustain dynamic development in the industrial district.

This point can be made clearer by contrasting two examples of industrial districts in the Valencian region. Industrial growth in this region has consistently outpaced development in most of the rest of Spain since the 1960s. In many respects this Spanish region has the most in common with the manufacturing region of central Italy: a strong export orientation; an emphasis on light consumer manufactures; a symbiotic relationship to agriculture in the early stages of industrial growth; a spatial pattern of specialised industry concentrated in particular towns or clusters of towns; and the dominance of small- and medium-sized firms, many of them family businesses.

However, here, as in Spain more generally, key social and political conditions shape a very different environment for industrial restructuring. One such difference is the social orientation of Valencian entrepreneurs. Small business owners in the region have been characterised as relatively conservative in the sense that they tend to view their firms as part of the family patrimony to be protected from undue risks. These men have for the most part a low level of formal training and past experience in production rather than management. They have shown a preference for investing the profits from their businesses in local real estate and other fixed assets rather than in research and development or other intangible, long-term business investments. The success of their firms has depended in large part on the capacity of the sectors to imitate international style and to produce a wide range of goods cheaply. Until the 1970s, comparatively low costs were assured by Spain's lower wages, and by the reliance in some sectors on part-time rural labour and lower-cost female homeworkers [see Picó, 1976; Sanchís et al., 1988].

The steady rise of wages and the slump in markets in the late 1970s forced adjustments here as elsewhere in Spain. One short-term solution was the rapid expansion of the informal economy in Valencian industry: an increase in the use of homework, a rise of off-the-books labour in established industry, and the appearance of many small, informal workshops. Observers agree that the informal economy became substantially larger in Valencia than in other industrial regions. Avoiding social security payments cut production costs directly, while relying on off-the-books subcontracting also allowed producers to displace much of the risk now associated with fluctuations in demand.

Longer-term solutions were equally obvious, but of course required more planning and co-ordination among firms; to continue to compete in the markets for the light consumer goods in which the region specialises, industry would have to devote resources to technological upgrading (Valencian industry is still lagging behind when compared with other EEC competitors), product innovation, enhancing the reputation of Spanish design, and promoting the capacity to propel fashion change rather than simply responding to it through imitation.

Valencian industries have reacted variably to this challenge, and their responses tell us something about the viability of industrial districts as a supportive environment for this type of adjustment. We will look first at a highly dynamic case, the ceramics-producing region centred in a cluster of towns in the province of Castellón. Here, local institutions have developed that have enabled the growth of industry based on increasing diversification and continual technological upgrading. In contrast, the shoe industry centred in the province of Alicante has stalled in its efforts to move Spanish production into higher-price, higher-fashion markets and is also now seeing its domestic market eroding under a rising tide of imports. Even though the shoe-producing towns display some of the same characteristics as the ceramics towns of Castellón, closer analysis shows crucial differences in the way local industry responded to the crisis. Some of the classic features of industrial districts - information-sharing among producers, for example - have actually worked in favour of short-term solutions to the sector's slump and against long-term growth. Technological differences in production in the two industries have something to do with their different responses at this conjuncture, but social and political conditions in the two communities are ultimately more important in explaining their divergent paths.

1. Two mono-sectoral industrial districts

About three-quarters of Spanish ceramics producers are concentrated in the province of Castellón, particularly in two towns, Onda and Alcora, and the surrounding district. None of the ceramics firms employs more than 350 workers, and about 80 per cent have fewer than 75 employees. A long tradition of ceramics work exists in the zone, although production with modern methods is relatively recent and dates from around the mid-1950s. Over one-fourth of the value of production is for export, and both total output and exports have shown rapid growth, especially in the last several years. The industry is clearly trying to position itself as a serious competitor to Italian manufacturers, who are still well ahead in technological capacity and design reputation.[24]

Compared to other sectors, the ceramics industry stands out due to the degree to which producers have aggressively pursued technological improvements. They have often done so, moreover, through co-operative efforts sponsored by the sector's employers' association. Efforts to modernise production were intensified rather than weakened during the downturn in markets in the late 1970s and early 1980s and have led to improvements that have supported the industry's bid to manufacture higher value-added goods. Co-operative initiatives have been successful, for example, in improving processes for raw materials preparation (clay atomisation or glaze production). The employers' association has also sponsored efforts to foment auxiliary industry to produce machinery locally; although less successful, this effort shows that producers recognise the danger of relying on Italian technology and are seeking ways to promote innovation in key areas of the industry.

These changes have been accompanied by the evolution of the traditional family-run firm. Many family firms were unable to keep up with the pace of technological change and closed during the recession. The number of firms has not diminished, however; new firms have been formed by investors from outside the industry, and the remaining family firms have incorporated professional managers. Particularly in the sub-sectors producing pavement and construction tiles, a growing number of university-trained entrepreneurs is appearing. In addition to drawing outside investors, the sector is attracting many of the offspring of businessmen already in the sector, some of whom have trained in areas especially relevant to a future in ceramics. This training of second-generation entrepreneurs is unusual in the industry of the wider region, where the sons and daughters of manufacturers who make it through university studies usually do so with an eye to escaping employment in industry [Sanchís et al., 1988].

The technological requirements of production in the industry clearly have had something to do with the level of inter-firm co-operation that has evolved in the district. Productive decentralisation in this sector was not a viable response to the crisis since production must centre around the operation of high-cost kilns on a 24-hour basis. Yet, producers might have sought individual solutions rather than banding together to pursue modernisation. We have found no good sociological study of the district to explain the origins of this collective strategy. However, existing studies suggest that inter-firm co-operation was enhanced by the conditions of the crisis. Producers in the region are acutely aware of the strategies employed in the Italian district of Sassuolo to achieve high-quality flexible production

---

24. For a brief but perceptive analysis of the Castellón ceramics district, on which much of the discussion in this chapter is based, see Castillo [1988].

there and may in fact be imitating the Italians not just in product design but also in organisational-industrial strategies.

The comparison to Sassuolo shows that inter-firm relationships in Castellón lack the complexity of relationships in that district. Without a strong auxiliary industry and greater technological independence, Spain's challenge to the Italians will continue to be hampered. Nevertheless, we are clearly faced with an exceptional case of strong inter-firm co-operation in the pursuit of well-defined goals to support international competitiveness. Community characteristics, such as the inter-generational transfer of entrepreneurial knowledge, seem to support these goals. Castellón is, in these respects, a good example of a successful industrial district in Spain.

Contrast this experience with the development of the shoe industry in the Valencian province of Alicante. Like the ceramics sector, the shoe industry is highly concentrated, with the majority of Spanish producers located in a cluster of towns in the Vinalopó Valley. Individual towns are noted for their specialisations: Elda in women's fashion shoes, Villena in children's shoes, Elche in sports shoes, and so on. In a pattern of growth similar to that of other Valencian industry, shoe production expanded rapidly in the 1960s; by the middle of the 1970s, Spain represented one of the leaders (just behind Taiwan) among newly industrialising countries supplying OECD markets [Edwards, 1979].

Although successful as exporters, Spanish producers were selling mainly their ability to produce medium quality shoes cheaply. Designs were routinely supplied by importers, particularly by clients from the United States, which was by far the largest customer. Foreign buyers also often supervised production and cemented close relationships with particular factories, which then became highly dependent on individual clients. Most factories modernised, introducing the assembly line and often substituting Taylorist methods for piecework, although the level of technological development remained only moderate, particularly in the underdeveloped auxiliary industry [Bernabé Maestre, 1976]. Further, industry participants were aware that the system for establishing wages through the state-run *sindicato* would soon be defunct, and the advent of true collective bargaining promised an increase in wages - an immediate blow to the industry's competitive cost advantage in international markets.

Clearly, then, Spanish industry was in quite a different position from the Italian shoe industry in facing the economic downtown of the mid-1970s. Whereas Italian producers were able to respond by diversifying production and capitalising on a strong position as design leaders, Spanish manufacturers cast about for short-term strategies to retain market position. The industry underwent a very rapid and dramatic process of spontaneous restructuring. Massive closures of established firms implied a crisis in the industry, but production in fact hardly slowed; throughout the Vinalopó Valley, low-cost, off-the-books subcontractors and a growing number of homeworkers were assuming productive tasks distributed to them by commercial agents and streamlined assembly factories. Estimates have placed the value of production in the informal sector in the early 1980s at as much as 40 per cent of the total.[25]

If this process of "informalisation" had been a temporary trend and had allowed the industry time to reformulate longer-term strategies - improving design, enhancing local technological capacity, or building a stronger auxiliary industry, for example - then we would be forced to evaluate its effects differently. However, we find that the sector is still losing ground in international markets and that imports have surged dramatically in recent years. Rather than diminishing, the informal sector has gained a certain stability in the Vinalopó Valley. The practice of firms' declaring false bankruptcies in order to write off social security debts (and to restructure their workforces, often placing some workers off the books) had become endemic by the mid-1980s. New informal-sector workshops were not establishing wider networks of clients, upgrading technology, or experimenting with more flexible systems of production. Despite increasing efforts on the part of the regional government to stimulate innovation in the industry, the dominant strategy remained one of achieving flexibility through subordinate, low-cost subcontracting.

Most significantly, characteristics of the Vinalopó Valley *as an industrial district* seem to have reinforced this lack of action on the industry's long-term problems. To begin with, the facility with which industry participants shared information in the district meant that employers learned quickly from one another how to conduct a false closure and maximise the benefits of informal labour use. As more factory owners took advantage of this option, it also became more socially acceptable; whereas interviews with owners in 1982 found that many were still resisting closure because they tended to view their firms as extensions of family property, this sentiment was lacking in 1985 interviews because the practice had become so widespread that it was established as a community norm [Benton, 1990].

Similarly, the close community setting of the industry tended to accentuate rather than mitigate tensions between factory owners and workers. A large-scale strike by shoe industry workers in the midst of the political transition was interpreted by many factory owners as a betrayal of the paternalistic pact that had earlier dominated relations in the small factories; workers, on the other side, came away disillusioned with collective action and sceptical about the benefits of maintaining good relations with employers. Both sets of attitudes encouraged participation in the creation of the massive informal sector, a process that often involved workers' agreeing to substitute under-the-table cash payments for job security and state benefits. Cynicism about workplace relations was further reinforced by the visibility of owners' and workers' consumption patterns in the Vinalopó Valley towns. Profits

25.   Ybarra [1982] documents this process of informalisation and its negative impact on conditions of employment. For a detailed discussion of the phenomenon in the shoe industry, see Benton [1990, Chapter 4].

from off-the-books operations fed a boom in luxury housing for "insolvent" employers, while some "unemployed" workers showed off new cars; each side accused the other of substituting individual, immediate interests for concern about the industry's future.[26]

From the mid-1960s until the mid-1970s, the Vinalopó Valley had many of the features of an emerging, dynamic industrial district. The area had a critical mass of skilled labour, an established tradition of entrepreneurship on the part of workers, a promising record of exports, a strong sense of regional identity, close social relationships among small factory owners, and a high degree of concentration of firms specialising in particular product lines. However, the political context of industrial restructuring during the next ten years shaped these relationships in ways that supported a rigid structure of subordinate subcontracting rather than the emergence of flexible specialisation. The close community setting could not by itself guarantee the quality of inter-firm and intra-firm relationships.

V.   Lessons from the Mondragón co-operatives

We would be remiss in our review of key industrial districts in Spain if we did not mention the interesting case of the Mondragón co-operatives. First formed in the unsympathetic climate of the Franco years, the Mondragón complex has grown to encompass 173 co-operatives, including 94 industrial co-operatives, and to employ over 19,000 worker-owners, most based in and around the town of Mondragón (population 30,000) in the Basque region. The co-operatives export about 30 per cent of their production and make over 190 different product lines, and thousands of products, many of which are related to their early specialisation in electrical home appliances. After paying a fee to join, worker-owners vote on broad matters of governance and receive compensation based on the ranking of their jobs (on a fairly flat scale of 1 to 4.5) and a share of the co-operatives' profits after set-asides for future capital investments.

There are some persuasive reasons for placing the Mondragón case on the margins of a discussion of industrial districts in Spain. The co-operatives owe much of their development to the fast growth of protected domestic markets, and their competitive strategy has had perhaps more in common with that of an oligopolistic firm than with the flexible adjustments of a network of small and medium producers.[27] Further, most observers have argued that Basque nationalism has played an important role in the co-

---

26.   The strike of 1977 and its impact on worker and employer perspectives of restructuring is covered by Benton [1990]. That work also describes interviews with industry participants that suggest how the town setting for industry exacerbates class tensions.

27.   I am indebted to María Teresa Costa Campi for this observation.

operatives' success; this claim suggests that the applicability of the Mondragón model in other regions in Spain is necessarily very limited.

Still, the case merits mention here because its features clearly lend support to the arguments made in relation to (other) industrial districts in Spain. Specifically, the Mondragón example confirms the need for strong local-level institutional co-operation in the face of unsupportive, or simply ineffective, industrial policy. The case also calls attention to the benefits to be gained from inter- and intra-firm co-operation and, more precisely, points to the significance of self-governance as support for these goals.

Further, some of the conditions that have made Mondragón suspect as an example of an industrial district may be changing. The success of the Mondragón co-operatives has been demonstrated not just by their growth but also by their ability to survive during economic downturns and consistently to outperform surrounding areas. Although the markets for Mondragón products were severely affected by the global recession of the mid-1970s and its protracted repercussions in Spain, the co-operatives managed to stay afloat without laying off many members. The loose organisational matrix of co-operatives permitted them to transfer members from the most troubled operations to more solvent ventures. At the same time, new co-operatives were being created to respond to new market opportunities. At least in recent times, then, the co-operatives have had to respond to similar market pressures requiring a flexible response, and they have come to have more in common with other industrial complexes around the country.

Other observations may also call into question the emphasis on Basque regional identity as a cornerstone for the co-operative movement. A recent study by Greenwood and collaborators from the co-operatives points out that in its Basque heritage and even in some features of its industrial past, Mondragón is not greatly different from the towns in the surrounding area, where no similar co-operative movement has surfaced [Greenwood and González Santos, 1989]. For that matter, the unifying function of Basque identity is somewhat ambiguous since nearly one-quarter of the town, and about the same proportion of co-operative members, are originally from outside the Basque region. The reasons for the success of the co-operatives, the authors suggest, have to be sought in the evolution of the co-operatives themselves, and in the internal politics of these institutions. Thus, in a broad sense, Mondragón may perhaps best be understood as a particularly successful experiment in building what Sabel in this volume calls "studied trust."

Certainly the town's long industrial tradition supplied a precondition for the experiment. Local ironworks were present in the thirteenth century. Industrial growth in the nineteenth century centred around activities related to the iron industry, and by the early twentieth century the town had developed a specialisation in locksmithing. By 1941, the year that the co-operatives' founder arrived in the town as a lay priest, Mondragón had a population of 8,000, an established union of locksmiths, and an apprenticeship school for locksmiths that was limited to sons of factory employees.

The co-operative movement had its roots in an effort to open greater opportunities to the youths of the town. A new technical school was founded and the first co-operative, Ulgor, was begun by some of its graduates in 1956 to produce heaters and petroleum stoves. A handful of other co-operative initiatives followed. Most significant, though, was the decision to seek to develop a system of self-financing which resulted in the joint founding of a bank, the *Caja Laboral Popular*. Support of the bank was crucial to expansion of the co-operatives during the 1960s. Organisational adjustments also helped. A new organisational unit - the co-operatives group - was formed in 1964 (the co-operatives today form 14 such groups) to allow for greater co-ordination in management and for economies of scale in production.

Through a process of ad hoc response to problems of organisation and management, the Mondragón co-operatives developed the mechanisms that have been the key to their success. Broadly characterised, the most important of these has been the willingness to extend the co-operative format in order to set up the necessary support systems for the core industrial co-operatives. The bank is only the most important example of this practice, which has been extended to the spheres of education, health and agriculture. Of the 173 co-operatives currently in existence, 45 are dedicated to education, including primary and secondary schools, a university-level technical training school (the *Escuela Politécnica*), and a business school. Because the co-operatives initially could not participate in the national social security and health insurance system, they set up a health care co-operative to provide insurance, retirement benefits, and other services to members. Other important ventures include a research and development co-operative which prevents co-operatives from duplicating their efforts in this area, and co-operatives formed to employ special groups, such as the one started by married women who were unhappy with certain unequal provisions in the established co-operatives. The credit bank, meanwhile, has grown to become the 22nd largest bank in Spain and now devotes less than 30 per cent of its assets to the capital requirements of the co-operatives, although it still functions as a key source of start-up funds for new co-operatives and is now establishing an independent unit to finance entrepreneurial activity [Greenwood and Gonzalez Santos, 1989; see also Whyte and Whyte, 1988].

By creating new co-operatives to provide needed services, and by maintaining an organisational structure that loosely linked these second-level organisations to productive ventures, the Mondragón co-operatives essentially filled the void for mid-level support institutions that until quite recently has been a feature of most Spanish industrial areas. The second-level co-operatives thus substitute themselves for the sorts of political alliances among local business, workers, and local government leaders that are evident in many of the Italian industrial districts. At the same time, the organisational structure has permitted a certain degree of flexibility in responding to market shifts and in developing new ventures. Some of this flexibility is apparent internally; the industrial co-operatives have experimented periodically with changes in the organisation of production to allow for greater worker participation in production decisions. Greenwood's study suggests that innovation in this area has slowed down in recent years and that members express considerable frustration over what they perceive to be growing tensions between democratic governance on a broad plane and hierarchical management in the production sphere. Resolving such tensions may prove to be crucial to the co-operatives' ability to continue to respond flexibly to market change, particularly since future growth, unlike past expansion, will depend on their ability to serve more demanding international markets rather than a protected and growing domestic market.

VI. Industrial policy and current policy options in Spanish industrial districts

The fact that we find *any* examples of vibrant industrial districts in Spain is itself perhaps surprising when we consider the nature of industrial policy in the last several decades and, until recently, its lack of support for local industrial development. Under the Franco regime, local-level planning, even of the most rudimentary sort, barely existed. Industrial planning was highly concentrated at the national level and was limited mainly to support for large-scale industry and ineffectual plans to redistribute industrial growth to designated growth poles around the country. Also absent were representative organisations that could mediate conflicts and build alliances in support of local industry. Neither representative unions nor employers' associations existed; the interests of both workers and management were supposedly represented in the sectoral "vertical unions" managed by the state. Finally, outward expression of separate regional identities faced severe repression under the regime and this further curtailed independent, local-level initiatives.

The situation has of course changed dramatically under the democratic government. But in industrial policy-making, some years passed before regional initiatives gained momentum. In the meantime, national industrial policy was complicated by the presence of numerous, often conflicting, goals: to mitigate the employment effects of the recession, to scale down heavy industry in preparation for Spain's entry into the EEC, to cater to well-organised industrial interests, and to contain social protest resulting from employment loss. At the same time, as in other areas of economic planning, changes in industrial policy were postponed during the transition period.

Beginning in 1981, the main vehicle for industrial policy at the national level became the industrial reconversion programme. The most immediate goal of the reconversion programme was to withdraw state support from costly and increasingly uncompetitive industries, particularly steel and shipbuilding (both of which also faced cutbacks as a condition for EEC entry). Somewhat haphazardly, other sectors were added to the reconversion programme, responding to political tensions and lobbying pressures [Segura et al., 1988]. In 1983, the orientation of the reconversion programme changed somewhat. It was by now clear that rising costs were making it difficult for Spanish industry to compete internationally and that profound changes were needed to revitalise industry [Fernández Castro, 1985]. The Socialist government thus made the reconversion programme the centrepiece of a general programme designed to enhance competitiveness. The emphasis of much of the programme continued to be, however, recovery from the crisis. A fund was set up to support workers who were unemployed through reconversion, and a programme was started to provide tax subsidies and other benefits to firms that were established in designated Zones of Urgent Reindustrialisation (ZURs).

In many important respects, the reconversion programme reproduced earlier patterns of centralised policy-making. Although business and labour organisations were invited to join tripartite commissions to discuss how reconversion should be implemented, they were required first to approve reconversion in the affected industries. Even organisations that largely supported the goals of reconversion - the socialist union, the UGT, or the leading business association, the CEOE - had little influence on the details of the programme's administration. Not surprisingly, results of the programme were disappointing, particularly in industries dominated by small or medium-sized firms with limited influence and, therefore, limited access to subsidies. In the shoe industry, for example, the government reluctantly agreed to introduce a subsidy programme under reconversion, then placed narrow restrictions on the types of firms that could qualify; in a sector of nearly 2,000 firms, only 195 applied for assistance and only 34 of these were accepted into the programme. In the electronics industry, the government conceded that the programme failed to help the sector as a whole; while the roughly 80 per cent of the electronics components sector that was made up of small and medium-sized firms did not benefit at all - only about one-third of the 28 larger firms that applied for assistance under the programme ever received help.

By the mid-1980s, it was clear that the industrial reconversion programme would not by itself support dynamic restructuring in industry. The national government enacted a series of other measures - increased access to credit, support for R&D, technical training, export assistance, and other related measures - designed to stimulate small as well as large firm growth. Yet, for obvious reasons, the national government found it difficult to reach small producers through centrally administered programmes. As the shortcomings of national policy became more obvious, the burden increased on local and regional governments to do more in support of their own industries.

The ZUR programme was the first industrial programme administered at the regional level. Like the rest of the reconversion project, the ZUR programme was located in response to local and sectoral political pressures and was conceived mainly as a way of palliating the effects of the crisis.[28] The ZUR programme was established in 1984 and affected various municipalities of Asturias, Madrid, Cádiz, País Vasco, Galicia, and Barcelona. The administration of the ZUR funds followed certain national guidelines; subsidies of up to 30 per cent were offered to new investments in fixed assets in the designated zones, and access to other types of fiscal assistance (credit, local tax rebates, etc.) was facilitated. The assignment of particular municipalities was itself subject to local political pressures inside the regions, and the programme was implemented somewhat differently by region. In Barcelona, a complex of 22 municipalities on the outskirts of the city - virtually the entire suburban industrial ring - was designated as a ZUR, and firms from any part of this area could apply for benefits. In Madrid, efforts to have the entire industrial periphery placed in the programme failed, and the subsidies were limited to a handful of municipalities (including Fuenlabrada). More significantly, Madrid policy-makers conceived of a way of using ZUR funds to support the development of a high-tech industrial park on the city's northern periphery. As part of this plan, a large part of ZUR funds were contributed to a package of subsidies and tax rebates offered to AT&T in order to persuade the multinational to open a computer chip plant as an anchor for the industrial park. That deal has attracted considerable criticism both because of the size of direct and indirect subsidies and because the chip plant is unlikely to develop extensive linkages that will benefit the burgeoning number of small and medium suppliers in the region [Estevan and Soto, 1987].

On balance, the ZUR programme clearly had some effects on local employment in industry, but its shortcomings as a centrepiece for regional industrial policy were readily apparent. At the same time that ZUR was under way, other local level initiatives to assist small industry were struggling for support. Consider, for example, the efforts of municipal leaders in Arganda del Rey, outside Madrid, to help local small industry. This Communist-led municipality had experienced much the same type of industrial growth of small firms as we observed in Fuenlabrada. Town leaders wanted to link that growth to increasing employment in the town by creating an industrial park for co-operatives founded by local residents. But funding and support from the newly formed regional government were not forthcoming, and the plans were placed on hold. Arganda was unusual, of course, in that it had any local-level industrial plans; more commonly, municipalities were struggling with administrative challenges that were

---

28.   See the analysis of the entire industrial reconversion programme by Segura et al. [1988]. For a more positive assessment of the ZUR program, see Lafuente Félez and Pérez Simarro [1988].

entirely new under the democratic government and that often placed them in conflict, rather than in alliance, with local firms (collecting local taxes and service fees, for example). Even in Catalonia, where regional autonomy was building on strong regionalist sentiment, the tradition of municipal-level planning has been very weak.[29]

Clearly, support for the emergence of dynamic industrial districts in Spain was of a very different order than that found in central Italy. The types of support for small firms by local government found there - for example, the establishment of special industrial parks for artisans or the setting up of local training programmes for workers and entrepreneurs - were almost entirely missing at a crucial period in the industrial restructuring process in Spain. However, there are some signs that the situation is now changing. The gradual strengthening of the role of the regional governments has included a growing interest in regional-level policies to support local industry. Some of these policies have particular relevance to the future of industrial districts. For example, various regional governments have initiated centres to promote technical development in particular industries and have encouraged access by small firms to these services. In regions where particular sectors are highly geographically concentrated, such centres may help to reinforce information sharing among firms in emerging industrial districts. Valencia, for example, has a new network of such centres distributed in industrial zones throughout the region. These "technological institutes" exist to support footwear and leather; ceramics; woodworking and furniture; toys and plastics; textiles and garments; metalworking; and food processing. Most regional governments have also introduced programmes to improve access to credit for small firms and for research and development.[30]

Yet, regional and local industrial policy has still clearly not reached the level of activism sometimes displayed in Italy, and there are some signs of a reluctance to move in this direction. In emerging industrial districts, government entities rarely involve themselves in efforts to create or sustain associations of producers, even though such organisations would not only help local development but also facilitate communications between officials

---

29. These conclusions are based on interviews with local officials in Madrid and Barcelona, including directors of industrial planning at the regional governments.

30. The most active regional governments (including those of Valencia, Madrid, Catalonia, and the Basque Country) are also sponsoring high-technology industrial parks. It is unclear what relationship these ventures (still very new) will have to industrial districts, but there is so far little evidence that they are playing a key role in stimulating growth in existing districts. Regional governments are also seeking to increase ties between universities and firms as a means of encouraging innovation, but these efforts begin from a poor baseline because of the isolation of universities and their lack of attention to research under the authoritarian regime. For profiles of some recent policy efforts in key regions, see Piqué i Camps [1988] and Veciana et al. [1988] on Catalonia; Rico Gil [1988] on technology institutes in Valencia, and del Castillo [1988] on industrial policy shifts in the Basque Country.

and factory owners. Local officials tend especially to support a "hands off" policy in areas where the informal sector has grown very large; local officials in Alicante, for example, speak of the potential for scaring off investors through over-zealous monitoring of local firms.[31] Furthermore, the robust growth of some industrial areas in the last several years has encouraged an air of complacency among some officials.[32]

Even where enthusiasm is great and state-of-the-art local development plans are initiated, some problems remain. To begin with, the regional programmes are very new and may have to struggle to establish industry confidence and acquire sufficient subscribers, particularly since industry participants have come to view most government assistance programmes with scepticism (a view that was reinforced by their experience with industrial reconversion). Furthermore, the success of industrial policy will be influenced by the way in which current tensions between some regional and local administrations are resolved. Key examples of places in which such tensions affect industrial policy are Madrid and Barcelona, where the city and regional administrations are led by different parties and a certain amount of passive non co-operation is evident in the implementation of policies initiated at one or the other level.

Clearly, there is growing awareness among policy-makers of the need to reorient industrial policy in Spain away from its traditional support of large-scale industry and organised interest groups and towards support for small- and medium-sized firms and particular geographical concentrations of industrial growth. Effective measures will include greater government support for local and sectoral associations among small firms, in activities such as marketing (particularly marketing outside Spain), management training, and technical assistance. Representatives of labour, too, must be brought into local planning, in recognition of the links between dynamic industrial growth and the promotion of worker participation in production decisions inside firms. Steps must also be taken to make it more difficult for established firms to declare false bankruptcies as a response to slight downturns and as a general strategy for periodic restructuring. Unless this loophole is removed, firms will have little incentive to invest in long-term plans to enhance the international reputation of their sectors and promote better relations with workers within their firms. Where the informal sector has expanded dramatically and subordinate subcontracting has become established as the norm, efforts must also be made to reach informal-sector

---

31.   Ybarra [1990] and Benton [1990] discuss this response to informalisation on the part of local officials.

32.   I noted such an attitude in an interview in the *Generalitat* (the regional government of Catalonia), with Modest Ginjoan, Director of CIDEM, the Centre for the Development of Small and Medium Businesses. He dismissed the need for greater attention to district-level development plans because Catalonian industrial growth has been so strong in the last several years.

participants with credit programmes, legal assistance, marketing advice, support for co-operatives, and other aid that will help fledgling firms and self-employed workers develop into more advanced, specialised producers capable of contributing to innovation in industry. They must be encouraged to capitalise off the benefits of their small size rather than remaining at the mercy of larger, better established clients. Most importantly, all the measures must be applied in ways that respond to the peculiar conditions of particular sectors or districts. No centrally administered or globally conceived industrial plan is likely to reach entrepreneurs and workers in the small and medium-sized firms that comprise the largest segment of emerging industrial districts.

VII. Conclusions

The introduction to this chapter emphasised the open-endedness of the widespread process of industrial restructuring that has led in some places to the consolidation of highly competitive flexible production systems centred in clearly bounded industrial districts. The examples from Spain confirm that although international pressures towards such trends remain strong, institutional and political conditions may block or at least postpone movement in this direction. In Spain, the relative weakness of local-level institutions, the legacy of the peculiar politics of the transition period (particularly the rapid accommodation of the unions and the parallel decline in the strength of sectoral and regional labour movements), and the tendency of firms to substitute short-term cost-cutting strategies for long-term collective strategies - these and other features have acted as a brake on the development of industrial districts that fit the "classic" pattern modelled after the Italian case. This is true even in places where other characteristics of the local setting clearly resembled those of Italian industrial districts; thus in Alicante, for example, we have observed the gradual deterioration of a seemingly vibrant industrial district in the wake of "spontaneous" industrial reconversion.

Nevertheless, we also learn from the Spanish examples that numerous patterns can develop that share some, though not all, of the features of classic industrial districts. These cases challenge the representation of a single model of industrial districts. In Fuenlabrada in Madrid, networks of dynamic firms co-exist with a larger number of marginal firms that are characterised by low technology and poor working conditions. In Castellón, a push for improved technological capacity and better design in the ceramics industry has been led by medium-sized firms inside the district but with the increasing participation and influence of outside investors. In Mondragón, a unique network of co-operatives responded to the weakness of local institutions by forming independent service, credit, and research organisa-tions, well before the Basque regional government was in a position to offer much assistance. And in the Vallés Oriental, a vibrant entrepreneurial culture and long tradition of employer associations have provided a framework for inter-firm co-operation. These examples of unorthodox successes in impelling local industrial development suggest that the concept of the industrial district is best used as a tool for investigating similar *processes* of industrial change rather than as *model* around which quite specific development strategies can be constructed.

The first approach leads logically to a more complex understanding of policy interventions. Rather than developing a list of policy prescriptions to promote flexible specialisation and the consolidation of industrial districts, we can serve policy-makers best by identifying the political processes that guide industrial restructuring and by helping them in the intensive fieldwork needed to evaluate the likely effects of particular measures on specific patterns representing those processes. This approach may not prove satisfying to many technocrats because it implies the need to engage in dialogue and joint planning with industry participants rather than merely dictating policy changes, but it is the only strategy worth pursuing. Policy-makers in Spain and elsewhere must explore the ways in which their actions can contribute to building a political atmosphere that will be conducive to inter-firm co-operation, participatory and flexible organisation of labour inside firms, and the strengthening of local-level alliances in support of these trends.

References

Amin, A.; Robins, K. 1990. "Industrial districts and regional development: Limits and possibilities", in Pyke, F. et al. (eds.): *Industrial districts and inter-firm co-operation in Italy*, Geneva, International Institute for Labour Studies.

Baiges, J. et al. 1988. "Notas sobre el sector industrial en Cataluña", in *Economía Industrial*, No. 263.

Becattini, G. 1989. "Sectors and/or districts: Some remarks on the conceptual foundations of industrial economics", in Goodman, E. et al. (eds.): *Small firms and industrial districts in Italy*, London, Routledge.

---. 1990a. "Chapter 4. Italy", in Sengenberger, W. et al. (eds.): *The re-emergence of small enterprises. Industrial restructuring in industrialised countries*, Geneva, International Institute for Labour Studies.

---. 1990b. "The Marshallian industrial district as a socio-economic notion", in Pyke, F. et al. (eds.): *Industrial districts and inter-firm co-operation in Italy*, Geneva, International Institute for Labour Studies.

Benton, L. 1989. "Industrial subcontracting and the informal sector: Restructuring in the Madrid electronics industry", in Portes, A. et al. (eds.): *The informal economy: Comparative studies in advanced and developing countries*, Baltimore, John Hopkins University Press.

---. 1990. *Invisible factories: The informal sector and industrial development in Spain*, Albany, SUNY Press.

Bernabé Maestre, J. M. 1976. *La industria del calzado en el Valle del Vinalopó*, Valencia, University of Valencia.

Brusco, S. 1990. "The idea of the industrial district: Its genesis", in Pyke, F. et al. (eds.): *Industrial districts and inter-firm co-operation in Italy*, Geneva, International Institute for Labour Studies.

Capecchi, V. 1989. "The informal economy and the development of flexible specialisation in Emilia-Romagna", in Portes, A. et al. (eds.): *The informal economy. Studies in advanced and less developed countries*, Baltimore, John Hopkins University Press.

---. 1990. "A history of flexible specialisation and industrial districts in Emilia Romagna", in Pyke, F. et al. (eds.): *Industrial districts and inter-firm co-operation in Italy*, Geneva, International Institute for Labour Studies.

Capellades, J. 1989. "Localisació de l'activitat econòmica de la població de Catalunya 1975-1986", in *Nota d'Economía*, No. 34.

Casals, M.; Vidal, J. M. 1985. "La economía subterranea en Sabadell", in *Papeles de Economía Española*, No. 22.

Castillo, J. J. 1988. *La informatización de las pequeñas y medianas empresas en España y sus efectos sobre el empleo y la organización del trabajo*, Madrid, European Community Commission.

---. 1989. *La división del trabajo entre empresas*, Madrid, Ministerio de Trabajo y Seguridad Social.

Celada, F. et al. 1985. *Efectos espaciales de los procesos de reorganización del sistema productivo en Madrid*, Madrid, Comunidad de Madrid.

---. 1990. *El distrito industrial de la periferia metropolitana del suroeste*, Madrid, Secretaria General Técnica, Comunidad de Madrid.

Costa Campi, M. T. 1988. "Descentramiento productivo y difusión industrial: El modelo de especialización flexible", in *Papeles de Economía Española*, No. 35.

---. 1989. "Los acuerdos de cooperación entre empresas industriales", in *Economistas*, No. 35.

---. 1990. "La organización industrial en el territorio: Descentralización y economías externas", in Parellada, M. et al. (eds.): *Estructura Económica en Cataluña*, Madrid, Espasa Calpe.

Cots Reguant, F. 1988. "Comarques industrials intermitges", in *Revitas d'Industria*.

del Castillo, J. 1988. "Evolución de la industria vasca y análisis de la política industrial", in *Economía Industrial*, No. 263.

del Castillo, J.; Rivas, J. A. 1988. "La cornisa cantábrica: Una macro-región industrial en declive", in *Papeles de Economía Española*, No. 34.

Edwards, A. 1979. *The new industrial countries and their impact on Western manufacturing*, London, Economist Intelligence Unit.

Estevan, A. 1984. *Relaciones interindustriales entre un grupo de PYMES tecnologicamente cualificadas en la Comunidad de Madrid*, Madrid, Comunidad de Madrid.

---. 1986. *La industria electrónica en la Comunidad de Madrid*, Madrid, Comunidad de Madrid.

Estevan, A.; Soto, P. 1987. *Actuaciones de promoción industrial y tecnología en torno a la factoría de AT&T en Madrid*, Madrid, Comunidad de Madrid.

Fernández Castro, J. 1985. "Una aproximación sociológica a la reconversión industrial", in *Papeles de Economía Española*, No. 22.

Greenwood, D. J.; González Santos, J. L. 1989. *The corporate culture of Mondragón: Social and cultural dimensions of industrial democracy in the Fagor co-operative group* (manuscript).

Lafuente Félez, A.; Pérez Simarro, R. 1988. "Balance y perspectivas de las ZUR", in *Papeles de Economía Española*, No. 35.

Linz, J. 1981. "A century of politics and interest in Spain", in Berger, S. (ed.): *Organising interests in Western Europe*, Cambridge, Cambridge University Press.

Lleonart, P.; Garola, A. 1989. "El sistema de ciutats de Catalunya a l'horitzó de l'any 2000", in *Nota d'Economia*, No. 36.

Martín Rodriguez, M. 1989. "Evolución de las disparidades regionales: Una perspectiva histórica", in García Delgado, J.L. (ed.): *España, economía*, Madrid, Calpe.

Miguélez Lobo, F. 1982. "Economía sumergida y transformaciones socio-laborales", in *Boletín de Estudios Económicos*, No. 117.

Muro, J. et al. 1988. *Análisis de las condiciones de vida y trabajo en España*, Madrid, Ministerio de Economía y Hacienda.

Oficina de Planeamiento Territorial. 1985. *La industria en suelo no urbanizable*, Madrid, Comunidad de Madrid.

Parellada, M.; Güell, X. 1988. "Factores de localización de nuevos establecimientos industriales en Cataluña", in *Colección Estudios FIES* (Madrid) (4).

Pedreño, A. 1989. "Un eje de expansión económica: Cataluña-Mediterráneo", in García Delgado, J.L. (ed.): *España, economía*, Madrid, Calpe.

Picó, J. 1976. *Empresario e industrialización*, Madrid, Editorial Tecnos.

Piore, M.J. 1990. "Work, labour, and action: Work experience in a system of flexible production", in Pyke, F. et al. (eds.): *Industrial districts and inter-firm co-operation in Italy*, Geneva, International Institute for Labour Studies.

Piqué i Camps, J. 1988. "La política de la Generalitat per a la promoció i ajut a la creació d'empreses", in *Revista Economía de Cataluña*, No. 9.

Portes, A. et al. (eds.). 1989. *The informal economy: Comparative studies in advanced and developing countries*, Baltimore, John Hopkins University Press.

Rico Gil, A. 1988. "La experiencia valenciana en la promoción de la inovación", in *Papeles de Economía Española*, No. 35.

Sabel, C. F. 1982. *Work and politics*, Cambridge, Cambridge University Press.

---. 1987. "The reemergence of regional economies", Cambridge, Massachusetts Institute of Technology (mimeo).

Sabel, C.; Zeitlin, J. 1985. "Historical alternatives to mass production: Politics, markets, and technology in nineteenth-century industrialisation", in *Past and Present*, No. 108.

Sanchís, E. 1984. *El trabajo a domicilio en el País Valenciano*, Madrid, Instituto de la Mujer.

Sanchís, E. et al. 1988. "La nueva pequeña empresa de la industria valenciana", in *Sociología del Trabajo*, No. 5.

Scott, A. J. 1988. *New industrial spaces: Flexible production and regional development in North America and Western Europe*, London, Pions.

Segura, J. et al. 1988. *La industria española en la crisis (1978-1984)*, Madrid, Alianza.

Solé, C. 1987. "El sistema asociativo empresarial en el sector textil español", in Solé, C. (ed.): *Corporatismo y diferenciación regional*, Madrid, Ministerio de Trabajo y Seguridad Social.

Vázquez Barquero, A. 1988. *Desarrollo local: Una estrategia de creación de empleo*, Madrid, Ediciones Pirámide.

Vázquez Arango, C.; Trigo, J. 1982. "Las vías de transformación de la economía formal en irregular", in *Información Comercial Española*, No. 587.

Veciana, J. M. et al. 1988. "La collaboració universitat-empresa a Catalunya", in *Revista Economía de Cataluña*, No. 9.

Whyte, W. F.; Whyte, K. K. 1988. *Making Mondragón: The growth and dynamics of the workers' co-operative complex*, Ithaca, ILR Press.

Ybarra, J. A. 1982. "La reestructuración de la industria del calzado español: Aspectos laborales y territoriales", in *Boletín de Estudios Económicos*, No. 117.

---. 1990. "La racionalidad económica de la industrialización difusa", Paper presented at the International Conference on Small Firms in the European Context, Alicante.

4   Industrial districts: Model and reality in Baden-Württemberg, Germany

Hubert Schmitz

I.   Introduction[1]

This chapter is addressed to an audience which includes both the practitioners in local industrial development and those who conduct research on it. The relationship between the two is not always an easy one. Researchers advising practitioners find it easier to pin-point what does not work than to recommend what does. At first sight, this chapter offers a chance of positive lessons since it focuses on one of the most celebrated success stories of regional economic development: that of Baden-Württemberg (B-W) in Germany. However, it should be made clear from the outset that the reader who expects ready-made prescriptions from this chapter will be disappointed. The success is clear but its causes are less so.

This volume focuses on industrial districts. The experience of the Third Italy and elsewhere suggests that such districts are a form of industrial organisation which facilitates growth, innovation and high employment standards. As a result, the stylised model of the Third Italy has become a reference point in the debate on local and regional policy. It is also the reference point for this chapter on Germany. It should, however, be mentioned that the Italian experiences are far from uniform and that not even industrial districts in the Third Italy always live up to the stylised model.

The chapter is structured as follows: Section II summarises the key components of the industrial district model. Subsequent sections examine *to what extent this model captures the reality of B-W and explains the success of the region*. This question is pursued step by step. Section III provides an overview of B-W's industrial structure, particularly on the relative importance of small, medium and large-scale enterprises and of their main branches of activity. Section IV examines the relationships between firms, especially vertical and horizontal inter-firm co-operation. Section V assesses the role of regional and municipal government in fostering growth and innovation. Sections VI and VII deal with the role of intermediary institutions and trade

1.   In preparing this paper, I benefited from discussions with many colleagues. I am particularly grateful to Harald Kohler for assistance in collecting data and literature and valuable sugestions on the institutional context for innovation in Baden-Württemberg.

unions. The concluding part, Section VIII reflects on some policy issues which emerge from this chapter.

II. The industrial district model

Over the 1970s and 1980s, B-W has experienced faster growth and lower unemployment than most other regions in Germany. This has led an increasing number of researchers to enquire into the causes of this relatively favourable economic and social development. This chapter does not contain a comprehensive review of this research. Its objective is more specific and modest. It examines B-W through the lens of a particular approach to industrial organisation: the industrial district model.

The significance of industrial districts as a hot-house for local industrialisation was recognised most clearly by Alfred Marshall at the turn of the century. He emphasised in particular the economic advantages that arise from the combination of geographical proximity and sectoral specialisation. Recently, there has been a revival of interest in industrial districts [see the collection of articles in Goodman and Bamford (eds.), 1989; Pyke et al. (eds.), 1990]. This was fuelled by "the rapid growth and competitive success of industrial districts composed of interdependent networks of small firms in parts of Italy, West Germany, Scandinavia, the United States of America and Japan" [Zeitlin, 1989, p. 367). In particular, the Third Italy gave rise to a new industrial district model [Becattini, 1990; Brusco, 1990] which is defined by more than *geographical proximity* and *sectoral specialisation*. Additional attributes are: the *predominance of small firms*, close *inter-firm collaboration*, *inter-firm competition through innovation* rather than through wage squeeze, high degree of *trust between employers and skilled workers*, provision of collective services through *self-help organisation* and *active regional and municipal government* strengthening the innovative capacity of local industry.

The model itself is controversial and is part of a wider debate on Post-Fordist industrial organisation, flexible specialisation and new regionalism [Piore and Sabel, 1984; Scott, 1988; Storper, 1989; Sayer, 1989; Hilpert, 1989; Fach and Grande, 1989; Amin and Robins, 1990; Best, 1990; Harrison, 1990; Hirst and Zeitlin, 1990; Schmitz, 1990; Murray, 1991]. The purpose of this chapter is not to engage in this general debate but to pursue a more specific task. The objective is to examine to what extent this industrial district model captures the reality of B-W.

Herrigel's [1987] analysis implies that there is a good match between the two. Similarly, Sabel et al. [1987] suggest that the key factors accounting for the success of B-W include "specialised but flexible firms that depend on the use of skilled, versatile labour and general purpose machines; subcontracting systems which allow firms to spread the risks of research and development, but above all encourage each production unit to learn its business as thoroughly as it can and share that knowledge with its collaborators; industry structures which co-ordinate specialisation among firms and provide the infrastructural services which allow individual companies to run all the risks associated with renouncing self-sufficiency; a state government which, despite temporary diversions, seconds these efforts at co-ordinated specialisation by shoring up the infrastructure of innovation within its own authority and resources" [p. 38]. Maier [1987] in his "Model Baden-Württemberg - Institutional Conditions of Differentiated Quality Production" gives a similar account.

Not surprisingly, this story of growth, innovation, differentiated quality production, collaboration amongst employers and workers, co-operation amongst firms, and supportive local institutions, has proved to be attractive. Indeed, B-W itself has become a reference point for research on industrial organisation and policy within and outside Germany [see, for example, Cooke and Morgan, 1990a; 1990b].

At this point, it is important to note that there is more than one "Model Baden-Württemberg": the one in the literature on industrial organisation coincides with that of the politician, Lothar Späth, Prime Minister of B-W since 1978. He stresses in particular the need for innovation policy, support to small and medium-scale enterprises (*Mittelstandspolitik*) and the consensus society (*Versöhnungsgesellschaft*). Some of the policy measures taken by his government are discussed in this chapter but it is not the purpose here to discuss Späth's project and the underlying political/ideological agenda. This has been done extensively in the German literature [see, for example, Erdmenger and Fach, 1986, 1989; Möller, 1988; Naumann, 1985; Schabedoth, 1989; Schmid, 1989]. As stated above, the agenda for this chapter is set by the recent debate on industrial districts.

III. Industrial structure in B-W

In area, B-W is the third largest *Land* in the Federal Republic of Germany and with 9.5 million people it has the third largest population[2] (see Figure 1). One of its chief characteristics is the high share of the secondary sector in both production and employment (see Table 1).

---

2. References in this paper to "Germany" or "Federal Republic of Germany" are pre-unification, i.e they do not include the former German Democratic Republic.

Figure 1:   Baden-Württemberg and its administrative composition

Table 1: **Sectoral distribution of production and employment in Germany and Baden-Württemberg (% in 1980)**

	Germany	B-W
Primary sector		
GDP	2.1	1.8
Population	6.1	5.3
Secondary sector		
GDP	47.3	54.4
Population	44.9	51.8
Tertiary sector		
GDP	50.5	43.8
Population	49.0	42.9

Source: Ott [1983].

In B-W, this secondary sector is almost identical with manufacturing industry. The purpose of this section is to examine three aspects of the structure of manufacturing which are central to the industrial district model:

- geographical concentration;
- sectoral specialisation;
- predominance of small firms.

The first point to make is that B-W is not a homogeneous economic region. It includes sub-regions with considerable variations of industrial density. The "Middle Neckar" region around Stuttgart is the industrial heartland of B-W (see Figure 2). In line with recent practice [see, for example, IHK, 1990], this region will be referred to as the *Stuttgart region*.[3] In 1989, it had a population of 2.4 million and 2,133 industrial establishments employing 456,308 people (= one-third of B-W). It is this region which is of prime interest in this chapter. Indeed, most of the discussion of the "model B-W" is essentially about this region, but it should be borne in mind that there are a number of other industrial agglomerations in B-W ([see Ott, 1983].

---

3.   To be distinguished from the city of Stuttgart or the *Regierungsbezirk* Stuttgart.

Figure 2:   Baden-Württemberg in relation to Germany and Europe

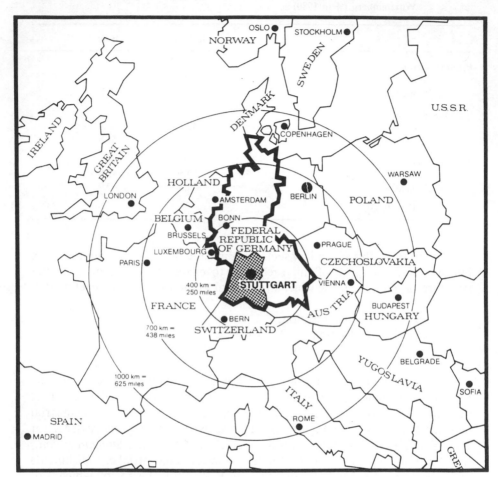

Note: The borders show Germany before unification.

If geographical concentration and sectoral specialisation are the necessary conditions for an industrial district, the Stuttgart region certainly qualifies.[4] Its main sectoral characteristic is a concentration in capital goods production which is high - even by German standards. Table 2 compares the share of the capital goods sector in total industrial *employment* for Germany, B-W and the Stuttgart region.

---

4.   As an industrial agglomeration, the Stuttgart region is, however, much larger than the industrial districts of the Third Italy, so much so that diseconomies of agglomeration, particularly traffic congestion, are beginning to constrain the region.

Table 2:   Share of the capital goods industry in total industrial employment in Germany, Baden-Württemberg and Stuttgart region in 1980 and 1988

	1980	1988
Germany	51.5	55.0
Baden-Württemberg	61.5	65.5
Stuttgart Region	73.5	78.2

Source: IHK [1990].

In 1988, the share of the capital goods industry in total industrial production was 79.3 per cent. The three most important sub-sectors were machine tools, vehicles and electricals/electronics with respective shares of 16.4 per cent, 29.4 per cent and 21.9 per cent in total production of the Stuttgart region. The international competitiveness of these three industries is underlined by their success in export markets. The share of production that is exported is 46 per cent for machine tools, 50 per cent for vehicles and 30 per cent for electricals/electronics. Capital goods production as a whole accounts for 90 per cent of industrial exports of the Stuttgart region. Some of the products of these industries (e.g. passenger cars) cannot strictly be counted as capital goods but this is of little concern to this chapter. More important is the degree and kind of division of labour between firms. Before this is explored, it is important to give an overview of the size structure of industry.

In the industrial district model, most production comes from small firms. Similarly, the backbone of B-W's industry is said to be the *Mittelstand*, for which the nearest English equivalent is small and medium enterprises. Definitions and statistical delimitations are arbitrary and indeed vary a great deal in the available literature but this has little effect on our main conclusion: small and medium scale industry is far from dominant.

Let us explain by putting B-W in the German context. B-W has the reputation of having a particularly well-developed small and medium scale industry. The statistics, however, suggest that it does not differ much from the German average. In 1987, 50.7 per cent of industrial employment in B-W was accounted for by enterprises of fewer than 500 workers; this compares with a German average of 47.4 per cent [IHK, 1990].

More important for our purpose is the size structure within the Stuttgart region which is shown in Table 3. In this industrial agglomeration, the share of industrial workers in enterprises of fewer than 500 workers is below the average of Germany and of B-W. Clearly, small and medium-scale industry carries relatively little weight in this industrial district. In 1988, the share of industrial workers in establishments of fewer than 500 workers was merely 36 per cent, compared with 50.6 per cent for B-W. The respective shares in enterprises of fewer than 100 workers were 14.6 per cent (Stuttgart

Table 3: Establishments and workers by size of establishments in Baden-Württemberg and Stuttgart Region in 1988

Size of establishment by number of workers	Establishments				Workers			
	B-W		Stuttgart		B-W		Stuttgart	
	No.	%	No.	%	No.	%	No.	%
1 - 19	1 063	11.5	148	6.9	12 086	0.8	1 747	0.4
20 - 49	3 486	37.8	826	38.5	114 199	7.9	27 249	6.0
50 - 99	2 023	21.9	492	23.0	141 333	9.8	34 596	7.6
100 - 199	1 280	13.9	325	15.1	180 445	12.5	45 415	10.0
200 - 299	528	5.7	136	6.3	129 989	9.0	33 669	7.4
300 - 399	242	2.6	48	2.2	83 701	5.8	16 164	3.6
400 - 499	153	1.7	35	1.6	68 161	4.8	15 923	3.5
500 - 999	262	2.8	66	3.1	180 240	12.5	44 386	9.8
1000 and more	196	2.1	70	3.3	532 199	36.9	234 436	51.7
Total	**9 233**	**100.0**	**2 146**	**100.0**	**1 442 353**	**100.0**	**453`585**	**100.0**

Source: Statistisches Landesamt Baden-Württemberg.

Region) and 18.5 per cent (B-W.)[5] This is a far cry from the industrial districts in the Third Italy where small firms seem to account for most of the employment and production.

There are, however, considerable variations in the size structure of the various industries. In the machine tool industry, large firms are much less dominant than in electricals/electronics. It is in the vehicle industry that large firms occupy the highest share in production and employment. Such inter-industry variations in size structure are not dissimilar from those in other parts of Germany or of Europe.

To conclude, B-W cannot be characterised as a small firm economy. On the contrary, the main industrial agglomeration of the Stuttgart region is dominated by large firms. It is true that there are some small industrial centres outside the Stuttgart region which bear a closer resemblance, in size and structure, to the industrial district model. One of the most interesting examples is Tuttlingen, a world leader in the production of surgical instruments [Maier, 1987]. However, such small firm industrial districts have relatively little weight in the B-W economy - particularly if compared with the Third Italy.

Does this matter? Sengenberger and Loveman [1988] doubt "whether it is the size dimension of business organisation *as such* that plays the crucial role in determining economic efficiency and vitality; and also whether there is something inherent in large or small firms that could make them particularly apt as job generators" [p. 3]. I would agree and extend these doubts to the industrial district model. There is another component of this model which is probably more important than size, namely inter-firm co-operation, which is examined in the next section.

IV. Inter-firm co-operation

Emphasising co-operation amongst firms does not mean a community without conflict. It is more about the balance between competition and co-operation. According to the industrial district model, there is intense competition between firms producing the same things and co-operation between firms producing similar but non-competing goods or between firms engaged in different stages of production. Such co-operation is part and parcel of the interaction of firms. In addition, there is formalised co-operation in which directly competing firms also participate. An example is

---

5.   These figures, derived from Table 3, under-rate employment in establishments of fewer than 20 workers, since *Handwerksbetriebe* (crafts) are counted under services, presumably because many of them engage in repairs and maintenance more than in production. The total number of such establishments in B-W is approximately 100,000 [Boelcke, 1987; Kohler, 1987].

the organisation of common services. (For further details, see Brusco [1986, 1990]).

In order to examine whether such co-operation exists in B-W, it is useful to distinguish between horizontal and vertical co-operation. The experiences which are reviewed come primarily from B-W's three main industries: machine tools, cars, electricals/electronics.

1.   Inter-firm co-operation in the machine tool industry

B-W's machine tool industry has a reputation for innovation and high quality. Its firms have prospered in the world market by producing specialised machinery adapted to the particular requirements of their customers. Co-operation amongst machine tool makers in B-W has been central to their success according to Herrigel [1987], who has conducted a in-depth study of this area. In his analysis, the B-W machine tool industry is a successful case of *co-ordinated specialisation*, the rationale for which is presented as follows:

> Small and medium-sized craft production based machinery firms are extremely flexible. Skilled workers with general purpose equipment could probably construct an infinite variety of machinery if given the chance. The problem is, if given that chance, markets would break down. Firms would be competing in all markets all at once with shops just like their own. At the first sign of a downturn in the business cycle, murderous price cutting and poaching of other firms' orders would break out as firms sought to keep their order books filled and workers employed[6] [p. 25].

> This problem repeatedly plagued the machinery industry ... gradually a solution to the problem evolved which took the form of co-ordinated specialisation. With the help and encouragement of the trade association - the VDMA - groups of machinery firms ... arranged their product palettes so that they did not compete with other members of the group ... [p. 26].

> Co-ordinated specialisation evolved as a process of continuous negotiation within confederations of firms concerning the definition and demarcation of markets and technology. This process of negotiation continues to take place today in the norm committee of the VDMA where norms and standards for machines and machinery parts are jointly negotiated by the member firms. The idea of the industry as an association of independent specialists, each with unmatched expertise and flexibility in a particular phase or type of production, shapes the process of negotiation [p. 26].

> Co-ordinated specialisation removed the albatross of competitive anarchy from the necks of producers. But in so doing, it created a number of other problems. Biggest of all, the system of specialisation increased each individual firm's vulnerability to both rapid technological change and to downturns in the business cycle. It thus placed pressure on firms to remain innovative [p. 27].

---

6.   To support Herrigel's reasoning, one can refer to the Brazilian machine tool industry during the recession in the early 1980s [see Porteous, 1990].

Herrigel [1987] suggests that the pressure to innovate deepened the vertical co-operation between firms:

> ... because the crux of co-ordinated specialisation meant that firms could not reduce losses by diversifying into new areas, they had to survive by improving or customising existing product lines. Progress in one phase of production naturally created bottlenecks in others, so firms were continually running into technological problems that they could not resolve with the resources they had on hand. This created a market for specialised supplier firms who could provide a particular technology or simply solid technological advice [p. 28].

This vertical division of labour and co-operation between firms deepened particularly in the 1970s and 1980s due to rising development costs associated with rapid technological change and shorter product life spans. As a result:

> ... firms have simply shifted some of the burden of innovation onto specialised subcontractors [p. 30].

> Greater reliance on subcontractors disperses the costs of innovation throughout a regional economy. Typically the machinery producer will cultivate a broad circle of suppliers with which it will work very intimately, providing manufacturing know-how and collaborating on production engineering of single parts and sub-assemblies. Many firms even help their suppliers purchase the equipment they will need to produce a given part, usually by guaranteeing a certain amount of orders so that the supplier firm can get the capital it needs from the local bank. The firm essentially ties its own existence to a network of suppliers [p. 31].

> At the same time ... firms generally refrain from becoming too dependent upon any one supplier. Most cultivate at least two sources for a part and confine their purchases from single suppliers to 10 - 20 per cent of that supplier's output. Suppliers are thus forced to develop similar relationships with a variety of ... manufacturers in the regional economy ... The decentralised industrial order in this way produces a pool of common know-how embodied in a multitude of co-operating and differently specialised firms.

Such vertical co-operation is, according to Herrigel, complemented by horizontal co-operation.

> Individual risk was socialised across institutions providing educational, technical and marketing services without which the specialised machinery firms could not survive [p.27].

The significance of some of these institutions will be examined in a later section, because they aim to cater not just for the machine tool industry, but for industry at large. The role of the association of machine tool makers (VDMA) has already been mentioned and indeed deserves further consideration.

> The VDMA and its many specialised sub-associations have evolved into indispensable institutions for small and medium sized firms. They provide market information, statistics, and legal counselling that firms could only with great difficulty get on their

own. More importantly, the specialised associations organise trade shows, arrange for export permits ..., promote the general exchange of market information and co-ordinate co-operative basic research projects at universities for member firms [p. 27].

I refer to Herrigel's [1987] work in some detail because inter-firm co-operation is central to the industrial district model. The extent and quality of such co-operation in B-W seems very impressive. But its actual existence has been questioned in recent research by Cooke and Morgan [1990b] who found that in B-W's machine tool industry "there was relatively little inter-firm co-operation"! [p. 46].

This view was confirmed by the VDMA who stated, both nationally and at regional level, that the machine-tool SMEs (small and medium sized enterprises) tended to be strongly independent, vigorous and specialised ... the VDMA had tried to encourage collaborative research and marketing because firms were too small to do these things themselves. However, despite numerous efforts the firms had resisted because they are competitors of each other [p. 46].

Even though the business associations that look after member firms in machine tools consider it wise for collaboration to be extended in, especially, research and marketing, firms are highly resistant to co-operation even where the results might be the penetration of new and potentially lucrative markets [p. 48].

Even if one makes allowance for the fact that Herrigel undertook his interviews in 1985/86 and Cooke and Morgan in 1990, their research results are contradictory. The incompatibility of findings, however, must not be exaggerated. It does not extend to the issue of vertical co-operation, but concerns mainly horizontal co-operation through sectoral associations. To clarify these issues, further research would be necessary.

Such research would indeed be useful, particularly for practitioners interested in applying lessons from B-W elsewhere. There is, however, a danger of concentrating too hard on consciously pursued co-operation. There is probably a great deal of co-operation which is not strategically pursued but "just happens" in the course of transactions between firms and in the course of contacts between their staff in and outside the place of work. Moreover, in an industrial district, firms benefit from each other's existence in ways which cannot be captured adequately with the term "inter-firm co-operation". I am referring here to external economies which are an important part of Becattini's [1989, 1990] analysis of the Third Italy. Such external economies are rarely planned and are hard to measure, but they are probably essential to the success of B-W's machine tool makers.

2.   Inter-firm co-operation in the car and electricals/electronics industries

The deep inter-firm division of labour noted in the machine tool industry is also present in the car and electricals/electronics industries. But there is also a major difference. In the latter industries, this division of labour is orchestrated by large firms.

This seems very different from the industrial district model outlined in Section II of this chapter. Sabel [1989], however, suggests that such differences are more apparent than real, that there is a general convergence of large- and small-firm structures "as the small firm industrial districts expand, they create centralised laboratories, marketing agencies and technology consultancies inspired by large firm models" [p.19]; meanwhile, large firms decentralise internally into semi-autonomous operating units and subcontract specialised suppliers. Contractor and supplier seek a stable relationship, not just for reliable delivery of parts and components but also for the shared development of improved designs. Contractors impose ceilings on the percentage of the supplier's output they will buy and encourage them to work for firms in other industries. The contractor thus benefits from the suppliers' exposure to other contractors and the suppliers do not tie their existence to fortunes of one single contractor [Sabel, 1989, pp. 33-35].

This general proposition is of direct relevance to the concerns of this chapter, even though the initial question needs to be reformulated as follows: to what extent are the large firms decentralising functions to internal units and external suppliers and thus approaching the organisation principles of the small firm industrial district model? In examining this question for the car and electrical/electronics industries of B-W, I concentrate on the subcontracting practices of the large firms since these affect the local industrial structure more than the large firms' internal developments.

The car and the electrical/electronics industries in the Stuttgart region consist of intermeshing webs woven by four large spiders: Daimler Benz (Mercedes), Bosch, SEL and, to a lesser extent, IBM.

Of these, Bosch comes closest to confirming Sabel's thesis. This is hardly surprising since it is largely based on his interviews in that firm's purchasing division. In fact, he refers to it as the "Bosch model" [Sabel, 1989, p. 37]. In the words of Herrigel [1990], Bosch:

> has adopted a strategy of transferring its own know-how in certain technologies on to outside firms, in order to be able to devote its resources to product development in its area of strength: the integration of micro-mechanical and micro-electronic technologies. ... It establishes its relations with subcontractors so that any given subcontractor only conducts approximately 20 per cent of its business with Bosch.[7] The rest the subcontractor must find from other producers in the Baden-Württemberg economy. The experience that the subcontractor gains from this diverse work, Bosch's reasoning goes, provides a valuable store of potentially useful know-how and expertise for Bosch [pp. 26-27].

Herrigel [1990] furthermore, suggests:

---

7.   According to Cooke and Morgan [1990b], "policy dictates that there is a formal ceiling of 30 per cent of turnover for the amount of output sourced from a given supplier by Bosch. However, in practice, the 30 per cent is often broken" [p. 33].

-   that Bosch is not an exception in B-W.;

-   that, while subcontracting has always been extensive, technological collaboration between contractor and supplier is relatively new;

-   and, more generally, that "large firms are not only beginning to interpenetrate with the smaller producers through the establishment of collaborative and subcontracting relationships, they are increasingly adopting principles of organisation and practices typical of the small and medium sized firm organisational field" [p. 25].

Other observers agree that there is a general increase in subcontracting by large firms, but also make important qualifications to the scenario drawn by Sabel and Herrigel. Loveridge stresses that technological co-operation between Bosch and its suppliers works well, because it is not new and has been practised for decades.[8] Cooke and Morgan [1990b] confirm that Bosch has increasingly farmed out the production of components but "there was no particular tendency to draw on Baden-Württemberg suppliers for this" [p. 30]. More significant was the fact that purchases from outside Germany were increasing at a faster rate. Similarly, in the case of Daimler Benz, the outsourcing is reported to be increasingly global or non-local. SEL, however, is not reducing its high level of local sourcing. Still, there remains a question mark, not over the decentralisation through subcontracting, but over the extent to which it is retained in the local economy.

There is also the question of the distribution of opportunities between large and small suppliers. Cooke and Morgan [1990b] report that amongst the subcontractors of Bosch, large suppliers were increasingly the winners over smaller ones. Semlinger [1989a; 1989b] provides a systematic explanation as to why this is likely to occur. Even though his work is not specifically concerned with B-W, his analysis implies a collision rather than a merging of the small and large firm structures.

3.   Conclusions

Inter-firm co-operation is a central feature of the industrial district model.[9] In B-W, vertical co-operation seems to be a common practice between enterprises of all sizes, but there are question marks concerning the extent to which small firms can feed into the collaborative subcontracting practices of large contractors. On the question of horizontal co-operation,

---

8.   Based on Loveridge [1990] and discussions with the author.

9.   Close inter-firm linkages are not necessarily conducive to success as shown by Grabher [1990] in his analysis of the Ruhr region in Germany.

there are contradictory observations on whether this occurs. The discussion in this section was, however, limited to sectoral associations in the machine tools industry. There are other intermediary organisations which are not branch specific and which are very active in B-W. Their role is discussed in Section VI of this chapter.

V. The role of regional and local government

The industrial district model emphasises the supportive role of regional and municipal government. Of all the components of the model, this is probably the one of greatest interest to the practitioner. Given the growth record of B-W and of the Stuttgart region, the practitioner's question is to what extent this growth was managed by regional and local government. The more it was, the greater the hope that such growth can be replicated elsewhere.

The current government of B-W presents itself as the creator or manager of this growth. In particular, new initiatives in technology policy have attracted a great deal of attention; not least because Lothar Späth, current head of the regional government, made it a centrepiece in his high-profile neo-conservative modernisation strategy [Späth, 1985; 1987]. One of the main arguments in this section is that the industrial success of the region can hardly be attributed to these new initiatives. The "Model Baden-Württemberg" was in place before they took effect. The recent measures may, however, turn out to be crucial in consolidating and strengthening local industry.

The above is also an argument for an historical perspective. If one wants to explain the success of B-W in the 1980s, one needs to ask about innovation policy pursued in previous periods. Here it is interesting to note that such policy has a long history in B-W, going back to the middle of last century [Reuss, 1986; Kohler, 1987]. In Württemberg, a regional organisation for manufacturing and trade was created in 1848. Its purpose was to support product and process innovation by making available technical advisers, technical information and finance. The first president of this institution was Ferdinant Steinbeis. He can be considered the founding father of innovation policy in the region. The main institution of current technology policy, the Steinbeis Foundation, is named after him.

Recent accounts of the success of B-W [for example Maier, 1987; Sabel et al., 1987] frequently refer to Steinbeis's initiatives and those of other local institutions but it is hard to assess their importance in the present context. It is true that some important principles in the adoption of current technology policy (to be discussed later) can be traced back to the last century. But this tells us little about the effectiveness of technology policy then or now. In fact, a critical observer could ask why - if the nineteenth century institutions were so important - did B-W remain poor for so long?

It is only since the 1970s that B-W has occupied a leading position within both Germany and Europe. Another critical observation to be made is that there is a good deal of discussion on technology policy in the middle of the last century and then again, almost a century later, in the 1970s and 1980s but very little on what happened in between.[10] Presumably, if the task is to explain the success of the late 1970s and 1980s, it would be particularly interesting to know more about policy in the 1950s and 1960s.

The purpose of these comments is not to belittle the new initiatives taken in the 1980s. On the contrary, they command attention and have stimulated the thinking on and practice of decentralised innovation policy both within and outside Germany. Practitioners would be paralysed if they only allowed themselves to take action once the effectiveness of measures has been "scientifically" proven. Hence, there follows a review of innovation policy at both the regional (*Länder*) level and municipal level.

1.   Regional technology policy

In what follows, regional policy is not understood to mean policy for the less developed sub-regions of B-W. It means policy adopted by the regional (*Land*) government. Lothar Späth, prime minister of B-W since 1978, has tried to rally society behind the objective of technological modernisation. Such modernisation cannot, in his view, be achieved by merely relying on market forces. His government, even though Christian Democrat, believes in and practises active innovation policy. What underlies this policy is a tripartite modernisation model of state, economy and science.

Innovation is affected by policy in various areas, in particular by incentives embodied in tax and trade policy and by explicit science and technology policy. Amongst these, it is in technology policy that regional governments in Germany have the greatest autonomy (vis-à-vis the federal government). This is what this section focuses on.

A.   Overview of technology policy

Technology policy in B-W covers a wide range of institutions and measures. For a broad categorisation, it is useful to distinguish between pan-enterprise (*überbetrieblich*) and single-enterprise (*einzelbetrieblich*) support.

(a)   Pan enterprise support

The government of B-W has tried to create an infrastructure which breeds technological innovation. This includes:

---

10.   Providing a continuous historical account would, however, be an elaborate undertaking because up to the early 1950s, B-W consisted of three *Länder* (Baden, Württemberg and Württemberg-Hohenzollern) which had undergone different economic and political developments.

(i) *Strengthening of research capacity both within and outside universities.* More so than in other parts of Germany, university research in B-W concentrates on science and engineering. There is special concern with *applied* sciences in, for example, the Institute for Microelectronics in Stuttgart, the research centre on informatics at Karlsruhe University, the institute for laser technology at the University of Ulm. Recent support has favoured in particular research into new materials (such as ceramics for machine tools) and automation technology. Equally, if not more important, are specialised research institutes outside the universities, notably the Max-Planck and Fraunhofer Institutes.

For research within and outside universities, government seeks the participation of the private sector, particularly in the applied sciences. The most recent culmination of the tripartite model of state, economy and science is the science city Ulm, an extraordinary newly fostered concentration of public and private sector research capacity [for details, see Schmid et al., 1990].

(ii) Of more immediate relevance to the concerns of this chapter is government support for *technology transfer*. There is clear recognition that innovation is costly and risky [Späth, 1985; 1987] and there are several institutions which provide or arrange advice at various stages of searching for or introducing new processes and products. The key actor is the Steinbeis Foundation which has the multiple task of working on technology policy strategically, acting as a centre which advises entrepreneurs who can help them, and providing specialised assistance itself through its technology transfer centres located throughout the region.

Some of these centres are attached to Polytechnics (*Fachhochschulen*) which themselves are expected to work closely with local enterprises and to assist with technical and related managerial problems. Thus, there exists a decentralised net of specialised technology support services. Industry contributes in varying degrees to the financing and organisation of these services. This applies also to the ten technology parks established in the region.

(iii) Taken together, the fostering of product and process innovation set out in (i) and (ii) are a means of furthering human resources. Indeed, public support for *education and training* is a central part of innovation policy and takes place at three levels:

- universities, including three technical universities;

- polytechnics (*Fachhochschulen*), whose curricula are closely linked to the needs of local industry;

- vocational training colleges (*Berufsschulen*) for apprentices who work three days a week in a local firm and spend two days at college (dual system of vocational training).

In its system of education and training, B-W differs little from the rest of Germany, except that collaboration with industry is perhaps closer here.

(b)   Single enterprise support

Innovation policy in B-W has attracted a great deal of admiration (even envy!) but also criticism from neo-liberal quarters [for details see Schmid, 1988]. The criticism is particularly directed at those measures which support single enterprises, as being against the principles of a market economy.

There are several programmes designed to provide financial support for entrepreneurs to (1) develop new products or processes; (2) put new techniques into practice; (3) set up new technology-intensive enterprises. The support consists primarily of subsidised credit; grants are less frequent. Between 1984 and 1988, over 2,600 enterprises benefited from these programmes, mostly for the second purpose, resulting in public expenditure amounting to DM214 million [Becher and Weibert, 1990]. However, it must be borne in mind that expenditure for these programmes ranks well behind pan-enterprise support.

B.   The significance of the policy

This brief account cannot do justice to the many institutions involved in technology policy in B-W. From the outside, this policy looks as impressive as B-W's recent economic development. It is tempting to make a causal connection between the two, but sober analysis forbids this for two reasons.

First, there is a great deal of description of the policy but - with a few exceptions [Becher et al., 1989; 1990] - there is little analysis of its effectiveness.

Second, other German *Länder* have adopted similar measures, but their industries have performed less well. Hence, if the success of B-W were policy induced, one would need to show that *more* was done, and that it was done *better* than in other parts of Germany. This is worth a brief examination, not least because it helps to locate B-W within the wider German perspective.

On the question of whether *more* was done, it is useful to remember that *implicit* innovation policy, i.e. setting incentives through tax, finance and trade policy, is largely in the hands of the federal government and is the same throughout Germany. This chapter has only considered *explicit* innovation policy and here variations can be observed. For example, according to Becher and Weibert [1990], in single enterprise technology support, B-W alone accounted for 39 per cent of total German expenditure (for comparison, its share in Germany's GDP was 16 per cent in that year). Similarly, it seems that B-W spends more on pan-enterprise technology transfer programmes, but comparative figures could not be found. With regard to the research capacity in universities and other institutions, there is less difference. For example, Kohler [1987] concludes that B-W and Nordrhein-Westfalen (where some of the declining industries are located) are broadly similar in expenditure, as well as in number and range of research institutes.

With regard to whether innovation policy in B-W is qualitatively *better*, a number of observations can be made:

(1)   In research and higher education, there is stronger emphasis on *applied* sciences and engineering than in most other parts of Germany.

(2)   B-W has pioneered a number of measures in technology transfer. One example is the "Furtwanger Model", a scheme under which academic staff can be temporarily released from their teaching function in order to help industry to develop and adapt new technology. This is now practised in most other parts of Germany [Kohler, 1987]. Of course, the fact that B-W has been a pace-setter in technology policy neither proves that it is better at executing it, nor that the existence of such policy matters.

(3)   In these respects, a study by Braczyk and Niebur [1987] is of interest. It compares small and medium-scale machine tool makers in the Stuttgart region and in the Ruhr region which is struggling to restructure. In both regions, there has been considerable expansion of technology advice services and the enterprises' views of these services differ little. They attach little importance to whether such services exist in principle and give a low rating to the quality of existing local services. Such responses lend support to those who question the relevance of regional technology policy.

(4)   Further critique comes from a study which examines another side of innovation policy in B-W. The chief instigator of this policy, Lothar Späth, claims that the creation of an innovative environment requires a tough stand on industries which are in decline. A detailed study by H. Schmid [1988] shows that this was indeed tried but that - in the affected sub-regions - local coalitions of employers' federations, trade unions and municipal governments were able to mobilise and obtain public resources for their ailing industries. Thus, contrary to the public image, this is a feature which B-W shares with other parts of Germany.

(5)   Innovation requires the active collaboration of workers. Späth's project of a *Versöhnungsgesellschaft* (consensus society) has its rationale in the

need for all forces of society to collaborate if innovation is the central objective. So far, however, labour institutions have played little, if any, role in B-W's innovation policy, unlike in some other parts of Germany such as Nordrhein-Westfalen [Kohler, 1987; Esser, 1989].

(6)   Finally, it is worth mentioning that Späth recognised that - in order to implement his vision - he required a more efficient and flexible administration. Yet the attempted administrative reform had to be abandoned.

The above observations are a very incomplete assessment, but help to provide a more realistic picture of B-W's celebrated technology policy in the 1980s. One should add that for some measures of technology policy, notably the fostering of research and development, it would be premature to undertake an assessment of their effectiveness; they tend to take more than a decade to bear visible fruit.

It would, however, be erroneous to conclude that nothing positive can be learnt from a B-W study on the role of regional government in technology policy. On the contrary, even if there remains a gulf between rhetoric and practice, there are a number of issues and principles that deserve attention and are highlighted by the B-W experience. These are set out below:

(1)   In the 1980s, the agenda of economic policy-making was set by the neo-liberals. In a neo-liberal world, market forces can be relied upon to maximise innovations. The startling success stories of rapid innovation and industrial growth, namely Japan, the Republic of Korea and Taiwan contradict this view [White, 1988], yet the neo-liberal agenda remains extremely influential. In Germany, *regional* governments have taken the lead in shaking off the simplistic neo-liberal prescription for innovation. B-W has made a significant impact in two respects. First, the government of Lothar Späth has been in the vanguard of making innovation policy a central concern for regional government. Second, it was a government of Christian Democrats that rejected the neo-liberal prescription. A mere reliance on market forces was judged to be insufficient even though B-W probably suffers less from market imperfections than most other regions in Germany or Europe.

(2)   There was a recognition that government required staff that could work on technology strategy, develop new practical approaches and co-ordinate the work of relevant institutions. It is interesting that this strategic role was not entrusted to an existing government department, let alone a new department created for this purpose, but to an institution which is not part of the civil service: the Steinbeis

Foundation.[11]   While working directly for the government and financed to a large extent by government, constitutionally it is a non-governmental organisation which reports to a *Kuratorium* consisting of representatives of craft, trade and industry, the scientific community, political parties and regional administration (but not of trade unions!). The point to be made is that the fostering of innovation requires an approach to policy-making which combines the capacity to think and act strategically, but works at the same time through decentralised institutions close to the enterprise.

(3)   In B-W, government support has traditionally been linked to self-help. It was a principle put forward by Steinbeis in the last century and remains a principle in current technology policy [Kohler, 1987; Maier, 1987].   The form and extent to which industry, trade and crafts contribute varies, but their active participation is in most cases a precondition for government intervention. This is discussed further in a separate section on self-help organisations.

2.   The role of municipal government

In the literature on industrial districts, it is not only regional but also municipal government that plays an important developmental function. The purpose of this section is to examine briefly whether this has also occurred in B-W.

In West Germany generally municipal government has become increasingly active during the 1970s and 1980s [Wollman, 1989].   This municipal interventionism can be observed in a number of fields (urban renewal, environmental protection and others). Technology promotion is one of the most recent areas of municipal activity, but the short experience has already brought out both opportunities and limitations of local authorities in this area (see, for example, the collection of articles in Hucke and Wollmann [1989], and in Dose and Drexler [1988]).   This is a lively and interesting debate which merits a separate paper.

The main points to be made here are that, first, there is relative silence on municipal governments in B-W compared with the noise surrounding the regional government. Second, the difference does not just seem to be in appearance but also in substance.   There is little, if any, indication that local government in B-W is more active in industrial policy than elsewhere in Germany or that it is more effective than elsewhere. This is an implicit conclusion one can draw from the recent literature on decentralised technology policy.

---

11.   The *Landesgewerbeamt* used to play an important role in B-W's regional innovation policy [Reuss, 1986], but its functions in this respect are now largely carried out by the Steinbeis Foundation.

Perhaps the most explicit evidence comes from a study which does not focus on innovation policy but deals with the wider issue of municipal promotion of economic activity (*Gewerbepolitik*). Nassmacher [1987] sought to uncover the reality of "economic policy from below" in an exhaustive study (covering 15 years) on three municipalities in various parts of Germany. One of them, Leonberg, lies in the Stuttgart region. Its local government was not more active in industrial promotion than the other two. If anything, it was geared towards improving and expanding residential accommodation rather than innovation and industrial growth (which were occurring anyway). Perhaps it is also worth mentioning an earlier study by Nassmacher and Nassmacher [1982] carried out in various municipalities of the Stuttgart region. It showed that there is little concept of and concern for local industrial strategy amongst leading local government officers and councillors.

3.   Conclusions

An essential component of the industrial district model is that regional and local government strengthen the innovative capacity of local industry. The objective of this section was to discuss whether and how the apparent success of B-W was fostered by regional and local government. There is no short answer to this question. What is clear is that regional government has an active innovation policy. Even if one makes allowance for the gap between projected image and practice, there is a well-developed strategy to improve the conditions for innovation and industrial growth in the region. It would, however, be misleading to attribute the success of B-W in the 1970s and 1980s solely to the neo-conservative modernisation strategy of Lothar Späth. The success preceded or coincided with his technology policy. At the same time, it would be unreasonable entirely to discard claims that the regional government helped industry to cope with the challenges of the 1990s.

Proving or disproving such claims will always be difficult. At present, it is too soon to assess the effectiveness of the policy; in particular the pan-enterprise support discussed above takes many years to bear visible fruit. With regard to single enterprise support, the results of a recent interim assessment are not clear-cut. According to Becher et al. [1989; 1990], over half of the enterprises benefiting from such support would have innovated anyway, but they intensified or speeded up the process because of the support; one-quarter of beneficiaries made no changes to what had been planned. Only one-sixth of the benefiting enterprises started innovation projects which would not have seen the light of day without support.

A great deal less is known about the role of municipal governments, but the evidence referred to above suggests they are relatively passive. There is a well-documented case of local political forces fending for local industry [Schmid, 1988], but ironically their action ran counter to the innovation policy of the regional government. It was a defensive local coalition seeking subsidies for a declining industry.

The overall conclusion of relatively passive local political forces may have arisen because the focus was on municipal governments. However, it must be borne in mind that there are other actors who make up local developmental coalitions, such as self-help organisations. The next section examines whether they have played a major role in facilitating local industrialisation.

VI. The role of intermediary institutions

Self-help organisations are an important component of the industrial district model. The purpose of this section is to discuss how industry in B-W helps itself through intermediary institutions, and to assess their relative importance for innovation.

Such institutions play a major role in some assessments, particularly that of Herrigel [1990, p. 5]:

> How has it been possible for so many small and medium sized firms to successfully combine technologically sophisticated specialisation with flexibility? My argument is that the success of Baden-Württemberg firms is based on a system that socialises risk across a broad array of public and private institutions. Small firms do not have to bear the entire burden of (a) developing new technologies; (b) finding new markets; (c) training skilled engineers and workers; (d) raising capital. The costs of specialisation are shared by or embedded in a thick network of inter-organisational relations, institutions and practices in the regional economy.

There could thus hardly be a closer match between this assessment of B-W and the industrial district model with its emphasis on regional institutions.

Some of the institutions referred to above have been discussed in the previous section on regional government; others are more clearly of the self-help type.[12] One such institution is the sectoral associations (*Industrieverbände*). The example of the association of machine tool makers (VDMA) was discussed in the section on inter-firm co-operation; it was found that it is not clear whether this association actually brings about "co-ordinated specialisation" (see Section IV). There is no doubt, however, that such associations provide some services. These concern technical matters such as product standards or industry-specific training needs. Some of them also advise member firms on labour issues such as rights and obligations towards their workers. These sectoral associations overlap with employers' federa-

---

12.   The main sources for this brief overview of self-help organisations are Boelcke [1987], IHK [1988], Kohler [1987], RKW [1988].

tions whose main role is to negotiate wages and terms of employment with trade unions.

Parallel to these associations representing particular sectors of industry, there are the chambers of industry and commerce (*Industrie und Handelskammern*), which represent all firms in a sub-region. Membership is compulsory for all industrial firms, as is the payment of a levy (calculated as a percentage of a local tax). Hence, it is a well-endowed institution able to deliver a wide array of services. The ones of greatest interest in the context of this chapter are training and technology transfer.

The chambers play a key role in Germany's dual training system, in the design and supervision of courses and in the examination of apprentices. The Stuttgart chamber, being one of the largest in Germany, also established a number of specialised training centres to which member firms can send their workers. In addition, it holds numerous courses which help technicians and managers keep up with new technologies and organisational practices.

As regards technology transfer, the chamber operates eight innovation consultancy bureaux in B-W. These either provide technical advice themselves or help member firms to locate the most appropriate firms or institutions that can help them. In this respect, it offers a service similar to that of the government's Steinbeis Foundation (see Section V.1; the relationship between them will be discussed later).

Self-help institutions also facilitate access to *finance* for innovative ventures. In instances where commercial banks find that loans for technical innovations are too risky, producers can turn to the *Bürgschaftsbank Baden-Württemberg*. This bank was set up by the chambers of industry and commerce and other self-help institutions to provide credit guarantees. Such guarantees are available for up to 80 per cent of a loan, at an annual 1 per cent commission and for up to 23 years. Since the upper limit is 1 million DM, it is of relevance mainly to small or medium enterprises. The same applies to another financial self-help institution, the *Mittelständische Beteiligungsgesellschaft*. It makes available venture capital up to 300,000 DM provided that at least 25 per cent of the total investment is the entrepreneur's own capital.[13]

Finally, it is worth mentioning that support from self-help institutions extends to foreign trade. The Foreign Trade Foundation (*Stiftung Aussenwirtschaft*) is an institution created jointly by the chambers of industry and commerce, industrial associations and the regional government. The Foundation's main task is to facilitate exports of small and medium-sized enterprises.

What has been provided so far in this section is not a complete list of all intermediary institutions and their functions. Nevertheless, this brief overview confirms that B-W has an impressive range of self-help

---

13.   In addition, this organisation acts as a conduit for venture capital of up to 1 million DM from federal sources.

organisations, some tied to regional government, others operating more independently. As mentioned in Section V.1, the self-help principle has a long tradition in B-W going back to the middle of the last century. The evidence indicates that this principle has reasserted itself in recent times. More than in previous periods, these organisations are now harnessed to a regional innovation consensus.

However, it remains difficult to assess how much they actually influence innovation and growth. One could argue that most of these organisations also exist in other German regions, including regions which have been less successful, and that such institutions therefore do not play a critical role. Since there is no comparative study on their relative weight and effectiveness, a conclusive judgement is not possible.

However, even without a comparative assessment, some observations can be made which have a bearing on the effectiveness of such organisations. What has emerged from Sections V and VI is that local enterprises have access to a variety of governmental, semi-governmental and independent institutions frequently offering similar, if not identical, services. This could be interpreted as undesirable overlap and duplication. This is not my view. To start with, there is complementarity and collaboration between these institutions, as stressed in official publications [*Ministerium für Wirtschaft, Mittelstand und Technologie*, 1990]. There is in addition, however, rivalry and competition, both among institutions and between them and the private sector. For technology support services, for example, Cooke and Morgan [1990] have pointed to the tension between the chambers of industry and commerce, the private consultancy industry and the Steinbeis Transfer Centres. Not surprisingly, the competing agents see this as a problem. Such competition could, however, be seen as a strength of B-W's institutional infrastructure. It gives the user a choice and makes the supplying institutions and enterprises more prone to cater to the needs of local industry.

In conclusion, B-W industry is well provided with services in technology, marketing and finance from self-help institutions. Similar services are offered by government agencies and - to some extent - also by private firms. Rather than making for undesirable overlap and duplication, competition between these service providers probably contributes to their effectiveness and relevance for industry.

VII. The role of labour and trade unions

A feature of the industrial district model is that competitiveness is not pursued by squeezing wages. The key competitive weapon is continuous innovation which in turn requires a highly-skilled and well-paid workforce. The purpose of this section is to examine to what extent such a high wage/high skill/high technology dynamic exists in B-W and what role the trade unions play in bringing it about.

If high wages and labour standards are essential components of the industrial district model, B-W fulfils these criteria probably more than the Third Italy. Industrial workers enjoy high wages and a short working week, particularly in the Stuttgart region. A shortage of skilled workers and low rates of unemployment for unskilled work has enabled trade unions to negotiate high wages and a step-by-step introduction of the 35-hour week.[14]

As mentioned above, the industrial district model also places an emphasis on skilled labour. B-W's reputation in Germany is one of a region which attaches great value to technical skills. Moreover, there is the evidence to support this high skill profile. Taking B-W industry as a whole, the share of technicians and engineers in its workforce is significantly above the German average [IHK, 1990]. But does this emphsis on skills extend also to other workers or is there a gulf between conception and execution of work?

One of B-W's advantages is that in its industry the separation of "head" and "hand" has rarely gone as far as in typically Fordist mass production. This is clearest in the skill-intensive machine tool industry. In B-W's mass production of cars and electronics there is, of course, fragmentation of work and use of unskilled workers, but observers of companies such as Daimler Benz, Bosch and SEL seem impressed above all with their training intensity. These companies invest heavily in the training of apprentices and technical and managerial workers [Cooke and Morgan, 1990b]. However, sector-specific comparisons of skill profiles and training intensity in B-W and other regions could not be found. As regards changes over time, there is contradictory information. Sources close to employers emphasise that the share of unskilled and semi-skilled workers has decreased [IHK, 1990] whereas a union commissioned study suggests a rising share of low-skilled labour [IMU, 1988].

The overall impression that comes across from available sources is that B-W industry comes close to fulfilling the Post-Fordist maxim: treat labour as a resource to be developed over time rather than a cost item to be minimised in the short run. Workers' representatives, however, stress that in many firms there is still a long way to go [IMU, 1988].

To the extent that B-W industry has treated labour as a resource, this does not derive merely from the wisdom of employers. It seems that trade unions have contributed to the emphasis on training, skills and innovation. More generally, it can be said that trade unions have accelerated rather than slowed down the innovation process. In order to elaborate, it is useful to explain briefly how unions are organised and to distinguish between different levels of union activity.

---

14.   Unlike the Third Italy, other institutions such as the church, government and political parties have little influence over wages and labour standards, but it should be mentioned that the conservative prime minister of B-W, Lothar Späth, has consistently argued against low wages [Schmid, 1988, p. 31].

German unions are organised by industry and not by profession. In metalworking, for example, all employees belong to the IG Metall regardless of their occupation or profession. Most of what follows concerns the IG Metall experience. It is the largest union in Germany, with around 2.7 million members. It is also the largest and most influential union in B-W, covering machine tool, car and even electrical engineering industries.

The role which unions play in the innovation process varies with the level and focus of analysis. At the micro-level, they have played an important role. The IG Metall has consistently warned against insufficient structural adjustment, innovation and retraining in the German steel industry, which is largely outside B-W [see Esser, 1982]. Similarly, within B-W, the union has had its eye on the future, arguing for innovation and investment in training, particularly for new skills. Co-determination at the company level (shop floor and supervisory board) makes it possible to channel such concerns into management decisions. IMU [1988], however, stresses that this does not always happen. Co-determination also exists in the vocational training system. Here, unions have sought to use their influence to bring about adjustments in occupational profile and training requirements.

In stressing this forward-looking attitude of the IG Metall,[15] it is not implied that employer-labour relations have been entirely harmonious. Far from it: in a number of respects these relations have been highly antagonistic, particularly in B-W. Effective strike action and negotiation has made the B-W unions a pacemaker in Germany. The IG Metall has been in the vanguard of the fight for a shorter working week and higher wages. Thus "destructive competition" [Sengenberger, 1989] by gaining advantages through squeezing wages and lowering labour standards had no chance. This pressure from the unions - made possible by the relative shortage of labour - contributed to creating a climate in which enterprises seek to become more competitive through innovation. This is of particular importance in a region which is both a producer and user of new technology.

While the unions play a major role in this high skill/high wage/high tech dynamic, this is not the case in the regional government's initiatives, discussed in Section V. To be sure, Lothar Späth's project of the consensus society embraces also workers and their unions [Späth, 1985], but in practice they have been excluded from taking an active role in the regional innovation policy [Kohler, 1987; Esser, 1989].[16] A partial exception is the establishment of the science city of Ulm, where the trade unions are represented in a new academic institution which focuses on socio-economic implications of

---

15. This forward-looking attitude is also brought out by the commissioning of a study on the economic prospects of the Stuttgart region in the 1990s by IG Metall [IMU, 1988]. The study concludes that there is an increasing risk of job losses in the 1990s. According to a prognosis of the Chamber of Industry and Commerce, however, this risk is remote [IHK, 1988]. A study of IAW/IFO [1990] tends to confirm the latter view.

16. For a general assessment of the role of German trade unions in regional industry policy, see Adamy and Bosch [1986].

new technologies [Schmid et al., 1990]. In conclusion, trade unions have been sidestepped in the regional government's innovation policy. It would, however, be wrong to conclude from this that trade unions in B-W are marginal to the innovation process.

VIII.   Conclusion

In this chapter, the B-W experience was set against the industrial district model - a model which is essentially based on the Third Italy experience. The comparison showed both similarities and differences. This is hardly surprising. As Pyke and Sengenberger [1990] note, just as with large corporations, no two industrial districts can be expected to be exactly alike.

This concluding section reflects further on the similarities and differences. It does so by focusing on two issues which are of particular relevance to those concerned with whether and how such local or regional industrialisation can be fostered. These are:

(a)   the critical importance of collective efficiency;
(b)   the pursuit of industrial policy at the regional/local level.

1.   Collective efficiency

The competitive strengths of industry in the Third Italy or in B-W cannot be grasped and cannot be furthered by focusing on individual firms. Their strength lies in their agglomeration and co-operative competition. Firms compete with each other - often fiercely - but also complement each other, either through vertical links and/or through horizontal collaboration to deal with specific common difficulties.[17] As a result, there is a collective capacity to adapt and to innovate. Elsewhere, I have suggested the notion of collective efficiency to capture such strength [Schmitz, 1990].

Such collective efficiency can be both planned and unplanned. The latter arises from the clustering of firms in a particular industry and location and from the external economies that this tends to generate. The former is consciously pursued through joint action to further common interests (for example, through associations, consortia and other self-help organisations). Clearly, both types of collective efficiency are present in B-W and the Third Italy.

---

17.   This is underlined by a fascinating case study which reached me after completion of this chapter. Semlinger [1991] shows how competing small and medium sized firms co-operated to cope with increasing quality requirements.

Having emphasised this similarity between the two regions, we also need to bring out the difference. Since the sectoral composition of industry is different, large firms play a greater role in B-W. Hence there is a greater degree of hierarchy. Particularly in the industrial agglomeration of the Stuttgart region, the interfirm division of labour is to some extent orchestrated by large firms. I agree with Sabel and others that this does not necessarily harm adaptive and innovative capacity. Indeed, the operating principles of large firms in B-W, particularly extensive collaborative subcontracting, seem to aid collective efficiency and flexibility.

However, differences in size structure are likely to have a bearing on policy. The larger and the more international the firm, the more difficult it is to influence its behaviour. This has been the experience of national governments and is even more true for regional and local government. Large firms like Daimler Benz and Bosch have their headquarters in the Stuttgart region and are probably more anchored in their home region than international firms generally are. Nevertheless, they have an essentially European or global rationale which is - inevitably - at times in conflict with that of the region and its government. This applies even more to the other two large firms in the Stuttgart region, SEL and IBM, since they are subsidiaries of French and US corporations. In the case of small and medium sized firms, there is likely to be a much stronger commitment to the region, because the economic and social standing of their owners is more closely tied to local factors - even if their firms produce for the world market. The argument is not that regional and municipal governments do not matter but that they have less influence in sectors which are dominated by large firms.

2. A new model of industrial policy?

In spite of the above limitation, there is a striking similarity between the Third Italy and B-W. Neither relies entirely on the market, both have regional or local institutions which support industry, particularly small and medium sized firms. Initiatives of these institutions have attracted national and international attention because there seems to be a causal connection between their interventions and regional prosperity. As stressed in Section V, such causality has to be treated with caution in the case of B-W. Much of the success was in place before the regional government under Lothar Späth launched its active industrial policy.

The same seems to apply to the Third Italy. In fact, Brusco [1990] distinguishes between an industrial district model Mark I and Mark II. Mark I refers to the early growth which was largely spontaneous. In Mark II, industry requires support from local institutions in order to speed up innovation, expand into new markets and thus consolidate regional growth. Such a distinction between the two phases seems useful also in the case of B-W. Therefore, although regional government policy did not create the industrial organisation which led to the observed collective efficiency, it would be hard to entirely dismiss claims that it has helped industry to cope with the challenges of the 1990s.

There is a policy implication which emerges from this similarity between the German and Italian experience. It is a conclusion which is almost obvious but which needs emphasising in view of the desperation with which poor regions observe those which are prosperous. Government or government-sponsored institutions cannot create an industrial organisation which competes on the basis of collective efficiency. However, once private initiative has led to a minimum concentration of industrial activity and know-how, they can play an important part in helping industry to innovate and expand.

Equally important, there is more than one way of pursuing such a policy. The Third Italy and B-W have a different balance between regional and municipal governments. In B-W, initiative and action emanate from the regional government, whereas municipal authorities play a greater role in the Third Italy. Murray [1991], who cast his net more widely in a review of regional and municipal government initiatives in Europe, notes the wide variety of experiences.[18] Similarly, Esser [1989] and Schmid [1990] emphasise the variety in the conduct of regional innovation policy in Germany. What these regional and local initiators have in common is that they are sceptical about relying entirely on the wisdom of the market and of central government.

More than that, they represent steps towards a new model of regional industrial policy which (1) emphasises delegation of functions to a diverse range of governmental and non-governmental institutions; (2) operates through institutions close to the enterprise;[19] (3) extends the concern with entrepreneurship from the private to the public sector; and (4) stresses self-help through business associations and producer consortia. This is a major political shift and is, in my view, a welcome one. Further research will have to show whether this shift - apart from being politically desirable - is also economically efficient. The critics have already raised their voices. Amin and Robins [1990] have questioned the potential of the industrial district in a paper on "the mythical geography of flexible accumulation". Fach and Grande [1989] stress that the connection between region and innovative capacity is far from clear. And no doubt neo-liberals will continuously (and justifiably) raise questions about the costs of municipal and regional government intervention.

---

18.   Murray [1991] also reminds us that "if the virtue of the local is action and diversity, its vice is parochialism". This has not, however, been the problem in the Third Italy and even less so in B-W. In fact, one of the main facets of Späth's [1985; 1987] project is that it formulates regional/local responses to international challenges.

19.   The case of B-W also brings home the risk of government-industry ties becoming too intense. In February 1991 (upon completion of this paper) Lothar Späth had to resign as prime minister of B-W, because his interactions with industry had become too close.

3. Final note

This concluding section has focused on collective efficiency and the role of regional industrial policy. Both are research issues in their own right, but in this chapter they have been discussed in the context of the current debate on industrial districts.

The purpose of this chapter was to contribute to this debate by examining to what extent the industrial district model captures the recent industrial development in B-W and explains the success of the region. To this end, the various elements of the industrial district model were disentangled and examined one by one. This is - I believe - a necessary and useful step in an exercise which has an empirical rather than conceptual purpose. However, there is a danger in disaggregating an "industrial order" (to use Herrigel's term) into its constitutive elements, because the key is to grasp how these elements work together. The whole is more than the sum of its parts. Indeed, after disaggregation, one needs to move to recomposition, but this is a much harder task. The trouble is that even if one were to succeed, it would not be easy to dismiss the cynical observer who says that B-W's success in the 1970s and 1980s was a matter of luck: the region happened to have mainly sunrise and few sunset industries.

References

Adamy, W.; Bosch, G. 1986. "Gewerkschaften in der Region - Impulsgeber oder Dulder regionaler Beschäftigungspolitik", in *Soziale Sicherheit*, No. 35, Volume 2, February.

Amin, A.; Robins, K. 1990. "The reemergence of regional economies? The mythical geography of flexible accumulation", in *Society and Space*, Vol. 8.

Becattini, G. 1989. "Sectors and/or districts: Some remarks on the conceptual foundations of industrial economies", in Goodman, E.; Bamford, F. (eds.): *Small firms and industrial districts in Italy*, London, Routledge.

---. 1990. "The Marshallian industrial district as a socio-economic notion", in Pyke, F. et al. (eds.): *Industrial districts and inter-firm co-operation in Italy*, Geneva, International Institute for Labour Studies.

Becher, G.; Weibert, W. 1990. *Technologiepolitik in Baden-Württemberg*, Karlsruhe, Fraunhofer Institut für Systemtechnik und Innovationsforschung (mimeo).

Becher, G. et al. 1989; 1990. *Zwischenbilanz der einzelbetrieblichen Technologieförderung für kleine und mittlere Unternehmen in Baden-Württemberg*, Part 1 (1989) and Part 2 (1990), Karlsruhe, Fraunhofer Institut für Systemtechnik und Innovationsforschung.

Best, M.H. 1990. *The new competition - Institutions of industrial restructuring*, Cambridge, Polity Press.

Boelcke, W.A. 1987. "Organisation und Politik von Industrie, Handwerk und Handel", in Schneider, H. (ed.): *Verbände in Baden-Württemberg*, Stuttgart, Kohlhammer Verlag.

Braczyk, H.J.; Niebur, J. 1987. *Innovationsdefizit und Nord-Süd-Gefälle: Ein Vergleich von Klein- und Mittelbetrieben des Maschinenbaus aus den Regionen Ruhrgebiet und Mittlerer Neckar*, Frankfurt, Campus Verlag.

Brusco, S. 1986. "Small firms and industrial districts: The experience of Italy", in Keeble, D.; Wever, E. (eds.): *New firms and regional development in Europe*, London, Croom Helm.

---. 1990. "The idea of the industrial district: Its genesis", in Pyke, F. et al. (eds.): *Industrial districts and inter-firm co-operation in Italy*, Geneva, International Institute for Labour Studies.

Cooke, P.; Morgan, K. 1990a. *Learning through networking: Regional innovation and the lessons of Baden-Württemberg*, Regional Industrial Research Report, Cardiff, University of Wales, Department of City and Regional Planning.

---. 1990b. *Industry, training and technology transfer: The Baden-Württemberg system in perspective*, Regional Industrial Research Report, Cardiff, University of Wales, Department of City and Regional Planning.

Dose, N.; Drexler, A. (eds.) 1988. *Technologieparks - Voraussetzungen, Bestandsaufnahme und Kritik*, Opladen, Westdeutscher Verlag.

Erdmenger, K.; Fach, W. 1986. "Späth-Absolutismus? - Uber die Zukunft der Vergangenheit des modernisierenden Staates", in *Blätter für deutsche und internationale Politik*, pp. 716-725.

---. 1989. "Profil oder Profilierung? Uber die politische Konstruktion der schwäbischen Moderne", in Hucke, J.; Wollmann, H. (eds.): *Dezentrale Technologiepolitik - Technikförderung durch Bundesländer und Kommunen*, Basel, Birkhäuser Verlag.

Esser, J. 1982. *Gewerkschaften in der Krise*, Frankfurt, Suhrkamp Verlag.

---. 1989. "Does industrial policy matter? Zum Einfluss industriepolitischer Konzepte auf die Technikentwicklung", in Fleischmann, G.; Esser, J. (eds.): *Technikentwickluung als sozialer Prozess*, Frankfurt, Gesellschaft zur Förderung arbeitsorientierter Forschung und Bildung.

Fach, W.; Grande, E. 1989. "Raum und Modernität - zur Regionalisierung des Innovations-managements", in *Perspektiven des Demokratischen Sozialismus*, Vol. 6, No. 3.

Goodman, E.; Bamford, J. (eds.) 1989. *Small firms and industrial districts in Italy*, London, Routledge.

Grabher, G. 1990. *On the weakness of strong ties - The ambivalent role of inter-firm relations in the decline and reorganisation of the Ruhr*, Discussion Paper FS I 90 - 4, Berlin, Wissenschaftszentrum für Sozialforschung.

Harrison, B. 1990. *Industrial districts: Old wine in new bottles?*, Paper presented to the 1990 Boston Meetings of the Regional Science Association, November (mimeo).

Herrigel, G. 1987. *The political economy of industry: Mechanical engineering in the FRG*, Working Paper, Cambridge, Ma., Massachusetts Institute of Technology, Department of Political Science (mimeo).

---. 1990. *The politics of large firm relations with industrial districts: A collision of organisational fields in Baden-Württemberg*, Paper presented to Workshop on the Socio-Economics of Inter-firm Cooperation, Wissenschaftszentrum Berlin, June (mimeo).

Hilpert, U. 1989. "Region zwischen Innovation und Marginalisierung", in *Perspektiven des Demokratischen Sozialismus*, Vol. 6, No.3.

Hirst, P.; Zeitlin, J. 1990. *Flexible specialisation vs. Post-Fordism: Theory, evidence and policy implications*, Birkbeck Public Policy Centre Working Paper, Birkbeck College, University of London.

Hucke, J.; Wollmann, H. (eds.). 1989. *Dezentrale Technologiepolitik - Technikförderung durch Bundesländer und Kommunen*, Basel, Birkhäuser Verlag.

IAW/IFO. 1990. *Baden-Württemberg und der EG-Binnenmarkt 1992*, Gutachten im Auftrag des Ministeriums für Wirtschaft, Mittelstand und Technologie Baden-Württemberg, Institut für Angewandte Wirtschaftsforschung Tübingen und Institut für Wirtschaftsforschung München.

IHK. 1988. *Prognose von Arbeitsplatzangebot und Arbeitsplatznachfrage in der Region Mittlerer Neckar bis zum Jahr 2000*, Stuttgart, Industrie und Handelskammer (mimeo).

---. 1989. *Bericht '89*, Stuttgart, Industrie und Handelskammer.

---. 1990. *Die Wirtschaftsregion Stuttgart - Strukturen und Entwicklungen*, Stuttgart, Industrie und Handelskammer.

IMU. 1988. *Stuttgart - Problemregion der 90er Jahre? Gefährdungen der Arbeitnehmer durch Umstrukturierungsprozesse in der Metallindustrie*, Munich, Regionale Branchenanalyse im Auftrag der IG Metall Stuttgart, Institut für Medienforschung und Urbanistik.

Kohler, H. 1987. *Konservative und sozialdemokratische Modernisierungskonzeptionen am Beispiel der Forschungs- und Technologiepolitik der Bundesländer Baden-Württemberg und Nordrhein Westfalen: eine vergleiche Analyse*, Diplomarbeit, Sozialwissenschaftliche Fakultät, University of Constance.

Loveridge, R. 1990. *Apocalyptic change, normative uncertainty and the control of knowledge*, Aston Business School (mimeo).

Maier, H.E. 1987. *Das Modell Baden-Württemberg: Uber institutionelle Voraussetzungen differenzierter Qualitätsproduktion - Eine Skizze*, Discussion paper IIM/LMP87-10a, Wissenschaftszentrum Berlin für Sozialforschung.

Ministerium für Wirtschaft, Mittelstand und Technologie. 1990. *Mittelstandsbericht 1990*, Stuttgart.

Möller, J.M. 1988. "Der Realist der Zukunft: Lothar Späth und das Modell Baden-Württemberg", in *Die Politische Meinung*, No. 236.

Murray, R. 1991. *Local space - Europe and the new regionalism*, Manchester, Centre for Local Economic Strategies.

Nassmacher, H. 1987. *Wirtschaftspolitik 'von unten': Ansätze und Praxis der kommunalen Gewerbestandspflege und Wirtschaftsförderung*, Basel, Birkhäuser Verlag.

Nassmacher, K.-H.; Nassmacher H. (eds.). 1982. "Lokale Eliten in der Gewerbepolitik", in Robert Bosch Stiftung GmbH (ed.): *Gewerbepolitik im Verdichtungsraum: Akteure und Instrumente im regionalen Wirtschaftsgeschehen*, Stuttgart.

Naumann, K. 1985. "Modell deutscher Möglichkeiten? - Späth Politik in Baden-Württemberg", *Blätter für deutsche und internationale Politik*, No. 7.

Ott, A.E. (ed.). 1983. *Die Wirtschaft des Landes Baden-Württemberg*, Stuttgart, Kohlhammer.

Piore, M.J.; Sabel, C.F. 1984. *The second industrial divide: Possibilities for prosperity*, New York, Basic Books.

Porteous, M. 1990. "Revolution in a recession? Advanced technologies and Brazil's machine tool sector in the crisis", in Schmitz, H.; Cassiolato, J. (eds.): *HiTech for industrial development*, London, Routledge.

Pyke, F.; Sengenberger, W. 1990. "Introduction" in Pyke, F. et al. (eds.): *Industrial districts and inter-firm co-operation in Italy*, Geneva, International Institute for Labour Studies.

Pyke, F. et al. (eds.) 1990. *Industrial districts and inter-firm co-operation in Italy*, Geneva, International Institute for Labour Studies.

Reuss, K. 1986. "Die klassische Gewerbeförderung vor neuen Aufgaben - Gewerbeförderung in Baden-Württemberg und ihre lokale Verankerung", in Maier, H.E.; Wollmann, H.: *Lokale Beschäftigungspolitik*, Basel, Birkhäuser Verlag.

RKW. 1988. "Sonderbeilage Industriestandort Baden-Württemberg", in *Wirtschaft und Produktivität*, Vol. 39, No. 10, October.

Sabel, C. 1989. "Flexible specialisation and the re-emergence of regional economies", in Hirst, P.; Zeitlin, J. (eds.): *Reversing industrial decline? Industrial structure and policy in Britain and her competitors*, Oxford, Berg.

Sabel, C. et al. 1987. *Regional prosperities compared: Massachusetts and Baden-Württemberg in the 1980s*, Discussion Paper IIM/LMP87-10b, Wissenschaftszentrum Berlin für Sozialforschung.

Sayer, A. 1989. "Postfordism in question", in *International Journal for Urban and Regional Research*, Vol. 13, No. 4.

Schabedoth, H.J. 1989. "Modernisierungspolitik im Widerstreit neokonservativer Machtsicherungsinteressen und gewerkschaftlicher Gestaltungsansprüche", in Kissler, L.; Kreuder, T. (eds.): *Der halbierte Fortschritt: Modernisierungspolitik am Ausgang des 20 Jahrhunderts*, Marburg.

Schmid, H. 1988. *Regionale Wirtschaftsförderung-Schranke des 'Modells Baden-Württemberg'? Eine Untersuchung über Gründe und Effekte des Festhaltens an einem umstrittenen Politikbereich*, Dissertation, Sozialwissenschaftliche Fakultät, University of Constance.

Schmid, J. 1989. "Modernisierungspolitik und Späth-Absolutismus in Baden-Württemberg - Eine parteilose Veranstaltung?", in Bröchler, S.; Mallkowsky, H.P. (eds.): *Modernisierungspolitik in der Bundesrepublik Deutschland*, Frankfurt.

---. 1990. *Industrialpolitik der CDU: Innovation, variation, diffusion*, Working Paper SIT-wp-2/90, Forschungsstelle für Sozialwissenschaftliche Innovations- und Technologieforschung, Fakultät für Sozialwissenschaften, Ruhr-Universität Bochum.

Schmid, J. et al. 1990. "Wissenschaftsstadt Ulm: Entstehung, Aufbau und Funktion", in *Forum Wissenschaft*, No. 10, Marburg, July. Extended version in *Informationen zur Technologiepolitik und zur Humanisierung der Arbeit*, Düsseldorf, Deutsche Gewerkschaftsbund (forthcoming).

Schmitz, H. 1990. "Small firms and flexible specialisation in developing countries", in *Labour and Society*, Vol. 15, No. 3.

Schneider, H. (ed.) 1987. *Verbände in Baden-Württemberg*, Stuttgart, Kohlhammer Verlag.

Scott, A.J. 1988. "Flexible production systems and regional development: The rise of new industrial spaces in North America and Western Europe", in *International Journal of Urban and Regional Research*, Vol. 12, No. 2.

Semlinger, K. 1989a. "Fremdleistungsbezug als Flexibilitätsreservoir - Unternehmenspolitische und arbeitspolitische Risiken in der Zulieferindustrie", in *WSI Mitteilungen*, No. 9.

---. 1989b. "Stellung und Probleme kleinbetrieblicher Zulieferer im Verhältins zu grossen Abnehmern", in Altmann, N.; Saver, D. (eds.): *Systemische Rationalisierung und Zulieferindustrie*, Frankfurt, Campus Verlag.

---. 1991. *Das Steinbeis-Zentrum für Qualitätswesen - Eine Kleinbetriebliche Kooperations-initiative auf dem Weg zum Erfolg*, Munich, Institut für Sozialwissenschaftliche Forschung (mimeo).

Sengenberger, W. 1989. *The role of labour standards in industrial restructuring: Participation, protection and promotion*, Discussion Paper DP/19/90, Geneva, International Institute for Labour Studies.

Sengenberger, W.; Loveman, G. 1988. *Smaller units of employment: A synthesis report on industrial reorganisation in industrialised countries*, Discussion Paper DP/3/87(rev. 88), Geneva, International Institute for Labour Studies.

Späth, L. 1985. *Wende in die Zukunft*, Hamburg, Spiegel/Rowohlt.

---. 1987. "Wirtschaftspolitische Umbrüche: Der Weg zur Innovationspolitik in Baden-Württemberg", in Buddenburg, H. (ed.): *Umbrüche - Neue Strukturen in Wirtschaft und Gesellschaft*, Herford, Busse Seewald.

Steinbeis Foundation for Promotion of the Economy. 1988. *Report 1988*, Stuttgart.

---. 1989. *Report 1989*, Stuttgart.

Storper, M. 1989. "The transition to flexible specialisation in the US film industry: The division of labour, external economies and the crossing of industrial divides", in *Cambridge Journal of Economics*, Vol. 13, No. 2.

White, G. (ed.). 1988. *Developmental states in East Asia*, London, Macmillan.

Wollmann, H. 1989. *Towards a new dimension and a new round of 'municipal inter-ventionism'?*, Berlin, Institut für Stadtforschung und Strukturpolitik (mimeo).

Zeitlin, J. 1989. "Local industrial strategies: Introduction", in *Economy and Society*, Vol. 18, No. 4, November (Special issue: Local industrial strategies, edited by J. Zeitlin).

5 Industrial districts in West Jutland, Denmark

Peer Hull Kristensen

I. Introduction

1. Background

In recent years, the Italian experience of small firm industrial districts has become famous as a novel form of industrial organisation that has succeeded in competing in industries that were thought to be either the preserve of the large fully-integrated corporation or destined to be monopolised by low-wage economies using cheap labour. Thus, it has been a surprise to many orthodox economists that traditional industries like clothing or furniture manufacture have not completely left the higher-waged advanced industrialised countries for the cheaper labour advantages of Third World or underdeveloped countries. The view that "the West" could only have a future with "modern" industries has been threatened by the successes of regions like the "Third Italy". Moreover, it would seem that the crucial factor lying behind this success has not been wage cost but, rather, the way industry has been organised. This has opened the prospect that "traditional" industries in industrialised countries can be retained without sacrificing labour incomes or, indeed, labour standards. Further, the fact that the basic unit of the Italian district has been the small firm has posed a challenge to those who believe economic efficiency and growth will only come from the promotion of large firms, and large firm economies of scale, whilst offering hope to underdeveloped regions lacking establishments of any size. The best approach for areas trying to develop their economies might not be to enter into regional competitions to attract footloose major capitalist enterprises but, rather, to give greater attention to helping and organising endogenous resources. The experience of the Italian industrial districts, then, is of great significance to policy-makers and those interested in fostering local regeneration.

In this paper, we propose to relate the Italian industrial district phenomenon to cases of small firm success in "traditional" garment/knitting and furniture industries in Denmark. It should be stated at the outset that our treatment of the subject will be somewhat tentative owing to the fact that so little research has been carried out in the areas that we will be discussing. In our view, this is the result, to some extent, of the fact that industrial analysts in Denmark have been focusing their efforts on trying to show how manufacturing industry has been unable to restructure from traditional to science-based, high-tech industries, and from stagnating world markets to high growth areas. If there had been an interest in analysing how such manufacturing industries could survive in Denmark, with its high wage levels and the need to finance a modern welfare state, there would probably have been more information available on the development of industrial districts.

There is general agreement that traditional branches, such as the garment and furniture industries, and small firms, both play comparatively larger roles in Denmark than in most OECD countries. It is our intention in this paper to offer some explanation as to why this might be so and to ascertain the extent to which elements of organisation analogous to the Italian success stories might have played a part. A major question of general interest is whether the Italian industrial district phenomenon is a historically, geographically, or culturally unique occurrence; or does it exist, in part or as a whole, perhaps in different forms but performing similar functions, in other countries? If the key to the Italian small firm district has been a particular kind of dynamic organisation, we will attempt to identify whether that has also been the case in Denmark and, if so, whether some of the principles of organisation are the same. Given that the Danish industries in the "industrial districts" that we will be studying have performed remarkably well, under difficult world economic conditions, we think that our findings are of considerable policy relevance.

2. The Italian industrial district and flexible specialisation

Piore and Sabel [1984] convincingly demonstrated how a series of changes in world markets, and in principles of state regulatory mechanisms, presented increasing difficulties to the former dominant industrial model of Fordist mass-production. The same factors, they argued, worked in favour of the industrial districts in the "Third Italy", where a number of economic, political and social elements combined to create an extremely flexible productive and distributive system, that was particularly well suited to meeting the competitive challenges of the 1980s and 1990s.

Since Becattini, in his reference to the Marshallian industrial district, shifted the unit of analysis away from the single firm to a number of firms connected together in a small area [Becattini, 1979], the research of Italian social scientists such as Brusco and Capecchi, and others, such as Zeitlin, Murray and Best, have greatly contributed to our understanding of how flexible specialisation and industrial districts function. The success of the Italian industrial districts seems to be the result of the total organisational impact of a number of factors rather than of any single factor or cause.

Of particular significance is the organisation of production along decentralised, small firm lines, with each firm specialising internally, and for the greater benefit of, the total district network. Characterised by high flexibility, both within individual units and in respect of the network as a whole, this flexible specialisation model of organising production contrasts sharply with the model of the completely centralised and integrated Fordist mass production unit, using principles of organisation based on special-purpose machinery which can only be adapted very slowly. Where the flexible specialisation production model occurs within a limited geographically bounded space, it takes on the character of an "industrial district of flexible specialisation" [see Capecchi, 1990].

Whereas Fordist production plants cater to a mass market and pursue a competitive strategy of capturing customers by minimising costs through ever-greater economies of scale, the plants of the flexibly specialised district are small-batch producers, more geared towards competitive strategies that emphasise quality, style, reliability, innovation and, above all, adaptability - that is the ability to react quickly to the latest fashions, tastes, and technical specifications. This emphasis on non-price factors does not mean that cost is irrelevant. From the customer's point of view, considerable costs are saved by being able to rely on quick, responsive suppliers. Time is indeed money. Even purely in terms of production costs, the most advanced industrial districts can be very efficient and (price) competitive because "as districts" they can achieve the economies of scale normally associated with the large integrated firm. Small firms can install expensive capital equipment knowing that "economic runs" can be achieved by virtue of having the whole district as their market. Further economies of scale are achieved by the organisation of collective services which individual small firms can call upon when needed.

The availability of "collective services" reflects another important organisational principle of the Italian industrial district, namely the strong role played by both competition and co-operation in the functioning of the economic community. Co-operation is manifest in the collective organisation of services, the strength and political influence of the small business trade associations, the collaboration between units in a production chain over questions of design and technology, and the general atmosphere of openness that encourages the spread of ideas and innovation so crucial to the district's success. The firms of the districts do not possess internal R & D departments in the manner of large companies and must therefore rely on inter-firm collaboration. At the same time, however, individual units maintain a competitive stance.

Labour is central to the success of the districts. A flexible strategy requires a different kind of internal social organisation than is to be found within the Fordist firm. Workers must be trained and adaptable, both within the firm and between firms and, if employers are to maximise productivity, innovation and flexible response, there must be collaboration and trust between all the parties concerned. The rigid divisions between mental and manual labour, as evidenced in the Fordist model, must be broken down. Good working conditions and remuneration provide a foundation for building trust. Collaboration between firms and trade unions to provide reasonable levels of pay and the taking of wage competition out of the picture further cements social trust while encouraging firms to pursue strategies based on innovation and productivity rather than those based on cheap labour.

In addition, the presence of an entrepreneurial spirit and dynamism is also important. In the Third Italy, there is a strong propensity for men and women to want to start their own businesses, and the confidence and opportunity to do so exists. There is considerable social mobility between the statuses of worker and entrepreneur. Local sources of finance and close collaboration between small firm co-operative organisations and financial institutions help to provide the necessary capital.

The extended reproduction of the system functions through these basic principles as the way work is organised enables workers to acquire the specialised skills needed to set up their own firms, gradually enriching and expanding thereby the industrial sector in which they have been trained.

As we shall see, many of these defining principles are present in the Danish context as well. But there is one major difference. There is no debate on industrial districts in Denmark. In the Third Italy, on the other hand, "industrial districts" and "flexible specialisation" are not just abstract concepts used by academics but rather part of people's daily perception of the world. The division of labour, functionally and vertically, among small- and medium-sized enterprises (SMEs) and the guidance from, and co-operation within, formal organisations (such as the National Association of Artisans), relating micro-politics to communal and national politics, create *in toto* a conscious sense of "system", which is brought to life in Sassuolo, Prato, Montegranaro, Cento, Nogara and the other geographical spaces that make up the Third Italy.

If sense of direction and strategy - i.e. self-consciousness - and its organisational expressions are criteria for evaluation, only the garment district of Herning-Ikast (see Section IV) would qualify as an industrial district in Denmark. As we have already pointed out, the current debate in Denmark is focused on other perspectives. The mass of self-employed people and SMEs in Denmark have not developed an alternative strategic view of the future. Moreover, even if industrial districts provide such an alternative strategy, the necessary links between micro- and macro-politics facilitating the formulation of such a strategy are at present lacking.

One root of the difference between Danish and Italian self-consciousness is a legal one. While many Italian craft organisations fall into a separate category in law which defines the special obligations and rights of firms with fewer than 20 employees, Danish law does not differentiate in such a manner and consequently large and small enterprises are all organised in the same trade, branch or craft. Larger firms often dominate the formulation of political strategies of such associations, and small- and medium-sized enterprises (SMEs) are left without the organisational means through which they could create a distinct identity, build self-consciousness and discuss strategies of development, whether aimed at the world market or in response to shifting fashions in political spheres.

Denmark's recent development has revealed phenomena (which will be discussed later) which show many similarities with the Third Italy. In particular, growth has been led by SMEs in peripheral areas which have shown remarkable adaptability and flexibility since the first oil crisis. However, as there has been no enlightened strategy to provide guidance, the ad hoc experimental nature of social initiatives can easily result in errors being committed and blockages to further growth being created. The development of the structures of industrial districts is only one historical possibility, which might as easily not occur. At the same time, however, Danish society may contain strong hidden self-reinforcing relations among its economic agents, which could serve to reproduce its SME structure, and its industrial districts, in spite of - even compensating for - its "false consciousness".

The focus of this chapter is on the way in which a set of historically-given institutions have channelled industrial development, albeit unconsciously, in favour of a system of small firm networks, organised in many ways according to principles similar to those found in the industrial districts of Italy. Whether or not the Danish cases develop further along these lines is an open question.

3.   Denmark and West Jutland

Over the past decades, regional development in Denmark has displayed a remarkable tendency to be highly differentiated. We show in Section II that, as is the case in Italy, growth has occurred in former agricultural areas, mainly in what have been considered the peripheral regions of Jutland (the Northern, Southern and, especially, the Western parts), and has been led by small- and medium-sized enterprises (SMEs) that have responded to the vicissitudes of the past two decades with a remarkable adaptability. Analysts trying to explain this surprising growth pattern using traditional development theories have basically failed, but what they have done is produce material indicating a number of organisational characteristics and strategies typical of flexible specialisation.

In the course of suggesting a historical explanation for the recent pattern of industrialisation of West Jutland, in Section III we show how small railway towns, which formerly functioned as service centres for the neighbouring agricultural areas, have served as seed beds for industrial entrepreneurial activity during periods of agricultural crisis during this century. This spatial organisation, together with the existence of national institutions like Denmark's apprenticeship and technical schools, partly explain why, and how, a peripheral region like West Jutland has been able, endogenously, to create industrial development. The reader will see in such features many similarities between West Jutland and the heartland of Italy's industrial districts: Emilia-Romagna (see, for example, Capecchi [1990]). But the differences are just as important. West Jutland has never fostered the sort of regional political consensus that exists in the Red Belt in Italy, which is reinforced by the strong representation of regional interests by trade unions, associations of artisans and other organisations. In West Jutland, recent developments have occurred primarily within very small towns indeed and the ability to consciously create coherent industrial districts has been limited. Rather, the districts have come about more by chance than has been the case in Italy, where business associations and regional political bodies have consciously helped to organise the economy.

The industrial districts which are the focus of this chapter have developed out of small railway towns. These towns often consist of fewer than 5,000 people, a size which is hardly sufficient for creating such complex structures as industrial districts. However, should chance favour a very high growth of one or two such towns through the expansion of a particular industry, or should a whole group of small towns concentrate on such an industry and integrate with one another, true industrial districts could be formed. In several instances in Denmark, chance has indeed worked in such a way. In Section IV, we discuss two examples. One is the knitting and garment district of Herning-Ikast which has developed, over the centuries, characteristics very similar to Prato in Italy. A second case and a much more recent phenomenon, is a network of furniture districts in Salling which evolved gradually since the 1930s because a number of small railway towns in the area all focused much of their activity on the same industry.

In both cases, the districts are located in West Jutland and explain, in part, the region's high growth rates during the last two decades. Their locations are shown in the map which follows and it can be seen that Herning-Ikast is within the boundaries of Ringkøbing County and Salling is included in Viborg County. Both counties feature very significantly in the statistics presented in the following sections.

In Section V, we try to explore how the type of politics existing in these two district cases can channel development along flexible specialisation lines from a basis of pure chance to one of coherent strategy. Our focus here is on education, the local political significance of which is its role in discouraging the emigration of young people. Vocational training institutions help to orient a regional population toward the same industry. We will demonstrate how this has been occurring in both areas.

In the concluding section, we try to summarise the similarities and differences between the Third Italy and West Jutland in order to draw attention to a few important political lessons.

Map 1: Districts in two locations in Denmark

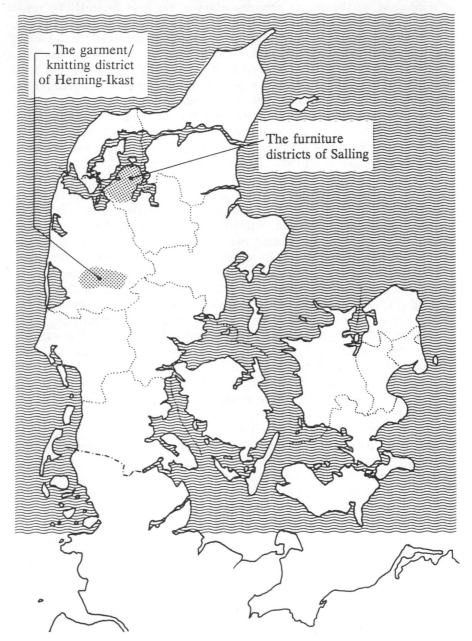

II. The surprising success of small firms in West Jutland

From nationally aggregated industrial statistics, readers can easily see that Denmark's industrial structure, in terms of size of enterprises, has been fairly stable since the beginning of the 1960s, and that growth and decline has been fairly evenly shared by large and small enterprises alike (see Table 1). A closer look, however, reveals that large firms suffered most in terms of employment during the crisis of the 1970s and 1980s, and that the generally even impression conceals a very varied pattern between growing and declining industrial branches.

Table 1: **Denmark's manufacturing industry. Number of firms by size (number of employees)**

Size of firm by number of employees	1963	1970	1980	1985	1987
6 - 9	1 300	1 245	1 213	1 239	1 280
10 - 19	2 000	2 013	1 961	2 056	2 236
20 - 49	1 850	1 976	1 754	2 033	2 119
50 - 99	822	850	740	800	876
100 - 199	411	470	423	454	438
200 - 499	272	274	238	249	278
500 -	95	93	91	101	87
Total	6 750	6 921	6 420	6 932	7 314

Source: For 1963 and 1970: *PPII, Bilag 3, 1974*, p. 53; for 1980 and 1985: *Statistisk Tiarsoversigt, 1987*, p. 67; for 1987: *Industristatistik 1987*, p. 50.

However, the single most important surprise appears when breaking down national industrial statistics into time series of regional distribution of industry. During the last 20 years, there has been a major redistribution of industry from the industrialised East to the agricultural West of Denmark.

To regional analysts in the 1970s, this development was contrary to all traditional theoretical expectations. By the mid-1970s, they expected the peripheral regions of Jutland to suffer most from the economic crisis. They argued that industrialisation in these regions in the 1960s was based on their ability to attract production units with the promise of low-skilled workers at lower cost. During a crisis these units were expected either to close down or to be relocated to regions with even lower wages (i.e. the Third World), while firms maintained their offices and high-skill facilities in the larger cities and in Copenhagen.

However, the opposite occurred, and during the 1970s, the developed areas in Western Jutland gained most in industrial employment and in the number of newly-established firms.

Table 2:   **Number of industrial enterprises and employment, 1972 and 1980, in Denmark's counties (dairies not included)**

	Number of firms		Industrial employment	
	1972	1980	1972	1980
Counties to the East:				
Copenhagen area	2 380	1 860	156 436	117 878
Vestsjaelland	353	331	19 208	17 780
Storstrøm	344	289	19 806	18 551
Bornholm	58	56	2 632	2 531
Counties in the middle:				
Fyn	629	617	42 917	36 689
Verjle	481	514	31 044	30 109
Aarhus	799	731	43 090	41 153
Counties to the West:	1 826	2 022	101 737	112 067
Ribe	243	255	13 890	15 015
Ringkøbing	544	616	23 035	25 331
Viborg	299	347	13 326	17 616
Sønderjylland	264	293	19 915	21 828
Nordjylland	476	511	31 571	32 277
Total	6 870	6 420	416 870	376 758

Source: Maskell [1982], pp. 26 and 28.

The Copenhagen area alone lost 520 enterprises and 38,558 jobs in industry from 1972 to 1980, while the Western counties gained 196 enterprises and 10,330 jobs, representing a growth of about 10 per cent in both enterprises and employment. A breakdown of growth in industrial employment according to the size of the towns which comprised a given municipality quite consistently demonstrated that the municipalities made up of the smallest towns had gained most in industrial employment. The larger the towns, the larger the drop in industrial employment. It is illustrative that while the Copenhagen area and the three largest provincial towns had 51 per cent of industrial employment in 1972, the comparative figure for 1980 had dropped to below 44 per cent. At the same time, the small towns had increased their share from 14 per cent to 19 per cent [Maskell, 1982, p. 43]. This phenomenon has been intensively investigated in order to find explanations, with surprising results.

A first explanatory hypothesis ran like this [Maskell, 1982]: Technological automation had reached a level where industry can take advantage of less skilled workers *by relocating production to agricultural areas*. However, investigations disclosed that workers in Jutland were just as skilled as their colleagues in Copenhagen. The proportion of skilled workers in the total economically active population varied between 10.1 per cent in the Copenhagen area and 13 per cent in Funen, and varied between 11 per cent and 12.5 per cent in all the Western Counties (figures for 1984, from *Undervisningsministeriet* [1988], p. 195). But this situation was not the result of a sudden relocation of the population during the 1970s. If we follow the single most important group, the skilled metal workers, we see that their number has continuously increased in the provinces and stagnated in Copenhagen since the 1950s.

Table 3:   **Fully paying members of the Metal Workers Union, 1950-1987**

Year	Copenhagen	Provinces
1950	23 115	26 537
1960	29 194	39 676
1970	27 268	58 474
1981	24 739	80 807
1987	22 286	89 520

Source: Torben Andersen and Sten Scheuer's Database, Institute of Organisation, Copenhagen School of Business Economics.

Though Denmark experienced a dramatic increase in the number of unskilled women in the industrial workforce during the 1970s, in general terms the 1970s broke the pattern obtaining in the late 1960s which was characterised by a declining proportion of skilled workers in the total labour force. For the whole country, the proportion of skilled blue-collar workers to all blue-collar workers increased from 31.7 per cent in 1973 to 33.2 per cent in 1981; in the provinces, the figure increased from 29.8 per cent to 31.9 per cent; and in the Copenhagen area, the change was from 35.8 per cent to 37.0 per cent [Pedersen, 1983, p. 114]. So rather than a de-skilling of the industrial labour force, it would appear that there was a general tendency to improve skills after a period of de-skilling in the 1960s.

The *relocation hypothesis*, however, was attacked from another angle, too. Hartoft-Nielsen [1985] demonstrated that employment did not increase in affiliates of firms which had their head offices located in larger cities. Growth in the peripheral areas came mainly from firms initiated locally. Concluding an investigation of a sample of firms he had followed for some years, Hartoft-Nielsen stated that: "industrial development in the small towns in the peripheral areas is to a large extent explained by growth in a number of firms, which were small in the beginning of the 1970s and still cannot be characterised as mass production firms" [Hartoft-Nielsen, 1980, p. 523]. He characterised the firms as rather young, export-intensive ones, producing in small batches, and making use of incremental innovations that recombined product technologies and production equipment in novel ways [ibid., p. 522]. At the same time, he showed that de-industrialisation and falling employment had occurred in large enterprises in large cities.

Essentially, he proposed that large enterprises in large cities had been relocating industrial plants and production facilities on an international scale (primarily to the Third World) while locally-owned firms, run by entrepreneurs, were all that was left to generate industrial dynamics in Denmark [Hartoft-Nielsen, 1985].

Maskell [1985] modified this picture somewhat by showing that a relatively high proportion of the growth of industrial employment in peripheral small towns could be explained by growth in municipalities in which a large enterprise was located (e.g. Lego in Billund, Danfoss in Nordborg, HTH-kitchens in Ølgod and Ecco-shoes in Bredebro).

In conclusion, the studies by Maskell and Hartoft-Nielsen appear to suggest that industrial growth in the peripheral areas has stemmed both from growth in the municipalities with a dominant large producer as well as from clusters of small, locally initiated firms. Industrial growth was experienced in 70 out of 79 municipalities with fewer than 5,000 inhabitants in their largest towns [Hartoft-Nielsen, 1985, p. 30].

However, the large enterprises mentioned were never "located" in these small towns; they were initiated there, some as early as the period of the 1920s and 1930s, as will be shown later. And this phenomenon of strong local ties seems to matter, as it is within the counties with the least "foreign" influence that industrial growth rates are the highest. Thus, whilst the tendency towards external control is very strong in old industrial centres of Jutland (such as Aarhus, Odense and Alborg - with an average 50 per cent), external ownership is lowest in the three West Jutland counties with the highest growth (Ringkøbing county, 11 per cent; Ribe, 19 per cent and Viborg, 20 per cent) [Planstyrelsen, 1990, p. 53].

On average, the decline of large enterprises in large towns and growth in industrial activity in peripheral Jutland reinforced the historical dominance of SMEs in Denmark's industrial structure. Already by 1914, Denmark was very much dominated by SMEs in comparison to other industrialised countries [Hastrup, 1979, p. 214]. As we shall see, this structure allowed Denmark a high growth rate during the 1930s, while post-war Fordism, especially in the 1950s, caused a reduction in the number of enterprises and in employment among the SMEs. However, it is interesting that the number of crafts and SME firms (with fewer than 20 employees) was fairly stable (around 22,000) between the late 1950s and the first energy crisis, while continuously increasing their employment figures (from 92,584 workers in 1958 to 131,400 in 1976) [ibid., pp. 334 and 234]. Since then, the average size of Denmark's industrial enterprises has continuously dropped: firms employing more than six people had an average size of 58.69 employees in 1980 compared with 64.35 in 1973 [Maskell, 1982, p. 32].

A *demand-oriented explanatory hypothesis* saw industrial growth in the peripheral areas as a short-term phenomenon. Entrepreneurs and the SMEs in the periphery were benefiting from increasing investments in agriculture after Denmark became a member of the EEC, and from public investments stemming from the decentralisation of the public sector during the mid-1970s [Grøn, 1985, p. 125]. It was predicted in the 1970s that should such investments decline, peripheral industries would face serious problems.

This prediction was soon put to the test as the greatest decline in agricultural investments in the post-war period occurred at the beginning of the 1980s, multiplying the difficulties industry was already facing because of the second energy crisis. From 1980 to 1982, the number of industrial establishments was reduced by 250 and more than 20,000 jobs were lost in the industrial sector. By 1982, however, in Viborg, Ringkøbing and Ribe counties, industrial employment was once again at the 1980 level and by 1983 the number of enterprises exceeded pre-crisis figures. However, the counties of the middle and eastern parts of the country were only part way to approaching the numbers of 1980 by 1984. Thus, decline was small, recovery fast and growth considerable in the West, while the middle of the country stagnated and the Eastern regions continued to decline.

Undoubtedly many enterprises went bankrupt in the Western counties during the crisis of 1982 but, as can be seen from Table 4, more new enterprises were soon established. The industrialisation in West Jutland since the beginning of the 1970s has undoubtedly been dramatic, involving much trial and error. Hartoft-Nielsen's investigation of a sample of 50 enterprises in North Jutland showed that 26 enterprises created 460 jobs between 1974 and 1977 (or an average growth of 80 per cent); 3 enterprises stagnated; 12 declined; and 9 closed. The last 21 enterprises mentioned lost 262 jobs, whilst 8 new enterprises were established in the locality investigated [Hartoft-Nielsen, 1980, p. 526]. What we are witnessing is clearly a very painful struggle for existence, involving high costs for entrepreneurs and employees.

However, the recovery since 1982 shows, beyond question, that development has passed the stage of pure luck or trial and error and that some kind of system of mutual reinforcement between economic actors has been established. A recent study produced clear evidence of this fact: from 1982 to 1987 all parts of Jutland experienced a growth in industrial employment. A total of 39,500 new jobs was created, but of these only 4,850 were in the Eastern part of Jutland, while five counties in South, West and North Jutland created 34,650 jobs; of these latter, only 4,500 were in municipalities with large towns, while 30,150 were established in municipalities with small towns [Planstyrelsen, 1990, p. 34]. Viborg county increased industrial employment by 72 per cent, Ringkøbing county by 43 per cent and Ribe county by 42 per cent.

Table 4:   Number of industrial enterprises and employment in Denmark's counties, 1980 and
           1984 (including mining and quarrying)

	Number of enterprises		Number of employed	
	1980	1984	1980	1984
Eastern counties:				
Copenhagen area:	1 874	1 846	118 802	105 860
Vestsjaelland	336	333	18 075	16 895
Storstrøm	297	285	18 774	16 737
Bornholm	57	60	2 589	3 039
Counties in the middle:				
Fyn	643	655	37 354	37 105
Vejle	534	561	30 599	32 312
Aarhus	756	788	42 215	42 583
Western counties:				
Ribe	282	306	15 801	17 821
Ringkøbing	644	692	26 007	30 676
Viborg	379	393	18 207	20 746
Sønderjylland	320	312	22 602	21 869
Nordjylland	561	586	33 305	34 961
The whole country	6 684	6 817	384 330	380 604

Source: *Industristatistik, 1984*, Copenhagen 1986, p. 29.

III. The historical roots of Denmark's regional development

1.   From the nineteenth century to 1950

The observed pattern of regional development characterised by high industrial growth rates in West Jutland and stagnation in the Eastern parts of the country continues to puzzle analysts who are trying to explain the phenomenon on the basis of past development theories. Development has occurred neither - as we have seen - as a result of the relocation towards unskilled workers of mass production technologies nor - as we shall see - as a consequence of the reallocation of resources towards modern science-based branches under the command of the central headquarters of huge financial groups. Instead of seeing the phenomenon as resulting from deliberate market strategies, we suggest that it can better be explained as the historical outcome of the fact that economic activity has been organised in areas which, over the last two decades, have been suited to, and benefited from, a situation in which world conditions have been in favour of flexible specialisation rather than Fordism [Piore and Sabel, 1984].

However, rather than being regarded as a reaction to the present crisis, the current industrial dynamic in West Jutland should be understood as being primarily a result of a population's fight against a series of agricultural crises in the 1920s, 1930s, 1950s and 1960s. During these four decades, these agricultural areas experienced stagnation, in the face of international trade barriers or depression. Although out-migration was the consequence most widely discussed, the gradual transformation of the population in these areas was far more important. From 1950 to 1965, the proportion of young people in Western Jutland acquiring an apprentice education increased from 25 to 49 per cent [Maerkedahl, 1978, p. 96]. In less than two decades, the population of these counties changed from being primarily oriented towards agriculture to being oriented towards crafts, industry, trade, services and administration.

Their yeoman inheritance as independent, self-employed farmers or craftsmen was a strong impetus towards the creation of their own businesses,[1] outside agriculture. Together, entrepreneurship and educational transformation created a self-reinforcing mechanism, with new small craft-based enterprises having strong inclinations to hire and educate apprentices,[2] who would then often create their own businesses in these areas.[3]

During the 1960s and 1970s, this mechanism found support from a general boom in building and construction and, after 1972, from increasing investments in agriculture after Denmark became a member of the EEC.

---

1.   In an investigation, 750 young men (aged 13-39 years) were asked whether they wanted to start their own businesses. Potential entrepreneurs plus those actually self-employed showed a very uneven distribution by region. In the Copenhagen area, the share was 22 per cent, in provincial towns 37 per cent, and in agricultural districts 43 per cent [Wickmann, 1985, p. 187]. "In short, one can conclude that the inclination to form an enterprise increases as you move west" [ibid, p. 196].

2.   In 1,325 enterprises formed between 1977 and 1981, 500 apprentices and students were employed by 1981. Four hundred of these enterprises were in manufacturing, employing 200 apprentices and students [Wickmann, 1985, p. 189].

3.   Danish studies have shown that a typical entrepreneur is between 30-40 years old; he holds an apprenticeship and has been employed in a similar enterprise to the one he starts; he comes from a home where the father was self-employed; and his motives are less economic than oriented towards the challenges, freedom and responsibility connected with starting one's own business [*Håndvaerksrådet*, 1983, p. 3 ff.]. It is quite fascinating that the old craft life-cycle seems to be quite intact despite industrialisation and an extremely high trade union organisation rate (more than 90 per cent of skilled workers and journeymen are members of a trade union). Goul Andersen [1979, p. 140 ff.] has shown that in some sectors, this life pattern is still surprisingly stable. In building and construction, of those who were skilled workers aged 15-24 years in 1940, 40 per cent had in 1970 become entrepreneurs. In 1970, after a dramatic decrease in the proportion of entrepreneurs and self-employed (especially in agriculture) as a percentage of the total population, 30.6 per cent of all men over 35 years of age were still self-employed. Another side of this phenomenon is that skilled workers as a group are much younger than other groups, implying that being "working class" is rather an educational position on a man's journey to something else.

Interviews with entrepreneurs in such areas[4] showed that many new enterprises were initiated in the construction sector, for example by cabinet makers and carpenters, and within the agricultural equipment sector by local blacksmiths, primarily serving a local market. A series of crises induced these small entrepreneurs to look for complementary businesses. Cabinet-makers and carpenters began carrying out subcontract work for furniture makers, and blacksmiths for machine-shops and factories, gradually evolving in the process into industrial enterprises. Consequently, the local market for building and construction, agricultural machinery and repair was left open for new generations of young entrepreneurs, later to be caught in the same traps and to react in the same way as their predecessors.

West Jutland in the 1970s witnessed the full consequences of this process. However, this does not explain how this dynamic began, nor how it was possible for the youth in these agricultural areas to enrol as apprentices in the early 1950s; nor how they could find a local market for their new businesses in times of agricultural crisis. To answer these questions, one must examine a peculiarly Danish pattern of economic organisation that explains why much initiative and entrepreneurial vitality still remained in agricultural areas rather than migrating east, thereby leaving open the option of a gradual development of industrial districts.[5]

The answer to these questions focuses on two historical circumstances: first, the existence of a high number of very small railway towns (or villages) serving as industrial service centres in and for local agricultural areas; and second, the existence of a national organisation of craft educational institutions linking these small railway towns into a horizontally very mobile labour market for skilled workers and potential entrepreneurs.

Both the institutions and the organisation of space were shaped by the reaction of social movements to a much earlier crisis than those

---

4.   Interviews were carried out by the author mainly in Salling during the spring of 1987, but the mechanism suggested in the paragraph has been supported by other conversations with entrepreneurs. In general, it seems that the construction industry during the 1960s and early 1970s attracted people who wished to become self-employed. Many found in the mid-1970s that they were journeymen in crafts for which there was limited demand, such as bricklayers, cabinet-makers or carpenters. However, beside their crafts, they had learnt to run building sites as master-craftsmen or as foremen, and some looked for jobs as middle managers in industry to learn new trades as routes to becoming self-employed. One example is a carpenter who by the mid-1970s had taken a job as a foreman in an embroidery factory in Odense, learnt to run the machines and then later set up his own embroidery factory in Herning to do subcontracting for other firms within this garment district (a subject to which we shall return in Section IV).

5.   In fact, by 1973, the post-war direction of migration from West to East stopped and was reversed; so people paradoxically migrated to areas with the lowest wages and the highest unemployment.

mentioned above, in that they were created during the last two decades of the nineteenth century.

The *first movement* was founded by small farmers, facing increasing competition on the British market from cheap corn from the United States of America in the 1870s. They created the well-known Danish co-operative movement whereby groups of farmers would create co-operatives in their localities to supply their own production and household needs, and also typically jointly establish dairies and sometimes slaughterhouses to sell products on the open market.

The movement started in West Jutland and moved gradually eastwards. At the same time, railways were being built from the East towards the West and, although railways implied concentration and centralisation of economic and industrial activity around Copenhagen - as was the case in the big towns in Great Britain and the United States - as the rails crossed Sealand, in Western Jutland, they became a means of connecting a great mass of villages, each one a small centre for manufacturing, trade and banking servicing the surrounding agricultural area. The railway became a means for this decentralising process, as it connected these tiny centres with national and international markets. Strong forces of local pride and independence were at work in these crucial decades at the turn of the century. Just as farmers had set up their own local savings banks in the mid-nineteenth century to gain independence from the merchants of larger towns, they now fought to retain this independence by setting up their own co-operatives, and to make themselves independent of owners of estates by setting up their own dairies and slaughterhouses. Educated in the Folk High Schools to organise their communities for the well-being of their members, the population contained such a mass of "social entrepreneurs" that each small community entertained high ambitions of developing a small "agro-industrial" centre of its own while treating the neighbouring villages as competitors and regarding them with distrust. Local archives contain rich material on the conflicts among small villages, their ambitions and their fights to have the railways come their way.

Yet the movement became an integrated whole as regional and national co-operative institutions were created to serve the local farmers in the manufacture of consumer and investment goods, the organisation of trade on an international scale, and the provision of other services. Often, each of the initiatives at this level was taken in order to compete with the activities of financial groups in Copenhagen. In effect, a national system of institutions ensured that growth in one region would help growth in others, creating in the process increasingly better living conditions for small farmers, for a while. Not surprisingly, in the decades that followed, Denmark experienced the establishment of an increasing number of small farms. Agricultural areas - especially in West Jutland - became richly endowed with people occupied in some form of self-employment.

For craftsmen facing increased competition from industry in the 1880s, these new railway town communities in the former wasteland of West

Jutland became a land of opportunity. Small craft shops were established, often combining production with a sales and service agency, enriching the agricultural areas with complementary skills, and adding employment and markets to already prosperous communities. Left alone, these craftsmen might have become the last generation of a craft-dominated Danish industry.

However, *a second movement* of craftsmen, in Copenhagen and the market towns, guaranteed that this would not happen. To these craftsmen, the competition from colleagues in small railway towns only added new problems to those they already faced after the destruction of their guilds (by law in 1862) and with increasing competition from industry. They consequently eagerly engaged in attempts to reorganise, imitating many elements within the farmers' co-operative movement.[6] Most of these attempts failed.

Nevertheless, in one area, the craftsmen's movement had great success. Between 1870 and 1900, 130 local technical schools were founded by local associations of crafts; by 1930, the number had reached 350. With these schools the crafts institutionalised their own reproduction at a time when most crafts in Western Europe were suffering from proletarisation. As these local schools began to form linkages with national schools of specialised crafts, where apprentices could finish their education, an institutional mechanism to secure the number of craftsmen and skilled workers grew continually. National standards of qualifications were created and all journeymen from a certain craft were joined into one horizontally mobile labour market. With the formation of the Technological Institute in 1907 an institution was added that could guarantee continuous adaptation to new technologies through the renewal of curricula at technical schools, through further training for masters and journeymen, and through the inclusion of new specialities (such as, for example, courses for mechanics and electricians) into the craft educational complex.

---

6.   These attempts included the organisation of their own banks, craft-controlled industrial enterprises to supply craftsmen with semi-finished goods and components, the organisation of groups of workshops in the same building to take advantage of the steam engine, and the organisation of joint purchases [Fode et al., 1984]. Had all their experiments been successful, crafts would have transformed Denmark into a very well-organised Emilia-Romagna well before the turn of the century. For at least two reasons, these attempts failed. First, the farmers' co-operative movement found support in laws institutionalised already during the agricultural reforms of 1789. Through heavy fines, the concentration of land in fewer hands was effectively stopped. After the prohibition of the guilds in 1862 this was no longer the case in the crafts. The death of some craftsmen often meant bread for others, as they had no institutions to protect them from unlimited competition. Secondly, the employers' associations typically organised according to trades and crafts, which gradually grew out of the old guilds, and never made the size of enterprise a political discriminatory criterion, with the result that owners of larger enterprises could often control the common initiatives for the benefit of their individual ends and use them as a means to oust smaller firms - reinforcing through organisational means the difficulties already created by a free market.

This educational complex had several implications for the role of craftsmen in the small railway towns. First, the educational complex ensured that these towns would be supplied with large numbers of craftsmen. Second, it connected these towns to a national labour market of skilled workers, organised by the divison of crafts in national trade unions, allowing a journeyman holding an apprenticeship from a small town to acquire additional skills by seeking employment in other areas. Third, through the system of further training of masters and journeymen at the Technological Institute, craftsmen could become channels through which new technologies valuable for the continuous modernisation of the railway towns and their agricultural surroundings could be introduced.

In the period up to the end of the First World War, these crafts and railway towns primarily served the needs of agriculture at a time when Denmark developed into a world leader in the export of high-quality bacon and butter. With the integration of the local co-operatives into a regional and national network of organisations, able to organise an expanding world trade, most railway towns were engaged in serving the surrounding local agricultural areas. Industrial development, focusing on agricultural machinery, dairy equipment and ships with freezing capacity for the transport of agricultural products to foreign markets, was still concentrated around towns in Eastern Jutland, Funen and Sealand, with Copenhagen as the unchallenged industrial centre.

During the structural crisis from 1918 to 1945, these tiny railway towns in agricultural areas became vital to the regeneration of the Danish economy. Crafts and small enterprises entered a highly dynamic development from 1925 onwards and throughout the 1930s. Although employment in manufacturing crafts and small enterprises only increased from 110,795 employees to 122,534 between 1925 and 1935, the number of establishments increased from 37,803 to 40,334, and in all crafts and small enterprises the growth in the number of firms was particularly high among machine-shops and furniture-makers [Hyldtoft, 1984, p. 268]. A total overview of the regional pattern of this development cannot be provided, but the regional redistribution of furniture-makers illustrates trends during the decade.

Table 5: Furniture makers in 1925 and 1935

| | Number of firms | | Number employed | |
	1925	1935	1925	1935
Copenhagen	506	524	1 959	1 556
Provincial cities	587	652	3 177	3 086
Agricultural districts	313	597	1 196	2 685
Whole country	1 406	1 773	6 332	7 328

Source: Hyldtoft in Dybahl, et. al., 1975, p. 149.

Another example is the garment industry. In 1925, Ringkøbing county's (in Western Jutland) 35 knitwear enterprises employed 266 persons; by 1935, the number of firms had increased to 132 employing 1,823 persons [ibid, p. 150].

What is remarkable is the pace at which the agricultural areas developed new enterprises during a period of crisis. Economic historians have explained the phenomenon by reference to a combination of market forces. They argue, first, that bilateralism in international trade created a protected market in which small enterprises, though less productive, could compete. Second, that high unemployment and decreasing wages in agriculture made it possible for such small firms to compete by hiring unorganised workers at below average wages, thereby gaining comparative advantages over their colleagues in market towns and Copenhagen.

Essentially, we would argue that the mechanisms suggested in the introduction to this chapter were at work during the 1920s and 1930s. Local craftsmen could switch to complementary production, reacting to economic, rather than seasonal, cycles, gradually opening up their shops to surplus population from the agricultural areas by enrolling apprentices who, in turn, gradually acquired the skills necessary to start their own businesses. In this gradual fashion, the ability of these local communities to face future challenges was increased.

The combination of growth in small firms and flexible restructuring in the large, craft-based enterprises [Dybdahl et al., 1975] gave Denmark an industrial growth period in the 1930s second only to the 1960s. The industrial structure was ideal for bringing the country through the Second World War, during which raw materials, machinery and equipment were scarce. The protected market further provided an opportunity for the development of new and complementary industries in sectors controlled elsewhere by large foreign mass-producers: e.g. radios, equipment to regulate heating systems, and chemical products. Some of these were established in the agricultural areas of Jutland such as, for example, B & O in Struer, and Danfoss at Als. In brief, it can be said that by the post Second World War years, the railway towns had frequently become relatively well developed centres for crafts and industries, unconsciously prepared, as it were, to receive as apprentices and workers the new generations that were to be pushed off the land by the agricultural depression of the 1950s and 1960s.

2.   1950-1970: Fordist expansion and the reorientation of railway towns

The ideology of mass production after the Second World War was in no way alien to the thinking of Danish politicians, unions or employers' associations. Since the 1930s, leading Social Democrats had favoured Fordism and had criticised the traditions of craft-organised production and the typical life careers of craftsmen. The leading industrialists in the Industrial Council reproached the new enterprises in the agricultural periphery for using unorganised labour and sweated labour to compete with the traditional enterprises during the periods of stagnation and difficulty in the 1920s and 1930s. As restrictions on imported raw materials and capital equipment during the Second World War were very tight, by the end of the war Danish industry looked very worn down, and vulnerable to criticism from those who saw American industrial organisation as an ideal to be imitated.

As in most other countries, large corporations in large cities were seen as expressions of modernity. The Danish SMEs, already under attack from international competition, were presented with further difficulties by the introduction of political reforms, and the growth of institutions aimed at supporting a modern mass production economy. Heavy investment in the vocational training system apart, the reproduction of a small enterprise economy was basically neglected. Compared to France under Monnet, however, Danish modernisers had few direct means to accomplish their ambitions. They could favour large firms through taxation and investments in, for example, Schools for Specialised Workers to train them for the repetitive tasks of mass production, but they had no means of destroying the SME sector itself. Nevertheless, aggregate statistics seemed to confirm that the political visions of the modernisers were being realised. From a peak in 1935, by 1958 manufacturing crafts and small enterprises (fewer than 20 employees) had lost nearly 18,000 enterprises and 30,000 employees [Hastrup, 1979, pp. 334 and 234], while the average size of enterprises in manufacturing industry had increased (from 35 to 66 employees between 1935 and 1967 [Hansen, 1970a, p. 27]). In addition, the class structure seemed to transform itself in line with the rules of Fordism combined with a modern Welfare State, as evidenced by the statistic that between 1935 and 1974 white-collar employees in the public and private sector increased from 20 to more than 40 per cent of the economically active population [Rasmussen, 1976, p.11; Andersen, 1979, p. 160], while the proportion of workers and self-employed fell.

Thus, the picture presented by aggregated national statistics should lead one to expect that the yeoman foundation of railway towns was being eroded. At least three other factors combined to confirm the general impression of decline. First, many railways and stations were being closed down as the transport system changed in favour of cars. Second, economies of scale entered even into the management of public institutions, leaving many small towns at longer distances from services. Third, many small communities lost their primary economic organisations when dairies, slaughterhouses and co-operatives were centralised. In short, railway towns appeared to have lost their role as local industrial service centres for the neighbouring agricultural areas and we might have expected that the combined effect of the factors mentioned above would have forced these railway towns into a vicious circle.

It is therefore surprising that between 1945 and 1955 the railway towns were amongst the fastest growing in terms of population [Svensson et al., n.d., pp. 86 ff]. But while the picture was not one of stagnation and decline, neither was it one of explosive growth - apart from a few exceptions. From national overviews it appears as though a process of cumulative growth in smaller towns had been initiated just after the war, gaining speed in the 1960s, and becoming population growth "poles" during the 1970s [Pedersen, 1989, table 4.2].

We suggest that this pattern can be explained as a transformation period during which the "yeoman republics" of railway towns moved away from servicing the agricultural areas to become localities for manufacturing industries in their own right. And although their yeoman foundation was at stake, the transformation was carried out by crafts and small enterprises. Though the number of self-employed in manufacturing crafts and SMEs was radically reduced during the 1950s, their shops were not ousted overnight. Rather, they closed gradually when owners retired. At the same time, the number of craftsmen in the building and construction industry experienced high growth rates creating new possibilities for self-employment in these small towns. The combined effect of this was very important. At a time of great difficulty for agriculture, the youth of agricultural areas enrolled as apprentices in rapidly increasing proportions, thereby creating the pool of human resources that underpinned the rapid growth of industry during the 1970s and 1980s.

Our knowledge of the specific character of development within these railway towns in West Jutland during the era of Fordism and the welfare state is very limited indeed. However, an investigation carried out into industries in small towns of North Jutland [IVTB, 1974], gives some clues to the general pattern of development. Between 1945 and 1965, the initiation of new firms seems to have been quite gradual. However, from 1965 to 1974, the pattern shifted very dramatically as both the number of firms locally initiated, and firms established locally by outsiders and localised production affiliates, increased very rapidly [ibid., p. 20]. By 1974, 50 per cent of industrial employment in the six towns investigated was in firms established before 1963, around 20 per cent in firms established from 1963-1968, and a final 30 per cent in firms established between 1969 and 1974 - growth in employment being primarily created through the newly-established firms.

IVTB [1974] suggested that the industrial make-up of such towns had run through a fast metamorphosis similar to the general industrial development pattern of industrial societies, but within a very short span of years:

> Around one-third of industrial workers in ... the towns ... have been employed earlier in agriculture. Others have earlier been employed in food industries, sawmills and other enterprises based on local raw materials, industries which were closed in the beginning of the 1960s. These industries were replaced by garment industries, furniture industries and iron and machine industries. Finally, at this moment it seems as if garment and furniture industries are now to be replaced ... by new industries." [ibid., author's translation].

Such an industrialisation logic fits perfectly with the traditional idea of industrial development as a movement from more traditional to more knowledge and science-based manufacturing branches, a development pattern in contradiction to the development of industrial districts *in senso stricto*. More important, however, was that the railway towns had developed a local concentration of skills that cut across a broad range of national crafts and industries. Such a variety of craftsmen and their apprentices provides a basis for a strong, flexible and heterogeneous industrial structure. Some of the railway towns have been able to make use of these, and other, advantages to develop strong industries, the organisation of which resembles in some ways that which characterises the Italian districts.

IV. Industrial districts: The garment/knitting district of Herning-Ikast and the furniture districts of Salling

Two cases of districts in West Jutland (see map on page 128) and key aspects of their organisation are described below. Both developed within the spatial organisation of a group of neighbouring railway towns.

1. The furniture districts of Salling

In Viborg county, there is a particularly high representation of "cabinet-makers and carpenters", when compared with the Danish average [*Undervisningsministeriet*, 1988, p. 208], and this can be regarded as being both a cause and effect of the development of this industry. In this county, there is an excellent opportunity to observe the evolution of industrial districts through the gradual industrialisation of railway towns.

In particular, the area of Salling is illustrative of a process of gradual evolution since the 1920s. Here, one finds a system of small towns that, even today, are inhabited by only between 1,000 and 1,500 people, yet each has a cluster of 7 to 11 furniture-makers or wood manufacturers together with small enterprises in the engineering and metal-using industry. The growth and prosperity of these small towns appears particularly impressive when we learn that they each had between 650 and 900 inhabitants at the beginning of the 1950s and that the 35 per cent increase occurred in a period during which they lost many of their basic enterprises: dairies, the slaughterhouses and the stations (together with their railways).[7]

---

7. These observations are based on an investigation I made in 1987, visiting enterprises, municipalities, local unions, and institutions. It is illustrative that when I was preparing this investigation, one of the two associations of furniture makers (*Førenigen Dansk Møbelindustri*) could provide me with a list of 36 members from the Salling area alone.

The wood and furniture industry has shown a remarkable post-war dynamism. Having moved from the east to the west in the 1930s, it stagnated towards the end of the Second World War. From the 1950s, it started to grow. The growth of value-added between 1950 and 1957 was 67 per cent compared with 48 per cent for all manufacturing industries [Hansen, 1983, p. 146]. Although by 1968 it contributed only 2.7 per cent of value added in the total Danish industry, its growth had continuously been 150 per cent that of the average growth of furniture industries in other countries [Kjeldsen-Kragh, 1973, p. 28]. The main reason was growth in exports. In 1950, it had contributed 1.6 per cent to industrial exports; by 1965 it was contributing 5.9 per cent [ibid., pp. 35-36].

Furniture alone has been a particularly strong growth industry. Measured by volume of production, the furniture industry increased more than any other in Denmark during the first half of the 1980s. While the index of employment for total manufacturing grew from 100 to 101.3 between 1980 and 1985, that of the wood and furniture industry grew to 116.1 during the same period [*Statistisk Tiårsoversigt*, 1986, p. 70].

The furniture industry is represented in most Danish counties, but there are particularly strong clusters of furniture enterprises in Viborg, Ringkøbing and Ribe counties.[8] In 1982, these three counties employed 37.8 per cent of all those employed in this industry while their share of employment in all manufacturing industries was less than 17 per cent [Hallund et al., 1985, Annex 1/45]. In the case of Salling in Viborg County, the gradual development of clusters of small firms can be traced back to the 1920s from which time family and master-apprentice relations have served as important development mechanisms.

2.   Herning-Ikast: a knitwear and garment district in Ringkøbing County

The railway towns of Herning and Ikast (and also the neighbouring town of Hammerum), developed into a garment and knitwear district comparable to Prato in Italy. While the Danish textile and garment industry as a whole either stagnated (in the 1960s) or declined (as in the 1950s and 1970s) [Thøgersen, 1986, pp. 36 ff.], these towns departed totally from this pattern. During the 1970s, the district surprised observers by creating increasing employment in an industry which was declining even in other areas of West Jutland. Ikast especially was very dynamic from 1970 to 1982 and increased employment in textiles and garments by 32 per cent [Hansen, 1984, p. 7], while Herning basically kept a stable employment pattern over the whole period. By 1980, 40 per cent of Danish textile and garment manufacturing employment was located in Ringkøbing County, of which

---

8.   However, furniture is by no means restricted to these areas and Fyn, Aarhus and Vejle county also have significant furniture industries.

Herning and Ikast alone accounted for a third of the national employment figure for this industry. The main reason for this impressive statistic was the concentration of knitwear firms in this area, accounting in Herning and Ikast for 75 per cent of national employment in this industrial sector [Maskell, 1984a, p. 22]. A feature of the developmental pattern of this industrial district was the gradual and mutual specialisation among the firms, stabilising the size structure among the small enterprises (a somewhat similar development probably stabilised the furniture industry as a sector of small firms).

Both the districts of Salling and that of Herning and Ikast demonstrate similar organisational features which might help to explain their success. These include the following.

(a)   In both cases the industries are *dominated by small, locally-owned firms*. In the case of the furniture industry nationwide, 55 per cent of employment is within enterprises with fewer than 50 employees (compared with the average for manufacturing industry of 55 per cent of employment falling within enterprises with fewer than 200 employees) [Hallund et al., 1985, p.15].

For the garment and knitwear district of Herning-Ikast, only one firm employs between 200 and 299 persons, while 59 per cent of the firms employ fewer than six [ibid., p.43]. Those with between 6 and 19 employees account for 45 per cent of all firms, while the same size group constitutes only 30 per cent of all enterprises in Denmark [Herning Kommune, 1982, Vol. 1, p. 32]. Herning municipality alone had 264 garment and knitting enterprises by 1980.

(b)   The districts of West Jutland can call upon *a strong tradition of entrepreneurship* and self-employment. In the Herning-Ikast garment and knitting district, the propensity to initiate new firms is above the average level in Denmark. The tradition of self-employment and free but small farms is stronger here than in any other region of Denmark.[9] For West Jutland, this tradition can be traced back to feudal times when farmers destroyed large landholdings by buying their farms using income earned through an export trade in knitwear, cattle and other goods. Had the small free farmers not been integrated into a system of co-operation - first through the community of villages and later through the establishment of the co-operative institutions mentioned earlier - they would have disappeared quickly. But thanks to the co-operative system they survived (in a manner similar to that which occurred in Emilia-Romagna) long enough to produce the entrepreneurial potential, which began to create, later on, the clusters of SMEs which are referred to here. In protecting their independence in this manner, they have, at the same time, created ideal conditions for continued

---

9.   For a more complete history of the early period of this area, see Hansen [1947].

entrepreneurship. Apprentices and workers are trained to acquire the general skills typically used in small batch production, and they also acquire the knowledge necessary for the running of small firms. Both Herning-Ikast and Salling are rich in biographies of men who have gone through a training and working period in small firms before setting up on their own. In Herning-Ikast at least, this yeoman tradition has served to increase political consciousness and encouraged people to create regional bodies through which they can organise and formulate strategies.

In the inter-war period, rather than looking with admiration at the entrepreneurial vitality of towns like Herning and Ikast, industrialists from other parts of the country treated their new small-firm colleagues to outspoken criticism and threats. The Industrial Association accused these small enterprises of dishonest competition based on the use of unorganised workers and the production of low quality goods, while large producers from Aarhus in a meeting with the small entrepreneurs from Herning, Hammerum and Ikast threatened them with a choice either of co-operating under the dominance of big firms or being destroyed in a price-war [Knudsen, 1979, p. 65]. They chose war, and this period no doubt played a very important role in renewing the self-awareness of the area and in keeping the ideology of self-employment and "free enterprise" alive. The entrepreneurs organised their own regional employers' association and were thus able to take decisions at a level which was lacking in most other regions.

(c)   Of particular significance is the fact that both the garment and knitting, and the furniture industrial districts appear to have deliberately pursued *strategies aimed at the high quality, design-conscious, export market.*

Between 1973 and 1984, the furniture industry increased exports from an index of 100 to an index of 667 [Hallund et al., 1985, appendix 4/2], which represented a growth in exports that was twice that of manufacturing as a whole. Thus, the furniture industry is particularly export-intensive, with 80 per cent of its production exported.

The knitwear industry was reoriented towards the international market during the 1960s,[10] with exports reaching a level of 70 per cent of total production in knitwear by 1981 [Maskell, 1984a, p. 14].

Design is of great importance. The "Made in Denmark" label has become associated with a certain image that raises expectations about the type of product being offered - in the same sense that "Made in Prato" might arouse certain expectations regarding Italian style and quality.

To become known as quality producers has not been an easy task for the small firms. The Herning firms began organising yearly fashion exhibitions on a collective basis, immediately after the Second World War, in order to attract the attention of the press and customers to their goods.

---

10.   From 1960 to 1970, exports grew from 17 per cent to 51 per cent of production within the sub-branch of knitwear [Maskell, 1984a, p. 14].

In doing so they changed their competitive strategy away from one based on lowest prices towards one aimed at continuous innovation and product development. The Herning exhibitions later turned the town into the country's leading exhibition centre. For the furniture producers of Salling, the introduction of national furniture exhibitions at the turn of this century has been a natural framework for a similar type of competitive strategy based on product innovation and high quality.

In the garment and knitwear district, there are firms which specialise in marketing and design and which subcontract out production to the other firms of the district; a new trend which seems to be evolving is one whereby manufacturing firms might develop a collection of products extending beyond the limits of their own speciality in order to present a whole clothing style, thereby involving, through various subcontracting relations, the firms of the district in general. In this sense it becomes a "Herning" or "Herning-Ikast" collection. This ability to organise activities beyond the limits of individual firms is crucial to the presentation of an image of being producers of quality fashion goods with well-known brand names, rather than of cheap bulk products.

(d)   In these districts, firms are able to make use of a *decentralised structure of small, specialised firms* to respond flexibly to new fashions and technical specifications.

During the 1950s, in the knitting and garments district, there was a major reorganisation of firms, and restructuring of relations between them. Until then, a typical enterprise integrated within itself most of the vertical steps of production. But in a context of difficult trading conditions leading factories began divesting themselves of many specialised activities, resulting in a decentralised production structure. The totally integrated factory was replaced by the familiar "Marshallian" picture of a network of specialised producers (specialised weaving mills, spinning mills, hosiery shops, dye works, textiles printers, suppliers of buttons, etc.). A whole cluster of former competitors made the shift during the same period [Knudsen, 1979].

Later, the basic principles of mutual specialisation initiated in the 1950s apparently continued, allowing the small producers to take advantage of new technologies and achieve collective economies of scale. In the 1970s, this phenomenon expressed itself particularly in a growing number of sewing workshops, associated with a very fast development of speciality equipment within the sewing sector.

Internally, firms have made full use of the traditional flexibility provided by knitwear technologies and have further increased productivity and flexibility through computerisation; as a consequence, the growth in the availability of computer and programming services in Herning-Ikast has been far above the average for the country. Moreover, this technological flexibility has increased design possibilities at a time when the traditional pattern of one or two collections a year has increased to four or more.

(e)   Flexibility, quality and a capacity for innovation is greatly facilitated
by *the maintenance of a craft tradition and capability*. Perhaps more than any
other factor, it has been the maintenance of broadly trained workers, capable
of redirecting their skills into new avenues dictated by the market, and with
the entrepreneurial desire to do so, at a time when flexible organisation and
flexible capabilities are of paramount importance, that explains the success
of the Danish districts.

The furniture industry is a typical example of craft-based
industrialisation. Sixty per cent of its male workforce are skilled workers
[Mathiesen, 1979, p. 261]; the proportion of white-collar employees is low
and the share of those with an academic education is half that of white-collar
employees in the rest of industry, while technicians with a background as
apprentices are predominant [Traerådet, 1978, p. 22].

From historical experience, it is clear that chance plays a major role
in whether the gradual and incremental development of localities like
Jutland's railway towns produce industrial districts focused on specific
industries. Yet there seem to be mechanisms which give chance a particular
direction and selectivity.

An industry may replicate itself more through an apprenticeship
mechanism than a profit mechanism. As we shall see later, it is in respect
of education and educational institutions that political activity is involved in
reproducing the "district" on an advanced scale. So today, with many
furniture firms already established, the reproduction, on an extended scale,
of the district character of Salling is beyond doubt. The incremental nature
of the way new firms are established both adds new complexity and makes
it easier for newcomers to find specialised niches, thereby creating an
expanding system in which individuals can take all the gradual steps
necessary for education as entrepreneurs within the furniture industry.

(f)   The districts can count on *well-developed local service infrastructures*.
Durup is a typical example of Salling's small town industrial districts. Today
it has 1,200 inhabitants after smooth growth during the 1950s and 1960s and
a rapid expansion during the 1970s. It has a rich variety of small tradesmen,
including all normal types of crafts for building and construction, a
blacksmith and two electricians; it has two savings banks of its own and a
branch office of the regional bank. A school, a public library, a town hall,
a church, a home for the aged, and a sports centre are the public institutions.
It differs in one respect from most of the other towns in that it still has a
dairy (a regional affiliation of the largest dairy company in Denmark), and
a private corn and foodstuffs company (which produces speciality fertilisers
and speciality mixtures for bakeries).

But the most dynamic part of the town - making it possible to
maintain this differentiated small town structure - consists of the nine
furniture enterprises which together employ a total of 450 people, 200 of
whom are in one firm, Magnus Olsen A/S.

The reproduction of Salling's furniture industry on an extended scale can only be understood by reference to the totality of such a small town. As we will discuss in more detail later, many furniture makers have traditionally used skills as carpenters and cabinet-makers to start up in the building and construction industry during boom periods in agriculture, in local industry and commerce or in housing. In such initial periods, the small local savings banks have been able to use their detailed local knowledge as bases for providing loans for the creation of new building and construction businesses. The existence of other furniture makers within these communities has served to provide models for imitation, as well as potential customers, for those turning their businesses away from building and construction during times of recession. Many of Salling's furniture makers followed this pattern not only in the 1920s and 1930s but also in the last two decades. When local banks have found themselves unable to support larger ventures, Salling's firms have had sufficient capital assets to be able to approach more distant banks.

In the Herning and Ikast area, the fusion of small banks has resulted in the creation of a strong regional bank capable of providing longer-term finance for the development of local firms. During recent difficulties, the population of the area proved itself ready to defend the regional bank from incorporation into one of the dominant Copenhagen banking groups.

(g)   *Close family ties*, together with craft-relations, play an important part. The firms of the districts are typically "family firms" and it may often be the case that the strategies of firms are more related to the contingencies of the family than of the market.

Durup is illustrative as a case of the furniture industry. The nine furniture enterprises of Durup were not created overnight nor during the last decade. Theirs is a story of fathers, brothers and sons, masters and apprentices, and involves the development of a genealogical tree where craft and family relations have become interwoven into 70 years of business history, in which enterprises were developed to compensate for seasonal or economic cycles and to stabilise incomes and employment within the very small and narrow labour market of a town of this size.[11]

---

11. It all began with "Durup Upholstered Furniture Factory", which by the 1920s had become one of the leading makers of upholstered furniture in Denmark. It still exists, but today is only a shadow of its former self.

The second enterprise, which became the first wood manufacturer, "Karl Plejdrup" started as a subcontractor for the upholsterer, manufacturing wooden frames. Its present name is Salling Chair Factory and its speciality is oak chairs, but a major part of its turnover remains frames for upholsterers, especially for "Skipper", now a leading manufacturer in upholstered furniture in Durup, and for a brother of the owner of "Skipper", who has a furniture factory in another town of Salling.

A third enterprise, the second wood manufacturer (now called Doca), was started by Karlo Plejdrup, a nephew of Karl Plejdrup, in the buildings of a former slaughterhouse, which had been run by Karlo's father. Karlo served an apprenticeship as a slaughterer, but he learnt the art of making furniture when his father sent him to work in his uncle's factory when the

Many furniture firms in Salling were created during the recessionary years of the 1970s and 1980s. The typical story is a repetition of the 1930s, as many carpenters and cabinet-makers faced with low activity in building and construction started to use their buildings and machinery to carry out subcontracting for other furniture makers, gradually moving into the business with their own products.

(h)　　　*Both competitive and co-operative philosophies and practices* exist side by side. Employers, especially in the knitting and garment district, are apt to collaborate in the organisation of common services. For several decades, the employers of Herning and Ikast have collectively organised common services for the benefit of the district. Thus, organisations to promote exports, collective travel arrangements for exhibitions, and the hiring of consultants for export promotion and production management have been set up. Recently, 11 firms have created an export company (including design, marketing, sales and distribution) to compete on the German market [*Netvaerksavisen*, 1, 1989]. Since 1959 in Ikast, through the co-operative body Danikast, employers have organised buses to bring women to work from the surrounding areas, have built a dormitory for young women, and have collectively purchased raw materials.

In the furniture districts, an unusual mixture of competition and co-operation has developed. Today, most furniture factories in Durup, for example, have a speciality which they sell to the final market. In addition, using specialised process equipment, they carry out subcontracting work for other firms in the area, and this often comprises the major share of their turnover. The general sentiment is typically against specialising in subcontracting alone, for fear of becoming too dependent. Few people believe that it is possible to enter into formal agreements of co-operation, as stories of how such agreements have been broken, and others' customers have been enticed away are part of the often-repeated myths of the area. Deliberate copying of "competitors'" products is another.

---

demand for slaughtering was slack. When the slaughterhouse closed due to its small size and low technology, Karlo had both the buildings and the necessary skill to turn it into a furniture factory (today Doca specialises in pine furniture).

Magnus Olsen came later. Before he started his business as a carpenter and cabinet-maker in 1937, he had worked as a journeyman in Karl Plejdrup's factory. But he started in building and construction and it was only to compensate for the cyclical downswing during the Second World War that he gradually moved towards furniture production during a phase when he carried out a mixture of activities, including subcontracting for Durup Upholstered Furniture Factory. In the 1950s, he moved into manufacturing high-quality furniture for the American market.

At least two apprentices from Magnus Olsen have crowned their careers, typically including their periods as journeymen in another firm and a period as foremen in a third, by setting up a furniture firm in Durup or in another of Salling's tiny towns.

Compared to practices existing in the Third Italy, where firms at the same horizontal level in the production hierarchy compete while co-operation occurs along the vertical axis of the production chain, the system in Salling seems less ordered. Here, all firms appear to relate to the final market as much as possible, with the consequence that a winning firm often has to use, as subcontractors, some of the firms which competed with it for the customer in order to be able to deliver the promised goods. This behaviour replicates the balance between co-operation and competition which generally obtains between contractors and subcontractors in the construction industry, in which many of the entrepreneurs learnt their ways of doing business.

In Salling, there appears to be no strong ideology fostering inter-firm co-operation; in fact, a perspective of competitive individualism appears to be more the order of the day. But this does not mean there is no co-operation. For example, one entrepreneur I recently interviewed was vehemently opposed to any formalised co-operation,[12] yet later during the interview, an upholsterer looked in to tell him that "their new sofa" had appeared on the front cover of a furniture magazine. Together they had not only produced the sofa, but had worked together several nights a week for six months to develop it.

Other forms of co-operation are also widespread. Many small furniture makers participate in trade fairs and exhibitions as part of groups, and there is a widespread tradition of engaging in longer-term co-operation in which one firm agrees with another to adhere to a certain speciality.

In Durup, Magnus Olsen broke out of a speciality agreement when his sons returned to the firm and became increasingly involved in co-operation with two furniture designers in Copenhagen to develop furniture for offices and organisations. Today, a whole group of firms co-operates around the two designers (four furniture makers, a fabric producer and a producer of applied art) on a range of activities, including marketing and the organisation of foreign exhibitions. The change in strategy has been successful as employment in Magnus Olsen has increased very fast from 20 to a level of 200 over a 5-year period. It is quite typical of the way in which firms co-operate that Magnus Olsen has joined a group of enterprises from

---

12. In this part of the country, this would most likely mean that he "gave his word" as there is a true distaste for written or, worse, legal contracts since people take pride in keeping their word. It is simply bad taste, a sign of distrust, to start an agreement by setting up a formal (written) contract. This way of doing business is very much related to the dominant form of firms, which are self-owned family units. Their confidence in any other form of firm is very low, as they know that only in the case of the self-owned company will the owner do all he can to pay his debts since not to do so might risk bankruptcy and the loss of his home and his family's well-being.

all over Jutland and one in Naestved in Sealand for which the general characteristic is extremely high quality and good design.[13]

It therefore may be that more co-operation occurs than is readily apparent because certain kinds of behaviour are taken for granted and are explained in terms other than "co-operation" (e.g. terms such as "obligations", "helping relatives or friends", etc). Possibly, from the outset, people in such districts are tightly knitted together by the local culture and family or neighbourly relations, besides being socialised through craft ethics and traditional ways of doing business. To some extent, the decisions to use, or function as, subcontractors, to collaborate or not, may not be seen as questions of choice so much as of conforming to obligations and normal practice. Thus, the larger structure of the industry may also be determined by non-decision.

Nevertheless, despite indications that more co-operation takes place than local philosophies would lead one to believe, competitive individualism is still a strong instinct amongst local entrepreneurs. Firms seem to use every opportunity they get to generate new *independent* businesses rather than institutionalise co-operative mechanisms. One telling example is the attempt to promote co-operation on exports. Some years ago, government funds were available for financing an export-agent if four firms worked together in co-operative export promotion. Several firms in Salling co-operated to exploit this opportunity. But, once public finance stopped, instead of building a co-operative trading company, several export agents established themselves as private self-owned independent firms exporting for others on normal market terms, helping the area to professionalise exports, but with co-ordination taking place through a "local" market rather than through "political discourse".[14]

The general conclusion, then, is that the furniture districts operate through a mixture of competition and co-operation as in the Third Italy, but the precise details must yet be investigated.

---

13.   Such forms of co-operation seem to be quite typical if co-operative representation in trade fairs can be taken as a sign of more continual contact. Furthermore, such co-operation seems to be evolving through the Network programme of the Ministry of Industry. *Netvaerksavisen*, No. 1/1989 mentions the creation of Alfabeticagruppen A/S, which was created by furniture makers from all over Jutland to co-operate on the development, production and marketing of furniture.

14.   This may change in the future. With the new "Network Programme" launched by the Ministry of Industry, new opportunities have arisen for gaining government support which seem to have had an immediate impact on co-operation within the furniture industry. One example is in Haarby, a small town in Fyn, where seven furniture makers (employing between 10 and 40 people each) have created Haaby Trading Company A/S which exports high-quality furniture designed by two designers on behalf of all the member firms, each firm specialising in a specific production phase [*Erhvervsbladet*, 4.9.1990].

(i)   People's craft identity is important for *linking individuals and firms to the larger, national labour market, the craft educational system and other enterprises throughout the country.*

This embeddedness within the larger national framework is very well illustrated by the case of the furniture firm Magnus Olsen. From the outset, national institutions such as the Technological Institutes in Copenhagen and Aarhus, and national trade fairs, have had a major influence on the orientation of the firm, including the choice of products produced, the selection of appropriate production equipment, and the maintenance of quality standards. The firm participated in the creation of "Danish Furniture-makers Quality Control" in 1959 [Sieck, 1987, p. 19] and in the creation as early as 1963 of a trade organisation (Domus Danica) consisting of different speciality producers from various parts of the country.

The experience of craft workers outside their own regions results in a broadening of horizons and contacts. For example, in the case of Magnus Olsen, both sons of the founder started their apprenticeships as cabinet-makers in Aarhus, and after having worked as journeymen they shifted between being at home, helping their father, and moving from job to job in the national industry to gain education and experience. One took courses in production management as a wood technician, was employed as foreman in a firm in Holbaek, and finished his education with a "merconom"[15] education from Skive, while he was a foreman in his father's firm. Having graduated from Aarhus School of Business Economics, the second son found employment as a furniture dealer, and later worked as a consultant in wood technology at the Technological Institute [see Sieck, op. cit.], acquiring a wide knowledge of the Danish wood and furniture industry as a whole. As a result of these backgrounds, they define their field of action more broadly than the locality of Durup and Salling, and make contacts with other individuals and firms from all over the country.

(j)   *The engineering and metal-using industry* plays a vital role in the proper functioning of clusters of small firms organised in industrial districts [Schmitz, 1990]. The existence of a technical capability, together with the informal social contacts among producers of the same locality, may be very important for a firm's ability to solve ad hoc problems and make innovations.

For a considerable period, the engineering and metal-using industry has had a significant place in Denmark's economy. In 1945, it accounted for 31 per cent of total manufacturing employment; by the end of the 1960s, the figure was 37 per cent [Hansen, 1970b, p. 20; 1983, p. 146]. While the number of enterprises in all industries fell by 22 per cent between 1950 and 1958, the number in engineering and metal-using was reduced by only 10 per cent. From 1958 to 1965, the number of enterprises increased by 25 per cent

---

15.   A two-year diploma in business studies usually taken at evening classes by engineers as a complement to their technical training.

(compared with 12 per cent for all manufacturing industries) and employment increased by 50 per cent [Kjeldsen-Kragh, 1973, pp. 29 ff]. The 1960s was a period of specialisation within individual enterprises. By the end of the 1960s, the Danish engineering and metal-using industry was comparatively specialised in machinery for agriculture and industry, whilst semi-manufactured goods had been reduced (contrary to experiences in Sweden and the United Kingdom, for example). In contrast to the Netherlands and the United States of America, Danish specialisation was low in R & D intensive products and high in consumer durables. The industry did not embark on the production of standardised mass produced consumer goods.

In Denmark, manufacturing crafts and industries lost a total of 52,000 jobs between 1972 and 1979, but in engineering and metal products, employment decreased by only 1,811 persons. However, this small movement conceals dramatic changes among sub-branches of the industry. Transport equipment lost most and declined with 4,831 employees; metal products lost 3,464 jobs; while the iron and steel and electrical machinery branches maintained stable employment. Machine shops and factories, however, increased employment from 96,220 to 101,950 jobs. The engineering and metal-using industry thus employed 43 per cent of the total national industrial workforce in 1979. Machine shops and factories alone employed 18 per cent of all manufacturing employment in 1979 [Frøslev Christensen, 1981, p. 30]. In 1976, the engineering and metal-using industries exported 43 per cent of their production compared to 32 per cent for the whole of industry. In machinery, the export share has been rapidly increasing, from 41 per cent in 1967 to 52 per cent in 1976 [Hartoft-Nielsen, 1980, p. 125-126].

This growth and change in the nature of the engineering and metal-using industry is highly influenced by what happened in the peripheral areas of West Jutland and elsewhere which, between 1958 and 1977, increased their share of total employment in this branch from 13.6 per cent to 28 per cent; during the crisis years, this achievement was caused in particular by growing employment in peripheral small towns (with fewer than 10,000 inhabitants). In Ribe, Ringkøbing and Nordjyllands counties, the average growth in employment in this industry between 1972 and 1977 was 60 per cent. This growth means an over-representation by 1977 of the machine industry in the peripheral areas, which by then had 40 per cent of Denmark's machine industry - this over-representation being caused uniquely by the small towns [Hartoft-Nielsen, 1980, pp. 134-138].

The general role of small engineering and machine shops or factories for industrial development is very important. Entrepreneurs in other manufacturing industries often attribute[16] their satisfaction with their locality to easy access to small machine and engineering shops in which they can have a new machine constructed at short notice, should they want to start

---

16.   During interviews carried out during my own research.

producing a new product. The widespread[17] knowledge all over the country of how machinery of different types functions also makes it easy to have machines repaired, or to have new tools constructed. In product development, this entire structure of small machine shops means that prototypes and experimental production equipment can be produced quickly by handing the work over to one or more of the many specialised producers.

Interviews with development engineers indicate that machine shops tend to co-operate in the same manner as master craftsmen in building and construction. As a customer, the development engineer contacts a machine shop or factory that has a special knowledge or ability of primary importance for the construction of the desired product or machine. This machine shop, the strength of which includes a knowledge of other specialists, subcontracts parts of the job to other speciality producers. Through this process of subcontracting to specialists, decisions about what to produce, and what to buy as standardised components from the international market, are parcelled out to people who know the cheapest and most competitive solutions.

Blacksmiths, plumbers, industrial electricians, cabinet-makers and carpenters are all crafts of which Denmark has an abundance, performing similar roles, with the consequence that many firms can easily have ad hoc tasks solved by contacting local craftsmen and SMEs, which then connect them to the larger national and international "networks". That the local community provides such an ad hoc system of industrial services for other industries essentially reflects a reorientation towards new needs of the whole railway town cluster of crafts, formerly serving the agricultural areas. A furniture producer once told me that he had often been irritated to learn that it was much easier to have a stand for a trade fair prepared and built in his local home area and have it shipped to, for example, the United States of America, than to have it prepared in the USA by their local agents, who maintained that it would be very difficult to organise the delivery of such ad hoc projects.

On the other hand, since the 1960s, semi-finished goods and standardised components have increasingly been produced outside Denmark. As this type of production is often the basis of permanent and quantitatively significant relations among firms in the industrial districts of the Third Italy or Baden-Württemberg, the nature of an industrial district in Denmark appears to be different from these "classical" ideal types.

(1)   *Industrial relations* and the *wage setting procedures* are significant elements. It is known that the railway towns and industrial districts have experienced fewer strikes and fewer days of sickness [Maskell, 1982]. On the one hand, one has high trust relations, high autonomy in the performance of

---

17.   Compared to countries like the United States of America, Sweden and Holland, the machine industry is relatively larger, while other sub-branches of the engineering and metal-using industry are relatively smaller [Hartoft-Nielsen, 1980, p. 126].

jobs, and an ease of communication between employers and employees, who are knitted together in close overlapping family and neighbourly relationships. On the other, one has somewhat narrow procedures of labour recruitment through personal ties, tightly drawn restrictions on behaviour, and a very strict discipline. For better or for worse, such a system of industrial relations is ideal for flexible specialisation.

Without unions, such a system could easily become very exploitative. Fortunately, while the unions in West Jutland are a little weaker than elsewhere, the rate of organisation is not much less than the figure of 80 per cent for all Danish workers organised by the Social Democratic unions.

Despite a preponderance of the "traditional" industries of knitting and textiles, furniture, and metalworking, and the large numbers of small firms, sweated labour and irregular labour contracts have not loomed large in the debate on the competitiveness of SMEs in the manufacturing sector of Denmark's peripheral regions. This is probably because, since the Second World War, the national unions have generally been able to regulate wages and labour conditions within the framework of broad-based collective agreements. With the high rate of unionisation in West Jutland, and with large and small firms not receiving differential treatment, it is likely that there exists a strong inhibition against organising production on the basis of cheap labour.

For skilled workers, there is, however, a geographical differential in the collective agreements in favour of workers in the Copenhagen area and against those of the peripheral regions, designed in theory to compensate for the higher cost of living in and around the capital although it does not do so in practice. In a comparison of living conditions of industrial workers in Copenhagen and North Jutland in 1973 IVTB [1974, p. 153] concluded:

> "A peripheral industrial worker with a full-time job the whole year through, and who owns his own house, has a higher income at his disposition (after tax and rent) than he would achieve in the Copenhagen region with a comparable quality of housing ..."

Living conditions for workers in peripheral areas were good at the beginning of the 1970s and, for industrial workers, have further improved relative to Copenhagen throughout the 1970s and 1980s. People in these areas own their own houses and cars to a higher degree than in the larger cities of the East. One aspect which might be thought to be worse in these communities is the general standard of public services and cultural activities.

Despite the higher cost of living in the Copenhagen area, the difference in average wages has in fact been continuously declining for industrial workers since the early 1970s. The decrease in wage differentials has not had the effect of slowing down the different rates of growth between the regions (as we saw in Section II).

It would seem, then, that whilst in the absence of concrete statistical information any conclusions about relative wage levels in the industrial districts of West Jutland must be tentative, nevertheless, the high degree of unionisation and the insertion into a national pattern of collective regulation would strongly suggest that workers in these areas share Denmark's renowned high standard of living. Such wage regulation and standard setting could then be at least partly responsible for the prevalence in the industrial districts of competitive strategies aimed at dynamic innovation, quality, and design consciousness, rather than those aimed simply at all-out price and cost minimisation.

The absence, in the industrial districts, of strategies aimed principally at cutting wage costs, together with smaller differentials than in Copenhagen between skilled and unskilled workers, and between industrial workers and white-collar workers, is very important for the cohesion of the small communities of the railway towns and the flexible co-operation among different groups of workers and managers within the firms. Since the coalition of bourgeois parties came into power in 1982, eagerly supported by the voters in West Jutland, the philosophy has been one of trying to increase differences between blue-collar workers and white-collar workers. On average, for the country as a whole, the policy has been implemented. From Figures 1 and 2, however, we see that the counties of West Jutland have run counter to this national policy. The differences between the average salaries of white-collar workers in the Western Counties and those in the Copenhagen Region have been widening, whilst differences for industrial workers have narrowed. Consequently, the small communities have in this respect counteracted the tendencies to increase class differences among their small populations.

The existence of relations of trust are important to the operation of the districts and there is some recent evidence that employers would be loathe to undermine it. When a new government came to power in 1982, advancing a programme of less state intervention and less equal incomes, the industrial relations of the railway towns and industrial districts might easily have deteriorated in the wake of the undermining of a sense of common interest by envy. When the government launched an incomes policy in 1985 to hold wage increases down to a 2 per cent limit, with the explicit intention of increasing profits, they received a promise from national employers' associations to help enforce it by fining members who exceeded the limit. The stage was set for the destruction of the trust underlying the industrial relations of the railway towns and industrial districts.

Probably it did happen in several places; but the furniture industry in Salling has been very creative in its handling of such a seemingly tightly controlled national policy. Experiencing a period of high growth and increasing profits, many local employers in Viborg county wanted to increase wages beyond the national limit; but they did not want to pay a fine to the employers' association. A way out of the dilemma was created. The solution was a radical change of the wage system such that it became difficult to compare new and old levels of earnings. In less than two years, all but one of Viborg county's employers within the woodworking branch had changed from a system of individual pay based on piece rates to a system of hourly wages with group bonuses, allowing wage increases far in excess of the

Figure 1:   Average salaries for white-collar workers in industry. Relative development: Western Counties and the Copenhagen area (= index 100)

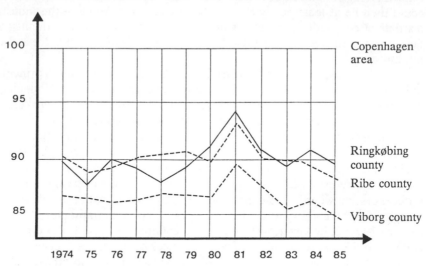

Figure 2:   Average wages for industrial workers. Relative development: Western Counties and the Copenhagen area (= index 100)

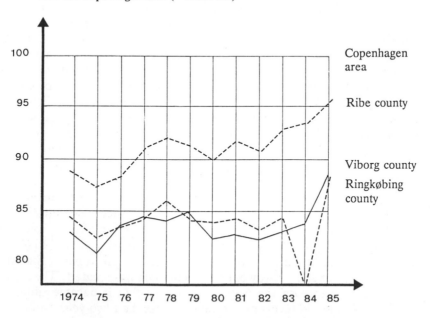

Note: Based on computations from the "Regsys" database of the Copenhagen School of Business Economics.

national limit, and preserving a sense of community and trust among workers and employers. Moreover, in the process, the wage system was transformed in line with the characteristics of small-batch flexible production and the workers were given more autonomy in the planning and execution of work. Salling woodworkers increased their wages by between 6.5 and 7 per cent.

V. Promoting industrial districts

In the transformation of localities into industrial districts after the Second World War, the railway town yeoman republics received little support from the national political level, which was preoccupied with the design and implementation, and later with the problems of a modern welfare state in the post-war period.[18] Yet, as explained earlier, the populations of agricultural areas were transformed into industrial classes through political institutions, apprenticeship and technical schools - which the constructors of the welfare state accepted and protected, though they never saw them as important parts of their attempts to modernise Denmark through a combination of Fordism and Social Democracy.[19]

In many ways, the functioning of the railway towns as yeoman republics was in direct contradiction to that of the welfare state. One example is their contradictory modes of stabilising incomes and business. Just as the entrepreneur in the railway town would look for production which complemented his main business in order to iron out instabilities caused by business cycles and seasonal slumps, the labourers of these tiny towns would look for employment in several sectors during a year, possibly taking building jobs in spring and early summer, changing to work in agriculture during harvest time, engaging in slaughtering in late autumn and accepting factory

---

18. This was no less the case for the small enterprise sector, which saw many government schemes in their favour reduced in the 1950s and 1960s [see Hastrup, 1979].

19. Since the 1930s, leading Social Democrats have been convinced that the craft-based labour market, together with craft ethics and the life cycle of a craftsman, were all components of an old-fashioned production culture, which mass production would soon make obsolete. However, when faced with the prospect of the degradation of work under the coming industrial regime - which they in all other respects welcomed - they wanted to provide individuals with an escape from monotonous work discipline. It was thought that individuals should have an opportunity through further education and training to escape from the factory floor. Consequently, new resources were channelled into the craft educational complex, organising new levels of further training into what was already a highly sophisticated system. Among these new levels of education were courses aimed at teaching people what was needed for introducing Fordism and Taylorism into Denmark's industrial establishments. In effect, it was often former craft workers who, after further training courses became the "sergeants" in the hierarchies of the industrial firms, reinterpreting Taylorism in line with their craft organisation [Kristensen, 1990].

employment during the winter.[20]   As the differentiation of the small communities into multi-functional societies owed much to this stabilisation policy, and vice versa, almost from its inception, the modern welfare state was in confrontation with one of the major principles of the yeoman republic. The rules of unemployment benefit do not encourage workers to shift from high income employment in building and construction to jobs at significantly lower rates of pay in agriculture or in factories, since they risk being paid lower unemployment benefits should they become unemployed after a period of factory work rather than after a period of work in building and construction. Similar mechanisms operate should they consider starting their own businesses, since they would risk losing the security of unemployment benefit during the period when they were initiating projects.[21] Some learnt gradually to live with modern welfare schemes in these yeoman republics, taking "black jobs" while on the dole, or basing newly started private firms on part-time moonlighting and destroying other local businessmen through "unfair" competition.

Yeomen of the railway towns had difficulty in recognising principles of solidarity in the Social Democratic welfare state. Instead they saw its schemes, rules and principles as a constant pressure towards criminal behaviour, or speculation; or for the few who resisted using it creatively, the welfare state was perceived as sheer robbery of which they were the victims.

The populations of the agricultural areas had proudly protected the tradition of sending their youth away for educational periods to folk high schools. Their experience told them that these young men and women would return with new ideas to set up a co-operative dairy, a small electricity plant, educate their neighbours in the sowing of a new type of seed, or set up a business, providing new employment opportunities for the local population. By sending their most able and intelligent sons and daughters away to distant towns, to university, or to other educational institutions, people expected their children to attain goals which their families had dreamt of for centuries. Then they found that their children were not returning to use their newly-acquired knowledge to the benefit of the small communities. In fact, for a while during the late 1960s, their university children were radical critics, censuring their parents for being capitalists and the welfare state for being too reformist. Later they embarked on careers in the hierarchies of the

---

20.   In many ways, workers in these peripheral areas could be characterised as more stable than those in the rest of the country. For example, they have fewer days of sickness and strikes [Maskell, 1985]. On the other hand, mobility between different jobs in different enterprises is rather high [see, for example, IVTB, 1974, pp. 145 ff.]. In Viborg County, the chairman of the regional department of the woodworkers' union told me that a quarter of his members change to other unions within three months.

21.   In the late 1970s, some of these rules were changed, as a reaction to Glistrup's taxpayer revolt, which we shall mention later.

public or private sector, which their families in the local yeoman republics either did not understand or believed they understood only too well.

Although causes for frustration amongst the people of the yeoman republics under the regulatory power of the welfare state were many, the reactions against it were few. For many years, the majority remained silent. In the 1973 election, however, resentment broke out in a wave of anger as people voted for Glistrup's tax revolt party.[22] His critique of public bureaucrats, leftist universities, high tax burdens and professionalised abuse of public money echoed so many dimensions of their own frustrations that the ideology of extreme selfishness, which framed his programme, was accepted unremarked.

After the 1973 elections Danish politics never returned to normal. Many right-wing parties became more critical towards public spending. Attempts were made to decentralise the public sector and reform the administration at state, county and municipal level. For the first time since the Second World War, small enterprises and entrepreneurs entered the arena of national politics. During the last half of the 1970s, Social Democrats were apparently looking for a new compromise between the yeoman republics and the welfare state. New programmes to help small enterprises with finance and technical assistance were introduced; technology centres were created in every county; and rules changed so that entrepreneurs could claim unemployment insurance; even programmes to help the unemployed start their own businesses emerged. By the middle of the 1980s, tax rules had been changed to remove discrimination against privately-owned firms compared to limited companies.

Apart from very general assumptions that the SMEs of today would be the large enterprises of tomorrow and that society's vitality depended upon its entrepreneurs, these reforms were never formulated into a national framework of industrial policy. Today, there has been a reversion to a discussion of the need for mergers and the creation of large enterprises in order to help Denmark's industry to engage in high-tech R & D projects and to market on an international scale. Now, political programmes are changing in favour of large enterprises while tax rules are reverting back to discrimination in favour of limited companies and against privately owned ones, based on the argument that what is modern and necessary is associated with "economies of scale". Yet, politics is in a state of confusion as the Government has also introduced the "network programme", an initiative aimed at learning from the Italian industrial districts experience by encouraging SMEs to develop on the basis of co-operation.

---

22. Support was strongest in West Jutland. It included workers as well as small employers and the self-employed. Leftist analysts later investigating Glistrup's voters were surprised to find that these people were very rebellious, often living in a close worker and employer relationship, not accepting the basic dividing lines which the welfare state took for granted. Many saw the welfare state as an egotistic society, destroying what these people considered to be a society built on solidarity and "self-help" at the local level.

The fact that the political voice of the yeoman republics of the railway towns is either silent, or caught up in sudden outbursts of reactionary party politics, reflects a missing link in Danish politics. Unlike the case of the Third Italy, Denmark has no organisations representing small firms at the local level. Thus, there are no organisations which could act as bridges between a locality's enterprises, communal and regional politics, and the national administrative and political bodies. The association of all crafts, which was formed after the prohibition of the guild system in the 1870s, had long been dead when the SMEs from the railway towns needed it. What existed in fact were associations built around specialised crafts, trades or industries, organising small and large enterprises together on a national scale. Politics of space and of size in such associations are difficult, and they work - as we shall see - very slowly.

The lack of adequate organisational mechanisms has at least two implications. First, there is no body continuously working for the creation of policies that favour the industrial districts which, we have argued, are coming into existence in various localities. Consequently, it would appear - at least according to official information made available to the public - that no-one is pushing for the creation of a system that could protect and advance flexibly specialised industrial districts. Second, there is no body in which businessmen can develop their knowledge of their strategic interests and combine size, trade and space into a unified concept.

1.   Making national political institutions respond to the needs of industrial districts

The implication is not that regions or localities are failing to influence the formation of institutions and the work undertaken by organisations within the public sector. However, this influence is being exercised "underground", hiding behind the curtain of public debate. A director of a local Chamber of Commerce and Industry, asked whether he was not annoyed with the changing programme of public policies, especially the change from policies in favour of SMEs and entrepreneurs towards those in favour of large enterprises, high-tech and large-scale R & D, responded most significantly that they were so used to such changes that, should stimulation be required at the local level, it was for them a matter of simply altering the content of applications for public resources rather than trying to change the plans of institutions and programmes.

Seen from the local level, national political bodies and state administrations produce a continuous flood of institutional initiatives and programmes. Localities - both at the regional and communal levels - have organised themselves in such a way as to be able to receive and translate such institutions and programmes for local use. The creation of a country-wide apparatus by local Chambers of Commerce and Industry and regional Centres of Information on Technology between 1975 and 1985, capable of making use of state initiatives and institutions at different levels, expresses their intent to transform the programmes and powers of national institutions into useful local tools. As we shall see later, such local transformation can be radical.

Consequently, the true significance of the roles of national institutions cannot be understood until in-depth investigation has been undertaken into how programmes are translated into the local context.

2. Orienting the national vocational training system towards the needs of industrial districts

A good example of local "shaping" of national programmes concerns technical schools and the schools for specialised workers.[23] During the 1960s, the state took over the large number of locally-owned technical schools which it had increasingly financed. The schools were concentrated in regional centres and the allocation of the different disciplines among them was carried out at the national level by bodies in which national unions, employers' associations and state administrators participated. A concentration on fewer schools, their integration into a national framework, and the development of new specialities with a greater range of levels, were seen as being part of a single, coherent strategy. Later - at the beginning of the 1970s - the EFG (basic vocational education) reform was initiated in this system. This reform basically meant that students, instead of enrolling as apprentices with employers, began with one year of theoretical basic training, to be followed, typically, by two-and-a-half years of practical work experience whilst attending school part-time. Today, all technical schools have some metalworking crafts, as well as special courses which they offer, in principle, to people all over Denmark. So, instead of a system of small introductory local technical schools, combined with final examinations at craft-specific schools at the national level, primarily located in Copenhagen, we now have a system of regional schools offering both basic training and higher level specialities.

If no local forces were at work in translating such a system into the local context, these institutions would at best be neutral to the development of industrial districts. But such forces are at work.

---

23. The last schools were created at the beginning of the 1960s. The main argument behind their creation was that Denmark needed short training courses to educate people for the simple, specialised, repetitive tasks of Fordism. Another argument was peculiar to Denmark: these schools were seen as a means by which the abundant workforce in agriculture could be retrained for industry, thereby making the Danish labour market more flexible at a time of great change. But they can also be interpreted from a different perspective, in which these schools are perceived as a way for the unskilled worker to compete with the skilled worker by the latter person's means [see Kristensen, 1989; 1990].

A good example concerns Herning Textile School, which today is a specialised institution within the national system of EFG education. The school educates around 100 students a year on a whole complex of subjects. A student can gradually build his or her programme of education through the combination of modules, and is able to move back and forth between periods in the educational institution and time spent at the workplace gaining practical knowledge of industry. The criterion for admission is a basic year of EFG education.[24] The lowest level courses take two years and the student becomes either a knitting, a clothing, a textile or a dye-works operator, who can operate, programme, set up, reset and maintain the relevant machines. Above this level, additional two-year courses are oriented either towards managerial positions or to teaching people to become clothing or knitwear technicians; then, a final level course for industrial designers, again of two years' duration could round off the whole educational career [Knudsen, 1979, *Hovedvejlederudvalget*, 1982]. Since 1985, a new programme has been designed to follow the dyer's course, gradually leading students to a qualification as "teknikum-engineer" in chemistry. In the 1980s, Herning successfully secured a decision that a department of the Clothing Technological Institute be established close to the school. Besides its consultancy role for firms, this institute experiments with new technologies, integrating new knowledge into the courses and training programmes of the school.

From the perspective of 1991, it cannot be assumed that a central allocation of courses and subjects would necessarily have differed from that which has been produced by local interests. However, the existence of the school in Herning has a long history. It dates back to the Second World War, during which the local employers' association and a local branch of the garment union agreed to utilise a new scheme for the training of unskilled workers under the auspices of the Work Technical School - for which the national union of unskilled workers and the national employers' association had successfully mustered political support. Local unions and employers had long been wanting to establish a Folk High School for garment workers. Within this scheme, undisturbed by its official national purpose (to give unskilled workers a technical training allowing them to compete with craft workers) an evening school - run over two winters - developed courses for experienced workers within the garment industry. These courses aimed at providing people with a basic theoretical knowledge of the trade and an introduction to new technologies. During these two years, the "school" had 60 students learning the general principles of the whole trade. Later, in addition, another two years of education specialising in particular fields was added. In 1968, when the garment school in Copenhagen was in need of modernisation and new buildings, employers in Herning moved quickly and

---

24. Apart from the Textile School, Herning has a normal - very large - technical school, providing a year of basic training and an abundance of specialities.

by offering a very beautiful building, Herning was able to have the school relocated (even though Herning had yet to become the main centre of the garment industry), thus providing a new institutional framework for their own educational needs. Since then, every educational reform and every new programme to advance knowledge on new technologies has been skilfully exploited to develop the school to serve the needs of local enterprises.

Much the same techniques seem to be employed in Salling with regard to the technical school located in the town of Skive. Among a small number of specialised subjects, there is both a course for traditional cabinet-makers and one for machine cabinet-makers, together with many associated courses offering further training. The initial allocation of these courses to Skive appears to have been no more than a consequence of a mixture of coincidence and trade-offs. The over-representation of cabinet-makers in the area, mentioned earlier, is undoubtedly partly a result of the decision to allocate these courses to Skive which, in turn, explains in part why industrialisation has worked selectively in favour of the furniture industry. Today, however, the fact that Salling contains a network of small furniture industrial districts has itself become an important factor in the continuous development of these centrally allocated educational institutions. Two examples are illustrative.

The first example concerns a new course for wood technicians above the journeyman level which gives experienced woodworkers an advanced knowledge of materials and technologies used in manufacturing, and provides insights into managerial techniques and methods of running a workshop as a master or foreman. To be able to negotiate the permanent allocation of this course to Skive, which is close to the furniture industries of both Viborg and Ringkøbing counties, furniture makers in these two counties had to agree to support the election of a particular person to the post of chairman of the National Guild of Cabinet-Makers. (The chairman has the right to negotiate in matters of vocational training for cabinet-makers at the national level.) The strategy was successful: Skive Technical School has now been allocated the new course and the present chairman is gradually pursuing his ambition to acquire a "teknikum-engineering" course for woodworking. However, this incident has another, more important, implication. The present pattern of interest formation in Denmark, mentioned earlier, which is less suited to the purpose of formulating politics in the interest of industrial districts, may gradually be transformed as the employers in these districts gain in power and representativity. At the same time, an increase in such power could easily result in conflict between interest groups from different industrial districts.

A second example of the ability of a locality to transform central institutions into a locally oriented system is even more significant. Although technical schools are administered nationally separately from schools for specialised workers, in Skive it has been possible to integrate the two into a system serving the needs of the furniture industry. The division between the two school systems occurs both in terms of interest representation - unskilled workers influence the Specialised Workers' Schools, while different craft workers' unions participate in the development of technical schools - and in that they fall under two different ministries and two budgets. Although debate at the national level has continuously stressed the rigidity of these two systems, maintaining that they ought to be better co-ordinated, this lack of central co-ordination allows local forces to shape events to their own advantage. In Skive, the two schools have co-operated to set up a very advanced system of further training, making it possible to provide industry with skilled workers at a time when the normal EFG apprentice education works too slowly to meet employers' needs. Unskilled workers start with a four-week course at the Specialised Workers' School, then continue with a four-week course at the technical school. Subsequently, two options are open to them: either they continue a short adult-apprenticeship scheme organised in collaboration with the local employers, or through a series of advanced courses for journeymen, with an introduction to the most up-to-date machinery and technology of the industry. Although aware of the ambiguity of its role, the woodworkers' union in Skive has agreed to encourage its new members to embark on these educational programmes, even at the risk of losing them to the cabinet-makers' union.

The local use of such institutions is extremely important for two reasons: firstly, it allows an industrial district to develop far beyond the limits of the natural boundaries of a limited labour market; secondly, it provides unskilled workers with a path to a career, during which an increasing number of options open up, enhancing their immediate bargaining power and the range of their future choices, including the possibility of setting up their own firms.

The examples mentioned here are not rare exceptions to the general rule. A representative from the Technological Institute in Aarhus - an institution which has traditionally developed new courses in advanced training for journeymen, masters and small entrepreneurs - recently told me that the Institute had lost its former business of further training to the technical schools. In Herning, which has been successful in establishing a number of different schools and educational institutions, the director of commerce and industry has moved away from a strategy of simply making occasional use of new opportunities, towards a purposeful approach to increase educational choice. School leaders meet monthly under his chairmanship to discuss plans or possibilities for new initiatives, courses or subjects, so that the schools can work together instead of competing for students, thereby maximising the region's ability to acquire support from government grants.

The philosophy underlying these attempts is not formulated with the idea of developing industrial districts. Nevertheless, the more moderate aim of ensuring that the locality's youth has an opportunity to acquire high levels of education in the region in order to halt the out-migration of the most skilled and intelligent, may eventually serve such an end. While the system of national craft education is still maintained over time, people's efforts to find educational opportunities as close to home as possible will create regional concentrations of skills and professions and reinforce the bonds of family and neighbourly relations. This has happened already - as we have seen - in the garment industry, and is moving in this direction for furniture makers.

3.   Making the welfare state work for industrial districts

The welfare state has been changing rapidly since the voters' revolt in 1973 and with its growing financial problems in the wake of the world recession. Responsibility for administering an increasing number of public activities has been directed towards the municipalities, while the state has simultaneously narrowed their budgetary freedom. Whether the municipalities are expanding and need to develop new institutions, or are going through a recession and need to support a large number of people on welfare, they share a similar experience: there is a growing need for integration across sectors and administrative boundaries of the welfare state and a need to solve socio-economic problems in the municipalities, which often feel that they need to take more power away from the state. One such example is that of municipalities wishing to influence the use of the state-run vocational training system and to integrate it into local programmes for employment creation and the provision of welfare payments.

Conflicts between state and municipalities cut across parties and often local members of political parties governing the state are critical of ministers for doing what is perceived from the local level as a poor job.

Though less visible in public debate, such divisions among the local and central levels within unions and employers' associations are increasing. Both shop stewards and managers are embarking on negotiations that go beyond nationally-approved rules and agreements, risking punishment for their local actions should there ever be a need to bring a conflict to the labour court.

Local ties among workers and managers are gradually growing stronger, while ties to the central organisations of the two groups are weakening. This process is independent of political class consciousness since, paradoxocally, it is often the more radical leftists among the shop stewards who are embarking on far-reaching experiments of factory reorganisation [Kristensen, 1986].

Micro-politics at firm level and in terms of factory organisation are becoming unsettled and opposed to centralised ideologies and policies, and projects involving the reintegration of the welfare state through micro and municipal politics certainly have potential. This situation could then rapidly change the possibility of the reintegration of the private and public sphere in support of industrial districts.

The following example brought Salling into the headlines of Danish newspapers.[25] It illustrates that while industrial districts have matured sufficiently to take the offensive in defending their own strategies for fighting unemployment, changing the definition of the working week, establishing further training, and other matters, they need the support of the welfare state to engage in such experiments in much the same way as anyone who takes a risk needs an insurance company.

At a time when there was a high demand for furniture, the head of the local commercial school in Skive suggested that furniture makers should move from one to two work shifts. If, instead of working eight hours, as was then the case, each shift would have worked six hours a day, the capacity utilisation of capital equipment and buildings over a 12-hour period would more than make up profit margins. Existing workers would have gained; employers would have gained; and especially the unemployed of the area would have gained from such a social contract.

The local union was prepared to change collective agreements in factories involved in the experiment, and found support at the national level of the union which - at the time - was in favour of a 35-hour working week. The unemployment fund agreed to count the 30-hour working week of the participating members as though it were 40 hours, should they become unemployed. Day-care institutions agreed to change their opening times. A special agreement on recruitment was made, whereby the employers would inform the unions about their need for workers while the unions in return would put unemployed members through courses at the Specialised Workers' School and the technical school. Special courses would be developed for this specific task. The expectation was that 140 new jobs could be created in the four factories initially involved in the experiment. In short, an entire local reintegration of the welfare state would take place within less than one year.

However, the experiment broke down because the four employers engaged in the experiment demanded to be insured against losses. Though calculations seemed promising, for them the experiment seemed very risky and they asked to be compensated in the event that increased production could not pay for the larger wage bill by the end of the experimental period. The unions suggested that what had been saved in unemployment compensation should be transferred to a fund that would pay employers who could prove a loss. This solution was totally rejected and another course was tried wherein applications were made to public and private foundations for resources. The two local unions persuaded their national union to promise to guarantee one million Danish Kroner each. But the employers' association not only refused to support them directly, they also cut off support from the private and public foundations they could influence. The national employers' association - according to one local union - feared that the experiment would prove that under certain circumstances a 30-hour work

---

25.　What follows is based on my personal interview with a local union representative.

week could pay for 40 hours of wages. Local employers did not fear such national political implications, but they had no way of changing the decision of the central organisation.

VI. Conclusion

It was said at the outset of this paper that there has been very little research carried out on what we have called West Jutland's garment/knitting and furniture districts and that therefore any conclusions must be tentative. Nevertheless, we have gathered together what information there is, more on some aspects and less on others, and we have been able to describe much of the historical background to the development of these districts and to outline what appear to be some of the main principles of organisation at work. Our main object has been to relate the undoubted economic success of these areas to the equal successes of districts in the Third Italy.

As in the Third Italy, the structure of Denmark's districts is oriented towards small, family-owned firms, organised on a decentralised, specialised basis, with the individual units and the networks to which they belong exhibiting great flexibility. There is not enough evidence yet to say how developed this model of "flexible specialisation" is but nevertheless, it is clear that the structure and organisation at least tends that way.

Also as in the Third Italy, Denmark's districts have developed against a predominantly rural background. Whether this means that agricultural areas are somehow more suited to this model is debatable. Capecchi [1990] argues that the kind of organisation found in industrial districts in Italy can also be found in neighbourhoods of large cities, like Bologna. Nevertheless, in Denmark's case, the land has been a source of surplus labour, and the agricultural history has, as in parts of the Third Italy, promoted an entrepreneurial ethos. Perhaps research would also show that the land has at times provided an alternative source of employment and therefore encouraged labour flexibility.

But the truly significant source of both entrepreneurial skills and labour flexibility in Denmark's case has been the extensive craft training system. It has been the ability of craft-trained workers to switch the focus of their employment in times of sectoral crisis or labour surplus that, together with the capacity of the small, family, craft-oriented firms to produce a supply of entrepreneurs, has provided the crucial dynamism in the districts' organisation. Not only does the craft basis support inter-sector flexibility and entrepreneurship, it also promotes flexibility *within* the small firm, giving it a capacity to respond to changing market requirements. This craft skill capability gives the whole network of firms the confidence that in total the district has an entrepreneurial capacity. Furniture firms know that if necessary they can call upon specialised engineering firms to produce customised parts or machines on demand.

Also significant are the industrial relations and wage-setting procedures. Both sets of districts - garment/knitting and furniture - have pursued strategies aimed at quality, design and innovation. They have deliberately avoided becoming involved in cut-throat price competition and battles for dominance of the cheap end of the market. This orientation towards the quality end is no doubt to some extent "forced" on employers by the existence of high unionisation and the maintenance of relatively high wage levels. On the other hand, the type of competitive strategy employers are pursuing does not encourage them to engage in aggressive attacks on labour and attempts to cut wages to the minimum. On the contrary, the pursuit of a quality, design-conscious, innovative strategy, works best in an atmosphere of trust and harmony. Co-operation, not conflict, is sought.

We have shown that, as in the Third Italy, various kinds of co-operation are also important in other areas, whether it be in relation to "speciality agreements", collective service institutions, or inter-firm consultation on design and technology. But the extent of the co-operation in Denmark's case is still not clear. Moreover, it *is* clear that there is also much competitive individualism. Exactly how the two - competition and co-operation - co-exist, and the relative organisational weights in the district systems we should give to these two principles, needs to be clarified.

At the beginning of this chapter, we said that one of the main questions to be answered was whether "the Italian industrial district phenomenon was a historically, geographically, or culturally unique occurrence". The evidence presented in this paper suggests strongly that the economic success story of certain parts of Jutland can indeed be at least in part explained by the working of organisational principles similar to those typical of the Third Italy. Clearly, Denmark is unique, with its own culture and particular history. Yet it has developed, largely by chance as we have seen, institutions and practices which carry out functions very similar to those of the Third Italy, albeit in a Danish way.

It would seem, then, that it is possible to have a Danish culture and Danish history and still develop organisational principles similar to those that have occurred in Italy. This is an important implication for other countries considering whether they can transplant some of these organisational principles into their own cultures and histories. One important facet of the working of Danish districts not mentioned very much in descriptions of Italian cases, or at least not emphasised, is the importance of the district locality's relationship with, and embeddedness in, networks that go beyond the area - into both national and international realms. This is important both in terms of marketing and supplies but also, perhaps less obviously, in terms of access to trained manpower. The small furniture districts in particular are fortunate that they can call upon trained labour, and have access to training institutions, which their own limited market and resources cannot supply. The networks that go beyond the immediate locality are also important conduits of new ideas.

Another important aspect, and different from the Italian experience, which we mentioned in the introduction, is that the Danish districts have largely lacked self-conscious direction to further develop their networks of small firms and supportive institutions. And, indeed, if the chance to build upon past success is to be seized then one recommendation would be a development of interest associations that cater specifically to the small firms of the districts.

The Danish experience should be of interest to policy-makers in the national and international organisations that seek to promote development in the developing world, Eastern Europe, and even the EEC and other advanced industrialised nations. In particular, it presents a challenge to those who think that development funds should only be directed towards "modern" industries, and that the promotion of "traditional" industries is a waste of time and money. It is clear that traditional industries and good pay are not incompatible. There is an alternative strategy to one based on cheap labour. Nor is it necessary to rely entirely on attracting foreign capital and large firms. The promotion of endogenous resources and small firm local networks organised as industrial districts offers an alternative.

References

Andersen, J. Goul. 1979. *Mellemlagene i Danmark*, Aarhus.

Becattini, G. 1979. "Dal settore industriale al distretto industriale: alcune considerazioni sull'unità d'indagine dell'economia industriale", in *Rivista di economia e politica industriale*, No. 1, pp. 7-21.

Capecchi, V. 1990. "A history of flexible specialisation and industrial districts in Emilia-Romagna", in Pyke, F. et al. (eds.): *Industrial districts and inter-firm co-operation in Italy*, Geneva, International Institute for Labour Studies.

Dybdahl, V. et. al (eds.). 1975. *Krise i Danmark*, Viborg.

Fode, H. et al. 1984. *Håndvaerkets Kulturhistorie*, Vol. 4, Copenhagen.

Frøslev Christensen, J. 1981. *Erhvervsstruktur, Teknologi og Levevilkar*, Vol. 2, Copenhagen.

Grøn, J.H. 1985. *Arbejde-virksomheder-regioner*, Esbjerg.

Hallund, C. et al. 1985. *Udredningsprojekt vedrørende informationsteknologi i trae- og møbelindustrien*, Teknologisk Institut, Tåstrup.

Håndvaerksrådet. 1983. *Ungskoven i dansk erhvervsliv, Ivaerksaettere 1977-80*, Copenhagen.

Hansen, H.P. 1947. *Spind og Bind. Bindehosens-Bindestuens og Hosekraemmerens Saga*, Copenhagen.

Hansen, S.Aa. 1970a. *Industri og Håndvaerk*, Copenhagen.

---. 1970b. *Early industrialisation in Denmark*, Copenhagen.

---. 1983. *Økonomisk Vaekst i Danmark, Vol. 2: 1914-1983*, Copenhagen.

Hansen, T. 1984. *Hern-Ika Omradet: Smørhullet for den danske tekstil- og beklaedningsindustri*, Upubliceret Speciale, Geografisk Institut, Aarhus Universitet.

Hartoft-Nielsen, P. 1980. *Den regionale erhvervsstruktur- og beskaeftigelsesudvikling*, Copenhagen.

---. 1985. "Industriens regionale udvikling i 1970érne", in Illeris et al. (eds.): *Industrien - koncentration eller spredning?*, Copenhagen.

Hastrup, B. 1979. *Håndvaerkets økonomiske historie, 1879-1979*, Copenhagen.

Herning Kommune, 1982. *Erhvervs- of befolkningsundersøgelse, 1980, Vols. 1 and 2*, Herning.

Hovedvejlederudvalget. 1982. *En oversigt over uddannelsestilbud i Ringkøbing Amt*, Herning Commune.

Hyldtoft, O. 1984. *Københavns industrialisering, 1890-1914*, Herning.

IVTB. 1974. *Erhvervsudvikling i Nordjylland. 2. delrapport: Industrien i sma Nordjyske Byer*, IVTB, DTH, Lyngby.

Kjeldsen-Kragh, S. 1973. *Specialisering og Konkurrenceevne*, Copenhagen.

Knudsen, L. 1979. *Efter Hosebinderne*, Herning.

Kristensen, P.H. 1986. *Teknologiske projekter og organisatoriske processer*, Roskilde.

---. 1988. "Virksomhedsperspektiver pa industripolitikken: Industrimodernister og industriens husmaend", in *Politica*, Vol. 20, No. 3.

---. 1989. "Denmark - an experimental laboratory for new industrial models", in *Entrepreneurship & Regional Development*, No. 1.

---. 1990. "Denmark's concealed production culture, its socio-historical construction and dynamics at work", in Borum; Kristensen (eds.):*Technological innovation and organisational change*, Copenhagen.

Maerkedahl, I. 1978. *Uddannelsesmønstre og erhvervsstruktur i Danmark*, Copenhagen.

Maskell, P. 1982. *Industriens regionale omlokalisering, 1970-80*, TTR, Handelshojskolen, Copenhagen.

---. 1984a. *Herning og Ikast Kommuners afhaengighed af tekstil- og beklaedningsvirksomhed*, TTR, Publication No. 33, Handelshojskolen, Copenhagen.

---. 1984b. *Ensidige industrikommuner, Bind 2: Danske Erfaringer 1972-82*, TTR, HHK, Copenhagen.

---. 1985. "Industriens omlokalisering 1972-1982", in Illeris, S. et al. (eds.) 1985. *Industrien - koncentration eller spredning?*, Copenhagen.

Mathiesen, A. 1979. *Uddannelsespolitikken, uddannelsesfordelingen og arbejdsmarkedet*, Copenhagen.

Pedersen, P.O. 1983. *Vandringerne og den regionale udvikling*, Esbjerg.

---. 1989. *The role of small enterprises and small towns in the developing countries - and in the developed*, CDR project paper 89.1, Copenhagen.

Piore, M.J.; Sabel, C.F. 1984. *The second industrial divide: Possibilities for prosperity*, New York, Basic Books.

Planstyrelsen. 1990. *Tendenser i den regional udvikling i Danmark*, Miljøministeriet, Copenhagen.

Rasmussen, G. 1976. *Det smaborgerlige oprør*, Copenhagen.

Schmitz, H. 1990. *Flexible specialisation in Third World industry: Prospects and research requirements*, Discussion paper DP/18/90, Geneva, International Institute for Labour Studies.

Sieck, F. 1987. *Magnus Olesen 1937-1987. En dansk møbelvirksomhed*, Fiskers forlag.

Statistisk Tiarsoversigt, 1986.

Svensson, B. et al. (eds.). n.d. *Danmark i støbeskeen. Egnsudvikling og Samfund*, Copenhagen.

Thøgersen, J. 1986. *Omstilling i Tekstil - og Beklaedningsindustrien*, Aalborg.

Traerådet. 1978. *Perspektivredegørelse for de danske trae-erhverv, 1978-1983*, Tåstrup.

Undervisningsministeriet. 1988. *Erhvervsuddannelserne, uddannelsessytemet og samfundet i ovrigt*, Copenhagen.

Wickmann, J. 1985. "Ivaerksaettere og deres virksomheder", in Illeris, S. et al. (eds): *Industrien - koncentration eller spredning?*, Copenhagen.

Part III: Policy perspectives

6 Small firms and the provision of real services

Sebastiano Brusco

I. Introduction

This paper has two aims: firstly, to venture a definition of the industrial district while examining a number of its controversial features; secondly, to describe a number of measures of industrial policy that, in the Italian experience, have proved capable of stimulating this type of industrial system. It is worth noting at the outset that many people are convinced that it may be possible to apply the said measures of industrial policy in many different situations, including one where the object is to stimulate the transformation of *groups* of small companies into company *systems* possessing the characteristics typical of the industrial district.

II. Towards a model of the industrial district

Economists base their definition of the firm on the provisions laid down by law. This, while being adequate as long as the company takes the legal form of a limited company, is clearly not so when there are several single companies owned by the same individual, or where there are productive units which, although legally discrete, are in fact linked by various kinds of co-ownership, agreements or partnerships. In either case the fate of the company is tied to events directly affecting other productive units, and it therefore becomes extraordinarily difficult to pinpoint the object of analysis. There is no shortage of evidence in economic literature of attempts to provide a precise definition of these sketchy and uncertain units of analysis. One might cite Richardson's concept of "co-operation" [1972] or the notion of "quasi-vertical integration" developed by Blois [1972].

The industrial district is another unit of analysis of the same type - lacking any clear-cut outline - but traced somewhat arbitrarily in such a way as to identify an "outside" and an "inside" within a continuum. As a result, the only possible strategy is to describe a simplified or - to take up Kaldor's ageing term - a "stylised" model.

Bearing such caveats in mind, it may be stated that an industrial district is a set of companies located in a relatively small geographical area; that the said companies work, either directly or indirectly, for the same end market; that their shared range of values and body of knowledge is so important that they define a cultural environment; and that they are linked to one another by very specific relations in a complex mix of competition and co-operation.

At this juncture, it is obviously essential to discuss and examine more closely the features enumerated. Many of the following sections will be devoted to this task which - it is worth stating explicitly and should be borne in mind - draw strongly on the Italian experience.

1.   The productive base

At the outset it is wise to consider the productive base of the district: its most immediately tangible feature. An industrial district normally comprises many mini-companies (with fewer than 20 employees), a fair number of small companies (between 20 and 50 employees), several medium-sized companies, and a few large companies. However, the relative proportions of mini-, small, medium-sized and large companies can vary considerably from district to district. In a district such as Carpi one may find that around 60 per cent of the workforce is employed by mini-companies; in other districts it may be the medium-sized companies that employ the bulk of the workforce. The overall size of the district varies from 5,000 to 30,000 or even 50,000, workers (including both employees and autonomous workers). In so far as its overall size is concerned, the structure of the industrial district is not, therefore, very different from that of a single medium- to large-sized company.

As has already been stated, all these companies operate within a relatively small geographical area within the same vertically integrated sector. An industrial district that manufactures shoes, for example, comprises not only shoe producers but also those companies involved in the advertising of shoes, those that produce shoe boxes, the manufacturers of glue, buttons, buckles, elastic bands, leathers, and patent leathers and also of course the manufacturers of machines for producing shoes. Viewed from this perspective, the district reflects in theoretical terms Sraffa's sub-system [1975] and, under certain conditions, the *filière* of French economists.

Industrial district companies can be roughly divided into three main categories. The first consists of companies that, regardless of the number of operations they perform, manufacture the finished product and deliver it either to the retail system (as with consumer goods) or directly to the companies that use the product (as almost always occurs in the case of investment goods). Firms belonging to the second category carry out one or several of the production phases needed to arrive at the finished product. In a metal and mechanical district, for example, some companies do lathe work, others do drilling, others produce metal structures, prepare dies or turn out moulded items. The third group of companies is the most heterogeneous of the three and comprises those companies that operate outside the sector to which the finished product statistically belongs, but which work for the vertically integrated sector.

Most small firms are involved in a particular phase of production. Yet one of the essential characteristics of industrial districts is that they also include many small companies supplying the market for finished products. On the other hand, the majority of large companies work for the end market. Yet even many of the larger companies operate at an intermediate phase of production. Size, therefore, is not a strong indicator of the role played by a particular company in the manufacturing process.

Many small firms that manufacture finished products supply the world market. One would be quite mistaken to imagine that small companies producing finished products turn out goods of inferior quality destined only for the local or, at most, the national market.

2.   Competition and co-operation

As has been noted, relations between companies within industrial districts are marked by the presence of strong elements of competition and co-operation. It is now necessary to pinpoint the modalities and the sites of each of these different relations. This will also shed light on the many hypotheses that see the district either as a network serving to link firms, or simply as a phenomenon of a strong division of labour or, on the contrary, as an informal structure of co-operation and even mutual assistance.

Typically, an extraordinary number of markets, in which firms buy and sell labour and activities, will exist side by side within the district. There is a market for each phase of the productive process: in a fashionwear district, for example, there are markets for loom or frame work, needlework, trimming and finishing, embroidery, ironing, and in some cases even for drawing. The buyers in these markets are either those firms that manufacture the finished product or those production-phase firms that undertake to produce a single complex component demanding more manufacturing processes than the aforesaid companies are themselves able to perform. In each of these markets, companies performing a similar work process or producing a similar product (not necessarily a finished product) will engage in lively and even fierce competition over price, quality and delivery and turnaround times. Of course the smaller the production run, the higher the quality and the shorter the delivery time, the higher the price. It is not difficult to explain why companies offering the same product compete so vigorously. The fact is that two of the key conditions underpinning competition are fully respected within industrial districts: the number of operators is high and the market quota of any individual company is low. The following remark should be unnecessary after what has been said, yet widespread suspicion on this point must be allayed: it is not possible for companies within the district to form agreements regarding sales conditions, production quotas or total quantities to be produced. This applies, of course, both to production-phase companies and to finished-product companies.

It is almost impossible to classify forms of co-operation. The most one can venture is a survey of the more frequent forms, grouping them according to the economic function they fulfil.

To start with, many business people are linked by behaviour characterised by straightforward friendliness: as when very small companies borrow one another's tools or even such raw materials as are not readily available on the market. Often - to fill a particularly large or urgently-required order - a firm may appeal for the co-operation of one of its competitors. This may involve a formal agreement (to the extent that both companies may then receive the order) or an informal agreement (so that as far as the commissioning company is concerned, only one firm guarantees the quality and delivery terms of all the work undertaken). The logic of agreements of this type is obvious: this kind of merely temporary co-operation, in which roles are frequently changed, enables individual companies on occasion to accept orders out of proportion to their normal manufacturing capacity, or to the manufacturing capacity they will have available once prior commitments have been honoured.

Between pairs of companies, that form of co-operation which often receives much of the credit for the industrial district's capacity for innovation also occurs: the relation between the commissioning company and the production-phase company. Often, an item or component is not ordered on the basis of a precise design, with detailed specifications. Rather, the customer explains to the subcontractor the intended function of the item, and is then ready to consider whether a standard component already on the market, and therefore less costly, might be used or, on the other hand, whether it might be preferable to stay with the original subcontractor, modifying the design of the component, if necessary, to make manufacture for the subcontractor easier. The element of consultancy in the relationship between customer and subcontractor is particularly striking when the production-phase company is a manufacturer of dies. Indeed only rarely are dies ordered to precise designs. More commonly, customers provide a particular item as a prototype which they wish to have reproduced. However, to reduce costs, they are usually willing to modify the prototype, providing this involves no sacrifice of efficiency. In some cases, co-operation between the customer and the production-phase company may result in considerable alterations to the finished product eventually manufactured, possibly engendering technical innovations. Almost always of the incremental type, these innovations may none the less have considerable value in the market.

There are many reasons why the manufacturer of dies, or indeed any other subcontractor, is so generous with his time and so willing to tackle a problem that does not really concern him or her directly. For example, it may be that the trouble taken in the first instance has a promotional effect leading to other production orders. Available information also suggests that consultancy time is usually accounted under general expenses: in the end, therefore, whatever algorithm is used in the calculation, the cost gets passed on to the customers. This implies that a greater degree of consultancy might be preferable (even though direct costs are inflated by higher general expenses) to less consultancy (and a smaller additional increase in direct costs). Moreover, hypothetically, in many cases such direct costs - specifically as a result of consideration and dialogue - may be brought down.

Unlike those forms so far described, co-operation can also involve many companies, requiring an agent to act as co-ordinator. The most widespread cases of this are: purchasing consortia in which many companies link up to obtain their inputs at a lower price; credit consortia, where firms join together to guarantee each other's bank loans and to negotiate with banks to secure a lower interest rate; agencies, which in Italy often take the form of trade associations, that keep the accounts and wages book for their member companies and, for a small consideration, fill in their income tax declarations. Moreover, trade associations often co-ordinate groups of members seeking to lower the costs of participating in trade fairs, or of promoting their products in a particular area, or of purchasing the necessary space for the development of their companies, or of constructing together, and therefore at a lower cost, the buildings needed to house their various factories. Even the classical role played by trade associations - negotiations with trade unions and representation of the trade vis-à-vis government authorities - can be seen as a form of co-operation.

The factors prompting the above-mentioned consortium-type practices are easy to understand and identify. Some jobs - like book-keeping or the purchase of inputs - cannot be performed very efficiently by each company on its own. The consortia described - or those organisations that function as consortia - simply provide a way in which small companies can assume the minimum size that is efficient in this or that activity. The aim therefore is to take advantage of all available economies of scale: "real" economies of scale, as in the case of book-keeping and the construction of factory buildings, and also "pecuniary" economies of scale, as in the case of purchasing or loan consortia.

Sales consortia, which might seem able to provide the same economies of scale in the field of marketing from which larger companies benefit, are in fact missing from the list given above. There is a reason for this. A common venture, be it a purchasing consortium or a trade association, presupposes that all those participating in it receive (or at least can expect to receive) equal treatment. But unless the products manufactured by the companies in a sales consortium are very similar, or are developed as a co-ordinated set from the design stage onwards, this is unlikely to be the case. Basically, this means that in order to co-operate over sales, through a single agency, the companies involved need to waive their independence to a far greater extent than when taking part in other forms of consortia - unless, of course, the companies in question produce virtually identical goods as is the case, for example, with agricultural companies, where sales consortia are indeed widespread.

Lastly, small companies may form associations, or be encouraged to work together, in the pursuit of goals more immediately connected with the urgent need to make use of new technologies or to reach new markets. This is not, however, the place to examine the problems posed by the sharing of such services - which might somewhat loosely be termed "superior" or advanced. We shall return to this issue in greater detail in the third part of this chapter.

3.   Cultural factors

It was stated at the beginning of this chapter that industrial districts share a number of clearly identifiable cultural features.

In districts, manufacturing and marketing expertise is very widespread: indeed this body of technical know-how forms an integral part of the overall social heritage. In some cases it dates back to very distant times, as in the case of Prato where Francesco Datini was already exporting fabrics in the fourteenth century. In other cases, expertise is more recent and linked to the development of large local companies or to important training schools. Furthermore, social mobility - in comparison to other areas - is very highly-developed, and there are many entrepreneurs who have worked their way up from the shop floor. This list of features could be continued, and each point would merit close examination. But this is perhaps a task more suited to other disciplines which, at least as far as Italian districts are concerned, have in fact devoted considerable resources to this issue, and with good results.

There is, however, a further characteristic that has an immediate impact on production costs and which therefore merits particular attention. It should be borne in mind that in industrial districts contracts between companies very often refer to the customary conventions of the particular area (although there is no specific provision for this). The existence of these implicit specifications, deriving from local customs and history and rooted in a language that is well understood by everyone, enables firms to draw up spot contracts with very low specification costs. Moreover, swindles and frauds are particularly rare and this also helps to reduce overall transaction costs. (Indeed, recalling what has been said earlier about the advantages of consultancy between firms, in many cases transaction costs may actually be deemed to be negative).

This rather special climate is a result of the fact that, alongside state regulations, there is a second set of rules that derives from the community to which all the companies belong. This set of rules, shared by everyone and to which everyone has to adapt, originates in civil society, and also carries a series of sanctions: whoever breaks the rules of the game is excluded from the community and can no longer work within it.

It is perhaps worth pointing out that cases where state rules are accompanied by another set of rules deriving from a smaller community are by no means rare. Quite apart from the influence in Italy of organisations like the Mafia, which have their own special codes of conduct, one need only think of the impact of traditions of discriminatory practices against one group or another involving marriage customs, admission to particular schools or access to particular jobs. More specifically, within the business community, there is the case of livestock markets, where contracts are concluded with a handshake and where certain frauds are permitted (in that there is general consensus that if you fail to notice the fraud you deserve to take the consequences) and other frauds not permitted. Another example is the stock exchange, where the very speed of transactions means that until the end of the morning no written records are made of any contracts concluded.

Customs can, of course, be changed very slowly by legislation. But a local system of rules can survive as long as it does not conflict in any way with the law, and as long as it is useful to the community that has developed it. It will last at least until a period of crisis prompts many people to violate it, thereby rendering it ineffective and unreliable.

It is perfectly possible to reduce this whole set of phenomena to a narrowly economic explanation. According to Von Weizsächer [1978], the low cost of transactions may be explained by the fact that industrial district firms pay great attention to their credibility and reputation, both of which have a high economic value and form the basis of their success. But this interpretation tends to impoverish the overall picture rather than making it easier to grasp.

In any case, whether it is interpreted as a local system of rules or as paying particular attention to the launching and reputation of the company, the lack of opportunism, the expertise and the social mobility mentioned earlier combine to give the area a character that sets it apart from other areas and from the surrounding region. Referring to these characteristics, Becattini has defined the districts in terms of a sense of belonging that distinguishes "us" from "the others", therefore outlining, in this respect also, a limit and a boundary.

4.   An operational definition?

So far, the features of the productive base of the industrial district have been pinpointed. It has been stated that competition between firms producing the same product is very vigorous, that firms find countless opportunities to collaborate, and that industrial district firms are linked by important cultural phenomena.

At this point, one cannot help but ask whether this definition can be put to work, whether it might in fact be applied in everyday research to distinguish what it is that constitutes an industrial district.

A number of difficulties are immediately apparent. Usually, a group of companies - whether end-market oriented or part of a production phase - who manufacture the same product, even if they are concentrated in a relatively limited area, are not bounded by any *clear-cut* geographical lines. The knitting district of Carpi has no clearly identified boundary. Within the manufacturing sector, the density of knitting firms decreases gradually as you go from Carpi to Mirandola and thence to Ferrara, so that to draw a line at any point along the continuum, marking it out as a boundary, would be wholly arbitrary. It is the same with regard to the silk district of Como or the textile district of Prato. Only very few districts - the stocking and sock manufacturing district of Castelgoffredo would be a case in point - have an indisputable geographical boundary that one can identify on a map.

Competition between similar companies is ubiquitous and therefore this aspect of the definition does not pose any problems. Co-operation, however, is a very different matter. The agencies that organise work sharing may be of a variety of types: consortia, trade associations, bodies sponsored and funded by local or provincial councils; or organisations that involve a whole range of bodies: local authorities, associations, trade unions and individual business people. Above all, the gamut of activities transferred from companies to collaboratively run agencies can be enormously varied. In Modena the CNA (small business association) does the book-keeping for 40 per cent of firms, whereas in Ancona this job is entrusted primarily to individual book-keepers and accountants.

No less complex are the problems that arise from the need to take account of such intangible and unmeasurable facts as the sense of belonging or the adherence to a style of inter-firm relations that stems from a local system of rules.

These difficulties become even greater as soon as one realises that, as is the case with large companies, the nature of districts changes over time. The proportion of companies enjoying a direct relationship with the retail system increases or decreases. The productive structure becomes more concentrated or more scattered. The forms of co-operation become more effective and widespread or fade away and are used less frequently. The sense of belonging weakens or extends over broader areas. The local system of rules grows stronger or becomes less consistent.

Under these conditions, it is hard to obtain all the data needed for any proper examination, and any attempt to reach hard and fast conclusions would therefore be misguided. Perhaps there is a basic flaw in any research strategy that sets out to examine a manufacturing system and to situate it, on the basis of all the variables described, according to a classification that only accounts for two types of production systems: the company group and the industrial district. The company group is defined simply as a concentration of firms within the same manufacturing sector which operates in a limited area, and the industrial district as a system in which inter-firm relations are strongly characterised in the way that has been discussed above.

A more subtle type of classification, perhaps more practicable and less arbitrary, might hinge on the idea of development and growth, providing no room for clear distinctions. It might make sense therefore to label districts such as Carpi or Prato, where the conditions of the stylised industrial district model are satisfied, as "highly developed", and to define those groups of secondary and poorly organised firms such as those working in the textiles sector at Sanluri, in Sardinia, as "backward districts". Between these two extremes, allowing for a whole range of intermediate shadings but still with reference to the ideal model, all the other sets of companies would find a place. And one might then also speak of districts in decline, like Vigevano, or of districts like the furniture district of Pesaro that are enjoying a period of growth and development.

III. Industrial policy and industrial districts

If the industrial district gains the status and the dignity of a suitable object for analysis, and if it is accordingly acknowledged that it represents a typical and, at least in certain countries, a commonly occurring productive system, a number of problems then arise, especially as regards industrial policy.

Current discussions on industrial policy in relation to industrial districts may be summarised as posing three questions:

- whether the model of growth by districts - which is implicitly assumed to be positive - can be exported ("replicated" as many people say) and under what circumstances. This is a debate that is carried on in particular in many newly-industrialised countries, and in a number of Mediterranean countries, such as Spain. And yet it has aroused no interest as regards the Italian Mezzogiorno, and one cannot understand why this should be so;

- whether anti-trust laws should be modified to allow the forms of inter-firm co-operation typical of industrial districts: this debate is confined to the United States, and relates above all to the terms of the Clayton Act;

- whether the district can survive the introduction of new technologies and competition with low-wage countries and under what circumstances: this is a discussion that is held mainly in Italy.

These three debates touch on very different issues. Here, we shall only consider the third. Of course the hypothesis that makes it possible to pose this question is that - except perhaps in particular sectors - no *optimal* manufacturing system can be identified; i.e. it cannot be argued that *in all cases* large-scale business is more efficient than the industrial district. Only if this hypothesis is well-founded does it make sense to ask what measures of industrial policy are required for the industrial district to grow and develop, and to prevent it plunging into a spiralling crisis. The need for tailor-made measures does not imply that the industrial district is by its nature at a disadvantage vis-à-vis large-scale enterprise: it simply means that industrial districts require special measures of industrial policy.

The measures to be introduced range over a wide variety of types: financial packages, training in technical, professional or management skills, and so on. But it is best to leave the analysis of these interventions out of the picture and to concentrate on what in Italy are referred to as *servizi reali*. The idea is to prioritise "real services" as against financial incentives, and to offer companies the services they need rather than the money to purchase those services on the market. The contrast is between meeting the needs of the companies directly and giving firms financial incentives to buy what they need.

1.   Real services: A definition

What are real services? All one can do is list a series of possible real services which are in fact already provided by a number of agencies.

The first example of what might be considered a real service is the provision of information regarding the technical standards enforced by law in various foreign countries: these often function as non-tariff protections. A small-scale producer of farm machinery - a small tractor, a hay baler, or a simple manure-spreader - wishing to export his products from Italy to Germany, France, England, Spain, Austria or Sweden, needs to be familiar with the technical standards in force in the various countries. The provision of this service involves setting up and equipping an office to which the entrepreneur can turn for the technical specifications with which manure-spreaders in Bavaria, for example, have to comply. Such an office would be able to give the entrepreneur details regarding minimum wheel size, minimum and maximum headlight heights, compulsory headlight size and voltage, etc. Since non-tariff protections are very rigorous and since small-scale producers of farm machinery are likely to encounter extraordinary difficulties in any attempt to find out about changes in standards, there is little point in offering an entrepreneur money so that he can go out and buy the required information. The entrepreneur simply would not know where to start looking for this information on the market.

Another example of a possible real service would be to provide firms with the software they require in order to design and manufacture their products. Such software could, of course, be produced by firms already operating on the market. In actual fact, however, existing software houses do not produce these packages or CAD-CAMs. This is because the potential users are either unaware of the existence of CAD-CAMs, or they underestimate their importance, or they believe them to be beyond their reach. Accordingly, software producers, before deciding to embark on this kind of work, would have to identify their potential market, carry out a feasibility study, and so on. In other words, they would have to be much more business-like and efficient than they really are. For there is another point that has to be borne in mind: all this preliminary work would have to be carried out not by huge companies such as Microsoft or Santacruz, which operate in quite different markets, but rather by the small locally-based software houses. Lastly, these software houses would also have to invest heavily in efforts to reach and win over potential users, i.e. to create a market for themselves, all of which is manifestly impossible.

A third example of a real service would be the testing of manufacturers' inputs. Small companies producing finished products, and indeed small production-phase firms too, often find it very hard to check the quality of the iron or silk or fibre that they have to work with. In Italy there is no public or private network of laboratories able to perform these analyses rapidly and at reasonable cost. It would therefore be useful to open a laboratory where an entrepreneur needing to check, for example, that the silk he has received from China is really top quality, can have the analysis of the silk carried out and receive a quick answer to his query. Or where a turner can take the steel he has bought from the wholesaler to an expert for checking that it is of the required grade for the manufacture of commissioned items.

Another example of a real service might be the translation of tenders advertised in foreign countries. In Italy, as no doubt elsewhere, it is quite easy to find out about such tenders: from the Chambers of Commerce, from the Ministry for Foreign Trade, and from various other sources. What is not so easy is to obtain a full text of the announcements, and an Italian translation that renders a correct account of the technical and legal terms. This, too, is a job that could be performed by a local services agency, one which might help smaller industrial district firms to compete with larger companies.

To sum up the points made so far, the provision of real services involves supplying companies, in return for payment, with those goods or services that they require, instead of giving them the money they need to go out and buy these goods or services on the market. Often, though not always, it is a matter of disseminating information.

2. Real services: Public provision because of market failure

Why must real services be supplied by public bodies rather than relying on private enterprise to step in? The reason is obvious: private enterprise simply does not supply these services. The question therefore needs to be rephrased: why does the market not function? Why is there no point in providing firms with incentives to buy those services? Why, instead, is it necessary first to supply the services required and then to encourage the firms to purchase them?

Basically, the answer is that we are faced with an imperfection in the market mechanism. There are a number of reasons why the market does not produce the services required. Firstly, the expertise needed to supply the real services in question is not to be found in the social environment in which the industrial district operates, and therefore has to be drafted in from outside. Secondly, even when, however well-concealed, the appropriate expertise is present within the district's social environment, very considerable investment is needed to produce the services required, and returns on this investment may take a long time to materialise. This is due to the fact that the patchy expertise available does not easily create much demand for the services or goods that it might eventually manage to provide. Thirdly, it may be that the very nature of an "information market" can make it difficult for private firms selling information on a commercial basis to become established. Information has in some respects the nature of a "public good".

The distinctive characteristic of public goods is that they may be enjoyed by the individual person or organisation free of charge. It follows, of course, that since no-one is entitled to derive profit from the sale of such goods, no-one is prepared to commit the resources necessary for their production. The example most frequently used to illustrate this situation is that of a garden that is open to the public but that no citizen will undertake to tend and guard. In such cases, text book theory proceeds, if the public good increases collective well-being, it will be produced and guarded at the expense of the community or of the State.

The distinction between public and other goods does not of course lie in the nature of the goods themselves, but rather in the rules that regulate the relations between such goods and civil society. A private good may be sold at a low price to many people, or at a high price to a few, or, lastly, may be reserved for the exclusive use of whoever produces it. In more concrete terms, this series of cases ranges from a garden open to all and sundry, followed by the garden of a duke open to all those willing and able to pay a small entrance fee, to the garden of a hotel - not in itself exceptional in any way - which for a considerable price is available to its few customers, and, lastly, to the private garden.

The rules and the market that operate in the field of information are similar, but not identical, to those described. Some items of information, like those broadcast on the radio, are free. Other kinds of information, such as that carried by newspapers, have a huge market and are available at a very low price. Others, such as confidential results on industries or countries made by specialised agencies (such as those provided by the Economist Intelligence Unit) are sold in a few thousand copies at a price which, whilst not huge, is also not negligible. Finally, there is information, such as that produced by the internal research department of a company (or a confidential report commissioned from a consultant) which is only available to its producer (or commissioner).

How does this all relate to services centres? Basically, whereas large companies are able to gather the information they need *directly*, keep it secret, and derive profit from it, small firms cannot. The small-scale nature of their operations means that the direct collection of information is too costly, and therefore not profitable. But neither can small firms buy the information they need in the market, because the market for information they require simply does not exist.

The fact is that a private firm producing the information required could not work for a "many customers, rock-bottom prices" market (the "newspaper type" of market referred to earlier) simply because the number of the potential buyers of the information is not large enough. For example, a specialised journal giving advance information on fashion trends in Italy would in fact have no more than 10,000 to 20,000 potential buyers - hardly a market sufficient to even cover costs.

Another market which is open to a firm producing this kind of information is the type referred to earlier as "few customers - not huge but not negligible prices". This market could be sufficient to allow the firm producing information to make a profit provided many of the potential buyers know of the advantages which the information could give them. Should this be so, a private firm could operate profitably and there would be no need for public intervention.

But, in fact, this is not the case. The need for information is there but *awareness* of this need is not. To sell information really means getting involved in the process of making that awareness grow, which is similar in many ways to a process of technology transfer. Fundamentally, what is involved is a kind of training activity, or at least any distinction between selling information and training activities is blurred.

The only market which could be profitable for a private firm would be the "one-client" market and in fact what happens in practice is that many of the large firms produce this information internally and keep it exclusive to themselves.

In conclusion, if we want most of the firms in the district to use the information being produced, we find ourselves faced with a contradiction: no private firm is prepared to produce the necessary information and yet its widespread use is essential for the welfare of the community and the growth of the whole economy. It is because of this contradiction that we have described this information as a particular kind of public good, and that public intervention directed at producing it and spreading its use is justified.

In our view, Hirschmann [1958] provides the most useful theoretical point of reference for an account of real services and for an explanation of the need for real services to be supplied by the public sector. The idea is that there are various bottlenecks acting as both obstacles and opportunities. Of particular interest here is the bottleneck created by a shortage of expertise. The social fabric identified within the industrial district needs greater know-how and finds this extra know-how very hard to acquire, in part because it has to be available to the entire fabric rather than becoming the exclusive property of a few. This constitutes a bottleneck and an obstacle to growth. To provide the social fabric in which the small companies operate with this know-how and expertise transforms the obstacle into an opportunity: new know-how, shared by hundreds or even thousands of people can unleash great creativity, originality and understanding not only at the product design stage but also at the process design stage.

3.   Real services: The mechanics of provision

At this point it is worth examining the "technical aspects" involved in the production of real services. It is my impression that the subject can be usefully subdivided by asking the following questions: to whom should the services be supplied? What services should be supplied? How should they be delivered? What price should be attached to them and how should they be assessed?

To whom must real services be delivered, for whom must they be designed? The basic point is that services must be supplied to a group of firms rather than to a single firm. This follows inevitably from what has so far been said: the operation in question aims to transfer a new technology into a social fabric where it was formerly absent, thereby carrying through that social process of knowledge acquisition which is an essential pre-condition for the expression of individuals' abilities.

In many cases, however, different strategies have been followed in pursuit of the same objective. The attempt has been made to introduce within a particular productive fabric a number of exemplary interventions, targeted on a single company, in such a way as to prompt imitative behaviour and to stimulate more rapid innovation. This strategic option often conceals an intention to reinforce the position occupied within a district by a single company, accelerating its growth, so that - once it has grown considerably larger than it was at the outset of the process - it is able to assume a position of leadership and then pull the entire fabric along behind it. This is certainly a reasonable objective providing one is aware of the hypothesis that underlies such an approach: that the industrial district as a productive system does not in fact work, and that there is another model - the company leader of a network - that is preferable.

It should in any case be borne in mind that to intervene at single company level can create many difficulties. Why is this? There are many reasons: an individual entrepreneur often fails to provide enough details for a sensible decision to be arrived at: he may wish to guard his role jealously and may not like to find himself in a subordinate position and faced with someone telling him how to do his job. Often a greater amount of confidential technical information is required when working with a small company, information of a quite different nature from that needed when intervening with a group of companies or when overhauling and restructuring a large company. Moreover, intervening in the affairs of a single small company often elicits paternalistic attitudes from the operators. Nor should it be forgotten that often, where individual firms are concerned, it is easy to make a variety of mistakes liable to create a climate of mistrust and open conflict around the intervening agency.

When one works with groups of firms, on the other hand, the whole nature of the operation changes: whichever firm is the first to accept the agency's proposals will depend mainly on the intention and the character of the individual entrepreneur. The main point is that the job of the real services centre has nothing in common with that of the individual consultant. The consultant works for an individual company, has all the relevant information at his fingertips, helps the entrepreneur to draw up a credible strategy, and is then paid a fee commensurate with the work he has put in. The real services centre does not aim to assist individual companies: its sights are set on a group of companies. Put in another way, the real services centre focuses on collective needs rather than individual needs. The individual needs of individual firms can be satisfied by individual consultants.

What services need to be provided? The notion that the real services centre is basically an agency for the transfer of technologies suggests a straightforward answer to this question. The services to be provided by the agency will be selected according to a wide range of considerations ranging from the ability to generate profit to the degree of ease with which the new techniques can be assimilated and incorporated into the firms. This, then, is the logic that has to be agreed upon between the agency and those with specialist knowledge of the productive fabric in question.

The foregoing should help to dismiss the widespread but mistaken notion that the right procedure is simply to ask firms what they need. Asking firms what they need is as pointless an exercise as asking a sick man what he needs. Indeed, the answers one is likely to receive are very similar. The sick man will say he wants to get better, and the company will say it wants to sell more of its products at profitable prices. Just as the doctor asks his patient to describe the symptoms of his illness and then decides what medicine is required, so the economist embarks upon a lengthy analysis designed to pinpoint the opportunities and bottlenecks (again, the theoretical framework is provided by Hirschmann), and in the process identifies needs of which the individual entrepreneurs are unaware or which they are unable to define with any precision.

There is a reasonably well consolidated strategy for identifying needs, based above all on research. This strategy entails a number of standard analyses. The first of these sets out to pinpoint which production phases are present in the area and which are lacking. For it may be that a number of specific production phases may not be covered by any of the firms in the district and that this is acting as a severe brake on growth. There is no doubt, for example, that the setting up of a company to do chromium-plating work or of a company to machine non-standard items can in some cases help to move the entire district on towards new levels of achievement. Another standard analysis sets out to ascertain the nature of relations between companies. The fact that a production-phase company or an end-market company has only a few or, on the other hand, a great many, customers may speak volumes about the bargaining power of this or that company. If a group of firms has very little bargaining power it may be useful to introduce into the district features designed to increase its ability to take action. Often, for example, it may be that a great number of production-phase companies are confronted with a very limited number of end-market companies, with the result that the latter are in a position to depress the profits of the former, thereby reducing their ability to spend money and thus preventing them from making the necessary investments in technical innovations. In such cases, measures may be developed to prompt the most successful of the production-phase companies to turn themselves into end-market companies. Alternatively, end-market companies may be brought into the district from other areas.

When undertaking this work, it is worth bearing in mind that public opinion often identifies the "baddie" incorrectly: great care has to be taken in this regard both in the creation of alliances and in the selection of one's battles. Attention should also be paid to the important role of ethnic, racial or gender issues in the division of labour and in relations with trade unions.

But above all, over the last few years, a special technique has been developed to identify the needs of industrial districts. This technique is based on comparative research focusing on productive systems in different countries competing for the same markets. It is worth rapidly recalling an example of research in the footwear market. Investigation in Italy, France and England [Courault et al., 1990] has shown that the different productive systems studied (eight Italian industrial districts, two French industrial districts, and a series of large English factories) each has certain advantages and disadvantages. The Italian firms turned out to be much more expert than the French or English ones in producing sample collections and in keeping one jump ahead of fashions. Also, they have at their disposal a more highly-skilled workforce, are able to work with advanced technology, and their wage levels are often no lower than those of other firms. In France and England, on the other hand, design technology is more advanced than in Italy and there is an ability to meet tough delivery deadlines that in Italy is quite lacking. The comparison between different manufacturers, both large and small, between different countries, and between manufacturers competing in different market segments, highlights the structural weaknesses of single districts and even of single large-scale firms requiring intervention. Comparative research, having defined a specific market, is thus able to pinpoint the relative strengths and weaknesses of the various manufacturers and to indicate which real services need to be provided. Once again the theoretical basis for this work is supplied by Hirschman and the notion of *bottlenecks*. The aim is to provide districts with a strategy either over the long term or involving market interventions that would be no different from the kind of strategy that larger companies are able to elaborate. Such a strategy need not necessarily entail any expansion in the size of the firms, but will certainly provide for an enrichment of the social fabric with a certain form of expertise and a certain type of technology.

In what form must these real services be delivered and what should be their characteristics? It is not simply a matter of supplying information in its most straightforward form: information needs to be provided in as personalised a form as possible. This follows from everything we have already stated: the basic problem is the shortage of expertise, and the market's inability to respond to this shortage. What has to be encouraged is the development of a group of companies or of a system of production able to foster more agile and more efficient technologies, industrial relations, and inter-firm relations. It is therefore necessary to supply new techniques and to stimulate the growth of new relations between companies in a manner that is appropriate to the groups of companies affected by the intervention.

One particular example of this springs to mind: the production by the national research organisation ENEA (Ente Nazionale Energie Alternative) of the software needed to facilitate and speed up design processes in the knitting and clothing industries. Here the goal was to design the new technology in such a way as to make it as similar as possible to previously-used techniques. The situation is not that of a hierarchical regime where the new technology could simply be imposed from above without any need for it to be understood. The climate is such that the new technology has to be understood and accepted by those who will be using it. It is therefore essential to encourage entrepreneurs and employees to work with the new technology, to tailor it to their needs and to improve it, and also to design the new techniques in such a way that they can be introduced without causing upheavals in the workforce, major shifts in the organisation of labour, huge alterations to company hierarchical structures, or vast changes to the organisation of the companies. In other words, the new techniques need to be introduced in the most painless way possible. There has to be an awareness that once the new techniques have been understood and adopted, they will grow further, provide benefits, be reinvented, undergo positive and perhaps not so positive changes, in line with the developing needs of the district and the creative input made by each individual. The underlying logic is to promote the transfer of technologies. The real services centre needs to deploy exceptional expertise to facilitate the introduction of new technologies. Once these have been installed, they will expand, multiply, and change in accordance with the imaginative and creative contribution of the various individuals involved.

At what price should the relevant agencies sell these services and how should an assessment be made as to the effectiveness of public money supplied to the agencies? The return on outlay can probably be evaluated by cost-benefit analysis. As has already been stated, the aim of the agency's work is to facilitate and accelerate the introduction or the spread of innovation. The costs involved comprise public money earmarked for the agencies plus the financial costs entailed in making private investments earlier than planned. The benefits to be gained are those resulting from the introduction into the productive system of a set of new techniques. However, the job of assessing these benefits is anything but straightforward. As a first approximation, the advantage to be gained from the initiative may be measured by the increase in the system's productivity during the period extending from the actual introduction of the innovation to the moment at which the innovation would have been introduced had no special intervention occurred. However, there are two reasons why this approach is in fact rather more complicated. Firstly, in the absence of any intervention, the district might become locked into a vicious spiral of decline. Then, as a result of this decline, the time lag prior to the introduction of the innovation might be further extended and its eventual introduction might take place either more hurriedly or more slowly than otherwise. Secondly, the introduction of the innovation may trigger responses that are precisely symmetrical to those just outlined, i.e. leading the district into a spiral of rapid growth. Should this in fact occur, one ought to include among the benefits not only the income secured by avoiding the delay in introduction but also the boost in income that, in subsequent years, will result from the creative use of the new technology.

Nor is it any easier to set a price on the intervention. In principle, a variety of models of optimisation might be constructed. One could, for example, maximise the income of the agency producing the service. Or, alternatively, one might maximise the income to the community, defining that income in the way that has been outlined. These two procedures would lead to very different results, laying bare the mistake made by those analysts who, despite the fact that the price of services provided is kept low to encourage the spread of new techniques, judge the success of the initiative not by the number of entrepreneurs using the service but by the agency's balance-sheet.

There are a number of other possible and reasonable strategies for setting the price of the services provided. For example, the decision might be taken to make a profit on those services with which firms are already familiar but to sell below cost those services the utility of which firms are not yet convinced. Equally, it might be possible to leave to the private sector the provision of established services and to concentrate on the introduction of new services. Lastly, when working out price strategies, it must not be forgotten that the goal of maximising the income of the community does not necessarily mean setting the price as low as possible. Often, within certain limits, as experience in Emilia-Romagna has shown, entrepreneurs value the usefulness of a service by its cost. Consequently, a relatively high price may in fact provide not only a saving but also a more rapid take-up of the innovation in question.

IV. Conclusions

Before the services described can be designed, a great many interviews will have to be conducted in order to gather types of data not normally covered by official statistics. A considerable commitment to research into the district's cultural circumstances will also be required ("cultural" intended here in the anthropological sense). Close links will have to be forged with research institutions possessing the appropriate expertise and ability to translate the most sophisticated technologies into terms comprehensible to small firms. Often, as has been said, there may be a need for comparative research between a particular district and large companies in the country concerned and in the most important competitor countries. This research would be designed to pinpoint the district's weaknesses and to apply greater precision to the selection of the intervention required. The district has to be viewed not only as a unit of analysis but also as a unit of initiative: as a fully-fledged and organically unified organisation, whose development is slowed down or impeded by bottlenecks that public action must turn into opportunities.

This view of the district as a complex but unitary organism has a number of implications. The first is of a purely theoretical nature. The interpretative viewpoint so far expounded gives grounds for believing that the functional mechanisms of the district can be more fully understood if reference is made to theoretical constructions developed from a study of single companies. And it is self-evident that the relations which, as has often been stated, link the actors within a single district to one another, are very similar to those that, according to Penrose [1963], bind together a group of people involved in running a company. Entrepreneurs and specialist workers in both production-phase and end-market companies, operators in companies providing services, and trade union leaders, all operate in a climate in which personal familiarity, a knowledge of the limits and strengths of each person, and an understanding of one's own abilities and expertise as well as those of others, play a role that is no different from that to which Penrose refers in accounting for the way in which different people manage to work in a unitary way. The industrial district, of course, lacks any unitary purpose or will. And yet there is an agreement as to the rules of the game, and a reciprocal respect.

Reference to Penrose can also help to focus the importance of the role that time plays, and the extent to which time is a necessary and essential factor in change. Penrose stated that time - the simple passage of time - was necessary to the growth of the managing group of a firm. Time is also required for an innovation to become widespread. Such periods of time cannot be shortened indefinitely: the rhythm of events and of growth cannot be accelerated precisely because the process that this rhythm punctuates is social rather than technical in nature. This framework also clarifies the role of public intervention: it is not a matter of forcing through a transformation but rather of activating it, of creating the conditions under which other people can bring it about. Incidentally, this is one of the reasons - perhaps the main one - why these interventions are at one and the same time both very difficult and very inexpensive. They are very difficult because it is a matter of *convincing* rather than of commanding; very *inexpensive* because once the process has been initiated it continues under its own momentum.

A complex and unitary organisation, as has been said, is co-ordinated not by a single central hierarchy but informed rather by the input from numerous knowledgeable agents. Such an arrangement - and this is the last implication - clearly demonstrates the pointlessness of comparing industrial districts with large firms in an attempt to identify once and for all which system of production is *better* in current economic circumstances. Each has strengths and weaknesses. Industrial districts - when they are successful - are creative, display originality, are often able to discover new markets, continuously introduce incremental innovations, some of which may prove important, and enhance social mobility and worker participation. On the other hand, industrial districts are slow to adopt new technologies, lack expertise in financial management, have little of the know-how required for basic research, and are unable to produce epoch-making innovations. Large firms - when they are successful - provide an inverted image of the one just described. Probably these two forms of productive organisation will manage to co-exist in the future: the latter with the help of sweeping trade agreements and tax laws; the former assisted by means of a painstaking and sophisticated intervention.

References

Blois, K.J. 1972. "Vertical quasi-integration", in *The Journal of Industrial Economics*.

Courault, B. et al. 1990. *L'industrie de la chaussure en Europe: Vers plus de flexibilité*, Paris, Centre d'Etudes de l'Emploi.

Hirschman, A.O. 1958. *The strategy of economic development*, New Haven, Yale University Press.

Penrose, E.T. 1963. *The theory of the growth of the firm*, Oxford, Blackwell.

Richardson, G.B. 1972. "The organization of industry", in *Economic Journal*.

Sraffa, P. 1975. *Production of commodities by means of commodities*, Cambridge, Cambridge University Press.

Von Weizsächer, C.C. 1978. *Efficiency, the invisible hand, information and extrapolation*, Paper presented at the IVth Annual Meeting of the European Association for Research in Industrial Economics, Brussels.

7 The role of local institutions in the development of industrial districts: The Canadian experience

Pierre-André Julien

I.   Introduction

In the industrialised countries, most industrial districts[1] have developed to such an extent over the last few years that it now seems reasonable to think that the age-old traditional movement towards company concentration may at last reach them, or that certain districts may vanish as happened at the end of the nineteenth and at the beginning of the twentieth centuries. But this change may also signal new forms of inter-firm co-operation enabling districts to maintain their principal features while ensuring their on-going development.

At the very least, this change presupposes the pursuit of new strategies by industrial districts to improve their efficiency and above all their flexibility as regards not only products and production processes but also distribution or exportation. These strategies relate to the very dynamics of the small firms system, but also to the development of the surrounding socio-economic network and the emergence of new forms of intervention adopted by the territorial government.

In this chapter, we shall first provide a rapid survey of some of the problems that industrial districts are currently facing. Then we shall show that any measures designed to promote their survival and development will have to entail a tighter control on economic information both internal and external to the district. But more often than not this control can only be achieved if special aid is granted by the territorial State, with the support of the central State. We shall conclude our analysis with a look at three examples of industrial districts in Quebec.

---

1.   Or localised systems of enterprises, local productive systems, diffuse industrialisation systems, territorial economies, specialised production areas, etc. On these different concepts, see Emanuel [1990].

II.   Changes to industrial districts

The principal dangers presently threatening industrial districts derive from the rapid transformation of their working environment in the face of increasing international openness. On the one hand, this opening-out entails the increasing segmentation and transformation of markets and hence more vigorous international competition. This competition is accentuated by the volatility of products demanding systematic innovation. But it is also stoked by fluctuations in exchange rates in customer or competitor countries, by the formation of new economic blocks, and by the development of visible or invisible barriers. On the other hand, this process of opening-out leads to an increased reliance on services, many of which can only be provided in the major towns and cities.

This international opening-out is also marked by the arrival of the newly industrialised countries (NICs), and also by advantages (in absolute if not in relative terms) deriving from the spread of new production technologies that make use of information technology or that permit new forms of organisation and flexible production. Thus some countries are now securing an almost unchallengeable lead thanks to their ever greater reliance on these new technologies [Thurow, 1987]. Moreover, this is occurring despite the efforts of several districts to bring in new technology. Put simply, we are witnessing a new confrontation between local economies and international markets.

But this opening-out is also effected through the various national communications media, thereby rapidly transforming the conditions and perceptions of social workers and women who are employed in large numbers in certain industrial districts [Capecchi, 1988]. This transformation receives an added impetus from improvements in educational standards. In other words, post-industrial values are beginning to reach into all environments, and are seriously undermining the traditional work ethic. Especially in the case of young people who no longer accept a shared economic project, this process threatens the kind of discipline that not only accounted for much of the competitive strength of the districts, but also underpinned the formation and gradual renewal of an entrepreneurial class [Trigilia, 1986]. In some cases, the social system that often constituted the very foundation of the cohesion of industrial districts may be breaking up [Tinacci Mossello and Dini, 1990].

Lastly, to these changes must be added the "new technological revolution" which, unlike previous industrial revolutions, makes available a range of equipment that is much better suited to the needs of small firms or to flexible or small-batch production. Some research has even shown that, for example, numerically controlled machine tools (NCMT) enhance the development of small and medium-sized enterprises (SMEs) more than that of large-scale business [Acs and Audrestch, 1988]. Other work has demonstrated that the take-up of information technology by SMEs has been gaining speed and that in certain sectors it has been occurring even more rapidly than in large-scale business [Julien, 1990b; Lefevbre and Lefevbre, 1990]. But, however necessary this revolution may be, it none the less transforms the working environment, opens up rifts between companies and tends to instal a new hierarchy. Lastly, it quickens the pace at which values are transformed.

III. Information control

At a time when industrial districts are facing such profound change in their environment, the problem of information control becomes crucial: information needed for the discovery or creation of new gaps opened up by market segmentation and by the development of the international market; information making it possible to understand and respond to the new aspirations of the workers; information and training to prepare the next generation of entrepreneurs; information to pinpoint which of the available new technologies can assist a particular firm in becoming more competitive; information on new services. Information is essential, in short, as a basis for greater flexibility, creativity, and innovation.

Vaggagini [1989] holds the view that industrial districts constitute areas of communication and that the sharing of economic, socio-cultural and political information accounts for their cohesion over time. They form special environments in which "communicational acting", as Habermas [1987] explains, ensures cultural reproduction and social integration within the family and hence within the community, at work and in the business world and thus in industrial development too.

As regards the economic dimension, industrial districts may be viewed as systems with "limited control over internal and external information",[2] in order to minimise transaction costs. These control systems can be explained by the greater gains that each individual entrepreneur derives from the sharing-out (between the firms in the district) of a broader pool of information as compared with the benefits to be enjoyed from keeping for one's own firm a more limited amount of information. These gains are not economic alone, but also social. In the districts themselves, this sharing-out or exchange of information has gradually become institutionalised and indeed accounts for their strong economic and social structuring. But as Vaggagini [1990] has observed, there appears to be a widening gulf between the district structures and "modernity", or between a more traditional community-based environment and an increasingly international and multicultural economy.

This constantly increasing openness in economic terms (markets), in technological terms (new processes, new products), or in sociological terms

---

2.   Or "systems of relative complicity", as we have called them [Julien, 1990a].

(affecting the value systems of workers and entrepreneurs) creates fresh challenges for information control. To survive and expand, industrial districts must on the one hand develop new national and international antennae while on the other hand developing new skills in the filtering, evaluation and use of information reaching them from this environment. In other words, the response of districts to the turbulence of their environment has to involve a heightened awareness of the development of national and international markets, a well-tailored adaptation of production organisations to the new aspirations of workers, and an increased sensitivity to technological trans-formations (as well as efficiency in introducing them), and a constant capacity for innovation. It is a question of technological and commercial "monitoring". But at the same time, to preserve their cohesion, districts must adapt this new information to their socio-cultural and political needs.

But this environmental monitoring - although also performed by small firms [Smeltzer et al., 1988; Zanka, 1990] - is harder to systematise in very decentralised organisations. In industrial districts, monitoring needs to be organised and controlled at the business community level. This requires a different kind of organisation and much more complex new forms of co-operation; it also entails institutional intervention.

Viewed systemically, as Maria Tinacci Mossello and Francesco Dini [1990] have observed, every system, in order to survive, during the course of its own evolution must minimise its complexity by continually checking its information relations with its environment. At the same time, it has to ensure that these relations are sufficiently complex to pick up all the information essential to it. This is why the development of a good structure of technological and commercial monitoring is the main challenge facing industrial districts as a consequence of increasing openness to the inter-national economy. In Italy, for example, it now appears that an increasing proportion of information between districts and the outside world is channelled through service companies located in the Milan metropolitan area [Capecchi et al., 1988]. These firms view their intervention in industrial districts as one operation among others and act principally in their own interests [Tinacci Mossello and Dini, 1990]. As a result, control over information is slipping away from the district. To regain it, a co-ordination of all the resources of the region in question is vital; and in most cases this co-ordination also has to secure backing from the territorial State.

IV. The role of territorial states: Long-term management of information and training

Given this growing complexity (the "hypercomplexity" of our socio-economic systems in Edgar Morin's view), one must highlight two main types of information essential to the smooth operation and development of the industrial district. The first type is short-term and conjunctural, and relates to markets and competition. The second type of information is long-term and structural and derives from research and development into products and technology and from changes in the system of values.

The first information group belongs to the capitalist domain and is in the possession of private firms or professional organisations within the district. Principally, it relies on the district's leading firms (those closest to the market or those who stand out as leaders in the last stages of the production process). It also relies on inter-firm co-ordination to promote, for example, gradual innovation through the process of "diffused innovation" [Bellandi, 1989]. The second information group derives above all from a kind of organisation that is oriented towards long-term change or is more collective or public in nature. This organisation cannot easily be founded in small-scale enterprises with short-term outlooks and resources that are too limited to support forecasts of prospects and radical technology transfers. Moreover, it is less characteristic of the private sector.

This is all the more true since short-term information is a factor in both competition and co-operation. If such information is not compensated for by reciprocal exchange, it becomes the fundamental element of differentiation.[3] In these circumstances, State intervention is either ineffective or liable to meet with rejection in the name of small firm independence, this independence being one of the main goals of small entrepreneurs [Brockhaus, 1986].[4] By contrast, long-term information, since it does not yet belong to anyone, is more neutral. Its production by a third party is easier to accept, and it is accordingly easier to share out.

This information must also cover new forms of accelerated training both for managerial or business personnel and for the skilled workforce. Here again one cannot expect SMEs or even districts to undertake reskilling or to develop on their own a more thoroughly self-trained fresh generation of entrepreneurs.

As regards the longer term, information can only be uncertain and subject to change and hence extremely complex. In information theory, the larger the set of signals and the more open the system of information, the higher climb the costs [Theil, 1969]: too high, in any case, for small firms or their professional organisations. Such information has to be a matter for the State. Yet it cannot be "efficient" unless it is oriented towards an

---

3. Baptiste and Michelsons [1989] have thus demonstrated that, in the case of the Alta Valdesa district, information exchange is generalised except as regards innovation: this is where competition comes in.

4. See the instance of the SPRINT project's "telematic programme" which was unable to operate because it tried to encompass all the information generated by the enterprises or craftspeople [Tinacci Mossello and Dini, 1990]. Other investigations have shown that SMEs tend to reject state intervention, especially in matters directly affecting competition [see Chicha, 1982].

"individualised" decision for each particular case [Chicha, 1982].[5] This long-term information has therefore to be developed in close co-operation with its users, while remaining sufficiently broad to satisfy more general requirements.

In the case of the industrial district (and this often applies to SMEs in general),[6] the State is represented above all by the territorial State, geographically closer, able to operate in close co-operation with the district or small firm and, most important, able to integrate the specific social and economic dimensions of each district, while respecting the wider environment and context.

It is obviously not possible for this territorial State, by switching from a strategy of national and regional development to one of socio-economic development (within the framework of the international division of labour) to establish on its own all the institutions able to fulfil the requirements. Yet it has to co-ordinate all existing institutions and ensure that they develop in such a way as to meet the needs of the enterprises and hence those also of the industrial district. It has also to secure the backing of the central State in order to provide those necessary but previously non-existent services.

As for Research and Development and technological transfer, the territorial State has a number of means at its disposal. On the one hand, it can work with research and innovative bodies at the regional level, for example with regional universities and colleges, and with company consultants,[7] in order to transfer information. If need be, it can develop special "antennae", with the help of agents at the national and international level, for instance, in order to pick up, filter and adapt information. Equally, the territorial State can seek to develop interface mechanisms to transmit information to companies according to their needs and respective resources. It can support special assignments or similar initiatives designed by central government for business managers at international fairs, or executive courses at foreign research centres. In short, it must harmonise territorial organisation with extra-territorial and international networks.

This problem of information is crucial, for example, to the spread and establishment of new technologies [Guesnier, 1984; Dosi et al., 1988]: access to information and its control constitute the prime factor (internal to the enterprises themselves) that distinguish between those SMEs that make use of new production technologies and those, on the other hand, that use traditional technologies. This information variable is much more important,

---

5.   In a piece of research that we carried out into the development of effective software for management and production, for example, in hospitals, we found that the best information systems were the ones that the users had themselves developed [Jacob et al., 1989].

6.   Just as the central State is the traditional counterpart of big business, so the territorial State is the small firm's normal counterpart.

7.   On the role of company consultants, see the interesting analysis provided by Chell et al. [1989] related to the clothing industry in England.

for example, than any financial constraint. The second factor is the level and type of management training [Julien et al., 1988].

The need for training increases with the growing complexity of production. As a result, the traditional "on-the-job" method of training entrepreneurs, with the gradual transmission of know-how accumulated within the district, is less and less efficient. This is because part of this know-how has to be regularly overhauled if not re-invented. Confronted with the new demands of the economic environment, there is a need for executives who are better able to understand and process complex information. As regards workforce training, reskilling is increasingly necessary, at least for technicians and key personnel. The territorial State must therefore come to terms with the educational resources of the region (which must themselves be renewed through contact with broader sources, in order to meet the needs of the district, even if this means developing ad hoc executive and staff retraining programmes).

Thirdly, the region has to obtain or promote consultancy and expertise in its area. The critical mass created by the existence of a great number of enterprises operating in the same sector should ease the creation of this expertise in the speciality in question; but when it comes to other types of support, it may be necessary to turn to entrepreneurs or enterprises from outside the region. In such cases, outside firms have to be prompted to develop a particular speciality for the greater benefit of the region. If need be, the creation of service firms should be promoted. Such firms should deal, for example, with the development of design skills, research and consultancy, technology transfer, international marketing, and export promotion.

Local government can play yet other roles, helping new firms to get started, making available risk capital, or providing technical advice for companies in trouble. But even if these functions may be necessary at the outset and during moments of crisis, they cannot replace longer-term functions.

In short, the manufacturing development of the district is increasingly tied to the development of services. And the development of this tertiary sector has to be stimulated by local government for the greater benefit of the region. Local government has thus to play the role of "catalyst" or "synergy facilitator" leading actors better to co-ordinate their actions with the help of or thanks to the provision of extra information. What is thus achieved is a "network" of resources of all kinds, relating to manufacturing as well as to services, supported by and supportive of the dynamism of the manufacturing SMEs, and backed by local government. It is essential that this network should function as the new linchpin for the economic and social cohesion of the district or territorial economy [Planque, 1983; Aydalot, 1986; Lund and Rasmussen, 1988]. It must make it possible systematically to enrich the endogenous forces of a controlled supply of exogenous information.

V.   Some applications

We have attempted to apply this conceptual framework to three Quebec districts: the first in the up-market area of pleasure boat production in the Grand'Mère and Shawinigan regions; the second in an industry that dates back to the beginnings of New France, the fur production district in Montreal; and the third in a more traditional sector, the furniture industry in the Victoriaville region.

1.   The pleasure boat district of Centre-Mauricie

The first of these two districts developed out of canoe and small crafts production at the turn of the century, to meet the needs of the paper industry for wood felling and floating to the north of Trois-Rivières. Gradually there developed a demand for boats from fishermen and hunters. But it was not until the 1960s that a number of firms in the area turned to producing motorised pleasure craft capable of sailing close to the sea coasts. Two of these firms expanded rapidly, drawing the others along in their wake. It is worth mentioning that this development occurred at a time when the region's main large-scale enterprises were declining.[8]

Overall, Quebec's pleasure craft industry has developed very rapidly. Between 1977 and 1985, the annual level of deliveries rose at a rate of 18.5 per cent in Quebec as compared to 13.8 per cent for Canada as a whole. The Centre-Mauricie district accounts for 55 per cent of production in Quebec. At present the district is home to the two leading companies (with between 250 and 350 production workers) and 29 other small firms (with fewer than 50 employees), many of which are subcontractors (divided into two levels: see Appendix 1). Roughly a third of these small firms are managed by former employees of the larger companies. Much smaller than the large districts (e.g. the Montreal fur district or the Italian districts, comprising several hundred small firms), Centre-Mauricie obviously matches the scale of Quebec's small regional economy. It does not, however, appear to have completed its growth cycle.

The district is therefore not in a position to produce and supply all the items demanded of it. However, an effort is being made to boost the rate of self-sufficiency (currently at 72 per cent). Indeed, the leading firms have recently created a purchasing group in an effort to concentrate their buying and to enhance their production within the district.

---

8.   The Centre-Mauricie region includes two small towns (Shawinigan and Grand-Mère) and about ten villages. In the 1950s and 1960s, the region was considered one of the richest in Canada. But the systematic closure of the large chemical firms and the slump affecting the paper and aluminium industries and companies in the 1970s had an adverse effect and led to a drop in population.

The district is supported by an industrial association (the Industrial Development Corporation of Centre Mauricie or CODICEM)[9] which co-ordinates development initiatives. One of the aims of the Corporation is to help renew the industrial base of the region through the creation of small subcontracting firms. Above all, this assistance involves what is known as an "incubator", offering a whole range of services to small firms during their early years.[10]

The Corporation promotes information exchange[11] via a "regional board of consultation", set up following the region's "socio-economic summit" held in 1987. It also co-ordinates the quest for risk financing, support for companies wishing to take part in industrial fairs or seek export openings, with the backing of programmes made available by the higher-level governments. Lastly, the Corporation works with the college of the region and with technical schools to promote the training of workers (in particular through the foundation of the Centre-Mauricie Nautical Training Centre)[12] and technical advice.

Yet the district still has a number of problems. The pleasure boat industry is in relative crisis in North America. First and foremost this crisis is due to a slowing-down in increases in income. Added to this is the Free Trade Agreement between Canada and the United States which has caused Canadian customs duties to drop 15 per cent in January 1987, as against 1.2 per cent in the United States. The US Merchant Marine Act, which bars the entry of any boats not used "for personal purposes", acts as a further brake on Canadian exports.

Already this year two major Quebec companies (neither of them located within the district) have had to close, in the wake of 12 others throughout Canada over the last five years. Even the top Canadian manufacturer of sailing boats had to seek new partners in 1987 in order to avoid bankruptcy. It also seems that several large American firms are facing difficulties [*Ministère de l'Expansion industrielle régionale*, 1988]. The only

---

9.   This Corporation intervenes not only in the district but also throughout the entire Centre-Mauricie region. In collaboration with the Quebec Enterprises Group, it sponsors a number of different economic bodies, such as the Risk Capital Financing Company (SOFICAR), Support for Youth Initiatives (SIJCEM), the Enterprise Creation Centre (CGEGEM), and an SME "club" (where industrialists can discuss their strengths and weaknesses).

10.   At present, the "incubator" is providing start-up assistance to seven subcontracting firms in the pleasure boat sector.

11.   A few years ago, for example, the Corporation created a data file on market opportunities in the region in order to inform industrialists about openings for subcontracting work. Later, however, the updating of the completed file was suspended.

12.   As regards training, most emphasis was initially placed on lamination and padding processes. At present, by contrast, most effort goes into cabinet work and CFAO.

possible solutions will have to entail an increase in productivity over the entire chain of companies, as well as a broadening-out of the market.

The computerisation of firms within this district has not yet made much headway. It is, however, true that production is pitched up-market. But reliance on design alone is not enough. Owing, for example, to the distance from the New England market, transport costs are high. An attempt has to be made to adapt or indeed to create new processes based on information technology.[13] Likewise, it is essential to adapt to the arrival of new materials and to seek new markets in Europe and Japan to offset fluctuations in the North American market. Lastly, training must be improved. To achieve all of this, long-term analyses are required. It takes time to train a skilled workforce, to elaborate managerial and marketing techniques, and especially to develop markets and forms of technology transfer. Yet short-term needs still seem to monopolise the energies of local institutions. In particular, there is a need to forge and develop links with the research and training facilities provided by the regional university.

2.   The Montreal fur district

The second example is that of the Montreal fur-producing district, which has emerged out of the fur trade that was carried on with the American Indians in the eighteenth and nineteeth centuries. Montreal was, at that time, a major centre for this trade. At the beginning of the twentieth century, most of the firms that processed furs had premises near the port, especially along rue Saint-Paul. But as the buildings grew older and fire insurance companies more exacting, they were gradually forced to move into the five-hectare rectangular area they still occupy, bordered by rue Major and rue St Alexandre, between de Maisonneuve and Sainte-Catherine. The district is therefore concentrated in the city centre (on the pattern of the fur districts in New York, London and, to a lesser extent, Frankfurt). Indeed, most of the district is located in twelve main buildings.

The Montreal fur district comprises 554 companies working in production (cleaning, dyeing, cutting, making up, finishing), distribution, sales, design and creation. The tanneries alone are located outside Montreal for obvious environmental reasons. Eighty per cent of firms have fewer than ten employees (a third have fewer than two employees, 4.1 per cent have more than 50 employees). The companies belonging to this district are particularly closely interlinked, with 80 per cent of them working on a more or less subcontracting basis. A lot of trading takes place from hand to hand, given the close proximity of companies. The leading companies are the larger ones or those with internationally famous brand names. Integration tends to

---

13.   Available technologies include canvas-cutting by compressed air jet, the use of robots for resin injection, wood-cutting by numerical control, etc.

proceed by formal pact (see Appendix 2). Most of the employees are women, many of whom are recent immigrants [Intermunicipal Commission on Metropolitan Development, 1989].

Production is predominantly up-market, taking advantage of Canada's fame as a fur-producing country. Lower range production is being left gradually to countries such as South Korea. More than 80 per cent of production is exported, either directly (50 per cent goes to the United States) or indirectly by sales to tourists visiting showrooms or from city hotels.

The district benefits from forms of direct institutional support for the fur industry such as the Annual International Montreal Fur Salon and the special training courses that are held at three Montreal colleges (even though some specialisations are not taught). The district is also helped by the Montreal fashion industry, with its two annual shows, and by its access to the Quebec Specialist Fashion Center, the Quebec Center of the Computerisation of Production, and to a range of aid packages developed by central and state governments. These include start-up programmes for entrepreneurs, strategic managerial training schemes, programmes designed to promote scientific employment, subsidies for trade trips abroad, help with promotion work, design, etc.

Competition in this industry is relatively low-key because of the fame of Canadian fur products. Free trade with the US can only benefit the industry, as company owners themselves acknowledge.[14]

However, the district is faced with at least three problems. First, it is now undergoing considerable pressure as regards property, caught as it is between office-boom areas. Secondly, it has to deal with growing pressure from animal protection groups. Lastly, new creative personnel and good designers are in short supply at a time when fashion is undergoing rapid change. There is also a growing need for greater computerisation in production.

As regards the first problem, the city is in the process of adopting a strategy designed to protect the area while promoting its modernisation. As for animal rights issues, a special tax is being levied on each processed hide so that world-wide counter-campaigns can be mounted. At the same time, there is a trend towards the use of increasingly pain-free ways of capturing animals. However, much remains to be done in this area. As for the third problem, there is still a lack of concerted action by the various actors involved (manufacturers, designers, specialised schools, council bodies, central and state governments, and so on). Indeed, even the business

---

14.   See the investigation carried out by Lavallin for CIDEM (Report on *La cité de la mode et le district de la fourrure*, Appendix 1, Montreal, April 1989). This investigation, using a representative sample of owner-managers, showed that 67 per cent of them felt "very optimistic" or "fairly optimistic" about the consequences of free trade.

associations needed for the lobbying have still to be created.[15] Lastly, the level of penetration, achieved, for example, by computer-assisted design (CAD) and computer-assisted manufacture (CAM), is still very low. It is true that new technologies are still ill-suited to this industry, but little or no effort is being made to develop such technologies further.

3.   The Bois-Francs furniture producing industrial district

Lastly, the small furniture-producing industrial district in the Bois-Francs region, an area that is still very rural, has been in existence since the beginning of the century. In 1989 the district comprised 37 firms, 74 per cent of which had fewer than 20 employees. Its location at the beginning of this century, around the periphery of the small town of Victoriaville, may be explained by the nearby forests which in those days supplied the species required by the industry. Regrettably, for a variety of reasons, the forests have been decimated and much of the wood needed is now imported. This has increased costs relative to some of the district's competitors.

Production here has long been aimed down-market. This has meant that when American production (in particular in North and South Carolina, where much of American furniture manufacturing is concentrated) was faced with a reduction in domestic demand, leading them to off-load their surplus on the Canadian market, it would spark off a crisis throughout the region.

The local authorities have developed two important long-term strategies. First, by dint of numerous representations, in 1964 they managed to persuade the government to establish in the region the only specialist school in Quebec to train students in furniture production and wood carving skills. The aim of this initiative is to create a skilled workforce able to develop traditional working methods. Following this, and in collaboration with the college of the region, the Bois-Francs Economic Development Corporation secured the creation of a training centre specialising in furniture design and production technologies. These policies have helped the industry to modernise, to improve its recruitment, to help a few of the firms to move up-market and, lastly, to enable some of the firms to specialise in particular fields and hence contribute to inter-firm co-operation.

However, as yet this strategy reaches only a few firms and competition is bound to grow tougher with the free trade agreements that will come into force by 1994, abolishing tariffs that currently stand at 15 per cent. At present, 88 per cent of exports of these products from Quebec are destined for the United States, whereas only 52 per cent of imports come from the United States, accounting for only 8 per cent of the Quebecois market. The district as a whole therefore still faces numerous difficulties.

---

15.   In the poll already cited (CIDEM), only 23 per cent of respondents were "wholly" or "mainly" in favour of such a body, with 22 per cent against and 55 per cent not answering!

Already, between 1985 and 1989, 30 per cent of the jobs in the industry were lost. Elsewhere in Quebec, however, this industry has managed to grow stronger, above all by reducing unit costs.

Here, too, long-term environmental monitoring remains quite inadequate. Marketing, design and distribution strategies to tackle consumer concentration are still ill-developed. Even available assistance from programmes such as the "Access-design" scheme is underused. Moreover, local institutions have been slow to address these issues, even though recently some encouraging efforts have been made.

VI. Conclusion

In view of current economic trends and the ability of districts to respond to the new international environment, the future development of districts, within the framework, for example, of the international division of labour, remains wholly questionable. Yet it is not the first storm that districts have had to weather, though perhaps this time the storm is more violent than before.

One thing appears certain: the districts will not be able to survive the storm on their own. They must get greater support from the State, and not merely of a short-term nature (start-up or "incubator" assistance, funding, enterprise creation) as before, but rather long-term economic aid. First of all, this support must involve the co-ordination of energies in both industry and the services, and also the creation of new information services to improve links between territorial organisations and extra-territorial and international networks of information.

With help from local government bodies, districts should promote the creation of broad networks comprising both production companies and service firms (distribution, creation, consultancy, information, etc.) as well as local institutions.[16] Such networks should provide further facilities for information monitoring and exchange within the district in order to promote an exchange of energies that would encourage the transfer of savings and investment, product innovation and organisation, new technologies and a highly specialised workforce that the district cannot itself train. The goal of this intervention is to create a "virtuous" circle of organisation/information/innovation. Put another way, districts, as they develop, with all their political, manufacturing and tertiary resources, need to behave as multinational companies both in terms of technological and commercial monitoring and of the renewal of internal resources. But they cannot

---

16.   On the role played by economic information networks, see, for example, Maillat and Perrin [1989] or Rothwell [1990].

undertake such long-term change on their own. They must be given support not only by local institutions but also by the territorial State.

This kind of change to the district's environment may mean its radical transformation, with the development, for example, of increasingly hierarchical relations between different enterprises. This may be the structural price for survival and continued development.

References

Acs, J.Z.; Audretsch, D.B. 1988. "Innovation in large and small firms: An empirical analysis", in *American Economic Review*, Sept., pp. 678-690.

Aydalot, P. (ed.). 1986. *Les milieux innovateurs en Europe*, Paris, GREMI.

Baptiste, F.; Michelsons, A. 1989. "Etude de cas de l'Alta Valdesa" in Ganne, B.: *Milieux industriels et systèmes industriels locaux*, Lyon, GLYSI, Université Lumière-Lyon II.

Bellandi, M. 1989. "Capacità innovativa diffusa e sistemi locali di imprese", in Becattini, G. (ed.): *Modelli locali di sviluppo*, Bologna, Il Mulino.

Brockhaus, R. 1986. "Entrepreneur: a psychological interpretation", Paper submitted to the Séminaire international sur l'entrepreneuriat, H.E.C., Montreal, 2-4 April.

Capecchi, V. et al. 1988. *La mobilità sociale in Emilia-Romagna*, Bologna, Il Mulino.

Chell, E. et al. 1989. "Competitive performance and the role of technical consultants in SMEs in the clothing industries", in Rosa, P. (Ed.): *The role and contribution of small business research*, Aldershot, Gower.

Chicha, J. 1982. *L'impact des certaines politiques horizontales sur les stratégies des PME*, Research report of GREPME, University of Quebec, Trois-Rivières.

Dosi, G. et al. 1988. *Technical change and economic theory*, London, Frances Pinter, p. 1121.

Emanuel, C. 1990. "Le polymorphisme des entreprises et du territoire: Une convergence possible des disciplines", in *Révue Internationale PME*, Vol. 2, Nos. 2/3, pp. 211-229.

Ganne, B. 1989. *Milieux industriels et systèmes industriels locaux*, Lyon, GLYSI, January.

Guesnier, B. 1984. "Développement local et micro-régional: Priorités à l'information", in *Révue canadienne d'économie régionale*, Vol. 7, No. 1.

Habermas, J. 1987. *Il discorso filosofico della modernità*, Laterza, Bari, cited by Vaggagini, [1989].

Intermunicipal Commission on Metropolitan Development. 1989. *La cité de la mode et le district de la fourrure*, Montreal, April.

Jacob, R. et al. 1989. "L'impact des nouvelles technologies de production sur l'emploi dans les centres hospitaliers", in *Administration hospitalière et sociale*, Vol. XXXV, No. 2, March-April.

Julien, P.A. 1990a. "La petite entreprise comme objet de recherche. Réflexion sur la renaissance des petites entreprises et ses effets sur la théorie économique", Paper submitted to ECT/GLYSI conference on "La PME comme objet de recherche", University Lumière-Lyon II, 30-31 May.

---. 1990b. "Le rythme de pénétration des nouvelles technologies de production dans les PME", in *Journal of Small Business and Entrepreneurship*, Vol. 2, No. 3.

Julien, P.A. et al. 1988. "Les facteurs de diffusion et de pénétration des nouvelles technologies dans les PME québécoises", in *Révue Internationale PME*, 1, 2, pp. 177-193.

Lefevbre, P.; Lefevbre, M. 1990. "Facteurs d'adoption des nouvelles technologies de production dans les PME manufacturières innovatrices", in *Révue Internationale PME*, Vol. 3, No. 1.

Lund, R.; Rasmussen, J. 1988. "New technology and social networks at the local and regional level", in Hyman, R.; Streek, W. (Eds.): *New technology and industrial relations*, Oxford, Basil Blackwell.

Maillat, D.; Perrin, J.C. 1989. *Innovation et territorialisation des entreprises*, Actes de la Table-Ronde du GREMI, Paris, Eresa-Economics.

Ministère de l'Expansion industrielle régionale (MEIR). 1988. *Profil de l'industrie canadienne de la construction des embarcations de plaisance*, Ottawa, January.

Planque, B. 1983. *Innovation et développement régional*, Paris, Economica.

Rothwell, R. 1990. "External networking and innovation in small and medium-sized manufacturing firms in Europe", Paper presented to conference on "Réseaux d'innovateurs", UQUAM-HEC, Montreal, 1-3 May.

Smeltzer, L.R. et al. 1988. "Environmental scanning practices in small business", in *Journal of Small Business Management*, Vol. 26, No. 3, pp. 55-62.

Tinacci Mossello, M.; Dini, F. 1990. "Innovation et communication sociale dans les districts industriels", in *Révue Internationale PME*, Vol. 2, No. 2/3.

Theil, H. 1969. *Information Economic*, Amsterdam, North Holland.

Thurow, L.C. 1987. "A weakness in process technology", in *Science*, No. 238, December, pp. 1659-1663.

Trigilia, C. 1986. *Grandi partiti e piccole imprese*, Bologna, Il Mulino.

Vaggagini, V. 1989. "Quatre paradigmes sur le district industriel", in *Révue Internationale PME*, Vol. 2, No. 2/3, pp. 253-273.

Zanka, D. 1990. *La veille technologique dans les PME manufacturières*, Research Report, GREPME, University of Quebec, Trois-Rivières.

Appendix 1

Inter-firm relations in the Centre de La Mauricie
pleasure craft industry

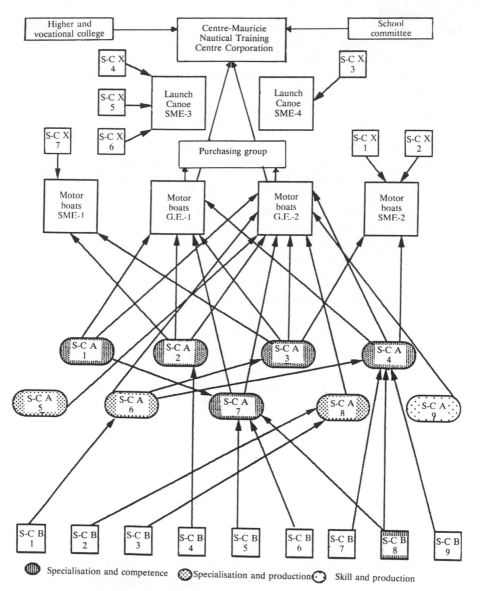

Source: Dumas, A. 1990. *Les relations de sous-traitance dans le secteur des embarcations de plaisance du centre de la Mauricie*, Doctoral thesis, Université du Québec à Trois-Revières, January.

Key to figure opposite

S-C = Sub-contractor

S-C A - 1: blown urethane
S-C A - 2: tanks
S-C A - 3: support bars
S-C A - 4: instrument panels and equipment
S-C A - 5: plexiglass window
S-C A - 6: fuse plates, strap hinges
S-C A - 7: instrument panels and equipment
S-C A - 8: fibre glass components
S-C A - 9: cabinet-work

S-C B - 1: welding
S-C B - 2: wood-cutting
S-C B - 3: strap hinges
S-C B - 4: accessory assembly
S-C B - 5: printing on instrument panel
S-C B - 6: machining
S-C B - 7: printed circuit base
S-C B - 8: printing on instrument panel
S-C B - 9: plastic box drilling

S-C X - 1: hook and rudder machining
S-C X - 2: canoe canvas
S-C X - 3: not yet decided
S-C X - 4: portage bars
S-C X - 5: padding work
S-C X - 6: launch pincers
S-C X - 7: cabinet work

Appendix 2

Diagram of the fur industry in Montreal

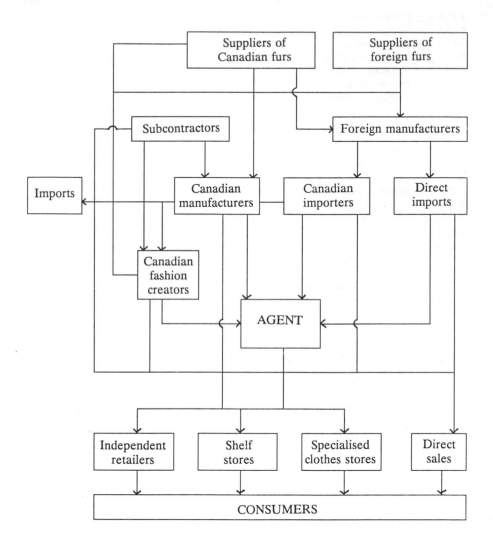

Source: Price Waterhouse, *Etude sur l'industrie de la mode de la fourrure*, CIDEM, April 1989

8   Studied trust: Building new forms of co-operation in a volatile economy

Charles F. Sabel

I.   Trust in a volatile economy

Trust, the mutual confidence that no party to an exchange will exploit the other's vulnerability, is today widely regarded as a precondition for competitive success. As markets become more volatile and fragmented, technological change more rapid, and product life cycles correspondingly shorter, it is too costly and time-consuming to perfect the design of new products and translate those designs into simply executed steps. Those formerly charged with the execution of plans - technicians, blue-collar workers, outside suppliers - must now elaborate indicative instructions, transforming the final design in the very act of executing it. But in a world of half-formed plans to collaborate in the production of highly specialised goods or services, any party can hold up the others - most ruthlessly by simply enticing a collaborator into dedicating resources to a joint project, and then refusing to dedicate the necessary complementary resources until the terms of trade are renegotiated in its favour. If trust is absent, no-one will risk moving first, and all will sacrifice the gains of co-operation to the safe, if less remunerative, autonomous pursuit of self-interest.

But it is frequently noted in practice and concluded in theory that collective appreciation of this dilemma does not resolve it. Indeed, the burden of experience and reflection is that trust can be found, but never created. In declining or threatened economic areas, for example, firm owners and trade union officials very often agree that labour and capital would both benefit if firms co-operated more with one another and with labour, yet despair of ever doing so. In each case, the outsider is given to understand, "our" industry has developed an unalterable tradition of universal suspicion. This tradition, exacerbated by the struggle to survive in hard times, precludes the co-operation necessary to reverse developments. In those areas which do prosper because of the collaboration which trust makes possible, on the other hand, these same actors regard their mutual confidence as a natural fact, as much an expression of their way of life as their language, and no less resistant to political direction. Here I am thinking in particular of the many small and medium-sized firm industrial districts in Western Europe and Japan. Each tells a different story of how trust became, for it, a fact of life; and the only common feature of these stories is that none could be reproduced elsewhere precisely because each depended on an improbable chain of fortuitous local circumstances.[1]

This fatalism is echoed, and subtly if indirectly reinforced, by disheartening theoretical conclusions. The theoretical arguments ring the changes on the hold-up theme. If there is a sufficiently high probability of a sufficiently costly breach of trust in the last of many exchanges, the argument runs, each economic agent will want to cease dealing at the last-but-one exchange. Repeated application of this logic of backward induction leads the parties to refrain from all exchanges, and thereby excludes experiences which might dispose them to be more trusting and trustworthy.[2]

From this perspective, co-operation is likely in two contrary and unusual circumstances. First, when the exchanges are many and the gains from future dealings highly valued in relation to current ones, then it can well be more advantageous to risk betrayal in the end than to forego the profits to be made in the meantime. Second, for reasons rooted in a common history - belief in the same god, dedication to the same political ends, or a common ethnic or cultural heritage - the parties may come to see themselves as members of a community of fate whose implicit (and sometimes explicit) conditions of membership exclude exploitation of the economic vulnerabilities of their fellows.

Neither circumstance, of course, justifies the hope that trust can be created where it is needed. In the first case, in fact, it would be wrong to

---

1.   For a good discussion of one such origin myth, see the analysis by Saglio [1991] of local accounts of the introduction of the injection moulding industry in Oyonnax, a town north-east of Lyons in France.

2.   In recent years, this line of reasoning has been challenged in two ways. One approach casts doubt on the validity of backward induction. According to this argument, the results of backward induction are dubious because they rely on conclusions drawn from situations which, following the repeated application of this very logic, could never have occurred. A paradox will illustrate the difficulty. Assume that a prisoner on death row is told on a Monday that he or she will be taken, by surprise, from the cell and executed before the next weekend. Plainly, the execution cannot take place on Friday because it would not be a surprise. Further backward induction suggests the comforting conclusion that the execution cannot be accomplished under the stipulated conditions at all. Thus fortified, the prisoner passes a tranquil week, only to be taken on Friday, very much surprised, to the place of execution.

The second approach seeks to demonstrate that doubts about the other's reliability (or doubts about the doubts) can encourage rather than obstruct co-operation. The claim here is that under certain assumptions about the cumulative value of the series of exchanges, it may be in each party's interest to dupe the other into thinking that he or she is a dupe by complying with the terms of the agreement. The result of the simulated honesty is outward co-operation. The question, from the point of view of the argument developed in this chapter, is whether the parties' reflection on the divergence between their motives and their actions causes them to reconceptualise their ideas of co-operation and trust and the relation between them. See, for these arguments, Dupuy [n.d.]. A good introduction to game-theoretic efforts to find the origins of binding relations in repeated exchanges is found in Kreps [1990].

associate co-operation with trust at all, because co-operation results from continuous calculation of self-interest rather than a mutually recognised suspension, however circumscribed, of such calculation. Here it would surely be more accurate to speak of a *modus vivendi* than trust.[3] In the second case, trust is a by-product of events which, to the extent they are planned at all, did not have the creation of trust as their goal. Seen this way, trust is one of those states, like drowsiness, spontaneity, or - archetypically - having no thoughts, which cannot be produced directly by willing them, and hence at first blush are inaccessible to individual or collective acts of volition. Surely, in this view, it is as self-defeating to try to cease continuous calculation of economic advantage because of the (calculating) conviction that it would be beneficial to do so as to concentrate on the thought of thinking nothing.[4]

The dominant theories of the role of politics and the state, moreover, reinforce these conclusions. These theories assume that politics sets the rules for and mediates the conflicts among groups in civil society with distinct interests. But those interests are as they are, and the state would overburden its rule-making and mediating capabilities, as well as abuse the citizens' mandate, were it to attempt to alter the definition of those interests - for example by encouraging the creation of trust relations. The success of mercantile states which do arguably reshape interests to meet new circumstances is regarded as just as anomalous as the existence of real trust among firms and explained the same way: by reference to a community of fate whose very definition includes the subordination of particular to general interests.[5] The expression "Japan Inc." expresses the bewilderment, anger, and envy of a world which recognises the apparently inimitable efficacy of the (alleged) historical fusion of a collective national identity and particular economic ambitions.

These observations lead naturally to a paralysing acceptance of history as destiny. Those rare clusters of firms or national economies in which trust is second nature will reap the benefits of their loyal dispositions in a world in which loyalty increasingly pays. Those who reasonably protect their self-interest will actually short-change themselves. Politics will spontaneously abet the co-ordination of the former and self-destructive defensiveness of the latter. Those firms and policies which cannot bear the burden of this passivity will, like wavering Puritans, make fitful efforts at co-operation, hoping that they will find themselves among the elect, but knowing that many are called, but few are chosen.

---

3. For a recent general statement of the distinction between calculating co-operation and co-operation framed by a moral order, see Rawls [1985, esp. p. 247].

4. Jon Elster has written extensively on such paradoxes. See, for example, Elster [1983, pp. 43-52].

5. For a nuanced discussion of the role of culture in Japan's economic success, see Dore [1986, pp. 244-252].

This pessimism is, I think, unwarranted. In what follows I will first argue that the theoretical views discussed so far mischaracterise human nature and, as a correlate, the malleability of trust. I know that many are sceptical of these theories and can readily cite one counter-example or another. I address the theories none the less because I believe that in times of crisis even many of the sceptics act on deep intuitions still shaped by the very ideas they dispute.

To escape their grasp, it is necessary to replace them with an alternative conception. The starting point for this alternative, I argue, is the idea that trust is a precondition of social life (Section II). Hence, the proper question is not how trust can be created from mistrust, but how and whether particular persons or relations come to be seen as trustworthy. I claim further that the extension of trust in any particular setting depends in part on the actors' reinterpreting their collective past, and especially their conflicts, in such a way that trusting co-operation comes to seem a natural feature, at once accidental and ineluctable, of their common heritage (Section III).

But if these two claims are sustained, the *prima facia* case for the futility of creating trust collapses, and it is no longer reasonable to dismiss as futile efforts by economic agents and public officials to improve economic performance in mistrustful environments. Thus, in the bulk of the essay (Section IV), I take up the case of current and arguably successful efforts to revitalise segments of the garment, foundry, injection-moulding and machine-tool industries in certain areas of the Commonwealth of Pennsylvania. The argument here is that the outcome depends on just the sort of redefinition of the actors' identity which the actors and many observers regarded - and may still in the abstract continue to regard - as contrary to the nature of economic exchange and political mediation. My aim is to show by this example how a new understanding of trust can lead to a new understanding of the role of government in economic development. A brief conclusion (Section V) reaffirms the central theme of the essay while cautioning against making too much of those arguable successes.

II.   Negotiated loyalty

Given what has already been said, the heading of this part is an oxymoron, because parties to a negotiation do not spontaneously share the very standards of fairness in all circumstances which the notion of loyalty supposes. None the less, I want to argue that oxymorons express the practical truth that the line between trust and mistrust is much more blurred and easier to cross than our theories suggest. This practical truth finds partial expression in such ambiguous phrases as "blind trust" and "undying loyalty", which frequently suggest abdication of responsible judgement, rather than a respect for duty. We (particularly "we" in the Anglo-American world) often fail to register this disjuncture between our idea of trust and our practice of it because of deep-seated ideas of personhood and human motivation. It is to these, their defects, and a communitarian understanding of individuality as an alternative to them that I now turn.

The notions of trust discussed so far rest on two complementary and widespread views of human nature. The first is the idea, familiar from neo-classical economics and rational-choice social theory, that individuals act to maximise satisfaction of their current desires, where these desires are given as the results of an unexplained and theoretically irrelevant process of individual development. Where this is so, co-operation is the result of an accidental complementarity of maximising strategies, and its culmination can only be a *modus vivendi* and never trust. The second is that, under rare circumstances, notably those associated with archaic or pre-modern societies, or modern communities which have retained key features of these latter, many persons have compatible preferences. Hence, they have compatible motives, know that they do, know that they know they do, and know that in their simple worlds the cost of obtaining all this knowledge and verifying its implications is not prohibitive. Consequently, they trust one another. On this view, a miss is again as good as a mile, because anything short of a synchronisation of preferences and motives so perfect as to be self-evident (and thus easily assimilated to the preconditions of collective life) sets in motion the backward inductions that transform the second case into the first.[6]

To this view of personhood and human nature I want to counterpoise a lawyer's list of alternatives, all of which blur the distinction between trust and mistrust and suggest passages from one to the other in ways that I shall spell out in a moment. By a lawyer's list, I mean a catalogue of arguments which could be simultaneously true, although it is unlikely that they are, and any one of which, if true, would discredit the claim to which all are opposed. A familiar American illustration would be the lawyer who defends a client accused of stealing a bucket by arguing that the accuser is not the rightful owner, that the bucket was in any case borrowed with his or her consent, worthless because it leaked, and returned in improved condition. I prefer this form of criticism of the liberal or neo-classical view to exposition of a single alternative for two reasons. First, those readers who already have doubts about the liberal picture are likely to have different reasons for doing so; and within the wide limits of the catalogue I am about to supply it is immaterial to the subsequent argument which these are. Following Rawls' principle of avoidance [Rawls, 1985, p. 231], I do not want to pick any fights to whose outcome I am for present purposes indifferent. Second, the variety

---

6.   For discussions of the fragility of trust-like relations from the point of view of methodological individualism by writers who adopt the point of view but are disconcerted by its implications, see Williams [1988, pp. 3-13]; and Elster [1990] concludes: "Why ... are we not in a state of nature? There is no general answer to this question. Altruism, codes of honour, and long-term self-interest all enter into the explanation. What seems clear is that self-interest cannot be the whole story." [p. 51].

of alternatives may itself sow some doubt where none currently exists, although after more than a century of explicit and inconclusive debate on these matters, I am aware that this seed takes root only under extraordinary and unpredictable circumstances. For ease of exposition, I will initially draw a crude distinction between criticisms that have grown out of sociological theories whose suppositions are antithetic to the methodological individualism of liberalism, and views which have emerged as the result of liberalism's own critical self-examination. This distinction carries less and less weight in current debate, and ideas from one source are more and more often combined with those from the other. Subsequently, I will treat conclusions drawn from both sometimes as complementary, sometimes as equivalent formulations.

The core of the sociological view of personhood is simply the idea that persons are constituted or can constitute themselves only in society. Individuality can only be expressed and appreciated as individual application of a complex body of common norms which define a shared universe of meaning and expectations: a community. Because it supposes this community, the only spontaneity there is, is co-ordinated; the only originality collectivised. Just as acquisition of a style or even creation of a new one (which, after all, only changes some of the prior constraints) simultaneously subordinates the artist to a common culture and enables expression of his or her otherwise ineffable individuality, so specialisation requires individuals to define themselves by means that in many ways reinforce the common culture within which and by whose lights they seek distinction.[7]

Notice, however, that this view does not require that all beliefs be completely shared or all behaviour harmonious or even pacific. Individuals in this world define their individuality, and their place in the social ranking of honour, in part by struggling to outdo one another in doing just what ought to be done in their society: for example, by giving magnificent gifts or accumulating vast wealth. In part and relatedly they achieve the same ends by struggling for social validation of practices once viewed as discrediting variations of orthodox ways. In either case, the community can be shaken by the conflicts which ultimately honour it. But even if it is shaken to pieces, individuals will maintain the same relationships with the fragments as they did with the whole, and nothing about the constitution of individuality will have changed.

In this perspective, of course, trust in the sense of shared expectations (and confidence that the expectations are and will continue to be shared) is the constitutive fact of social life. What needs to be explained here is how the boundaries of a particular community are drawn or, collaterally, how mistrust arises. One way would be as the result of disputes that begin as disagreements (prompted, say, by the struggle for honour) over the interpretations of common norms, and end as the articulation of

---

7.   An elegant development of this view appears in Bourdieu [1977].

irreconcilable views of the world. Another would be as the result of the clashes of different cultural worlds which were, so to speak, irreconcilable from the first. But whatever the answer to this question, so long as social life is possible, the realm of trusting behaviour can always in principle be enlarged by extending to new realms the shared understandings which make sociability possible in the first place. The contentious interpretations can be reinterpreted to re-establish consensus; two alien cultures can discover - each in its own way but prompted and provoked by the other - the grounds for a common self-definition. Put another way, every *modus vivendi* can be made a trust relation simply by assimilating it to the kinds of exchanges regarded as just by the common culture - a culture whose very existence is denied in the liberal characterisation of the modern world.

There are, moreover, variants of this view which connect the social constitution of individuality to specific spheres of social life, and in the spirit of lawyerly listing I mention two of these. One is the idea, central to certain strands of Marxism, that work is the collective activity - the artistry of material survival - which simultaneously subordinates the individual or groups of individuals to common constraints, yet thereby provides the material means for self-development upon which the emancipation of humankind from these and subsequent constraints depends.[8] Another is the notion, central to much of late twentieth-century philosophy, that we constitute ourselves and our humanity by trying to make ourselves intelligible and understanding others' efforts to do the same: in short, by speech acts. With all its ambiguities and lacunae constantly revealed by application in social situations (whose central issue is precisely the struggle to impose or agree on meanings), language here becomes the medium of socialisation and individuation.

Because language is so imperfect, and mutual intelligibility so dependent on hard-fought collaboration, shared understandings and hence trust are always extensible in this view, too. Unless individuals constantly assumed that others, like themselves, were seeking common meanings - the assumption which Donald Davidson calls the "act of charity" necessary and sufficient to produce mutual intelligibility - there could be no communication at all.[9] But these same acts of charity constantly create (without necessarily realising) the possibility for the substantive agreements which are the foundations of trust. A world in which all know that no-one can think his or her own thoughts without conversing with the others is a world which is constantly reminded how much it has to lose from the selfish exploitation of ambiguity. In this world it is literally impossible to discuss how trust is

---

8.   The fullest treatment is in Lukács [1984-86].

9.   Donald Davidson, "On the very idea of a conceptual scheme", Presidential address delivered to the Seventieth Annual Eastern Meeting of the American Philosophical Association, Atlanta, 28 December 1973, and reprinted in Rajchman and West [1985, pp. 129-144].

possible, because if trust as the willingness to make mutually intelligible sense of the ambiguous were not a primitive characteristic of human nature, it would not be possible to talk about anything at all. Rather, the question here, too, is how boundaries between communities are formed, and under what conditions they may be revised.

Conclusions that overlap these can be reached through criticism of liberalism's core idea. The characteristic claim of this critique is that the notion of an individual maximising satisfaction of an arbitrary bundle of current desires simply cannot capture crucial aspects of our intuitions of what it is to be a person, especially our capacity for prudential action and even our capacity to understand and draw moral conclusions from what it means to be a person.

Take first the problem of prudence.[10] To act prudently is to do something for which there is no current motivation, but which one will have want to have done at some time in the future. But unless the notion of current desires is implausibly stretched to include the desire to do things that one would regret not having done in the future, it is unclear why the desires of my future self should influence my current behaviour at all. Indeed, why should I care for the satisfaction of the bundle of desires which by accident will define my future self any more than the satisfaction of the desires which define any one of my immediate contemporaries? If persons are capable of, and in part defined by, the capacity for prudential action, as I take them to be, then they must have a view of their personalities as extended in time. Because of this extension, present desires lose their absolute motivational priority; and now is a particular time, one among many in the life of a being aware of its continuous existence, and not the locus where identity forms.

An analogous argument connects the ability to grasp others as persons - and hence to achieve some conception of personality which is not an extrapolation of one's own unique experiences - with the need to view the self as one among many: a someone. To understand someone else as a person, it is necessary to fix what they have in common with you. But to do that, it is necessary to ask how the other, posing the same question, would view you. Thus, to imagine someone else as a person, it is necessary to view oneself impersonally as a someone. Just as the capacity for prudential action supposes the existence of a personality that encompasses the present in an extended lifetime, so the capacity to grasp the very idea of a person supposes a personality which can understand itself as one self among many. And by demonstrating that the self is not hostage to its own selfish present, and indeed by its very nature entertains thoughts about what would be good for persons (of which it is one) in general or itself in the future, this criticism of liberalism creates the preconditions for a psychology or even metaphysics of the person in which the question, What would happen if everyone did *that*?, can always be asked, and hence trust is always an arguable proposition.

---

10.   The argument here follows Nagel [1970, esp. pp. 33-76].

These critical arguments directly suggest the common theme of all the entries in my lawyer's list of objections to the neo-classical picture of the person and the pessimism about the possibility of trust which follows from it. The theme is that the self is always a virtual or reflexive self. Its defining capacity is the ability to choose through reflection which possible self will actually motivate action. The choices express and elaborate a personal identity which is shaped by consideration of the future and other, and which can in principle be increasingly shaped by them. Writers in the tradition of self-critical liberalism will refer to this self creation as the ordering of preference orderings, or, as Sen puts it, "rankings of rankings" [Sen, 1979, pp. 317-344]. Writers in the sociological tradition may prefer to speak of self-creation hermeneutically, as the definition of an individual personality through the struggle to make sense of one's self in relation to one's own (constantly redefined) community of shared but ambiguous norms.

Either way we have a conception of personality, and by extension community, which escapes the liberal's dismaying oscillation between a conception of the self and the group which can perceive the benefits of trust but cannot act to obtain them (because of a paralysing belief that present preferences inevitably rule), and a conception of the self and the group which benefit from trust, but cannot conceive how others might similarly benefit (because, as an accident of history, they share values whose commonality is taken to be irreproducibly accidental). The reflexive self, which on this account is the one we actually have, can entertain and act on the idea of creating or extending common values regarding loyalty and forbearance in the face of vulnerability precisely because it knows that other selves can entertain and act on the same idea. Whether and under what conditions such a change is likely to occur is an empirical question, whose answer depends, among other things, on the prevailing economic conditions and their history, as well as the agents' skill in reinterpreting these. The crucial point is that there is in this view nothing mysterious, in principle, about the creation of trust in economic affairs. Mutual dependence is the precondition of both individuality and sociability, and it is in some sense known to be such. What precise bearing this mutual dependence has for economic exchanges is another open question, to which one might expect a wide range of answers, depending on circumstances. The answer one would *not* expect is precisely the one liberalism, in the sense intended here, has taught us to count on: that by our nature we cannot discuss the question as though the discussion could be consequential.

Notice, finally, that from this viewpoint trust in economic affairs becomes much less of an all or nothing psychological gamble on the reliability and verifiability of guesses about the harmony of our motives and those of others. A community of reflexive selves is by definition both prudent and other-regarding. It can imagine a trusting world and imagine others imagining the same. It can also devise stratagems for testing and encouraging these beliefs. These stratagems, moreover, will appear to be part of the continuous and inevitable process of individual and collective self definition in a mutually dependent world, rather than leaps of faith hedged by various fall-back strategies.

Seen this way, trust is both a thick and thin human relation. It is thick in that each party must suppose, as I have argued that they should, that the others have at least an intuitive understanding of what it means to make oneself vulnerable to others and are capable - because there is no other choice - of sometimes doing so. But it is thin in that it supposes that each party might decide after due and prudential deliberation, and well understanding the gravity of the act, to put its trust elsewhere. Trust in this sense is like a constitutional, democratic compact which requires of the parties only that they agree to resolve disputes in ways which do not violate their autonomy, and roots this agreement in the citizens' recognition of the connection between the assertion of one's own autonomy and respect for that of the others'.[11]

In such a world, loyalty could be negotiated and trust vigilant without fomenting disloyalty and mistrust precisely because the elaboration of norms of collective behaviour as a concomitant and precondition of the elaboration of one's own or group personality is exactly what the exercise of autonomy is all about. Blind trust and undying loyalty are here regarded as deformations, at once admirable and deplorable, because they bespeak a suspicious renunciation of the self's or the group's powers of self creation. By the same token, it would be possible for individuals and groups to outwit themselves and achieve, by indirect means, changes which could neither be willed directly nor made accessible to a single act of collective volition.

This view of trust relations as makeable and breakable because more "political" or "prudential" than commonly thought is corroborated by both ethnographic accounts of trust-based dealings and the sociology of organisations. Dore's account of subcontracting relations in the Japanese textile industry and Lorenz's account of subcontracting among metal-working firms in Lyons both emphasise that trust obligates partners to behave loyally in the present, but does not obligate them to refrain from asking - out loud - whether and under what conditions they should continue to do so in the future. Nor is it regarded as a breach of trust to make provisions - for example, by recourse to a second supplier - for the possibility that trust could be breached. Conversely, the absence of trust does not prohibit joint discussion of the conditions under which it might exist. No wonder, then, that Lorenz characterises the partners' views of each other by exclusion: vendor and customer are "neither friends nor strangers" for one another [Dore, 1983, pp. 459-482; Lorenz, 1988, pp. 194-210].

The sociology of organisations emphasises the ways in which elements of systems not built on trust can be used to construct ones which are, and hence, by extension, the surprising facility with which an organisation of one type can pass from one side of an apparently

---

11.   See, for the conditions of such a compact, Rawls [1985].

unbreachable barrier to another. Stinchcombe, for example, demonstrates in his study of the Norwegian oil-drilling industry how contracts - the symbol and instrument of market relations - can be used to construct complex dispute-resolution regimes of the kind usually associated with communities of (trusting) firms. He argues as well that trust relations can emerge from a series of exchanges whose initial intent was the achievement of short-term advantage [Stinchcombe, 1985, pp. 121-171]. Eccles and Bradach extend the argument by showing how elements of the market system such as prices can be used to facilitate non-market exchanges precisely by setting standards and thus removing potential sources of dispute which might threaten the latter [Bradach and Eccles, 1989, pp. 97-118].

In sum, the more one looks, the harder it becomes to draw a clear line between states of mind or kinds of organisations which are trusting or mistrustful. But if that is so, why do the agents themselves seem so sure that such lines can be drawn? In the next section, therefore, I want to return to the broad-brush characterisation of the agent's view of trust to see whether on closer examination their experience does not lend support to the views arrived at here.

III. Reconciliation and genesis amnesia: The politics of trust

The views of economic agents, it seems, tend to confirm neo-classical expectations on two central points: those who suffer the costs of mistrust can imagine the benefits of trust, but despair of obtaining them given the motivations of persons such as themselves; those who profit from trust think it an historical accident that they and the (few) others in similar situations do so. In this part, I want to focus on this second perception, although I will touch at the end briefly on the first before discussing it at length in connection with the analysis of the case of Pennsylvania.

In re-examining the reports of trust as historical good luck, I do not, of course, mean to challenge the existence of such reports or the good faith of those who repeat them. I myself have heard or read different variants of this tale, each emphasising the particularities of local circumstance, in at least a baker's dozen industrial districts in Italy, West Germany, Austria, France and Denmark. For what it is worth, all strike me as sincere and guileless in the sense of concentrating on themes and events which everyone in a particular locale regards as important to their collective self-definition. Indeed, once you have come across one of these stories about how misery in a particular place was turned to prosperity through the co-operative exploitation of folk ingenuity galvanised by the genius of a few widely-travelled native sons (daughters in these tellings tend to stick to their knitting, quite literally; but that is another story), you can be sure of two things: so long as you keep the conversation on that plane, you will hear almost exactly the same story again and again; and what you hear will be different in many details - for instance, whether the setting is in the city or the country - from similar stories about similar places. But it is precisely these two regularities - that accounts of the same place are always the same and those of different places always different - which, I think, ought to arouse the suspicion that the story you are getting is not the whole story.

What is suspicious or at least curious about the similar stories is that they sound similar enough to have been if not reheared, then at least repeated with proverbial frequency. But rehearsed or repeated for whom, and why? Surely they do not circulate for the benefit of outsiders. As a rule, the stories themselves explain why the local society is different from, morally superior to (because capable of greater solidarity), and hence in some profound sense inaccessible to outsiders. On this point, the story does seem to be the whole story. There is nothing put on, so far as I can tell, in either the self-effacement or the pride contained in the remark periodically heard in the Italian metal-working district of Emilia-Romagna: "America is here!".

But why should the insiders, the members of the local society, tell themselves these homilies so often that they sound rehearsed? In the most austerely liberal account of psychology in these societies, everyone simply has the same or compatible motivations, and there is no need for anyone to advertise that fact. In less austere versions, there might be room for a little sociological folklore in which the common knowledge is ritually publicised to reassure everyone that their assumptions about shared expectations still hold. Even taking account of that possibility, however, it is hard to see why people who do rely on one another, and allegedly believe that it is a matter of (cheerfully accepted) historical inevitability that they do, spend so much time getting straight what they are all supposed to take for granted.

The obvious alternative explanation in the light of the preceding discussion of the reflexive construction of self and community turns the liberal account on its head. It is that the stories are articulated when persons or groups which once had incompatible stories agree on a common history which resolves or renders irrelevant those differences: the stories continue to circulate because they set bounds on subsequent disagreements. Instead of expressing a consensus, the stories in this view are part of the process of creating it: they create a past in which the prior conflicts resulted from mistakes and misunderstandings rather than fundamental differences, and suggest a future in which all subsequent conflicts will be limited in virtue of being defined in advance as family fights. Seen in this way, it is not us outsiders but themselves that the tellers of these stories aim to fool; and it is no fault but our own if their efforts to induce a kind of genesis amnesia in themselves lead us to believe that their history was actually without conflict.

A deliberately shocking example from the practices of the Ilongot headhunters of Northern Luzon in the Philippines will illustrate the process I have in mind. The Ilongot bear grudges, and bear them hard. Offences to certain classes of their kin produce in the young males of the society a resentful anger that can only be relieved by severing the head of someone appropriately related to the offender and hurling it joyously in the air. In this way, feuds start and ramify, with the result that in time the very survival of the society is jeopardised. When they believe things reach this point, the feuding groups meet and - here is the crucial point - try to reinterpret kin relations in such a way that the original offence need not have obligated a revenge killing, nor, because of the understandable error, the revenge killing a feud [Rosaldo, 1980]. If this sounds far-fetched as a description of a dispute resolution mechanism that might apply in any way to advanced industrial societies, consider how insistent formerly hostile nations are that, as an indispensible part of their reconciliation, the textbook history of their hostility be rewritten in a mutually recognisable way as a series of tragic misunderstandings. A nineteenth century example is the United States and Great Britain; twentieth century examples include France and West Germany, the United States and Japan, and currently Japan and China and South Korea. Letting bygones be bygones requires a collective act of self-redefinition, not simple forgetting.

But let me add, to avoid any suggestions that these mechanisms are self-activating, that nothing requires that bygones *be* bygones. If they always were, disputes would never proceed far enough for the issue to become explicit and there would never be cases, which there manifestly are, of mutually destructive conflicts. The point is merely that when social cohesion is threatened domestically or internationally, the parties generally know it, and that efforts to reinterpret the past or recreate a new collective identity are indispensable to resolution of the problem.

As I do not want to break stride to introduce the historical evidence that would buttress my argument about the creation of trust relations in particular economic settings, I will merely mention a few *prima facia* cases in favour of my interpretation and indicate several well-documented instances of the "discovery" of historical conflict in industrial districts that once did or do today tell stories about themselves which exclude such possibilities. The *prima facia* cases are the twentieth century experiences of countries like West Germany, Italy, Austria and Japan. All of these came to the brink of or actually fought civil wars in the 1920s or 1930s. Yet all today enjoy, reasonably, in the light of their economic performance, a reputation for putting to productive use a national culture of co-operation which is itself a source of national pride and identity. The power of current success to blind nationals and foreigners alike to the obvious fact that these "co-operative" cultures did not exclude the possibility of fratricide cannot be overestimated. I recall, for instance, once being told by a group of AFL-CIO trade union leaders that certain West German institutions of labour-management co-operation were unsuited to United States conditions because German employers could never think of doing to German unions what American managers did to organised labour here.

The historical "discoveries" I have in mind concern industrial districts such as the modern woollens centre at Prato, near Florence; the Sheffield cutlery industry which saw its heyday in the late nineteenth century; the centre of injection moulding in Oyonnax, near Lyons.[12]   One common feature of all these districts - and every other one of which I have knowledge - is a history of complex struggles between shifting alliances of merchant factors or converters, high-volume producers of semi-finished goods, artisans making highly differentiated finished products and working independently or in large factories, and less skilled workers employed directly or as nominally independent subcontractors by the independent artisans or the large firms. A second common feature is that whenever the parties to these conflicts regulate their disputes through arbitration boards or councils which police quality or set and monitor wage schedules, the districts flourish; when not, then not. The third common feature, and the reason "discoveries" is set in quotation marks, is that the preceding two are immediately obvious in historical retrospect, but almost completely invisible (because taken for granted and obscured by tales of a co-operative culture) to contemporaries so long as the districts are prospering. A visitor to Prato today, for example, will hear lots about how trade unions and employers' associations are working (as they apparently always have) to solve the problems of industrial adjustment, but nothing about the fact that for almost a decade after a wave of decentralisation in the late 1940s, the unions and manufacturers were unable to sign a single collective agreement.

This view that conflict and an almost mythologically extolled consensus co-exist in high-trust systems is, moreover, supported by the few ethnologically sophisticated studies of such systems in action. "Negotiated loyalty" is the title of an oral history of labour-management relations in a United States shoe firm in the 1920s [Zahavi, 1983, pp. 602-620]. In Dore's account of subcontracting by large Japanese firms, "co-operative pursuit of common goals" and "vigilant monitoring of the distribution of the costs and benefits of co-operation" are two sides of the same coin [Dore, 1989, p. 6]. Surely these characterisations evoke worlds that mistrust blind trust without being for all that mistrustful.

Consider next the diversity of (unique) stories about the history of particular districts. A few diverse histories supports the liberal assumption that trust is a rare accident. Many diverse histories, on the other hand, suggest that there are many paths that end in the creation of trust relations or, to connect the point to the earlier discussion of the reflexive self and community, that many groups of producers can reinterpret themselves and their history in such a way as to make trust the natural outcome of their common experiences. Whether there were few or many or - above all - an increasing number of industrial districts and other trust-based economic systems is, of course, a matter of considerable debate. To caricature the positions: those who see a large number of trust-based systems claim any instance of co-operation as a case of trust. Those who see a small number

---

12.   On Prato, see Trigilia [1989, pp. 283-333]; on Sheffield, see Lloyd [1913]; on Oyonnax, see Ravèyre and Saglio [1984, pp. 157-177], and Saglio [1991].

claim any instance of conflict as a proof that trust does not and cannot exist. From what was said before, it should be clear that this kind of exhaustive dichotomisation makes it impossible to say whether trust is present in a particular case or not. Co-operation that is not more or less institutionalised in a system which enlists public sanctions in the defence of shared values may be no more than a *modus vivendi*. But it should also be clear that conflicts can lead to the creation of trust and that they can persist, transmogrified and limited, even after the trust has been established. How many production systems have crossed or are crossing the *modus vivendi* threshold and institutionalising conflict in a way which does not obstruct flexibility I cannot say. But my strong suspicion, watching developments in Western Europe, Japan and the United States, is that the number is growing. If that turns out to be true, then the history of the contemporary period will treat the switch to high-trust systems much as history has treated the whole process of industrialisation beginning with Great Britain: apparently impossible for any country to do until it does it, and dependent on some short list of rare preconditions which is successively extended as new cohorts of nations or regions prove that it is in fact possible to industrialise under conditions different from those of their predecessors.

Finally, I return to the first of the two confirmatory reports of economic experience: the complaints of those in declining or threatened regions that they are incapable of the trust required. Again, it would be foolish to deny the prevalence of such complaints or impugn their sincerity. Taken at face value, they suggest that the agents themselves recognise the force of the theoretical conclusion that it is impossible to create trust by an act of will. And in this, the theoreticians and the actors may be right. But the interesting question, we saw, is not whether trust can be created at will. If the reflexive view of self and society is correct, then the real problem is how trust can be built in particular circumstances through a circuitous redefinition of collective values. In the next section I provide an example of one way this can be done by reporting on recent developments in the Commonwealth of Pennsylvania, a large industrial state just south of New York whose declining mass production industries and efforts at economic revitalisation mirror the dilemmas and possibilities of industrial America as a whole.

IV. Studied consensus: learning to co-operate in fragmented industries

This section tells a tale-within-a-tale about the revitalisation of the foundry industry near Pittsburgh in the south-west part of the state, plastics firms in the north-west on the Lake Erie shore, apparel firms in the Lehigh Valley in the north-east, and four scattered clusters of tool-and-die firms.

The larger narrative concerns the reorientation of economic development policy both nationally and in Pennsylvania. In the last 15 years, that policy has shifted from a strategy aimed at providing individual firms with the services needed to increase their innovative capacity to one aimed at helping the actors in particular industries and locales - firms, trade associations, trade unions, educational institutions, and local governments - define collectively which services they need severally and collectively. Put in a way which resonates with the language of the preceding discussion, the consensus is drifting from the view that individual actors know their interests, and that government's role is to remove obstacles to realising them, to the view that it is only by recognising their mutual dependence that the actors can define their distinct interests, and that government's role is to encourage the recognition of a collectivity and the definition of particularity.

The smaller, interior story, and the one on which I concentrate, concerns this two-fold process of identity formation. The aim here is to show how, in coming to a common, and generally surprising view of an economic situation which each thought it had understood fully, mutually suspicious groups can redefine their relations and (prudently) begin to construct communities of interest - yet another practicable oxymoron - where none had seemed possible. These beginnings are no more than that and I will underscore their fragility later. They are none the less worth discussing because they have already gone beyond the limits of what the conventional liberal view of the wellsprings of co-operation suggest is probable; and should they in fact revitalise their respective local industries, the projects will have demonstrated that it is possible to create vigilant trust in settings - declining industries in the heart of mass production, unrepentantly individualistic America - where theory and practice would rule it out entirely. If economic community can be discovered in Erie or the Lehigh Valley or the environs of Pittsburgh, then it can certainly be discovered in many other places. Not least for this reason, as we shall see, those concerned with economic development in the United States are following developments in Pennsylvania with increasing attention.

In retrospect, of course, it is easy to trace the changing direction of economic development policy in the United States. For case of exposition, I will distinguish three successive models, although they in fact overlap and the seeds of the later ones are contained in the earlier experiences.[13]

By the second half of the 1970s, traditional mass production industries in the leading manufacturing states had come under increasing domestic and, particularly, foreign competition. As the federal government

---

13.   For a comprehensive survey of changes in economic development policy, particularly at the state level, and further description of the programmes and institutions referred to in the following account, see Osborne [1988]. A succinct presentation of recent developments is found in Herbers [1990, pp. 43-500]. Interpretations of the political appeal of the various policies, however, reflect my own discussions with administrators, legislators, managers, and trade unionists in the relevant states during the last five years.

proved less able and willing to cushion, much less reverse the changes, state governments were forced to articulate new strategies of economic development. To Republicans on the right and Democrats on the left, two points seemed clear. First, "smokestack chasing" - the use of tax incentives to attract branch plants of large, typically mass production corporations - did not work. Study after study showed that firms' locational decisions were rarely influenced by the universal (and hence self-defeating) offers of tax breaks; and when they were, the kinds of firms that were attracted by such means tended to close up shop at the first sign of economic trouble. Second, it was therefore necessary to foster the state's existing economy, particularly by encouraging the foundation and growth of firms in new industries such as computers, semi-conductors, or test equipment, where competition depended on the ability to innovate rather than reduce manufacturing costs. Both convictions seemed well-founded in the product-life-cycle theory of industrial development: the view that new products and industries are born in the most sophisticated and technologically advanced economies, and then diffuse to less advanced and lower cost settings as the products and production processes become standardised and hence easier to master and transfer. From this perspective, the only plausible strategy was to stop chasing smokestacks - the "mature" industries - and encourage the transition to the youthful, technologically dynamic ones.

The upshot was the first new strategy of growth, which might, for want of a generally accepted name, be called the development-bank model. Given the assumptions about the self-directing powers of the market and its close relation to technological development on which the product-life-cycle view rested, the problem for policy was simply to reduce the barriers to innovation for firms. These were seen to be of two kinds. One was access to capital: banks were very reluctant to accept new ideas as collateral for loans, and hence it was difficult to finance their translation into commercial products. The other was access to technology: somehow the ideas developed in university laboratories had to be brought within the reach of the economy. State-funded development banks in various guises could solve both problems. By providing grants or guaranteeing or matching private-sector loans to firms with innovative projects, the banks could address the capital problems. Use of similar instruments would encourage joint industry-university research efforts in areas of benefit first to individual firms, but by extension to whole sectors of the state economy. Massachusetts, pushed by the decline of its textile and shoe industries and pulled by the prospect of distributing the treasure-trove of ideas accumulated (and in part already commercialised) at the Massachusetts Institute of Technology and Harvard, led the way. But it was followed in the early 1980s by Pennsylvania, which created the Ben Franklin Partnership (BFP) to fund joint research and development projects, and Michigan, which passed legislation allowing a portion of the state employees' pension funds to be invested in uncollateralised ventures. The idea was attractive because, beyond its resonance with deep-seated conceptions of economic growth, it promised a lot for a little and appealed to a wide spectrum of political interests. As was widely noted, the development banks affected the economy beyond their immediate radius of action. By demonstrating the viability of certain kinds of investments, they drew private and semi-private capital such as pension funds into previously avoided areas, thereby vastly multiplying the effect of the state's own lending activity. For those on the free-market right of American politics, moreover, all this could be seen as a remedy for clearly limited market failures, and hence a way of reinforcing the broader appeal of a market economy. For those on the New Deal left, it could be seen as a form of French-style indicative planning or a publicly controlled variant of the co-ordination of private firms exercised through long-term loans by German universal banks. The ambiguity of these viewpoints and the coalitions they permitted recalls the Progressives' efforts to establish social welfare programmes in the United States in the first decades of this century by creating public insurance schemes which were meant to serve as both an alternative and a compelling model to private insurers.

By the mid-1980s, a second, extension-service model began to take root in the undergrowth of the first one. One cause was the discovery that even firms in the new, high-tech sectors of the economy needed a longer list of services than originally imagined. If access to capital and technology were problems, so, too, were access to managerial expertise in areas ranging from marketing to manufacturing, as well as training of technicians and workers. A second cause was the realisation that often, indeed typically, the solution to industry's problems lay not in abandoning current markets for new ones (the recommendation of the product-life-cycle theory), but rather in introducing high technologies into the products and production processes of the "mature" industries (the strategy in firms in such advanced economies as West Germany, Japan, Italy, Sweden, and Switzerland which were out-competing their United States counterparts). To do that as well, new services were needed, particularly for small- and medium-sized firms. Their modernisation was indispensable to the success of their larger clients because the reintegration of conception and execution requires increasing reliance on collaboration with sophisticated suppliers. But the latter had been so weakened by the crisis that they could not afford the necessary help. In the United States, the Agricultural Extension Service of the Department of Agriculture had successfully provided general consulting services to family farms since the Great Depression. It was therefore a convenient model - or, rather, analogy, as few agricultural institutions were actually transferred to the industrial sector - for state governments moving from the provision of resources which firms combined as they saw fit to the provision, through consulting services, of knowledge about how best to combine resources. The Technology Deployment Service in Michigan (later part of the Michigan Modernization Service), which serves primarily the automotive parts suppliers, the Co-operative Regional Industrial Laboratories in Massachusetts (now called Action Projects), which serve the Springfield machine-tool industry (Machine Tool Action Project, or MTAP) and the New Bedford-Fall

River garment industry (The Needle Trades Action Project, or NTAP), as well as the nine Industrial Resource Centers (IRCs) spread through Pennsylvania are all examples.

In this case, too, the model was in part palatable because it was consistent with politically divergent interpretations of its underlying motivations. For the right, the extension services could be seen as an elaboration of the preceding, market-perfecting activities: marginal interventions needed to make further, and consequential, state intervention unnecessary. For the left, the new activities could be seen as part of a comprehensive effort to reshape markets through politics: to establish, by new institutional means, new boundary conditions appropriate to the current conditions of competition, as the New Deal had done by the then appropriate use of regulatory agencies and the like.

Once again, however, a new model has begun to grow in the underbrush of the old. This third, incipient model of economic development, which I will provisionally call associative or co-operative, also has twin roots.[14] One is the discovery by those immediately involved with economic

---

14.   I call the new model, amorphously, "associative" or "co-operative" because characterisations with more definitions have misleading theoretical echoes. One candidate would be auto-poetic (literally: self-creating) or reflexive systems. These are systems in which the logic governing the development of each of the elements is constantly reshaped by the development of all the others: the parts reflect the whole and vice versa. It is easy to see affinities between this logic of reciprocal institutional influence and the kind of mutual adjustment of identities under discussion. The difficulty is that the idea of auto-poesis is typically embedded in theories of social evolution in which epochal institutional change is connected to increasing organisational complexity. Increased efficiency at first requires increased differentiation of spheres of activity and tasks within those spheres. Law becomes separated from religion and morality; agriculture becomes distinct from industry, and production within each is decomposed into more and more specialised operations. As society becomes still more complex, however, the costs of specialisation exceed the gains. The solution is de-differentiation, the costless, automatic, and - above all - self-adjusting form of co-ordination called auto-poesis or institutional reflexivity. One general problem with this view is that there is no convincing metric of social complexity, and without one it is impossible to make sense of, let alone evaluate, the theory's evolutionary core. A more particular historical difficulty, which corroborates the first one, concerns the role of auto-poesis in American constitutional thought. As suggested above, Jaffe's idea of law-making by private groups can be interpreted as an argument for the legalisation of reflexive institutions. That the collective bargaining institutions built in part on the basis of those ideas did not prove adaptive or self-reforming shows either that the ideas did not capture the essence of auto-poesis, or - more plausibly - that the auto-poetic character of institutions is always limited by the historical circumstances under which they come into being. If the latter, then strictly speaking, there can be no unqualifiedly auto-poetic institutions at all. In any case, given the New Deal precedents, it would be necessary in the United States to speak of neo-auto-poesis - a word which is hard to mouth even as a neo-logism and harder to swallow as a concept. For an exemplary formulation of the auto-poetic view of the development of law and state structures, see Teubner [1983, pp. 239-285].

A second way to characterise the new development model would be as neo-corporatist. In the late 1970s and early 1980s, neo-corporatism referred to a system of interest representation in which the national state and the peak organisations of labour and capital

development that what makes the successful extension services and development banks work is that their operation creates more or less informal networks of business persons, trade unionists, local government officials, bankers and educators who together discover ways to bring resources to bear efficiently to the problems at hand. These resources include, but are hardly limited to, those provided by the state or local authority. Indeed, the original programme, redefined to serve ends only distantly connected to the intent of its originators, often comes to play a subordinate part in a package of resources which could not have assembled without the efforts of the network - whose own formation would in turn have been unlikely but for authorisation of the now marginal programme. Thus, programmes such as the Springfield machine-tool project worked only at one remove, and for reasons not anticipated at the time of their conception.[15] The second root was the growing realisation that the systems of West German, Italian, or Swedish firms whose success had played an important role in casting doubt on the product-life-cycle theory and in suggesting the plausibility of the extension-service model, themselves depended on (often highly formalised) networks of a similar type [Katzenstein, 1985].

In short, the more carefully United States observers studied domestic or foreign industrial structures well adapted to current economic conditions, the clearer it became that what mattered was the social system by which packages of programmes were defined and administered, rather than the precise definition of any single programme or service. But if that were so, then instead of trying to define programmes directly - extend the extension services - state government should try to design programmes which encourage the actors to define their own needs. In so far as the definition of needs depends on the creation of certain types of local co-operative networks, this means programmes which encourage the creation of the appropriate forms of co-operation among the actors in particular industries in particular locales.

One of the first, and certainly the most comprehensive programmes of this sort, or at least to learn how to create one, is the Manufacturing

---

established policies which ideally minimised inflation and unemployment, and maximised growth. Since then, national economic performance has come to depend less on national, macroeconomic policy, however co-ordinated, and more on co-operation at the plant, regional, and sectoral levels, as suggested above. Neo-corporatism has been accordingly qualified and extended to include micro(-neo)-corporatism, meaning plant-level co-operation, amd meso(-neo)-corporatism, meaning regional or sectoral co-operation. But if the concept is thus extended to cover any form of economically advantageous co-operation, or even any institutionally mediated form of such co-operation, why not speak directly of co-operative or associative institutions? Better a place-holder that reveals the outline of the terminological gap clearly than a stop-gap term with blurry contours. For an extensive treatment of neo-corporatism as the system of pre-contractual institutions that makes possible not only contingent claims contracting but "production coalitions" between labour and management of, presumably, any kind, see Streeck [1987, pp. 241-246, esp. p. 244]. A more nuanced statement of this view is given in Streeck [1990, pp. 105-145].

15.   Discussions in 1990-91 with Robert Forrant, director of MTAP.

Innovation Networks (MAIN) project announced by the Commonwealth of Pennsylvania in the spring of 1989.[16] The programme's sponsors, all in their 30s and early 40s, held responsible staff or line positions in the Commonwealth's Departments of Labour and Industry, or the Department of Commerce, or worked directly for the governor. All had come of age in government in the late 1980s, just as ideas of economic development were changing most rapidly. One, Jacques Koppel, had helped found the Commonwealth's industrial-extension service, the IRCs. Another, Robert Coy, who was chiefly responsible for organising MAIN and currently directs the programme, had served as executive director of a committee to foster labour, management, and government co-operation on a range of state-wide economic development issues. All were familiar with the related efforts of other states, and Coy was particularly knowledgeable about the situation in Western Europe. All were aware of the shortcomings of discrete services, no matter how appropriately designed, and sensed the possibility of improving the performance of all the pieces of the already extensive economic development programme by integrating them first locally, and perhaps later at the state level as well. No-one, however, had a clear idea of how to do this, and the MAIN programme was in large measure an experiment to see whether, as current fashion had it, the actors themselves could play a decisive role in solving the problem.

The programme itself was straightforward and fiscally modest enough to be almost negligible. In the spring of 1989, the Commonwealth invited groups of firms in a particular locale and serving common markets to submit, together with trade associations, unions, and any relevant public entities, plans for assessing the strategic situation of their industry and the utility, if any, of more co-operative arrangements among themselves. Small- and medium-sized firms were to have preference for reasons having to do with the general shift in policy towards the weakest part of the traditional industrial base. But plans contemplating increased co-operation between large and small firms were also encouraged. The proposals also had to stipulate the membership of a steering committee, composed of representatives of all these groups, whose task would be to oversee administration of the project. The applications were due less than two months after the Commonwealth's Request for Proposals was announced, and the four submissions judged best by a committee of the programme's originators were to be funded for one year in amounts of not more than $100,000 [Departments of Commerce and Labor and Industry, 1989].

By giving the applicants little time, the Commonwealth could be sure that only industrial agglomerations already toying with the idea of new forms

---

16. The following is based on numerous meetings and telephone discussions with participants in the MAIN project. Here is the place to disclose that I have acted as a consultant to MAIN since its inception; in addition, I serve on the Strategic Investment Committee of the Ben Franklin Partnership, whose purpose is to review the performance of that institution and recommend ways of improving it.

of association would be likely to enter the competition. The kind of collective "strategic audit" (a consultants' term of art for an assessment of a firm's competitive possibilities) which the Request for Proposals called for would only seem worthwhile to assemblies of distinct groups which had begun to contemplate themselves as collectivities. By making the grants small, the Commonwealth insured that no group of firms already co-operating in the way envisioned would bother submitting a proposal: the effort was simply more trouble than it was worth for a going concern. By forcing the applicants to present a single steering committee of the "relevant" groups, the Commonwealth brought to the surface submerged conflicts which might have thwarted subsequent efforts had they remained hidden. In fact, in several cases, different groups claiming to represent the same industry in the same area did submit or consider submitting competing proposals. Only Coy's mediation composed the differences.

Given these constraints, then, it was no surprise that the projects selected came from industrial agglomerations whose situation makes it nearly impossible, on the liberal view, to establish trust. On the one hand, all had long traditions of entrepreneurial independence; and competition among firms, generally considered a fact of business life, had turned cut-throat in the late 1970s and early 1980s. The Pittsburgh area foundries, to begin with, went into crisis with their traditional customers, the steel industry. The Erie plastics firms came on hard times as their customers in the automobile industry were battered by imports, and as foreign injection-moulding firms began to compete in the United States. For firms in Erie, the only way to survive was often to shoot and ship plastic cups and other low value-added products, where relentless price competition increasingly pitted local firms against one another. The situation was similar for the apparel firms in the Lehigh Valley. In the 1950s and 1960s, these firms had prospered as subcontractors (or simply contractors, in the industry's language) for the large New York manufacturers who essentially dictated fashions and provided the corresponding piece goods to the giant department store chains which dominate retailing in the United States. In the 1970s and 1980s, however, most of the traditional manufacturers were pushed aside as the retailers began to design garments themselves and subcontract production to new, usually foreign firms (private labels), or to a new more flexible kind of manufacturer able to keep abreast of more rapidly changing fashions in large measure by also using foreign production sites. Men's wear, women's wear and sportswear firms in the Lehigh Valley were left chasing the business for reorders of those items which proved more successful than anticipated. Given the relatively high price they commanded, these reorders could be resupplied on short notice by relatively high-cost local producers. For the tool-and-die producers from Pittsburgh, Philadelphia, Erie, and the Pennsylvania Dutch area in the centre of the Commonwealth, the decline of domestic industry and the rise of imports had also apparently led to an intensification of local competition.

Although it is impossible to get strictly comparable figures for the clusters of firms concerned, several summary statistics indicate the extent of the economic trauma: between 1979 and 1988, some 262,381 jobs were lost in the apparel industry in the United States; in Pennsylvania, 47,551 jobs in the same period (a decline of 35 per cent). Of these, 8,484 were in the two counties of the Lehigh Valley area (a decline of 43 per cent). In the same period, the Pennsylvania foundry industry lost 13,027 jobs (a decline of 58 per cent, as against a decline of 48 per cent for the industry in the United States as a whole). Nineteen of 134 foundries closed, a drop of 15 per cent. In the greater Pittsburgh area, including Allegheny, Washington, and Montgomery counties, the number of firms declined by just under 28 per cent, from 28 to 20, and the number of jobs in the industry by 60 per cent, from 2,601 to 1,037.[17] The Erie plastics industry was the only case in which employment grew through the 1970s and 1980s, but this was widely perceived to be the result of an explosive growth in demand for plastic goods of all kinds, rather than a sign of the technological prowess of the local firms. During this period, other firms grew in number without strengthening their competitive position.[18]

On the other hand, all four industry groups had had in the more or less recent past some experience of inter-firm or labour-management co-operation which, together with their increasing awareness of the organisational basis of their foreign competitors' success, made it plausible to think that each could benefit from rethinking its current forms of association. The most extreme case was apparel, where unions had long played a role in stabilising the industry. Unions put a floor under wages by controlling the flow of work from unionised manufacturers to unionised contractors; they even provided industrial-engineering services to small shops to help the latter operate efficiently enough to pay the higher union-scale wages. But Erie, which billed itself in the 1920s as the "plastics capital of the world", was evidently for a time an industrial district quite similar to Oyonnax, near Lyons. The plastics industry there grew out of the activities of two resistor manufacturers (which accumulated experience with the new materials) and a zipper-maker (which trained several generations of highly skilled tool-and-die makers, who turned their knowledge to mould-making). Most firms in the area still trace their lineage back to one of these three companies. Awareness of this common heritage, and many of the friendships and associations on which it is based, seems to have survived the increased competition of the 1970s and 1980s. In the foundry and tool-and-die industries, an analogous role is played by craft pride and the cognate sense

---

17. All figures are drawn from the US Department of Commerce, County Business Patterns, appropriate years.

18. In Erie county, for example, employment in firms producing plastic products increased by 106 per cent between 1972 and 1987, from 1,726 to 3,562 persons. See US Department of Commerce, County Business Patterns, appropriate years.

of membership in a community where everyone has something to learn from the others.

Thus, the situation of the four project groups could at first glance be assimilated to either of the two views of trust presented earlier. They were balanced, as the liberal view suggests they would be, between the view that efforts to organise co-operation would founder on calculations of current self-interest, and a longing for the benefits of co-operation which would prove futile precisely because it was too imprecise to evaluate. But they were also balanced, as the sociological view suggests would be the case, between two possible identities, each with its own referents in recollected experience. In a very loose sense, then, the changing self-conception of the groups constitutes a kind of primitive demonstration of the greater explanatory power of this latter perspective.

The ability of the MAIN project to tip the balance in favour of trust depended, as almost all the participants seemed to realise, on the utility of a simple device. By "studying" their industries jointly, it was hoped, the parties would at best discover new sources of vitality which could serve as models for collective reorganisation. At worst, it was further hoped, they would discover a reality different enough from the one they expected to force reconsideration of their traditional assumptions. This reconsideration would, in turn, lead to formulation of new ideas of best practice. Just as insomniacs can be led to forget their insomniacal thoughts, and fall asleep, by the request that they write down the symptoms of their insomnia, so the industry groups were invited, or invited themselves, to connive in a form of self-distraction which would allow them to catch sight of new possibilities. I will call the kind of consensus, and the associated forms of economic transactions which theoretically result from such a process, studied trust.[19]

---

19.   Students of weakness of the will or *akrasia* may want to distinguish the strategy of self-transformation described here from the strategy associated with Pascal's wager. Pascal argued that if there was any chance that a god capable of granting infinite satisfaction existed, then it was reasonable for any self-interested person to believe in the existence of that god. Because there are reasons to believe god exists, belief is reasonable. But, the argument continues, a conclusion founded on such reason has nothing to do with the unreflective affirmation of the existence of a supreme being which we commonly understand as belief in god. To believe unthinkingly what we have reasonably concluded to believe, therefore, we act as *if* we believed that way, practising all the religious ceremonies which express unconditional faith. Because the ceremonies become habitual and habits are by definition unthinking, calculated belief finally becomes true faith.

The situation described here is like Pascal's wager in that the actors in some sense choose what they eventually want to believe. It is also like Pascal's wager in that actions occasioned by their choices are self-reinforcing. But the situation is crucially different in that this self-reinforcement leads rarely, if ever, to suspension of self-reflective, and hence in some sense calculating, evaluation of one's current situation. If the self-reinforcement of initial choices *did* have this effect, the world could consist of nothing but trusting zones like Japan and mistrustful ones like Sicily. But, as the preceding discussion has suggested and the subsequent argument will reaffirm, such cases are the exceptions. The rule is that persons define and experience trust in a way that allows them to distinguish that condition from both

The "trick" seems to be producing such studied trust because the groups are capable of redefining their community interests, as the previous discussion has suggested they could, and because they have reason to do so given the results of their investigations. Most generally, all have found that they overestimated the costs and underestimated the benefits of co-operation. This was because the estimations were typically based on the experience of the crisis years of the early 1980s, when the firms were truly competing head-to-head and co-operation would have been meaningless. But the firms that survived that period did so largely by specialising in mastery of a particular production process or manufacture of a particular product. Hence, many had become more and more dependent on the provision of complementary products or processes by local companies without, however, grasping the cumulative significance of the incremental changes. Even as it was becoming more pervasive and mutually beneficial, co-operation among specialists was still generally regarded as an exception to the old rule of cut-throat competition and, in any case, assimilated to traditional forms of neighbourliness or craft solidarity.

These findings were not self-evident. Entrenched views and interests of the trade associations, firms, and unions drew attention away from those situations which might have alerted them to emergent changes in the environment. The Commonwealth's role was to bring these limiting assumptions to light, either by bringing in consultants to suggest alternative ways of looking at the situation or by using the surprises encountered by one project to jog the others. It was this process, of course, which created the possibility for redefining collective identities and cleared the way for studied trust. Had it been otherwise, the groups would have solved their co-ordination problems long before they were identified as such.

Some examples will clarify the sorts of barriers which obstructed joint efforts and how the groups have begun to dismantle them in the name of a new collective self-definition. The Lehigh Valley project was initially conceived as an effort to improve relations between the unions and the unionised contractors. The initial participants were aware that there was a growing non-union sector of recent Vietnamese, Lebanese and Syrian immigrants. But to the Italians and Jews who dominated the firms and unions in the organised sector, the new firms were essentially sweatshops, and the problem - to be addressed in part by the project - was how to make operations there conform to union standards, whether the workers themselves were organised or not. From the point of view of the new immigrants, a number of whom had adopted best-practice technologies and were paying wages well over minimum union rates, the established groups and the unions in particular were simply taxing them: firms which subcontracted work to non-union shops are forced to pay an amount into the union social welfare

---

distrust and unquestioning faith. For an excellent discussion of Pascal's wager, see Elster [1984, pp. 47ff].

funds equal to the contribution which a unionised subcontractor would have made, and this regardless of the level of wages and benefits actually paid by the non-union firm. To the extent the non-union firms absorbed the penalties paid by their unionised clients, they were subsidising union members at the expense of their own employees and profits. But through meetings and shop visits, employers from unionised shops and union officials became more aware of the dynamism of parts of the non-union sector. Conversely, representatives of the latter began to similarly distinguish a dynamic part of the unionised sector which was prepared to trade services with them and a stagnant sector which counted on enforcement of old rules and practices to assure its flow of work. As this happened, the problem became less one of regularising sweatshops (the original "union" view), or outwitting an out-dated but still powerful monopolist (the new-immigrant view), and more a question of rethinking the collective needs of the new specialist firms in the Valley, their relation to one another, and ultimately their relation to the manufacturers and retailers in New York.

The Pittsburgh foundries provide a second example. Their trade association is the Pennsylvania Foundrymen's Association, a for-profit organisation which sells its services to individual foundries. The principal service is workmen's compensation insurance, which the Association, through one of its entities, can provide at advantageous rates because it has identified and taught its members to eliminate the chief hazards in foundries. Because the Association is run by persons who do not come out of the industry and think of themselves as providing discrete services, they do not have a detailed grasp of changes in the foundry technology or the structure of the industry: for example, the customers' growing emphasis that foundries provide design services and furnish products which require little, if any, further machining. Nor did they learn of these changes from their current members, because these latter tend to be the oldest, most traditional, and often economically most desperate of the surviving firms. Again shop visits, organised by outside consultants with little prior knowledge of the industry, turned up facts that surprised the more traditional shop owners and trade associations alike.

The first was that many foundries were in fact selling foundry-related services or, rather, providing customers with services which went far beyond the simple pouring of metal according to the client's specifications. Of the 42 (of 45) foundries in the area which responded to a questionnaire, 20 provided just-in-time delivery, 29 machining services, 20 welding services, 20 drafting services and 15 engineering services. Plant visits revealed, moreover, that the firms had begun to systematically co-operate in the provision of complementary services. Some went so far as to bid jointly on jobs; many were enthusiastic about advertising the region as a foundry centre. The industry, finally, was attracting a surprising amount of investment. Eight of the firms, or nearly 20 per cent, had either been purchased by new owners, sold to management, merged into joint ventures, or started from scratch. All of those, domestic or foreign, who entered the business were foundrymen, and all brought knowledge of the latest technologies [Pennsylvania Foundrymen's Association, 1990].

The strategic audits also uncovered less surprising surprises: situations which confirmed widely-held views about common problems, but which cast those views in a new light and led to unexpected conclusions regarding their implications for the organisation of particular industries. Training is the chief example. It is banal to remark that United States workers have not been trained for the tasks which the new competitive conditions require of them. All four project groups observed in their applications to the Commonwealth that collective provision of training was a crucial area in which they expected gains from co-operation, and none were disappointed. What was surprising was the precise relation in each case of training to other problems of organisation. In apparel, for example, training was crucial to the flexible use of new garment-routing technologies: unless sewing operators mastered several tasks, there was no point in introducing conveyance systems which allowed managers rapidly to reconfigure the shop for new products. In the tool-and-die industry, shop-owners and managers were compensating for skill deficits by programming machines and organising work themselves. As a result, they had little time to manage, and considerations of long-term strategy were sacrificed to the daily struggle for survival. Increased training in this industry is thus literally the precondition to thinking through other changes. As foundries expand into foundry services, to take a final example, they discover the need for broad training in metal-working which overlaps with the needs of the mould-makers in plastics and the tool-and-die industry. Hence, co-operation in training soon came to include the idea of co-operation across industry lines, and raised the possibility of collaboration well beyond what had been imagined by each group in isolation.

All of these discoveries, surprisingly, or less so, reacted in turn on the organisation of the parties to each project and ultimately on the Commonwealth as well. The dynamic firms are gently emarginating the more traditional ones in the Foundrymen's Association, and the Association's leaders see the possibilities of leading an expanding sector, rather than administering the decline of a moribund one. Non-union firms are playing an increasing role in the apparel project, particularly in the important committee which has been established to investigate the full range of new technologies appropriate to producers in Lehigh Valley. These changes have just begun, but everyone concerned with the projects remarks on the new, and more numerous, faces which appear at meetings; and this shift of public is itself a strong hint that the institutional identities of these industries is in flux.

The Commonwealth's role has changed in at least two ways. First, whatever the outcome of these projects, the state is now part of the social system within which firms in these industries decide their future. In this sense, it has become an unobtrusive participant rather than an intrusive spectator. Information about the economy flows to the state because the state has helped create the system by which that information is generated. The better informed the state is, the better it is, presumably, at making decisions of all kinds regarding the economy.

Second, as the projects learn to co-ordinate the efforts of their member groups and the latter define the services they need, the state has begun to learn how to define and co-ordinate the provision of public services. To make the extension-service Industrial Resource Centers and the community colleges more responsive to the needs of the MAIN groups means to change the administrative structure of both, and raises the question of their relation to the development bank, the Ben Franklin Partnership. Just what this will require is still unclear, but even a cursory backward glance at the unruly profusion of economic-development institutions in Pennsylvania shows that something must be done.

Consider the following administrative tangle.[20]   At present the Partnership disburses about $25 million a year to fund its various projects. The bulk of the projects are proposed to the BFP's governing board and, upon approval, administered by four technology centres. These are non-profit corporations, governed themselves by boards of officers of universities and private firms. The technology centres may use BFP funds to support technology transfer (including research and development), the operation of existing university centres of excellence, the development of entrepreneurial skills, training for the workforce, and incubation of small businesses. In addition, the BFP has created 45 centres of excellence at educational institutions in the Commonwealth. These are to acquire expertise in particular technologies selected in consultation with the companies which serve on or can be attracted to their governing boards. The vast majority of the Partnership's projects involve one or a very small number of firms. Although some undoubtedly demand a level of technological sophistication beyond that of the IRCs, many apparently do not. Many consulting services which are or could be offered by the BFP also overlap those currently or potentially offered by the IRCs. There is, therefore, no clear line distinguishing the jurisdiction of one organisation from the other. More important, there is no consensus regarding the most effective relation between projects aimed at influencing the behaviour of whole sectors and local economies through encouragement of inter-firm co-operation - the associative model - and projects aimed at influencing the behaviour of individual firms - the extension-services model.

---

20.   For the BFP's administrative structure and the composition of its budget, see Board of the Ben Franklin Partnership Fund [1988]. The following was written before the first meeting of the BFP's Strategic Investment Committee on October 24, 1990, and reflects, therefore, the views of persons closely associated with and responsible for the BFP before that date. Information brought to light by that committee has changed those views, to the surprise of many, myself included, for the better. I plan to report on these findings later in a broader analysis of changes in the Commonwealth's internal governance structure and relation to the private sector.

With the Commonwealth's help, the actors will ideally be able to define the public services they require, as well as the balance between services provided to collectives of firms as against services provided to single enterprises. But arriving at such a definition will be hard and institutionalising it harder still in the face of the entrenched opposition of those who find the current situation acceptable. The state's ability to reshape indirectly the economic actors' identity and change their interests will thus be indispensable to its own reorganisation. Coy's promotion from Director of the MAIN project to Director of the Office of Technology Development in the Department of Commerce, with responsibility for, among other things, the BFP, the IRCs, and MAIN, assures that this will be on the agenda.

The project is also likely to have repercussions on local and state politics. In the much longer term, it may even lead to a reordering of national institutions as well. You do not have to be a Marxist to recognise that economic crises discredit the political classes responsible for averting them, whereas economic successes accredit their political sponsors. It is too early to tell what effects the continued revitalisation of Pennsylvania industry will have on the political composition of the relevant communities and the Commonwealth as a whole. But an analogous process in the French town of Annonay and the more strictly comparable experience of MTAP in Springfield, Massachusetts show that the new trust relations established through the reorganisation of production do tend to create a new group of local notables.[21] What unites the group is the sense that the reorganisation of production in the plant depends on collaboration among firms and between them and the private sector.

The first political ramifications of the Springfield project, which began in 1986, are already apparent. The mayor of the city ran successfully for a seat in the United States House of Representatives on a platform which promised the extension of the co-operation between the groups of firms, government, and educational institutions. The last president of the Western Massachusetts' chapter of the National Tooling and Machine Association (NTMA), was closely associated with the project. He has become the head of the NTMA's model technical school in Rochester, New York. Meanwhile, his place in Springfield has been filled by one of the machine-shop owners who was one of the founding members of MTAP's governing board. The head of the local community college is beginning to make a career as a reformer in the state educational system; and the director of MTAP, Robert Forrant, not only sits on the boards of several technical schools, but also participates in the Commonwealth of Massachusetts' certification of particular training facilities as degree-granting institutions. The trade unionist (from an electrician's union) who followed the development of

---

21.   On the relation between changes in factory organisation and the recomposition of social groups in Annonay, see Ganne [1983; 1989]. The discussion of developments in Springfield is based on conversations with Robert Forrant.

MTAP most closely and encouragingly has become president of the Greater Springfield Central Labor Council. It may be, of course, that all of these persons took an interest in the project because they are interested in everything that is novel, and that it is their energy and curiosity rather than anything learned by affiliation with MTAP which explains their subsequent progress. But by all accounts they have been influenced by the project. If the latter continues to succeed, it seems reasonable to expect that they will try to extend and apply what they take to be its lessons elsewhere in Massachusetts. The MAIN projects could in time have similar results in Pennsylvania.

Finally, the project may have national repercussions as well. Reinvigorating and systematising a technique of political innovation that culminated the New Deal, the governors of the US states have taken the initiative in experimenting with new policies on their home ground, and then orchestrating national implementation of their successes.[22] The recent reform of the welfare system was elaborated by the National Governors' Association before being presented to and enacted by Congress; and a reform of the education system is being prepared in the same way. The governors have also expressed interest in economic development, especially of the sort undertaken in Pennsylvania: the working group preparing the governors' deliberations in this area in 1990 discussed an analysis of economic development which draws heavily on the experience of the MAIN project.[23]

There is thus likely to be a public and political airing of the obvious question: what might be done nationally to encourage the creation of new relations of trust in local economies? While it is hard to say what, if anything, will come of such deliberations, it is possible to focus consideration of possible outcomes by indicating an important continuity and an important discontinuity between efforts to draw out the national implications of the new economic-development localism and New Deal experience. The continuity concerns the constitutional interpretation of the powers of self-governance of groups engaged in productive activities - an issue which has been at the heart of constitutional disputes in the advance of capitalist countries throughout this century. Earlier I referred to a regulatory tradition in which expert administrative boards create a framework of rules for whole industries.[24] But there is a second, sometimes competing, sometimes complementary, New Deal tradition of regulation through economic self-

---

22. The actual policies of the New Deal depended, of course, on a complex interplay between state-level innovations, the outcome of fights within the federal bureaucracy, and the balance of power between Congress and the executive branch. See generally on these themes, Weir, Margaret et al. [1988].

23. For the comprehensive document that framed the governors' discussion of economic development in 1990, see Bosworth [forthcoming 1991].

24. The classic statement of this position is in Landis [1983].

government. This tradition emphasises the right of groups, in a society formed of groups, to create by mutual agreement and with a minimum of administrative supervision, legal regimes which suit their needs. In this view, associated with the work of Louis Jaffe, if groups acknowledge mutual economic dependence and hence the need for trust in the sense used here, they are constitutionally entitled to devise institutions for policing behaviours which, uncontrolled, might undermine the possibility of collaboration [Jaffe, 1973].

Under the New Deal, the crucial instance of such law-making and such groups was collective bargaining between unions and management. The unions were granted exclusive jurisdiction in the company or plant bargaining units whenever they represented a majority of non-supervisory employees. The managers were obligated by law to bargain in good faith with labour. Until the last decades, these bargaining regimes were analogised to miniature democracies in which the citizens reconciled the differences using collective bargaining contract in place of the constitution which governed disputes in the larger polity [Van Wezel Stone, 1981].

But as originally articulated, the argument for self-governance was not meant to empower particular groups to the exclusion of others. Many of the most persuasive constitutional glosses validating collective bargaining assimilated such contracting to the broader category of what Jaffe called "law-making by private groups". A paradigmatic case, which recalls many of the economic-development activities considered above, would be the creation, with governmental approval, of special tax districts to finance improvement of local infrastructure [Jaffe, 1973].

Seen in this way, the MAIN projects are simply returning to these first principles by sanctioning the participation of educational institutions, trade associations and government entities in the kind of bargaining about the conditions of economic development which were in the post-war period the privileged reserve of trade unions and employers. Those on the right will see this broadening of participation, especially when disassociated from "preferential" treatment for labour and capital, as a means of enabling entrepreneurs or those who want to become entrepreneurs, to realise their ends. This is community capitalism in which the stronger the economic community, the more numerous the capitalists. Indeed, it is noteworthy that a number of leaders of the trade associations participating in the MAIN projects and the consultants with whom they are working hold such Ripon Republican views.[25] Those on the left, on the other hand, will stress the government's responsibility to ensure that the public sanction of more extensive and effective forms of group co-operation does not reinforce, and if possible reduces, disparities of power between the participants. But what unites left and right is the realisation that to secure the economic actors the

---

25. See, for example, Krauss [1990]. Krauss conducted the survey of foundries referred to above.

legal autonomy needed for the collaborative pursuit of their respective interests, it is necessary to set, or allow *them* to set, rules which redefine and even blur the distinctions between their identities. Were it indeed to flourish in the law, this view would give authoritative expression to the claim that groups engaged in production constantly redefine those they trust by redefining their own self-conceptions and redirecting - not abandoning - their vigilance. In short, the view developed earlier of trust as a local constitution would itself become constitutional doctrine.

The discontinuity between efforts to draw national implications from the Pennsylvania projects and New Deal experience goes to a paradoxical ambiguity in the very idea of state or local government as, in the famous phrase, laboratories of democracy: the sites where new plans of governance are proven before being extended to the national polity. This notion is self-explanatory so long as it makes sense to think of applying experimental programmes in something like their local form to national problems. Obvious cases where such a transfer does make sense are social insurance programmes, where coverage can be extended without changing the principles governing eligibility, contributions and distributions of benefits. Thus, the influence of state-level experiments with unemployment insurance on the corresponding New Deal programme is a standard illustration of the role of the states as laboratories of democracy.[26]

---

26. Although standard, the illustration is inaccurate in a way which casts doubt on the tenability of at least the garden-variety version of the laboratories of democracy view. The Federal Unemployment Tax Act financed federal unemployment benefits by a 3 per cent tax on payrolls. Employers could deduct contributions to state unemployment insurance programmes from their federal tax liability up to a limit of 2.7 per cent of their payrolls. But the law also provided that monies which firms were excused from paying into state funds because of superior records of employment stability or because of compensation paid to unemployed workers could be included in the sum offset from the federal tax. The intent was to reward employers who organised production to provide stable jobs, and to encourage others to emulate them. But different states rated firms' employment experience and credited payments by firms to the unemployed in vastly different ways. The result was that firms in many states were soon meeting much of their federal tax payroll obligations with state tax credits which would not have been granted in the others; and, not surprisingly, where states were most generous in excusing firms from tax liabilities, benefits for the unemployed were the most meagre. A general lesson might be that at least in the federal systems which are most likely to see localities as laboratories of government, there can almost never be a direct transfer of local experiences to the national level: the very success of the local model programme argues for allowing other localities to choose between some version of it (thus permitting further experimentation) and the national programme which it inspires. To do otherwise - say through the imposition of uniform national rules - would invite the accusation that the central government was destroying the preconditions of its own self-improvement. But freedom to choose between national and local plans in combination with the subsequent exercises of local discretion in the elaboration of the programme, means that the national system creates a framework within which different local variants proliferate, rather than generalising a particular local situation. On unemployment insurance in the United States, see Altmeyer [1963].

But what if, as in the case of Pennsylvania, the lesson of the local experiment is precisely that programmes of a certain type must *remain* local if they are to function at all? In that case, the only sense in which the national government could generalise a local experience would be by creating conditions under which other localities could, *mutatis mutandis*, emulate it. The national programme in such instances would thus complement rather than duplicate and extend the laboratory experiment as in the stylised account of the origins of the New Deal.

Besides a permissive legal environment of the kind just described, the obvious national complement to MAIN-type projects would be a system of grants-in-aid to distressed localities. The monies would be spent at the discretion of the local economic actors to formulate and begin execution of an adjustment strategy. The transfers could be organised as a national or (in, for example, the European Economic Community) supra-national reinsurance system: prosperous regions would pay into the fund in the expectation of drawing on it when they themselves needed to restructure. At the least, such a system would encourage rationalisation of the current hodge-podge of subsidies to distressed areas, sectors, groups of workers and the unemployed, which in many countries amounts to a badly co-ordinated, inefficient analogue to such a system. At the most, it would bring into the open and encourage public recognition of the economic locales' mutual dependence, giving each a stake in the others' prosperity as an ultimate guarantee of its own, and extending, perhaps, local trust relations beyond local boundaries.[27]

V. Some pessimism of the intellect

But here the strains of what the Germans call future music are drowning out current concerns. At the outset I said I would conclude by reaffirming the central theme of the essay and cautioning against overly enthusiastic conclusion, and I intend to do just that. I have argued that liberal pessimism about the possibility of creating trust is theoretically untenable, and that the actors' echo of it can be reconciled with the alternative view that trust is a constitutive - hence in principle extensible - feature of social life. The example of Pennsylvania, I think, supports this scepticism about neo-classical claims. But it does not prove that there is even one sure - let alone Pennsylvanian - way to actually extend trust when the actors believe it is in their interest to do so. Many economic development projects, as everyone knows, are either well-intentioned failures or publicity-minded frauds. This one is indubitably neither. But it is only a year old, and it would be foolishly premature to celebrate its success. The most that can be said, and I think it enough, is that it has done well enough

---

27. For a discussion of this kind of reinsurance system, see Sabel [1989, pp. 17-70].

to strengthen confidence that something like it will succeed if it does not - and that such success will further loosen the hold of ideas that undermine trust where trust is possible.

References

Altmeyer, Arthur J. 1963. "The development and status of social security in America", in Somers, Gerald G. (ed.): *Labor, management, and social polity*, Madison, University of Wisconsin Press, pp. 123-159.

Board of the Ben Franklin Partnership Fund. 1988. *Challenge Grant Program for Techno-logical Innovation, Five Year Report, March 1, 1983 - February 29, 1988*, Harrisburg, Pennsylvania Department of Commerce.

Bosworth, Brian. 1991. *State strategies for manufacturing modernization*, Washington D.C., National Governors' Association (forthcoming).

Bourdieu, Pierre. 1977. *Outline of a theory of practice* (Richard Nice, trans.), Cambridge, Cambridge University Press.

Bradach, Jeffrey L.; Eccles, Robert G. 1989. "Price, authority and trust: From ideal types to plural forms", in *Annual Review of Sociology*, pp. 97-118.

Davidson, Donald. 1973. "On the very idea of a conceptual scheme", Presidential address delivered to the Seventieth Annual Eastern Meeting of the American Philosophical Association, Atlanta, December 28, 1973, and reprinted in Rajchman, John; West, Cornel (eds.): *Post-analytic philosophy*, New York, Columbia University Press, 1985.

Departments of Commerce and Labor and Industry. 1989. Commonwealth of Pennsylvania, *Request for proposal for industry-specific development plan initiative*, Harrisburg, 15 April.

Dore, Ronald. 1983. "Goodwill and the spirit of market capitalism", in *The British Journal of Sociology*, Vol. 34, No. 4, pp. 459-482.

---. 1986. *Flexible rigidities: Industrial policy and structural adjustment in the Japanese economy 1970-80*, Stanford, Stanford University Press.

---. 1989. "The management of hierarchy", Paper presented to the NOMISMA Conference on Industrial Policy: New Issues and New Models, the Regional Experience, Bologna, 16-17 November.

Dupuy, Jean-Pierre. n.d. *Communauté et common knowledge*, CREA-Ecole Polytechnique, Paris (manuscript).

Elster, Jon. 1983. *Sour grapes: Studies in the subversion of rationality*, Cambridge, Cambridge University Press.

---. 1984. *Ulysses and the sirens* (revised edition), Cambridge, Cambridge University Press.

---. 1990. "Selfishness and altruism", in Mansbridge, Jane J. (ed.): *Beyond self-interest*, Chicago, University of Chicago Press.

Ganne, Bernard. 1983. "Conflit du travail et changement urbain: transformation d'un rapport local", in *Sociologie du Travail*, Vol. 25, No. 2, April-June, pp. 127-146.

---. 1989. "PME et districts industriels: quelques réflexions critiques à propos 'du modèle italien'", in *PME Revue Internationale*, No. 2-3, pp. 273-285.

Herbers, John. 1990. "A third wave of economic development", in *Governing*, June, pp. 43-500.

Jaffe, Louis. 1973. "Law making by private groups", in *Harvard Law Review*, Vol. 51, No. 2, December, pp. 201-253.

Katzenstein, Peter J. 1985. *Small states in world markets*, Ithaca, Cornell University Press.

Krauss, Jordan P. 1990. "Producing growth: Infrastructure improvement, enterprise zones and sound economic policy", in Eberly, Don E. (ed.): *Leading Pennsylvania into the 21st century: Policy strategies for the future*, Harrisburg, The Commonwealth Foundation for Public Policy Alternatives.

Kreps, David M. 1990. "Corporate culture and economic theory", in Alt, James E.; Shepsle, Kenneth A. (eds.): *Perspectives on positive political economy*, Cambridge, Cambridge University Press, pp. 90-143.

Landis, James M. 1983. *The administrative process*, New Haven, Yale University Press.

Lloyd, G.I.H. 1913. *The cutlery trades*, London, Longmans, Green & Co.

Lorenz, Edward H. 1988. "Neither friends nor strangers: Informal networks of subcontracting in French industry", in Gambetta, Diego (ed.): *Trust: Making and breaking cooperative relations*, New York, Basil Blackwell, pp. 3-13.

Lukács, Georg. 1984-86. *Zur Ontologie des gesellschaftlichen Seins*, 2 vols. Benseles, Frank (ed.), Darmstadt, Luchterhand.

Nagel, Thomas. 1970. *The possibility of altruism*, Oxford, Clarendon Press.

Osborne, David. 1988. *Laboratories of democracy*, Boston, Harvard Business School Press.

Pennsylvania Foundrymen's Association. 1990. *Quarterly Report, January 1, 1990 to March 31, 1990, Southwest Pennsylvania Foundry Industry, MAIN Project*, 20 April, on file at the Department of Labor and Industry, Commonwealth of Pennsylvania, Harrisburg.

Rajchman, Jon; West, Cornel (eds.). 1985. *Post-analytic philosophy*, New York, Columbia University Press.

Ravèyre, Marie-Françoise; Saglio, Jean. 1984. "Les systèmes industriels localisés: Eléments pour une analyse sociologique des ensembles de PME industriels", in *Sociologie du Travail*, No. 2, pp. 157-177.

Rawls, John. 1985. "Justice as fairness: Political not metaphysical", in *Philosophy and Public Affairs*, Vol. 14, No. 3, summer, pp. 223-251.

Rosaldo, Renato. 1980. *Ilongot headhunting, 1883-1974: A study in society and history*, Stanford, Stanford University Press.

Sabel, Charles F. 1989. "Flexible specialisation and the re-emergence of regional economies", in Hirst, Paul; Zeitlin, Jonathan (eds.): *Reversing industrial decline?*, New York, St. Martin's Press.

Saglio, Jean. 1991. *Industrie locale et stratégie des acteurs: Du peigne à la plasturgie dans la zone d'Oyonnax*, Lyon, Groupe lyonnais de la Sociologie industrielle (manuscript).

Sen, Amartya K. 1979. "Rational fools: A critique of the behavioral foundations of economic theory", in Harris, Henry (ed.): *Scientific models and men*, New York, Oxford University Press.

Stinchcombe, Arthur L. 1985. "Contracts as hierarchical documents", in Stinchcombe, Arthur L.; Heimer, Carol A. (eds.): *Organization theory and project management*, Oslo, Norwegian University Press, pp. 121-171.

Streeck, Wolfgang. 1987 "Industrielle Beziehungen, soziale Ordnung und Beschäftigung: Ein Kommentar", in Matzner, Egon et al. (eds.): *Arbeit für alle ist möglich. Uber ökonomische und institutionelle Bedingungen erfolgreicher Beschäftigungs- und Arbeitsmarktpolitik*, Berlin, Edition Sigma.

---. 1990. "Status and contract. Basic categories of a sociological theory", in Sugarmand, David: Teubner, Gunther (eds.): *Regulating corporate groups in Europe*, Baden-Baden, Nomos, pp. 105-145.

Teubner, Gunther. 1983. "Substantive and reflexive elements in modern law", in *Law and Society Review*, Vol. 17, No. 2, pp. 239-285.

Trigilia, Carlo. 1989. "Il distretto industriale di Prato", in Regini, Marino; Sabel, Charles F. (eds.): *Strategie di riaggiustamento industriale*, Bologna, Il Mulino, pp. 283-333.

Van Wezel Stone, Katherine. 1981. "The post-war paradigm in American Labor Law", in *Yale Law Journal*, Vol. 90, No. 7, June, pp. 1509-1580.

Weir, Margaret et al. 1988. *The politics of social policy in the United States*, Princeton, Princeton University Press.

Williams, Bernard. 1988. "Formal structures and social rality", in Gambetta, Diego (ed.): *Trust: Making and breaking cooperative relations*, New York, Basil Blackwell.

Zahavi, Gerald. 1983. "Negotiated loyalty: Welfare capitalism and the shoeworkers of Endcott Johnson, 1920-1940", in *The Journal of American History*, Vol. 71, No. 3, December, pp. 602-620.

9 Industrial districts: The point of view of the unions[1]

Paulo Brutti

The level and maturity attained by research into industrial districts convinces me that it is now possible to take an important step forward in the identification of development strategies based on small and medium-sized firms. A particularly significant conclusion from the research is that analysis and interventions, whether by the institutions in general or by the trade unions in particular, are now compelled to abandon the more familiar and simpler level of the single firm and come to grips instead with the greater complexity of a local system of firms. This shift is not easy, especially for trade unions. There are cultural, ideological and political obstacles, which merit a brief description.

Trade unions have always found it hard to accept the idea that a small firm may represent a specific social and productive world different from that of a large company. This has been particularly apparent when attempts have been made to use company size as an argument in favour of warranting exceptional contractual status. In such circumstances, argument has tended to focus exclusively on the need for small firms, seen as weak industrial units, to be given special structural protections, particularly ones that will hold down labour costs.

In such viewpoints, the thesis that small firms are simply companies caught at a youthful stage in their development, and that locally-organised systems of firms merely represent retarded phases in industrial development, has taken hold. The industrial system's own process of development is expected to perform the task of marginalising such pockets of productive backwardness. The trade unions are expected to wait for such firms to get over this necessary period of incubation, while proposing policies designed to support and promote the transformation of small firms systems into large-scale, concentrated, solid manufacturing ventures on the lines of the classical model.

This approach has yielded few results in terms of contractual uniformity, whilst forecasts predicting industrial and productive concentration have proved incorrect. Not only do small firms continue to proliferate, but

1.   A version of this article was also published in Italian in *Il Ponte*, No. 12, December 1990.

their development, even over the last years of the 1980s has, in terms of employment growth at least, been positive.

It cannot now escape the notice of trade unions that the move towards greater flexibility in the productive activities of large firms tends to follow models that copy the organisational methods developed by specialised locally-based small firms systems. It is a fact that while the industrial district, as a defined concept, struggles to make headway in legislation and contractual procedures, the organisational form of the specialised multi-unit system is in the process of becoming one of the most successful models in the productive reorganisation of large companies.

The nub of the whole issue lies in the answer one gives to a crucial question: whether or not industrial areas of so-called flexible specialisation or, if one prefers, "industrial districts", possess the features of a distinct economic-productive and social system. My answer, with all the necessary caveats, tends to be "yes".

This is not an ideological approach, nor does it suggest the re-emergence of an abstract and doctrinaire concern. My approach is based on empirical fact and the experience of a specific kind of industrial development. In fact, it is only by strongly emphasising and promoting the economic and social "distinctiveness" of industrial districts that it is possible to argue the need for industrial policies and trade union relations to be thought through from scratch, rather than simply adapted from other situations. The more the status of this distinctiveness is asserted, the greater will be the opportunity to make structural innovations in the field of industrial policies, such as in regard to incentives, trade union relations and contractual relations.

So far, industrial districts have grown spontaneously amid the indifference of the powers-that-be. They have not been able to count on policies targeted specifically at their needs, but instead have had to rely on interventions directed at small firms in general. Despite current received wisdom, industrial districts have developed with the greatest exuberance precisely where they have been able to rely on the openness of markets and on the growth of the international market. Although such districts are locality-based, they do not survive by remaining oriented to the local market or even the domestic market. The output of the districts is aimed at export, and the widespread efficiency that is encountered in the districts generates productivity levels that are fully comparable with those attained by other kinds of organisation.

Labour in the districts is not the same as in traditional firms. In particular, it is characterised by enterprising attitudes and behaviour, making use of creative faculties and a capacity for adaptability and skills. The spread of an enterprise "mindset" is a condition decisive for the success of a district. The continual rearticulation of productive activity, the division of production into different enterprises, each facing market uncertainty, and the high birth and death rate of firms, all mean that the frontier between employee labour and independent labour is continually confronted during the life of any single worker.

The creative input by labour in industrial districts is an aspect of the greater opportunity for workers to participate in the production organisation; an input which at times makes it possible to deploy the full range of existing technologies, from the least complex to the most sophisticated. This participation does not derive from ideological or political principles. Rather, it is a feature that workers in industrial districts must possess in order to make up for the comparatively modest service "apparatuses" that district firms generally have at their disposal relative to those available for larger-scale companies.

Such work features are at the root of the difference between district workers and workers in traditional businesses. In districts, for example, work may be paid for by a combination of earnings and a share in company ownership. Those workers who possess the greatest professional skills are in a position to use this as a lever on the labour market and hence to move from one firm to the next until they are offered a real stake in the ownership of the firm for which they work.

The problem now facing trade unions and business associations is how to highlight the "specificity" of industrial districts, as places where particular trade union relations must apply. Indeed, what can be achieved in the case of industrial districts may not necessarily be achieved in the traditional labour market through the operation of traditional trade union relations (and, of course, the opposite must also hold).

This means that districts must become the ground for a development in labour rights, moving not in the purely quantitative direction of "equal rights" but rather in the qualitative direction of rights of "equal opportunity". What is needed is to devise a strategy for rights that can safeguard and reinforce the specificity of labour requirements in industrial districts.

Industrial district workers are interested, for instance, in a range of labour market provisions, such as: professional training, the removal of inhibitions on labour mobility, the guaranteeing of company shareholdings, and mechanisms to protect incomes from the ups and downs of workloads. Workers are also naturally interested in devices designed to prevent work accidents and reduce environmental hazards. This last aspect is of huge importance given that district-based productive organisations often present large, mostly urban, areas, with the problems of pollution and toxicity that accompany extensive plant. Lastly, industrial district workers are interested in the development of the best technologies, including technologies designed to minimise the risks of work accidents.

The satisfaction of these needs places the issue of labour costs in a new light. I shall not now address the controversial question of the creation of area funds for purposes of insurance, salary, savings or investment. Instead, I should like to draw attention to two important matters: first, the local determination of work contracts. Districts do not all possess the same potential and the same development levels. Trade union bargaining accordingly needs to operate at two levels: at the national and at the district level. These two levels should keep their processes separate and avoid any interaction, thereby leaving local bargaining to determine levels of pay increases, working hours and rights, while national bargaining addresses itself to the general conditions of negotiating status. This would enable districts to achieve what the workers on their own cannot secure: district negotiation of the conditions under which labour is supplied, conducted in accordance with the forms and instruments of collective action and autonomy.

However, a tricky problem arises, bringing us to the second issue I would like to examine: how a correct relation can be established between trends in labour costs and fluctuations in a district's productivity. This is no academic question, as would be appreciated as soon as district bargaining begins to develop within a logic of pay increases and reductions in working hours linked to hoped-for rises in productivity. The solution has perhaps to be sought at a global level, taking account of the various activities of a district. In this context, it might be possible to devise instruments such as district funds to cover agreed productivity target payments. These funds could be stocked by payments from the firms and regulated on the basis of the average productivity of the system.

In my judgement, there is a common failure to truly understand the phenomenon of industrial districts. They are not recognised in legislation. When it comes to either incentives or real services or policies designed to encourage restructuring processes, public intervention knows nothing of districts. Indeed, employment crises affecting entire districts are handled as crises focused on a myriad of separate industrial points, often with differing levels of social protection. It is necessary to overcome this lack of identity and absence of even legal recognition.

Finally, I would like to say that, for underdeveloped areas, industrial districts are of more than marginal importance. And yet in Italy no conscious interventions aimed at promoting new industrialisation have sought to establish industrial areas on the district pattern. On the contrary, preference has been given to developing a diversified industrial base and avoiding the risks involved in productive specialisation. Yet the success stories of newly-industrialised countries, where the industrial district has acted as the main basis and condition for the organisation of production, are plain to see.

10 Flexible specialisation in small island economies: The case of Cyprus[1]

Robin Murray

I. Introduction

For the last 30 years, the debates on industrial development have been mainly conducted in terms of the problem of markets: import substitution versus export promotion; whether internal markets should remain unconstrained or be subordinate to a plan; whether distortions in price structures meant a bias against small-scale and labour-intensive technology. There was little said about the strategy of production and its organisation, the nature of work processes or of product design. The assumption was that it was mass production which offered the main path to increasing productivity and lower product prices. Development depended on supplying the factors and creating the conditions for mass production to work: capital for fixed investment, blueprints and machinery from abroad; the right mix of skilled and semi-skilled labour; modern management; and an approximation to mass markets at home and abroad. The supply of these factors and the creation of these conditions have been the basis of three decades of development policy and academic discussion. Flexible specialisation has challenged all this.

The academic work on flexible specialisation (FS) that has gathered pace in the 1980s has focused attention on the strategy of production, in particular questioning many of the assumptions of the mass production approach. In doing so, it has cast a new light on old issues - the choice of techniques, firm size, inter-firm relations, the implications of multinational investment, of foreign technology supply, the appropriate forms of financial markets and institutions. Of particular importance has been the spotlight it has thrown on the question of forms of economic organisation. It has asked how firms can be effectively structured, how they relate to markets, suppliers

1.   This article summarises the work of the UNIDO/UNDP Cyprus Industrial Strategy team carried out between 1987 and 1989 and I would like to thank all those who contributed: our colleagues in Cyprus, in UNDP and UNIDO, and other members of the team - John Bessant, Michael Best, David Evans, Jane Humphries, Raphael Kaplinsky, Paul Levy, Mario Pezzini, Jim Rafferty, Drew Smith, Peter Snell and Jonathan Zeitlin.

and their direct competitors, and how governments and quasi-public institutions can most effectively implement industrial policy.

The bulk of the recent literature has analysed operating examples of flexible specialisation. It has provided a new way of looking at the economic landscape, a re-reading of what is and what has been. It has rescued small firm industrial districts and networks from the shadows, suggesting that, far from being relics of the past, they contain within them a sustainable model for the future; a model, furthermore, which is in many ways more appropriate for smaller Third World countries and vulnerable regions. It has done this by showing how existing industrial districts and flexibly specialised firms have been holding their own against, if not outcompeting, conventional mass production industry and it has analysed the nature of the operating systems that have allowed them to do so.

The industrial districts themselves were not organised on an explicit principle of flexible specialisation. Nor was the local and regional government support which has proved so important. The districts grew as a result of particular circumstances, and the public policies were responses to felt needs. They were not driven by a theory. Each case - and it is as true of dispersed networks as much as districts - had its own specific history. Flexible specialisation as a concept emerged as a way of recognising the significance of these cases, and suggesting their potential as an alternative to mass production.

There has been much less experience of trying to implement an explicit strategy of flexible specialisation *ab initio*. Indeed, some have argued that the conditions which allowed the development of successful industrial districts have been so specific that they cannot be replicated. Such a conclusion would necessarily reduce the significance of the many studies of flexible specialisation as it actually exists. But I do not think it is warranted. For it is one of the features of the FS approach that particular productive systems should not be replicated. It is the mass production model that leads to a Ford factory in Cologne being laid out and operated in the same way as a Ford factory in Australia. Ford, like McDonalds, mass produces or replicates a particular system of production. Flexible specialisation seeks to adapt its system to the particular circumstances and histories of the places where it is applied. You cannot create a Carpi in Bombay nor in Kingston, Jamaica. But what you can do is to seek to use the insights of the FS approach to develop new methods of production appropriate to the societies in which the economies are embedded. Just as an FS firm seeks to customise its products to its customers, so an FS strategy would seek to customise the policy as a whole to the specificities of place.

But is it possible and how should it be done? This is when theory is no substitute for experience, and experience is still limited. In this chapter, I want to report on the initial stages of one such attempt to develop an FS strategy. It is the case of Cyprus, whose government has explicitly adopted flexible specialisation as its approach to industrial restructuring.

II. Cyprus: The economic background

Cyprus achieved independence in 1960. During the 1960s, it grew modestly, with manufacturing accounting for little more than a tenth of GDP at the end of the 1960s, and only a fifth of commodity exports. From 1970 there were signs of an industrial take-off. Between 1970 and 1973, manufacturing value added rose by more than 50 per cent. Then in July 1974, the Turkish army invaded the island, cutting it in two with 45 per cent of manufacturing capacity remaining in the Turkish-held northern part of the island. The Greek population from the North moved South. Unemployment in the South reached 40 per cent. In 1975, manufacturing value added in the South was 45 per cent down on the 1973 figure for the whole of the island.

By 1977, unemployment had fallen to 3 per cent. By 1980, the economy had grown by more than 70 per cent of the 1975 figure, and manufacturing value added had doubled (all figures in real terms). Private consumption had also doubled, and at the same time investment was running at 23 per cent of GNP by the late 1970s. The events of 1974 had given way to an economic miracle in the Greek section of the island, centred round a construction boom following the Government's rehousing programme and commercial rehabilitation, and a manufacturing export boom to the post oil price rise markets of the Middle East.

Between 1980 and 1985, growth slowed (with consumption growing at 5 per cent per annum as against 10 per cent per annum in the late 1970s) with the main dynamic in the internal economy shifting from construction to tourism. Manufactured exports faced an increasingly competitive and slower growing Middle East market, though with heavy protection Cypriot producers continued to supply three-quarters of the home consumer market. By 1983-85, manufacturing was contributing less than 10 per cent to the overall growth of the national economy, and by 1986 it experienced negative growth for the first time in a decade.

At the same time as this slow down, the Government decided - largely for political reasons - to apply for associate membership of the European Economic Community. This would involve reducing tariffs on manufactured imports whose nominal rates for clothing, footwear and furniture ranged between 63 per cent and 72 per cent. With declining export markets and with signs of a slackening in tourist growth and domestic consumption, manufacturing faced substantial cut-backs during the late 1980s and 1990s. It was at this point that the Government decided to draw up a Cyprus Industrial Strategy (CIS). It wanted to see what could be done to upgrade Cyprus industry so that it could reorient itself from the Middle East to Europe, and hold its own in an increasingly open home market. To this end, it enlisted the help of a team of economists and sector specialists centred at the Institute of Development Studies, University of Sussex, United Kingdom, who had been working on small-scale industry in developing countries, and development banking by local government in the United Kingdom and the United States of America.

III. Proto mass production

The team worked in Cyprus for the month of January 1987, with follow-up visits during the first half of that year. They visited some 110 plants, and held discussion meetings with sectoral industry associations, with parastatals and with government officials. The picture which emerged from this work was of an industry geared towards mass production. The rapid growth of internal and external demand meant that there was a premium on output rather than quality. Many of the industrialists who 15 years before were artisans - butchers, tailors, shoemakers and carpenters - were encouraged by the demand boom and capital incentives to buy equipment from abroad, to copy foreign designs and recipes, and then to concentrate on volume. In the second half of the 1970s, when labour was plentiful, their growth was extensive. When the labour market tightened in the 1980s, they looked to new capital equipment to substitute for labour, raising the growth rate of productivity from 1.4 per cent per annum in the latter 1970s to 2.6 per cent by 1985.

There were, however, inherent difficulties in pursuing mass production strategies in Cyprus. Firstly, the internal market is small, the Greek section of the island having a population of only 600,000, with an annual tourist flow which was forecast to reach a million.

Secondly, because of the small market, machinery was often used at under-capacity, or could not be justified in the first place. The capacity problem was particularly marked in the meat processing industry where five firms had modern machines, each of which could have supplied the Cypriot market on its own. In footwear, the downturn in the Middle East left a number of firms stranded with specialised equipment which could not be turned over to other uses. In tetrapak juices, knitwear and underwear, and large batch furniture production, equipment designed for long runs was operating at low capacity or lying idle.

Thirdly, as island producers, manufacturers face a long supply line for their imported intermediate goods, and where they are produced locally this is usually by one, or at most a few, suppliers. The long supply lines were particularly damaging for the fashion industries, with industrialists in the footwear and clothing sector commenting on the danger of fashion obsolescence when material might take one to three months to arrive.

These problems were compounded by the structure of industry. Cyprus was a small firm economy. Out of 6,616 manufacturing firms in 1985, only 56 had more than 100 workers, and only one had more than 500. The 56 accounted for less than a third of manufacturing value added, and a fifth of employment. The great majority of producers were family firms. In 1984, imputed wages and salaries for proprietors and their families came to a third of all payments to labour. Only 20 per cent of firms with more than 50 workers were public companies. The resulting fragmentation of ownership was made more serious by the lack of specialisation between firms. In furniture, for example, many of the producers had their own shops and were thus forced to produce a full product range, most of the items in small batches. Far from competition having encouraged rationalisation and specialisation, it led if anything to product diversification.

Mass production, even in large markets, has always been vulnerable to market fluctuations, supply failures and capacity utilisation. It has always had quality problems. For these reasons, it has tended to carry high stocks and work in progress as a buffer against uncertainty, and to exhibit low stock turns (stock:turnover ratio). It has also run up against labour supply problems in a boom, and continuous labour turnover of its semi-skilled workforce in boom and slump. These difficulties have been offset by the scale economies of production.

For a small island economy like Cyprus, the scale economies are necessarily limited, while the problems of mass production are enhanced. A country with a small internal market is particularly subject to the effects of world market fluctuations. It has few labour reservoirs. Most of its machinery and intermediate goods have to be imported (in 1984, the figures were 69 per cent for intermediate goods and 81 per cent for capital goods) and this compounds the problem of long supply lines. Coupled with its capacity utilisation problems, this leads to low stock turns. Of the sample firms analysed, the majority had stock turns of less than 4; 16 per cent of the metalworking firms had a ratio of less than 1, that is to say their stocks exceeded their annual turnover. For manufacturing as a whole in 1985, the ratio was 5 (in contrast, say, to Toyota, who achieve a ratio of 90, their stock turning over once every four days).

In sectors where there are volume economies, small country mass producers will need protection for the home market and/or the advantages of raw materials or cheap labour in order to export. But limited quantities of labour - when coupled with the disadvantages of mass production in such economies - mean that the capacity to sustain a mass production strategy is limited. Cyprus faced these constraints by the mid-1980s.

The public policy response both by the employers' organisations and the Government had been largely developed within the same strategic framework. The Government's incentive schemes were focused on fixed capital: up to 45 per cent of capital expenditure qualified for an investment allowance, any capital expenditure was allowed as a deduction from income in the year it was spent, and there was a tax reduction from 42.5 per cent to 25 per cent on profits set aside for investment in new machinery. The Government encouraged amalgamation, public companies paying only 25 per cent profit tax, and there has been pressure to establish a stock exchange to further shift industrial ownership away from the family towards professionally managed public firms. There have also been attempts to attract foreign mass producers through the establishment of a Free Trade Zone at Larnaca, and other fiscal incentives.

All these policies have by and large failed. During the first half of the 1980s, firms with under 20 workers increased their share of manufacturing output from 27 per cent to 34 per cent, while the share of firms with more than 100 workers fell from 41 per cent to 34 per cent. By 1987, the Free Trade Zone had only a dozen firms, and much of it lay unutilised. Singapore and Hong Kong were located close to sources of labour. The same was not true of Cyprus.

For their part, the firms which were facing declining markets and increased competition in the Middle East attempted to reorient themselves to the internal market and towards Europe. There was increased price cutting competition within Cyprus by 1987 (notably in metalworking), and a move into retailing (footwear). Some were trying to diversify into other products (a switchgear producer seeking to start printed circuit board production, for example) while others aimed to become importers of goods from other parts of Europe, using the retail outlets they already owned (as was the case in the furniture industry). However, none of these defensive strategies offered the long-run prospect of overall industrial growth.

A number of firms saw their future as subcontractors to other European manufacturers, and regional service points for their products. In clothing, for example, Cyprus manufacturers had for some time undertaken Cut, Make and Trim (CMT) subcontract work for London wholesalers. In 1983-84, a survey found a third of a sample of 70 clothing companies engaged in CMT work. In our own 1987 sample, the figure had risen to 45 per cent and one industry source estimated the figure as 70 per cent for industry as a whole. Other volume clothing firms had established longer-term contracts - one providing shirts to three large European jeans manufacturers, another underwear to Germany. In footwear there were three "sourcing" plants, and in furniture three exporters of pine chairs.

At the same time, a number of footwear and clothing firms established technology agreements with other European firms, giving them access to design and brand names in the Cypriot and regional markets. Of 12 such contracts studied, five limited sales to Cyprus, four restricted them to regional markets, and only three served wider markets, including those in advanced industrial countries.

There was clearly some potential in both these strategies. Cyprus was well placed to act as a European shop window for the Middle East. There has also been a tendency for European light industrial production to move processes to the southern periphery of Europe, and the evidence suggests that Cyprus still has a wage cost advantage over EEC countries, with the exception of Portugal and Greece, though a disadvantage in relation to North Africa.

Yet the margins on both licensed and subcontract production are narrow. The fees on the technology contracts ranged from 4-10 per cent of sales, while pre-tax profits in a sample of 19 clothing firms averaged only 6.7 per cent in 1986. For the subcontractors much depends on wages - it is the decisive advantage - but, with tight labour supply and a strong trade union movement, wages have been increasing faster than in the rest of Europe (by 58 per cent as against 17 per cent between 1980 and 1985), thus narrowing the gap. The employers had been pressing for the de-indexation of wages (which had long been a feature of Cypriot industrial relations). They have contested wage settlements more vigorously, and there has recently been an increase in labour migration from North Africa. But any of these will only marginally affect the central issue - that there are geographic, demographic and political limitations on Cyprus being able to act as a long-term platform for cheap labour subcontracting to the rest of Europe. Other economies which have followed a path of labour-intensive volume production - Ireland, Hong Kong, South Korea, Singapore - have all evidenced a tendency for wages to rise and foreign-owned or contracted production to move to a new set of lower wage countries. In each, a labour-intensive stage has been followed by an attempt to upgrade production. Cyprus has been through its labour-intensive stage.

The University of Sussex team concluded, therefore, in its report "Cyprus Industrial Strategy",[2] that volume production did not have a long-term future for Cypriot producers. The internal market was growing more slowly and was due to lose its protection. Low wage competition could be expected to intensify in both domestic and overseas markets. Quality products made under licence promised limited growth, while labour supply constrained the future of subcontracting. "Cyprus will not become the Hong Kong of the Eastern Mediterranean on the basis of low wage volume production", the report concluded.

The question was posed, therefore, of whether there was an alternative strategy, one centred on upgrading, and, more specifically, on the application of the principles of flexible specialisation.

IV. The potential for flexible specialisation

Curiously, a number of the features which had worked against efficient volume production provided a basis for a strategy of flexible specialisation. Most immediately, the small, family-owned firm structure had many parallels with those in the industrial districts of the Third Italy. Cyprus was itself small - a similar population to, say, Modena in Emilia-Romagna - and had a strong civic and national cohesion. Industrialists tended to know each other, as well as local and national politicians. As in Emilia-Romagna, there was a strong Communist Party (the Communists and Socialists accounting for some 40 per cent of the national vote in Cyprus) and, since 1975, there has been a social pact between labour and their employers reflected in the continuation of wage indexation and substantial state welfare provisions. The threat from Turkey acted as a force of national cohesion.

---

2.   Institute of Development Studies. 1987. *Cyprus Industrial Strategy*, Report prepared for the United Nations Industrial Development Organisation on behalf of the Government of Cyprus, Brighton, University of Sussex.

In many ways, too, the Cypriot economy in the late 1980s was markedly sophisticated. The Cypriot domestic and tourist markets, though small, are quality-conscious and demanding; acting as a stimulus to design-led strategies in the consumer goods sector. There is a strong tradition, too, of education: the proportion of graduates in Cyprus is one of the highest in the world. Having no university of its own has meant that Cypriot students have been educated at universities and polytechnics in many different countries, and this has contributed to a cosmopolitan culture. Many of the sons and daughters of industrialists are among those trained abroad, and this second generation is already bringing a new approach to Cypriot industry.

It is not surprising, therefore, that there are already a number of firms following a policy of upgrading. The dairy producers have been actively marketing Cypriot "niche" products in Europe. In clothing, there is a medium-sized children's wear firm where designers make up 9 per cent of the workforce. As a result, the firm has been able to establish and promote its own brand name in the Cypriot market. Its owner, who had at one time worked as an engineer for a European quality car firm, had brought many of the quality lessons with him, as well as an emphasis on management information systems and skilled labour. This firm is exporting to Sweden and Holland under its own brand name. There were other clothing firms like this: one exporting 100 per cent of its fashionwear through relatives in the United States of America, another producing leather clothing for export, a third producing knitwear, buying its collection each year from a freelance designer based in Milan. So there were already working examples in Cyprus of an alternative production strategy.

A number of points which showed the contrast of these firms to the traditional mass producers emerged during sector association meetings attended by the Sussex team. All of them were competing on design and quality rather than price. The fashionwear clothing firms spent considerable sums on keeping abreast of design intelligence from abroad, one firm spending C£800,000 a year on fashion forecasting reports, foreign travel and salaries for its 10-person design staff, or 4 per cent of its total turnover. Others have sent their daughters to London and Paris for specialised training in garment design. In the shoe industry, a number of firms had subcontracted design to Italy as a step towards making themselves competitive in Europe. In furniture there were cases of outstanding design, but here the problem was how to shift from being one-off luxury producers to being more automated, low priced yet still high quality firms.

Such firms also placed importance on the quality of their labour force and on good industrial relations. In the clothing industry, for example, it was the quality conscious firms which undertook training, and who were unanimous in the view that moderate increases in wages would not pose major difficulties for their businesses. In the footwear industry, there was a clear correlation (0.75) between average wages and value added per worker.

It was also striking that all these firms remained independent of foreign firms who wished to use them as subcontractors. One design-oriented furniture firm had refused an offer for a joint venture with Habitat, a large United Kingdom retailer, on the grounds that the contract stipulated 100 per cent Habitat designs. The design-oriented clothing firms preferred to subcontract design abroad rather than tie themselves to a licensing and trade mark contract which restricted them to the Cyprus and regional markets. Only one of the designer clothing firms had entered into a subcontract with European firms, in this case French and British designer companies. The French company sent its designers to Cyprus several times a year to work out final samples with the local Cypriot management. The Cypriot factory produced for the French market and was allowed to sell the output anywhere outside France. The Cypriot firm had its design team working with the French designers, developing original designs of their own for the regional market. In this case, the owner/manager saw the link-up with the overseas designers as a means of learning about the requirements of design in the European market, rather than as a long-term substitute for developing its own designs.

In this case, the Cypriot firm sold in Europe and elsewhere, and it was a feature of all the firms that they had "turned towards Europe" in a different way to the low-cost subcontractors. The new wave firms were taking upon themselves the responsibility for overseas marketing and design, many of them using the tourist and Cypriot home market as a testing ground for their products. They saw the domestic market less as a place for high mark-ups to finance their competition abroad than as a site for product development for eventual expansion into developed country markets.

It was quite clear that these firms had a quite different outlook to the traditional mass producers, and that the strategies they were pursuing were similar in some ways to those followed in the successful industrial districts in Western Europe.

The question was how firms of this sort could further develop along the lines they were following, and whether it was possible to generalise the approach to other firms in the key sectors. In none of the sectors did it appear that flexible specialisation would be easy. But what became generally agreed - by industrialists, and the Government - was that it was a more promising strategy than the alternative of volume production. The "Cyprus Industrial Strategy" (CIS), which was delivered in draft in the autumn of 1987, outlined a number of paths by which the strategy could be pursued.

V.   The turn towards flexible specialisation: where to start

The key features of flexible specialisation can be summarised as follows:

(i)   the adaptability of production systems to movements in market demands;

(ii)   the customisation of products to particular segments of the market;

(iii)   a capacity for continuous innovation in both process and product (in the case of Cyprus this was more through design than research and development);

(iv)   a focus on the economy of working capital, through such means as Just-in-Time production, low defect rates, and making to order;

(v)   a focus on continuous learning both within enterprises and between any one enterprise and its suppliers, its final markets and its competitors. The enterprise is opened up to the external world which is seen as a source of stimulation and new ideas rather than a hostile arena;

(vi)   the labour in the enterprise is seen as an asset rather than a cost - a repository of skills and ideas, and crucial to ensuring quality at the point of production;

(vii) the organisation of the productive system as a whole involves a mixture of decentralisation (to small firms and plants) and centralisation (of certain indivisible or collective services), as well as inter-plant specialisation to ensure economies of scale.

Flexible specialisation is not about small firms or small batches, but rather about a productive system which can produce either large or small batches with flexible production systems, without the costs of excess capacity and stock build-ups characteristic of the mass production system. It is about intra-organisational flexibility in response to changing external requirements.

VI. Micro-level restructuring

All these imply a different way of looking at production, at organisation, and at economic relationships. The starting point is necessarily at the level of the enterprise. The firms themselves have to recognise the nature of the alternative strategies and see the potential of the flexibly specialised path. To this end, the manner of producing the strategy is itself the first step in its implementation. New industrial policy cannot be satisfactorily developed by economists - whether indigenous or from abroad - advising the Government on changes in state instruments. It must start from those immediately involved in production - both management and workforces - for it is on them that all change in the economy ultimately depends. In the case of the CIS, the recommendations emerged from the sectoral discussions, firm visits, and public meetings and were seen as a first approximation to be further developed.

The employers' organisations played an important part in this process. They not only hosted the sectoral meetings, but translated the relevant parts of the draft strategy into Greek, distributing them widely throughout industry and organising a series of discussion meetings by sector. These continued for many months and were followed by a series of seminars in the new approach funded by the industrialists themselves.

One important initiative centred on one of the new wave clothing firms. The owner/manager came to the United Kingdom at his own expense to attend a 6-week seminar on flexible specialisation, then returned home to further reorganise his production. He introduced a new cellular layout with each worker performing 3-4 different tasks at 2-3 different machines, whereas previously each had done a single repetitive job at a single machine. Batch size was cut (from 400 to 120), and lot sizes cut to 5-6 pieces, providing only limited buffer stocks between workpoints. Each worker was made responsible for quality at source, and no faulty goods were to be accepted by the next worker. He also established a joint venture with a Cypriot softwear writer and developed a computerised integrated database containing the detailed characteristics of all orders, their cut details and the delivery data. It automatically provided a bill of materials - helping to reduce raw material and final product stocks; it provided more accurate orders to raw material suppliers abroad, and up-to-date detail on which items were selling well. It also helped production scheduling, allowing control of the scheduling to pass to production staff, thus freeing senior management. Finally, the need to integrate design, production and marketing and the flexibility offered by the new form of production led the firm to open its own chain of shops.

The result of this reorganisation has been as follows. First, work in progress and final stocks have been drastically cut. This gave a once and for all reduction in working capital requirements which itself more than covered the costs of reorganisation and enabled a saving in annual interest charges of C£6,000 a year. Sales per worker increased by a third. Space requirements fell by 28 per cent, the value of the space saved alone being equivalent to more than the total cost of restructuring. Throughput time has fallen from nine to three days, and production lead time from six months to three. Product flexibility rose from 15 to 20 varieties and the system has the capacity to handle up to 40 different varieties without negatively affecting production efficiency. Overall, the reorganisation produced once-off net savings of 25 per cent of annual sales, and annual net savings of 7 per cent of sales.

These are striking results and they have recently been written up by the manager together with one of the original Sussex team to provide a case study of the difficulties (for there were some) and the benefits of restructuring. It is clear that such firm-level restructuring needs to be an important component of any broader strategy, centred at first on a small number of "new wave" firms and then extended through a system of consultancy and advice.

VII. Sectoral restructuring

Micro-level restructuring is a starting point, but it is not enough. For in a small firm economy like that of Cyprus, there are many economies internal to large firms which have to be achieved through sectoral planning and co-operation. The first of these is specialisation. It was clear from the Sussex team's studies that there were many potential economies of horizontal specialisation which were not being developed through the market. The furniture industry, with so many of the medium-sized manufacturers having their own retail outlets, was a case in point. If the manufacturers shared retail outlets, and then specialised between themselves, they would be able to move to larger batch sizes.

With the support of the Cyprus Development Bank, a group of 12 (now 13) Limmasol furniture makers did this. They agreed to open a joint retail shop, for which they would produce newly-designed products on a specialised basis. One firm was charged with kitchen furniture, another with bedroom suites, a third with children's furniture, a fourth concentrated on upholstery and so on. Each firm would submit designs for its speciality to a design committee, bearing in mind the styles being produced by others. The members of the consortium (known as the A-Z Consortium) were allowed to keep their own retail shops and their lines of production, but the specialised furniture could only be sold in the joint shop.

There were two immediate economies. Firstly, unit costs in the specialised furniture fell by 20-25 per cent as the result of longer runs, and the new lines have allowed one of the manufacturers to move into larger facilities, and several others to invest in new, more specialised machinery. Secondly, there have been clear retailing economies. The consortium can employ a specialist interior designer at the point of sale; it offers a wider variety of product (economies of scope); and has two marketing staff to engage in research and propose new product development. It also has a joint delivery system, and can afford a greater level of advertising than any of its members did previously.

What was soon evident was an extension of these economies of specialisation back into production and purchasing. Joint retailing required careful costing, and a costing subcommittee of the consortium was established to visit each manufacturer, examine his or her costs, and advise on costing methods and materials and production itself where the costs were out of line. By such means, the consortium provided a way of spreading the most effective methods. They were also able to fund specialist consultants from Italy and, by joint purchasing, cut material costs by up to 25 per cent.

The results have been strikingly successful. The consortium now has shops in each of the major towns in Cyprus. Its consortium sales exceeded those projected in the initial feasibility study. In 1989 they won a major export order to the Soviet Union and have become successful exporters to Saudi Arabia. From being a group of small manufacturers competing for the domestic market, they have become - if all their employment is added together - the second largest manufacturing concern in Cyprus, with a growing export record.

This is one kind of consortium. There are potentially others - in exporting for example, or finance, or the provision of common services. These are the kinds of consortia found in Italy. As part of the development of sector strategy, a group of clothing manufacturers, and another of furniture makers, visited Emilia-Romagna and the Milan region, to examine the experience of consortia and the centres of "real services". The example of the latter at Carpi has been taken as something of a model for Cyprus, as a centre - to be run and part-funded by the industrialists themselves - to provide a mixture of market intelligence and technological information, as well as to provide access to Computer Aided Design equipment.

A further area of sectoral action is the improvement of the quality of input supplies. In some sectors, the problem was the price and quality of inputs from existing local facilities (lasts, for example, for the footwear sector are supplied from a single source and have been found to be of lower quality and more expensive than imports). In both furniture and food there was a tension between the final manufacturers and the suppliers, each blaming the other for low quality and poor production techniques. The sectoral discussions also produced suggestions for new input facilities - an expansion of the textile dyeing capacity, a third leather finishing plant, a joint steel stockholding facility, and a collective converting operation in the clothing industry by which a consortium of clothing firms would buy up grey cloth and have it finished in line with members' requirements.

These are all examples of projects emerging from a sector strategy. Some can be taken forward by groups of firms. Others require broader sectoral support, not least in the development of a sector strategy itself, on a rolling basis, as a context for enterprise and government initiatives. In some countries - notably France - the industry associations are publicly funded to produce sectoral strategies of this kind, but in many others, including Cyprus, the capacity for sector strategy remains limited.

VIII. Inter-sectoral and national policies

Beyond the enterprise and sectoral levels, there are also some factors which require inter-sectoral and national action. One of these is finance, another is design, a third is education, training and the whole area of labour policy, a fourth is industrial estates. There is also the question of the system of financial incentives. I will deal with each in turn.

1.   Finance

Many of the manufacturers complained about the commercial banks. They were, it was said, passive, lending for the most part on the basis of collateral with a short- or medium-term time horizon. They lacked sectoral expertise, and gave little technical support to their borrowers. This is a complaint often heard against commercial banking - notably in Britain.

It was clear that some of the working capital needs could best be addressed by improving the use of working capital through firm-level restructuring. One firm complaining of a lack of working capital had three years of steel stocks in an under-used factory. This was not primarily a problem of the banking system.

But it was also clear that a flexible specialisation strategy did require a much more supportive industrial banking system capable of taking a long-term developmental view, in the manner of the Cyprus Development Bank (CDB). The CDB, like the great majority of development banks, was established to do all that the commercial banking system did not do - provide long-term funds; look at projects and potential bankruptcies from the viewpoint of national development rather than solely in terms of the balance sheet; give hands-on advice and other support services to domestic industry, and so on. The CDB has done all these things, and is one of the few Cypriot institutions to have developed sector specialisation. As we have seen in the furniture sector, it has also actively intervened to encourage sectoral restructuring. It has, however, suffered from a restriction of public funds, and on the freedom to diversify into new fields which would give it access to sources of private funds.

The CIS argued that development banks had a central role to play in promoting industrial restructuring - indeed, this should be seen as the main function of a development bank, beyond its role as a project defined institution. It suggested that the function should be greatly expanded, primarily as a front-line agency to give hands-on advice and support to firms and sectors reorienting themselves along flexible specialisation lines.

2.   Design

Design is one of the pivots of the new competition and, with notable exceptions, Cypriot firms had little, if any, design capacity. This reflected a lack of a design culture within Cyprus more generally - in spite of a keen consumer awareness of its importance. Thus, while individual firms could take steps to strengthen their design staff, what was needed were more widespread measures to raise design skills and design consciousness in Cyprus as a whole. The CIS proposed a number of ways this might be done: through establishing a Cyprus College of Art and Design linked to a Museum of Contemporary Art and Design; through the Ministry of Education, extending art and design teaching in secondary schools, and giving priority to students intending to go to design colleges in its selection guidelines for study abroad. These ideas arose from discussions with members of the small design community in Cyprus and with educationalists and industrialists. Their aim was to strengthen the educational and cultural infrastructure in the design and, more generally, the visual field.

3. Labour and education

Cyprus already has an Industrial Training Authority (ITA), funded by a levy on employers. The ITA has produced some of the best sector studies that exist in the country, and has been working on skill programmes with employers and unions. Some of these reflected the division of labour and responsibilities characteristic of mass production, but the ITA was among the first to embrace the implications of a flexible specialisation strategy for its training programmes.

The ITA studies suggested that the problem was less the supply of trained labour than the way labour was employed. The level of wages and poor working conditions meant that labour turnover was high in manufacturing. In metalworking there was a clear substitution of inexperienced and unskilled workers for the 78 per cent of workers leaving their jobs who were skilled or semi-skilled. It was common for workers with specific skills to be doing jobs requiring quite different training. There was a notable lack of child-care facilities - particularly serious in a manufacturing wage labour force of which 55 per cent were women.

Thus, any new policy which treated labour as a key asset in the production process required not only a reorientation of training, but a transformation of the conditions of employment, of the design of the work process and of industrial relations, if it were to succeed. The strategy therefore called for the preparation of a detailed Labour Plan for manufacturing - covering new payment systems, working conditions, health and safety, child-care, incentives for firms to employ quality-of-work consultants, the operation of the labour market, the future supply of labour, the employment of women, industrial relations and productivity increases, as well as the whole field of training and education.

4. Industrial estates

The government had for some time run a successful industrial estates programme, but the estates had not been operated in such a way as to encourage sectoral concentration and industrial districts. There were two small traditional industrial districts in the centre of Nicosia which the urban planning authorities wanted to remove, and the CIS encouraged both the municipal authorities and the Government to plan for sectoral districts, which provided common facilities and services.

5.   Financial incentives

Cyprus operated a range of tax allowances and incentives geared to encouraging investment in fixed capital, new product development, exports, mergers and the formation of public companies. There were three main problems with the system as it stood. First, tax evasion and avoidance was widespread. The Ministry of Finance estimated that only 30-40 per cent of firms actually filed tax returns, and many of those which did showed little, if any, profit. Incentive schemes based on tax allowances cannot therefore be expected to have much purchase. Secondly, the take-up of many of the schemes was low. There were only four applications for the generous new products scheme in 1987, for example, and the general guarantee scheme for loans to industrialists was running at a rate of three approvals per year in early 1989. Three of the schemes alone accounted for 78 per cent of the usage. Part of the problem was the lack of incentives in tax relief, as mentioned above; a number of the schemes were administratively complex and this was a further disincentive; nor did some of the incentives apply to the key concerns of manufacturers (in clothing, footwear and furniture, design is at least as important as R & D).

This touches the third problem which was that the incentives encouraged investments in hardware rather than software. Because of the generosity of the capital allowances, some industrialists - like the meat processors - clearly over-invested in machinery. The allowance system encouraged investment in surplus capacity. The areas that received much less encouragement were investment in training, the development of management information systems, design, or marketing structures. The Industrial Strategy therefore proposed a switch of emphasis in the incentive programme from hardware to software.

The proposals that have been developed over the past two years suggest that this is done not simply by changing the items of expenditure that are eligible for allowances. Rather, they propose incentives which are geared to a process of firm-level restructuring of the kind I described earlier. Firms would be encouraged to engage an innovation consultant who would act like a General Practitioner in the medical field, in identifying where the key problems were and, as in medicine, advising the firm to move on to a specialist consultant in, say, management information systems. The Government would cover part of the cost up to a limit, but responsibility for the consultants and part of the finance would be with the firm. One of the results of this process would be to identify where investment - both in hardware and software - is needed, some of which would qualify for government support on the basis of the consultants' assessments.

Variations on such schemes have recently been developed in Europe, and one of their advantages is that they have encouraged the development of innovation consultancy itself. They have customarily been delivered from outside the normal civil service structures by a managing agent - the Design Advisory Service in the United Kingdom is run by the Design Council, an independent non-profit body concerned with promoting better design standards. In Germany, the administration of schemes is often given to research organisations; for instance, the scheme to promote computer-aided design and manufacturing is managed by a small branch of the Nuclear Research Centre in Karlsruhe. In such centres, administration is normally handled by two or three people, with a minimum of form filling, who build up an approved list of consultants in order to exert a measure of quality control. The Cyprus government is currently considering the adoption of such a scheme.

IX. Industrial strategy and the flexible state

Industrial planning and strategy are normally associated with the state. They are national issues and part of public responsibility. But responsibility is one thing, the means of developing a strategy and implementing it quite another. In the field of industrial policy, it is as important to apply the principles of flexible specialisation to public administrative practices as it is to encourage its adoption in productive enterprise.

In traditional forms of economic administration, the government sets the rules and the terms within which industrial enterprises operate. It may have some public production - in the case of Cyprus the Ministry of Industry and Commerce ran the largest bakery, and was the main timber producer - and provide some infrastructure, but for the most part it stays off the field of play and attempts to influence action by changing the rules of the game and the macro-economic environment. Ministries of Finance and Planning are generally at the centre of such management. Ministries of Industry and Commerce are responsible for the administration of incentives schemes, tariff protection, anti-trust regulations, and so on. They may also be charged, particularly in developing countries, with a development role, being involved in promoting sectoral restructuring, innovation, and upgrading.

This is where difficulties arise, for civil services are structured to be mass producers of administration. The Weberian model of the state - with its mixture of Prussian administrative practice and Taylorist principles - is based on rules, a clearly specified division of function, hierarchical levels of graded authority, an intentional separation of the bureaucracy from the receivers of the service, and lifetime employment with impersonal criteria for appointment and promotion. Like all such structures - whether in the private or the public spheres - its advantages are its permanence, and its efficiency in delivering standardised outputs (an immunisation campaign, for example). Its weaknesses are its inflexibility, its role-based rather than task-based orientation, its discouragement of innovation, and the distance that stands between it and the community it administers. All these make it an unsuitable structure to perform a developmental role.

In the industrial sphere, some bureaucracies of this kind have seen planning in terms of the principles of their own structures: as a set of detailed plans (like a rule book or code of practice), which the subordinate economic agents are required to follow. But the problems of information, incentives and control have all contributed to a bias in such planning towards large-scale public projects, and have made it quite unsuitable for the operation and restructuring of smaller-scale economic sectors. What has happened as a result is that planning ministries have retreated into providing a structure for the co-ordination of public projects within the context of broad macro projections, while sectoral ministries have concentrated on administering developmental schemes on the basis of the application of impersonal guidelines. What is lacking is a sense of strategic direction for particular industries and for broader sectors of the economy which can connect the many parts of the government with all those involved in industry. This is the function of an industrial strategy.

This conflict between administrative structure and developmental tasks applies to governments all over the world - East and West, North and South - as it does to international institutions like the United Nations or the World Bank. It applies to Ministries of Agriculture as to Industry, to Energy and Water as much as to Health. It is no surprise, therefore, that the Government of Cyprus - in spite of an able and highly qualified civil service - has been beset by this problem in its economic administration.

How can flexible specialisation help? First, by its emphasis on the importance of decentralisation within the context of a commonly-agreed overall plan. Economic strategy cannot be adequately drawn up by the centre and administered from the centre. Indeed, I have suggested that the starting point should not be the centre at all but those directly involved with production. Each firm needs its own strategy, which it will put into practice. But equally, for the reasons I have outlined, micro-level strategies are by themselves not enough. There is a need to establish links between firms, within sectors, between sectors, and across the national economy as a whole. The image of the Russian doll is more appropriate than that of the pyramid.

In order to encourage these different levels of strategic reorientation, the process of making the strategy, and continuously remaking it, is of the first importance. It must involve all those party to its implementation. Thus, modern corporate management has recognised that the old Taylorist division between head and hand is quite unsuitable for a world of continuous innovation. In the development of corporate strategies, workforces should be involved. At the national level, employers, trade unions and different parts of the Government, as well as user groups and special interest groups like women's organisations, need to take part. The wider the representation, the richer the strategy, and the more effective the implementation.

To date, this has been one of the most successful sides of the Industrial Strategy process in Cyprus. I have already touched on the work of employers' associations in translating and sponsoring discussions amongst its members. But the Government, too, insisted that the CIS should be widely circulated and discussed. There have been public meetings, working parties and discussions within the Ministries, and the President has set up a task force, headed by an industrialist, to carry forward the ideas. The Strategy has been extensively covered in the newspapers and on television - "flexible specialisation" is no longer an academic phrase in Cyprus.

Where there has been an intense debate within the Government is on the question of how this strategic work should be organised. It is generally agreed that there is a need for a representative Strategic Council, with a small secretariat to service it. Its *modus operandi* would be to form temporary teams to focus on particular sectors - the teams to be made up of people with knowledge of the industry from inside and outside the public service and supported, where necessary, by specialists in the field of international industry. These teams would then report to the Council for approval, agreement and action by the parties concerned. The debate has been about how this new structure of strategic planning should link in to the existing government structure - a matter which has only recently been positively resolved.

The point about strategic planning is that it is a skilled task, and it is a skill which all parties require in order to be fully effective. This applies to the government Ministries - for whom in general the tasks of day-to-day administration have reduced their strategic capacity - as much as to parastatals and those directly involved in industry. The Government has a clear role in bringing all parties together - within its own structures as much as in the civil society - and in ensuring that it has an adequate strategic capacity within its main departments to fulfil the tasks in hand.

The strategic function is therefore a central one for Government. When it comes to support services and the allocation of funds, the public task is usually best administered by decentralised bodies. A support service needs to be tailored to the needs of those receiving the service, and should, where possible, be under their control. The requirements of the service rather than the institutional structures of the server should be paramount. In the industry field, this means that an industrial advice service should at least work hours in common with the industrialists they are advising, and the advisers should have the scope to update their own direct knowledge of the industry. This does not happen in Cyprus any more than it does in many public industrial extension services. When it comes to technology advice and "real services" the Sussex team have strongly recommended that they be run from centres controlled and funded partially by the industrialists. The same would be true of export marketing organisations.

In the allocation of funds or services where there may be a conflict of interest between the individual receiving enterprises and any independent body, it is still important for fund and service providers to have a day-to-day knowledge of the industry. This can be achieved by the circulation of staff between the donor agencies and industry, by frequent firm visits, and by placing a measure of responsibility on the provider for the success of the recipient. None of these functions can effectively be carried out by officials at a head office - whether the head office is private or a public ministry. The task of a head office is to allocate tranches of funds to local funding agents and to judge their performance. This is why the new incentive scheme proposals envisage independent units and agencies with a specialist administering the schemes.

Whether the services are general or specific, the same principle of decentralisation should hold: training provisions, productivity programmes, or export promotion. The central state should exercise its responsibility through (a) approval of the structure of control, ensuring that the governing boards represent the proper range of interests; (b) the broad terms of conduct of the organisation; (c) powers of information, inspecting and reporting by independent assessors; and (d) finance.

What is imperative for any such programme of public decentralisation as proposed in Cyprus is the existence of an independent public auditor. In the United Kingdom, the Audit Commission has played a useful role in local government by a close examination of services and comparisons between different service providers. It has over-emphasised the financial aspects of the audit, at the expense of services and needs, but this could be rectified by a change in the terms of reference, and strengthening its non-financial personnel. For Cyprus, an Audit Commission would need to be established with the same professional ethos as legal judges; they would need the rights of full access, as well as the right of reporting at cabinet level; and they could be asked to approve the annual report of the quasi-public body in the same way as financial auditors approve the accounts. They should also themselves be subject to audit, and replacement where necessary.

A further guiding principle is that of pluralism. There is a danger that an Audit Commission might seek to impose a particular view of how a service should be provided, and unreasonably discourage alternative experiments. Experimentation should be one of the criteria against which quasi-publics should be judged, and where relevant more than one provider should exist to encourage pluralism. A Weberian model would criticise this as duplication. In the production economy, it is called competition, though the form of competition in the quasi-public sphere would differ from that of the market.

Such an approach to economic administration removes routine administration from the key ministries, allowing them space to develop their strategic role, to ensure the delicate task of co-ordinating other parts of the government around the strategy, to administer their funded bodies (securing general finance, allocating funds to the front-line allocators, assessing their performance), and finally to stimulating short-term initiatives which might later be directed to one of the independent institutions.

I have referred to this as a flexible rather than a Weberian state, not simply because it allows the decentralised services to establish their own relevant procedures and organisational cultures, and to take a much greater measure of responsibility for their action than has been possible in centralised state structures. But also it establishes a different relationship between the service providers and those for whom the services are provided. The front line staff in this system become the prime units in the model of administration, as though the organisational pyramid had been stood on its head. They are able to establish close relations with those whose needs they serve, in much the same way as flexible specialisation develops sustained two-way relations between a firm and its suppliers and customers. Such contacts are then a basis for service innovation - which may need to be approved by the Ministerial funder but which would have been unlikely to have been initiated by them. In such a structure, the former centre of authority - the Ministry - becomes a supporter, funder, adviser, and overall strategic stimulator of the front line rather than the controller.

X. Conclusion

The "Cyprus Industrial Strategy" represents an attempt to redirect industrial policy and its public administration along a path of flexible specialisation. It remains to be seen how successful it will be. What we have learnt so far is that the open process of making a strategy - along the lines I have described - itself begins the process of implementation. Irrespective of formal government approval of the strategy, firms themselves and a number of the quasi-public institutions like the CDB and the ITA have already been exploring the new directions.

In general, steps which require agreement between independent organisations - public or private - have been the slowest to proceed (the A-Z furniture consortium being a notable exception, due in significant part to the prompting of the Cyprus Development Bank). The delay has been particularly marked over new national level institutions. This suggests that any such process should focus first on the micro level - at what existing institutions can do for themselves, without further public funds - before moving to the sectoral and the macro levels. The latter are necessary but are likely to take longer, and the difficulties encountered should not hold back developments at the micro level. What is clear from the Cyprus case is that there is considerable space for the micro institutions to re-orient themselves as they stand. The process of industrial strategy-making brings to the fore those firms, individuals, and public institutions who have the spirit to apply the strategic principles immediately in whatever way they can. This is important because they become the key points for further stages of diffusion - both as models of experience, and as people to contribute to the wider strategic movement.

This underlines a second point which I necessarily touched on in discussing the strategic process. It is that strategy at all levels gains from a strong "civil society". This has been a lesson from the East, and from the West. Governments and enterprises too often regard trade unions, environmental groups, consumer organisations, or community groups as an inconvenience, an interruption to the task in hand. But what the Sussex team has found is that such groups have been centrally important in shaping the direction of an economy in a way which is both productive and socially unifying. They have been the spur to innovation, to improvements in quality, and to service delivery. Firms and states which have recognised and even supported them have found themselves to have benefited in all sorts of fields.

Cyprus has a long-standing trade union tradition, and this is a strength for the prospects of flexible specialisation. It is less strong in its consumer movement, but already the Cyprus Consumer's Association (again with the support of the Cyprus Development Bank) has taken the initiative by pursuing one of the proposals of the CIS, to publish a Good Food Guide as a means of raising quality in the food processing industry, and improving tourism. A thriving economy depends just as much on organisations like this as it does on the technocrat or planner.

Thirdly, the experience with Cyprus has shown the value of the sector strategic approach as against the generic one. By the latter, I mean organising a strategy around such things as training, foreign investment, export promotion, manufacturing versus services, new technology, and so on. One of the complementary studies to the CIS was a Cyprus Technology Strategy, which argued that new technology could often best be delivered sector-specifically, defining the sector, however, as a *filière*, a thread which often ran across traditional statistical categories. It looked in particular at the water, energy and agricultural *filières*, each including primary, secondary and tertiary industries, each needing specific forms of support services. It affirmed the need for customising the generic policy concerns to the sector since the sector is the prime contour of the productive economy. One of the reasons why the Cyprus Industrial Strategy has been so widely discussed is that it was organised sectorally, that is along the grain of daily experience and economic organisation.

These lessons have long been learnt in the industrial districts of Europe. This is why their structures and directions are so suggestive for industrial policy in the developing world. But one further lesson of these districts must also be remembered: that each has a long history, and that successful flexible specialisation takes time to grow. In Cyprus, it is now five years since a new strategy along the lines we have described was begun. That, too, has seemed a long time: but against the background of an Emilia-Romagna or a Jutland, it is still a mere beginning. The prospects it offers, and is already beginning to show, are encouraging enough to reward its patient supporters. In the matter of industrial strategy, as in economic management, it is the outlook of the gardener rather than the mechanic which is now the most relevant.

Part IV: Overview and comment

11 Industrial districts and local economic regeneration: Overview and comment

Jonathan Zeitlin

I. Introduction

Industrial districts have captured the attention of a substantial body of researchers and policy-makers across a wide range of countries and organisations. Three principal factors largely account for the districts' appeal, as Werner Sengenberger and Frank Pyke observe in the opening chapter: their economic performance, as measured by exports, employment, flexibility and innovation; their capacity for endogenous regional development; and their ability to sustain high wages and labour standards in the face of international competition. Much of the debate about industrial districts has rightly focused on how far and under what conditions particular districts in fact fulfil these high expectations. A considerable body of research on these issues is now available, much of it summarised in this book and in the previous IILS volume on *Industrial districts and inter-firm co-operation in Italy* [Pyke et al., 1990]. Such empirical studies provide a strong *prima facie* case for the economic and social robustness of industrial districts in a variety of sectors and regions though, as we shall see below, their findings are neither univocal nor free from ambiguities.

But once it is accepted that industrial districts do constitute a potentially attractive model of regional development, two central questions arise for policy-makers in governments, trade unions, employers' associations and other relevant organisations. What role can conscious policies play in sustaining established districts in the face of new competitive challenges, whether commercial, technological or organisational? What role can policy play in stimulating the emergence of new districts, whether in declining industrial areas or in developing regions? Each of these questions quickly runs up against a widespread view of successful industrial districts such as those of the "Third Italy" - shared by many of their own inhabitants - as unique social artefacts which are the product of a singular, and therefore unrepeatable, history.

The contributions to this book contain a wealth of insights about the ways in which policy-makers can help to sustain and diffuse industrial districts. Taken together, they represent a significant advance in our understanding of the strategic opportunities and avenues for fostering industrial districts by conscious political means. At the same time, however, the various chapters both contribute to and require a recasting of received ideas about the nature and dynamics of industrial districts in order for their policy implications to be fully appreciated.

This concluding chapter therefore proceeds in three main steps. Section II examines contrasting models of the industrial district in the light of recent research such as that presented in this volume. It argues for a "thin", "open" model of the industrial district which leaves considerable room for geographical and historical variations in organisation and performance, rather than a "thick", "closed" model abstracted from stylised descriptions of particular cases such as the "Third Italy". Section III considers the respective roles of culture and institutions in the operation of successful districts, highlighting the importance of formal mechanisms for conflict resolution and the provision of collective services in sustaining trust and co-operation among economic actors. Section IV then returns to the possibilities for fostering, through public policy, the simultaneous creation of the institutional infrastructure and collective actors required for the emergence and reproduction of successful industrial districts.

II. Industrial districts in theory and practice

The most widespread conceptual framework for understanding industrial districts is undoubtedly that derived from the work of the turn-of-the-century British economist Alfred Marshall. As is well known, Marshall argued that external economies could be obtained through the concentration of a large number of small firms engaged in a single industrial sector (including "subsidiary industries" such as machinery manufacture) within a localised geographical area. These external economies assumed three main forms in Marshall's analysis: economies of specialisation arising from an extended division of labour between firms in complementary activities and processes; economies of information and communication arising from the joint production of non-standardised commodities (assimilable to modern notions of transaction costs); and economies of labour supply arising from the the availability of a large pool of trained workers. More dynamic but less narrowly economic in character were the advantages Marshall attributed to the sedimentation in long-established districts of a distinctive "industrial atmosphere" which facilitated the acquisition of specialised skills through socialisation and the diffusion of innovation through frequent interchange between local actors.[1]

---

1.   For Marshall's own views, see Marshall [1975, pp. 195-198; 1922, pp. 267-290]; 1927, pp. 283-288]. For helpful modern commentaries, see Becattini [1989]; Bellandi [1989].

Marshall originally developed the concept of the industrial district with reference to contemporary British examples such as Lancashire cottons, Sheffield cutlery and South Wales tinplate. During the late 1970s and early 1980s, Italian scholars such as Giacomo Becattini, Sebastiano Brusco and others revived Marshall's concept as a framework for interpreting the explosion of small-firm development occurring in the central and north-east regions of the country. In applying the concept of the industrial district to the Italian experience, however, these scholars both extended and modified Marshall's original ideas in significant ways. Most writers on the Italian districts emphasised their classic Marshallian characteristics like the extended division of labour between firms, the accumulation of specialised skills and the diffusion of innovation. But a number of the most influential formulations, notably those of Becattini and his collaborators, also sought to elaborate Marshall's notion of "industrial atmosphere" by including a set of more explicitly "social" features drawn from a stylised account of the Italian districts. Among the new elements thereby introduced into the "canonical" model of the industrial district were a non-metropolitan, small-town environment; a set of shared values such as hard work, co-operation and collective identity; and a social structure based on the preponderance of small entrepreneurs and industrial workers. This recasting of the industrial district as a "socio-economic notion" was reinforced by the complementary work of sociologists such as Arnaldo Bagnasco and Carlo Trigilia who highlighted the influence on the genesis of "diffused industrialisation" in the "Third Italy" of historical inheritances such as the extended family, sharecropping and peasant proprietorship, and local political subcultures, both "red" (Socialist/Communist) and "white" (Catholic).[2]

This reinterpretation of the Marshallian industrial district has proved immensely fruitful both in focusing attention on the distinctive social and historical features of Italian small-firm development and in stimulating the search for analogous phenomena elsewhere. But the policy implications of the Italian experience were highly paradoxical. On the one hand, the industrial district appeared to constitute an attractive and coherent model of economic and social development which policy-makers elsewhere might wish to emulate. On the other hand, however, the wider policy relevance of the Italian model remained uncertain because of its apparent dependence on a highly specific socio-historical context.[3]

More recent research both confirms and challenges the canonical model of the Marshallian industrial district developed within the Italian

2. For a useful overview of the Italian literature, see Brusco [1990]; and for his own version of the model, see also Brusco [1982; 1986; 1989]. For major formulations by Becattini and his collaborators, see Becattini [1987; 1989; 1990a; 1990b]; Sforzi [1989; 1990]; and Bellandi [1989]. For syntheses of the work of Bagnasco and Trigilia, see Bagnasco [1988]; Trigilia [1986, 1989a, 1990]; and also Becattini [1978].

3. See, for example, Amin and Robins [1990]; Ganne [1990]; Courault and Romani [1989]; Bagnasco [1988, ch. 5]; Messori [1986].

literature.[4] The broader relevance of the industrial district as a dynamic form of economic organisation has been confirmed by the discovery of successful counterparts in a wide range of sectors and regions outside the Third Italy, as well as by the effective adjustment of many (though by no means all) Italian districts to the new competitive conditions of the 1980s. But the proliferation of industrial districts with diverse origins and internal organisation also challenges the idea of a canonical model based on a stylised account of a single national experience, as too do the significant changes observed within the Italian districts themselves. The remainder of this section briefly discusses these research findings before going on to outline an alternative and more compatible model of the industrial district.

The first and perhaps most striking finding of recent research, as we have already noted, is the sectoral and geographical range of districts identified outside the Third Italy. Drawing only on the contributions for this book, examples of established or emergent districts examined include: Baden-Württemberg in Germany; West Jutland in Denmark; Fuenlabrada, Castellón, Mondragón and the Vallés Oriental in Spain; parts of Pennsylvania in the United States; and Centre-Mauricie, Montreal and Bois-Francs in Quebec, Canada. Among the better-documented cases missing from this list should be added: Silicon Valley, Route 128 and parts of greater Los Angeles in the USA; Oyonnax and Cholet in France; Småland, in Sweden; Sakaki in Japan; and a host of districts such as Biella, Brianza, Brescia, Como and the Canavese in the north-western Italian regions of Piedmont and Lombardy.[5] As in the Third Italy itself, many of these districts specialise in light, labour-intensive industries such as clothing, textiles, shoes and furniture, but an increasing number have now been identified in more technologically-demanding and capital-intensive sectors such as metalworking, machine tools, ceramics, plastics, semiconductors, computers, motion pictures, aerospace and industrial automation.

In some of these districts, the historical matrix of development bears some affinities to that of the Third Italy. In Baden-Württemberg, West Jutland, Oyonnax and Cholet, for example, agrarian smallholdings, independent artisans and a "white" or "red" political subculture also appear to have played important roles in the formation of industrial districts. In other cases, however, district-like forms of organisation have emerged by very different routes, whether from urban professional milieux as in Silicon Valley, Route 128 and Turin or from declining large-scale industries as in Fuenlabrada, Pennsylvania or Sesto San Giovanni near Milan.[6]

---

4. In addition to the contributions to this book and Pyke et al. [1990], for surveys of recent research on industrial districts and public policy in Italy and elsewhere, see Hirst and Zeitlin [1989a], Zeitlin [1989]; Regini and Sabel [1989], and Brutti and Ricoveri [1988].

5. For a general survey, see Sabel [1989a].

6. For an elaboration of this argument, see Sabel [1989a, pp. 45-52].

These newly-identified districts display a similar diversity in economic performance, internal organisation and social complexion. Some are world-renowned centres of technological innovation with commanding export positions, while others are still struggling to establish their position in domestic and international markets. Small and medium-sized family firms overwhelmingly predominate in some cases, while large-scale enterprises and external capital play a more significant role in others. Some districts have formalised co-operation among local actors through a variety of collective institutions, while others have experienced greater difficulty in forging common interests among competing firms and social groups. Some districts are heavily unionised, with earnings levels and working conditions above the national average, while others remain poorly organised, with sub-standard wages and conditions. Although the most economically successful districts are typically characterised by high wages, high union density and institutionalised co-operation, no single organisational model may be said to prevail.[7]

Similar problems are raised by recent developments within the Third Italy itself. The canonical model of the Marshallian district took as its point of reference the experience of the 1970s, when small-firm growth was at its most rapid and Italian exports took off dramatically in world markets. Conditions in the 1980s, as Trigilia and Brusco in this book, and Ricoveri [see Ricoveri et al., 1991] each point out, have differed in a number of respects from those prevailing during the preceding decade: increased competition in international markets from both advanced and newly-industrialising countries; accelerated diffusion of new, microelectronic technologies; and a less favourable macroeconomic environment (fixed exchange rates within the European Monetary System, devaluation of the dollar since 1985, slower growth of world trade). The districts of the Third Italy have responded to these challenges with varying degrees of success: thus, for example, the metalworking districts of Modena and Bologna have maintained or even enhanced their competitive position, while the textile districts of Prato and Carpi have experienced greater difficulties in readjustment.[8]

In each of these cases, however, the 1980s have also seen significant changes in the structure of the districts themselves. One change is the growing intervention of local government in the collective provision of "real services" to the firms, a shift which marks for Brusco the transition to a qualitatively new model: the Industrial District Mark II [Brusco, 1990]. A second change emphasised particularly by Trigilia is the enhanced role of trade unions and employers' associations in negotiating the terms of flexibility and restructuring within the enterprise, a process in which local authorities

---

7.   For similar variations within the Third Italy, see Brutti and Ricoveri [1988].

8.   On Modena and Bologna, see Perulli [1989], Alaimo and Capecchi [1990], and Brutti and Ricoveri [1988, pp. 254-263]; on Prato and Carpi, see Trigilia [1989b], Bursi [1988] and Brutti and Ricoveri [1988, pp. 224-238, 272-285].

also play an important part [cf. Regalia, 1987]. A third change is the emergence of more formalised groups of firms, sometimes controlled by larger companies outside the region: it is now estimated that there are some 400 groups of firms in Prato, for example, while five large groups (one of them owned by de Benedetti) now control much of the automatic packaging machinery sector in Bologna.

Some observers have seen in this last development a fundamental transformation of the districts through a process of "concentration without centralisation" [Harrison, 1989; Bianchi, 1989], but such a conclusion seems decidedly premature. In Bologna, for example, the formerly independent packaging machinery companies appear to be devolving increased responsibility for production and design to external subcontractors within the district, at the same time as they are profiting from the common marketing and after-sales services provided by their parent groups [Alaimo and Capecchi, 1990]. Moreover, as is pointed out by Sengenberger and Pyke as well as Trigilia in this book, large companies themselves have been decentralising, devolving and disintegrating their operations into looser networks of semi-autonomous subsidiaries, franchisees, subcontractors, joint ventures and strategic alliances. Rather than signalling the imminent eclipse of the industrial district, therefore, the developments of the 1980s seem better understood as part of what Sabel calls the "double convergence" of large- and small-firm structures, as small firms in the districts build wider forms of common services often inspired by large-firm models, while large firms seek to recreate among their subsidiaries and subcontractors the collaborative relationships characteristic of the small-firm districts. This process of double convergence is giving rise in turn to an observable proliferation of hybrid forms of organisation which fall between the canonical models of the industrial district and the vertically-integrated corporation, as well as a multiplication of more explicit alliances and exchanges between firms of both types [Sabel, 1989b; Regini and Sabel, 1989].

Taken together, therefore, recent research underlines the diffusion and dynamism of industrial districts as an economic and social phenomenon at the same time as it highlights the limitations of the conceptual framework within which they are normally understood. Despite its many valuable insights, the canonical model of the Marshallian industrial district now appears too rigid, too exclusive and too closely bound up with the experience of a particular time and place to accommodate convincingly the diversity displayed by contemporary districts both inside and outside the Third Italy. One possible solution proposed by Brusco and taken up by Sengenberger and Pyke in this book is to distinguish between "advanced" and "backward" districts depending on the degree of correspondence to the stylised model (e.g. commercial and technological autonomy, inter-firm linkages, co-operation), with Carpi and Prato at one evolutionary extreme, the textile districts of Sardinia or Queens at another, and a variety of cases in between. But this proposal, helpful though it is in opening up the model of the industrial district to encompass a wider range of observable situations, remains problematic because of its teleological premise. For why should we expect "backward" districts to evolve towards a single model given the changes under way within the "advanced" districts themselves?

In the face of these difficulties, it seems necessary to move away from a "thick", "closed" model of the industrial district based on a stylised account of a particular national experience towards a "thin", "open" model capable of generating a variety of empirically observable forms. Such a model might take its point of departure from Marshall's original definition of the district as a geographically localised productive system based on an extended division of labour between small and medium-sized firms specialised in distinct phases of a common industrial sector. And it might also draw on Brusco's notion (Chapter 6 of this book) of intermediate or hybrid cases defined in terms of their distance from the ideal-type: e.g. the degree of localisation, the size distribution of productive units, and the extent of inter-firm linkages. But it would not assume that industrial districts so defined are necessarily innovative, flexible, consensual or otherwise successful, since stagnant or declining districts also display many of the same structural features, nor would it assume that as districts develop they will necessarily evolve towards the pure model. Put another way, industrial districts are neither necessary nor sufficient conditions for flexible specialisation, understood as the manufacture of a wide and changing array of customised products using flexible, general-purpose machinery and skilled, adaptable workers, but rather one possible organisational framework within which this form of production may flourish.[9]

For industrial districts to realise the economic and social possibilities envisaged by Marshall and documented by recent research, however, they also require a set of collective institutions to sustain the innovative recombination of resources by balancing co-operation and competition among productive units. For the decentralised structure of the districts characteristically poses two major institutional problems: the provision of common services which are beyond the capacity of individual firms to supply for themselves, such as training, research, market forecasting, credit and quality control; and the resolution of conflicts among local actors which threaten to displace competition from what Sengenberger and Pyke in this book term the "high road" of product and process innovation to what they call the "low road" of sweated wages and conditions. While these dilemmas are intrinsic to the general model of the industrial district, the institutional solutions may vary considerably in form, participants and effectiveness from one district to another, as we shall see in the next section. And it is this disjunction between common functional requirements and diverse institutional solutions which opens up a space for policy intervention in fostering the districts' development.

---

9. For a theoretical exposition of flexible specialisation in these terms, see Hirst and Zeitlin [1990].

lture and institutions

Among the most frequently noted features of successful industrial districts is the interpenetration of social relations and economic exchange. Firms in these districts typically combine competition and co-operation in ways that are difficult to reconcile with a pure market model of economic behaviour; trust relationships are widespread not only between legally separate enterprises but also between workers and employers; and it is hard to say in many cases where the local community stops and industry begins. Thus, experienced observers of the Third Italy speak of "a thickening of industrial and social inter-dependencies", "the social construction of the market" or the primacy of other-regarding "action" over self-regarding "work" in seeking to capture the social dimension of economic activity in industrial districts.[10] There can be little doubt that co-operation, trust and community have indeed been crucial to the economic success of industrial districts such as those of the Third Italy. But it is precisely these social features - so distant from prevailing conceptions of economic rationality - which lead many commentators to regard such districts as unique historical artefacts which can be found but not made. Only a common and exceptional culture, in this view, could account for the apparent harmony of individual preferences and motives observed in the industrial districts.[11]

Yet recent research on industrial districts, past and present, has cast increasing doubt on this view of trust relations as the product of a pre-existing cultural consensus. Just as studies of new districts outside Italy have identified a wider set of formative milieux, so too have they discovered that a common cultural heritage in a narrow sense is neither a necessary nor a sufficient condition for their emergence. In the Spanish case, for example, the success of the Mondragón co-operative is often attributed to the strong Basque identity of the region; but as Lauren Benton points out in Chapter 3, this Basque identity can be found in many towns which have not turned into successful industrial districts, while a quarter of all Mondragón members are not of Basque origin. Nor can such cultural inheritances account for the contrasting trajectories of other initially similar areas such as the declining shoe and thriving ceramics districts of Valencia. Elsewhere, too, the pre-existing bonds which can give rise to trust relations in industrial districts turn out to be exceedingly diverse: small enterpreneurs' common background as "alumni" of a particular large firm (plastics in Erie, Pennsylvania or wooden furniture in Salling, West Jutland); a common professional identity (high-tech engineers in Silicon Valley or Turin); craft pride (foundries and tool-and-die shops in Pennsylvania); as well as more obvious ties such as family origin, ethnicity, religion or political affiliation. Under the right

---

10. For these formulations see, respectively, Becattini [1990b]; Bagnasco [1988]; Piore [1990].

11. For a critical exposition of this view, see Sabel's contribution to this book.

circumstances, it would appear, almost any set of common experiences can form the basis of a common culture, since as Charles Sabel argues in Chapter 8 of this book, a minimum degree of trust in the sense of shared communicative expectations may be taken as a constitutive rather than an aberrant fact of social life.

A second finding which undercuts the view of trust as the product of a pre-existing cultural consensus has been the rediscovery of overt conflict within the histories of industrial districts themselves. Careful studies of any district, however successful, typically turn up evidence of recurrent tensions between different groups within the local economy: merchants and manufacturers; assemblers and subcontractors; employers and workers; craftsmen and labourers. In many districts which now represent themselves as co-operative and consensual, moreover, such tensions erupted into open and bitter conflicts at some point in the not-so-distant past: a frequently-cited case is that of Prato, where no collective bargaining agreements were signed between unions and employers' associations for more than a decade after a series of unsuccessful strikes in the late 1940s [Trigilia, 1989b]. Often, too, as Sabel notes, participants in these disputes subsequently disclaim any knowledge of these events, as if an act of collective amnesia were required for relations between social groups to be redefined in co-operative terms. Where a more individualistic ethos prevails, conversely, as in the West Jutland districts described by Peer Hull Kristensen (Chapter 5), entrepreneurs frequently deny the existence of co-operative relationships with other local firms even when these are readily observable in everyday practice.

Given these discoveries, trust relations in industrial districts seem more a consequence than a precondition of practical co-operation among local actors, and social consensus less an antithesis of conflict than an outcome of its successful resolution. These conclusions are reinforced by a third major finding of historical research on industrial districts: the dependence of their long-term success on institutional mechanisms for the resolution of collective conflicts. As Sabel aptly observes of districts such as Prato woollens, Sheffield cutlery, Oyonnax plastics and Swiss watches (and one could add a host of others, past and present), "whenever the parties to these conflicts regulate their disputes through arbitration boards or councils which police quality or set and monitor wage schedules, the districts flourish; when not, then not." (Chapter 8, p. 228). While the social consensus necessary for the smooth operation of a decentralised industrial structure may build on formative experiences in the past, it can only be sustained over the longer term through the creation of formal dispute-resolution procedures whose operation remains broadly satisfactory to all the parties concerned.[12]

Many of the contributions to this book likewise underline the crucial importance of institutions for the provision of collective services in

---

12. For fuller accounts of conflict resolution in industrial districts and a wider range of historical cases, see Sabel and Zeitlin [1985; forthcoming].

developing the innovative capabilities of contemporary industrial districts. Whereas informal co-operation among local firms such as exchange of tools, advice or subcontracts may have appeared sufficient during an initial phase of development, most successful districts have felt the need to create more formal collaborative institutions in order to compensate for the disadvantages of a fragmented industrial structure. While the institutionalisation of co-operation is most advanced in well-established districts such as those of Emilia-Romagna and Baden-Württemberg, promising initiatives in this direction can also be discerned in the emergent districts of West Jutland, Spain, Quebec and Pennsylvania, to cite only examples taken from this book.

As the chapters show, there are considerable variations among these districts in the precise range of services offered. Some services are primarily concerned with marketing, from information gathering and research (forecasting fashion trends, translating tenders, monitoring foreign technical standards) to co-operative sales initiatives (catalogues, exhibitions, stands at trade fairs, local trade marks and even jointly owned retail outlets or export companies). Others are more focused on production, from technological information and consultancy, subcontracting registers and quality control to co-operative R & D and joint operation of large-scale equipment such as CAD/CAM systems or silicon foundries. Still others deal with key inputs such as bank finance and credit, raw materials purchase and testing, or the training of skilled workers and technicians. Often, too, it is difficult to draw a line between the provision of such services and regulation of competition among local firms: thus collective marketing arrangements, as Brusco notes, can only work well where firms specialise on complementary products, as they do by formal agreement in Baden-Württemberg and West Jutland; while quality control certification and local trade marks also serve as a means of preventing companies from cutting costs by adulterating raw materials or finished goods. In this way, institutions for the provision of collective services join hands with those for collective wage setting and dispute resolution: both encourage small firms to compete through continuous innovation and upgrading rather than through squeezing labour and reducing product quality.

Just as the range of services available varies widely from district to district, so too does the institutional framework within which they are produced. Sometimes collective services are provided directly by local government; sometimes by an independent agency run as a public/private partnership; sometimes by artisan, trade or employers' associations; sometimes by co-operative enterprises or consortia of individual firms; and sometimes by ad hoc teams of business people, public officials, trade unionists, bankers and educators. The key to their success, as Sabel remarks, is that the relevant local actors come to constitute a more or less formal policy network within which effective solutions to common problems can be jointly discovered. While no universal model of organisation can be therefore drawn from the various chapters, two generalisations do emerge about the institutional requirements for the formalisation of co-operation within industrial districts.

The first requirement concerns the autonomy of local government. Only local authorities are in a position to acquire the detailed knowledge of the local economy and broker the social consensus among local actors needed for the effective provision of collective services, as in the cases of Baden-Württemberg or Emilia-Romagna. Where the financial and policy independence of local authorities are sapped by central government controls, as in Mrs. Thatcher's Britain, industrial districts are unlikely to flourish and promising experiments in collective service provision may wither on the vine.[13] Conversely, where political decentralisation has enhanced the autonomy and powers of regional government, as Benton shows for Spain during the 1980s, the reorientation of industrial policy towards local interests and objectives may give a crucial boost to the development of industrial districts.

The second requirement concerns the role of collective actors. Collective services, as Trigilia observes, often take the form of public goods to whose creation individual firms or workers may be reluctant to contribute however great their advantages for the regional economy as a whole. Hence the production of these collective services requires strong local interest organisations such as business associations and trade unions which are capable of internalising both their costs and their benefits. Such organisations are equally necessary for the operation of collective wage determination and dispute resolution systems whose importance in sustaining social consensus and productive flexibility we have repeatedly underlined. Where business associations and trade unions are weakly organised, lack territorial autonomy or are dominated by the interests of larger firms, as to varying degrees in southern Italy, the industrial periphery of Madrid, West Jutland and much of the United States, co-operation among local actors within emergent industrial districts is more difficult to institutionalise than where the opposite conditions prevail, as in Emilia-Romagna, Baden-Württemberg and Barcelona. At the same time, however, successful experiments in co-operation and consensus-formation among local actors may also stimulate the reinforcement of weak interest-group organisations, as in the Pennsylvania manufacturing districts discussed by Sabel.

IV. Politics and policies

What role, then, can public policy play in sustaining and diffusing dynamic industrial districts? The contributions to this book suggest two sets of conclusions, one negative and the other positive. The negative conclusions concern the inappropriateness of two conventional policy instruments for

---

13.   For a more extensive discussion of the British case, see Hirst and Zeitlin [1989a; 1989b]; Crouch and Marquand [1989].

promoting regional economic development: strategic industrial policy on the left, and free-market deregulation on the right.[14] Strategic industrial policies assume that the state can promote development by co-ordinating the investment policies of large firms and concentrating resources on advanced sectors and technologies. But the various chapters of this book suggest that "traditional" industries such as clothing and furniture may form the basis of dynamic regional economies just as much as "modern" ones such as electronics; that regional development is better promoted by building on existing specialisations rather than by seeking to transplant wholly new productive activities; that collective services aimed at a group of firms are more effective in diffusing innovation than strategic interventions targeted on a single company; and that central state officials often lack the local knowledge needed to assess the policy requirements of established or emergent industrial districts.

Deregulation policies assume that economic development can be promoted by encouraging competition and removing institutional constraints on the free working of product, labour and capital markets. Yet the articles in this book suggest that the collective inputs and services on which industrial districts depend are public goods which will not be provided by market mechanisms alone; that institutional mechanisms of wage setting and conflict resolution are vital for sustaining trust and co-operation among economic actors; and that unrestrained competition may undermine the productive flexibility and innovative capabilities of industrial districts (as illustrated most graphically by the case of fraudulent bankruptcies in Spain - see Chapter 3).

On the positive side, the texts suggest that policy-makers can stimulate the development of industrial districts by simultaneously fostering the creation of the institutional infrastructure and the collective actors required for their sustained reproduction. Thus, political authorities can upgrade the local industrial structure and encourage co-operation among economic actors by supporting the provision of collective services such as marketing, research, technological consultancy, low-cost credit, and training, as well as the construction of collective mechanisms for wage-setting, dispute resolution and quality control. At the same time, however, local and regional governments need to orchestrate the formation of broad policy networks within which a variety of relevant actors can collaborate in solving common problems - what Paul Hirst and I have elsewhere termed an "industrial public sphere" [Hirst and Zeitlin, 1989a] - while also seeking to reinforce the capacity of business associations, trade unions and other interest organisations to internalise the costs and benefits of collective services and regulatory mechanisms.

These double imperatives mean that the crucial task for policy-makers in promoting industrial districts is that of social and political leadership. Establishing a dialogue and building a consensus among local

---

14.   For an elaboration of these criticisms, see Hirst and Zeitlin [1990].

interests becomes inseparable from the process of analysing the weaknesses of the regional economy and constructing effective institutional solutions. Rather than drawing up blueprints for collective services themselves, therefore, public authorities should devise programmes which encourage local actors to co-operate in defining their own needs, as in the case of the Pennsylvania Manufacturing Innovation Networks described by Sabel in Chapter 8. The industrial policy-maker's role, in this view, is less similar to that of a doctor, to use Brusco's image in Chapter 6, who prescribes an appropriate medicine after examining the patient's symptoms, than to that of a psychoanalyst, who assists the patient to cure him or herself through an extended process of self-examination and discussion. And just as the modern psychoanalyst is continually driven to reassess the therapeutic role as a result of his or her interaction with the patient,[15] so too the industrial policy-maker must be prepared to reconsider the role of government in the provision of public services as a result of the dialogue among local actors, as the Pennsylvania experiment once again suggests.

A final set of policy issues raised by the chapters of this book concerns the relationship between local, regional and national institutions. Industrial districts, as we have repeatedly stressed, require strong and autonomous local institutions which can formulate effective policies tailored to local needs. These requirements are most evident in the case of local government and industrial policy. But as a number of the authors argue, promoting industrial districts also demands a reorientation of national policies in other spheres such as social welfare, taxation and vocational education. In Denmark, for example, as Kristensen observes, the social security system long discriminated against patterns of self-employment and occupational mobility characteristic of the West Jutland districts, vocational education has been geared to training semi-skilled workers for large firms, and taxation rules favour large-scale limited companies over small privately-owned enterprises. In Italy, similarly, Brutti and Ricoveri advocate a far-reaching reform of the contributory basis of the social security system from wages to value-added in order to redistribute the tax burden between labour and capital-intensive activities as well as between small and large firms [Brutti and Ricoveri, 1988, pp. 104-113].

But as several chapters also emphasise, the reorientation of state policies to suit the needs of industrial districts is not simply a matter of decentralisation. Thus, as Trigilia suggests, for many problems such as technical education, applied research, environmental protection or transportation and communications infrastructure, a reinforcement of regional authorities is also necessary in order to co-ordinate local initiatives, avoid duplication and overcome constraints of scale. And as Brutti and Ricoveri [1988] argue, the devolution of responsibilities to local and regional

---

15.   For a discussion of the changing understanding among psychoanalysts since Freud of "countertransference" (the analyst's reactions to the patient), see Samuels [1989, pp. 144-150].

governments - whether in the sphere of industrial policy or social welfare - needs to be anchored in a new national framework of legislative guidance and support. Hence promoting industrial districts does not mean the dissolution of national policy-making, but rather a new distribution of tasks between different levels of government - local, regional, national and even supranational, as in the case of the European Community.[16]

Local and regional autonomy, moreover, is no less important for interest-group organisations such as trade unions and employers' associations than it is for government. Highly centralised bargaining procedures can also constrain local experimentation with new collective agreements adapted to the employment patterns of industrial districts, as Kristensen shows in this volume in the case of work-time restructuring in Denmark, or Benton in Chapter 3 observes of national tripartite pacts in Spain. Interest-group organisations therefore need to strengthen their negotiating capacities at the local and regional levels, not only in relation to one another but also to government authorities. Here, too, as both Trigilia in this book and Ricoveri [1991] emphasise, what is at issue is not the abandonment of central negotiations, but rather the development of new forms of articulation between bargaining at different levels from the individual firm through the district, region and industrial sector to the national economy as a whole. Hence for trade unions and employers' associations, as for the state, promoting industrial districts involves not only a reorientation of existing policies but also a restructuring of their own organisations and practices.

References

Alaimo, A.; Capecchi, V. 1990. "Un caso di specializzazione flessibile: l'industria delle macchine automatiche a Bologna (1920-1990)", Unpublished paper forthcoming in Annale. Istituto per la storia della resistenza dell'Emilia-Romagna.

Amin, A.; Robins K. 1990. "Industrial districts and regional development: Limits and possibilities," in Pyke, F. et al. (eds.), pp. 185-219.

Bagnasco, A. 1988. *La construzione sociale del mercato*, Bologna, Il Mulino.

Becattini, G. 1978. "The development of light industry in Tuscany', in *Economic Notes*, No. 5-6, pp. 107-23.

---. (ed.) 1987. *Mercato e forze locali*, Bologna, Il Mulino.

---. 1989. "Sectors and/or districts: Some remarks on the conceptual foundations of industrial economics," in Goodman, E. et al. (eds.): *Small firms and industrial districts in Italy*, pp. 123-35.

---. 1990a. "The Marshallian industrial district as a socio-economic notion," in Pyke, F. et al. (eds.): *Industrial districts and inter-firm co-operation in Italy*, pp. 37-51.

16. For a more general discussion of the possible relationship between industrial districts and the national welfare state, see Sabel [1989a, pp. 53-59; 1989b].

---. 1990b. "Chapter 4. Italy", in Sengenberger, W. et al. (eds.): *The re-emergence of small enterprises. Industrial restructuring in industrialised countries*, Geneva, International Institute for Labour Studies.

Bellandi, M. 1989. "The industrial district in Marshall," in Goodman, E. et al. (eds.): *Small firms and industrial districts in Italy*, pp. 136-52.

Bianchi, P. 1989. "Riorganizzazione e crescita esterna delle imprese italiane," in Regini, M; Sabel, C.F. (eds.): *Strategie di riaggiustimento industriale*, pp. 335-366.

Brusco, S. 1982. "The Emilian model: Productive decentralization and social integration", in *Cambridge Journal of Economics*, Vol. 6, No. 2, pp. 167-84.

---. 1986. "Small firms and industrial districts: The experience of Italy", in Keeble, D.; Warner, E. (eds.): *New firms and regional development in Europe*, London, Croom Helm, pp. 184-202.

---. 1989. *Piccole imprese e distretti industriali*, Turin, Rosenberg & Sellier.

---. 1990. "The idea of the industrial district: Its genesis," in Pyke, F. et al. (eds.): *Industrial districts and inter-firm co-operation in Italy*, pp. 10-19.

Brutti, P.; Ricoveri, G. (eds.), 1988. *La quarta Italia: Il lavoro e la politica industriale nei distretti e nelle aree integrate in Italia*, Rome, Ediesse.

Bursi, T. 1988. *Piccola e media impresa e politiche di adattamento: Il distretto della maglieria di Carpi*, Milan, F. Angeli.

Courault, B.; Romani, C. 1989. "La flexibilité locale à l'italienne", in *La lettre d'information du CEE*, No. 14, Noisy-le-Grand, Centre d'Etudes de l'Emploi.

Crouch, C.; Marquand, D. (eds.) 1989. *The new centralism: Britain out of step in Europe?*, Oxford, Blackwell.

Ganne, B. 1990. *Industrialisation diffuse et systèmes industriels localisés: Essai de bibliographie critique du cas français*, Geneva, International Institute for Labour Studies, Bibliography Series, No. 14.

Goodman, E.; Bamford, J. with Saynor, P. (eds.) 1989. *Small firms and industrial districts in Italy*, London, Routledge.

Harrison, B. 1989. "Concentration without centralization: The changing morphology of the small firm industrial districts of the Third Italy", Paper presented to the International Symposium on Local Employment, National Institute of Employment and Vocational Research, Tokyo, Japan, 12-14 September.

Hirst, P.; Zeitlin, J. (eds.) 1989a. *Reversing industrial decline? Industrial structure and policy in Britain and her competitors*, Oxford, Berg.

---. 1989b. "Flexible specialisation and the competitive failure of UK manufacturing", in *Political Quarterly*, Vol. 60, No. 2, pp. 164-78.

---. 1990. "Flexible specialization versus Post-Fordism: Theory, Evidence and Policy Implications," Working Paper, Birkbeck Centre for Public Policy.

Marshall, A. 1922. *Principles of economics*, 8th ed., London, Macmillan (1st ed. 1890).

---. 1927. *Industry and trade*, 4th ed., London, Macmillan, (1st ed., 1919).

---. 1975. *The early economic writings of Alfred Marshall, 1867-1890*, Vol. 2, ed. J.K. Whitaker, London, Macmillan.

Messori, M. 1986. "Sistemi d'imprese e sviluppo meridionale: Un confronto fra due aree industriali", in *Stato e Mercato*, No. 18.

Perulli, P. 1989. "Il distretto industriale di Modena," in Regini, M.; Sabel, C.F. (eds.): *Strategie di riaggiustimento industriale*, pp. 249-82.

Piore, M.J. 1990. "Work, labour and action: Work experience in a system of flexible specialisation," in Pyke, F. et al., (eds.): *Industrial districts and inter-firm co-operation in Italy*, pp. 52-74.

Pyke, F. et al. (eds.). 1990. *Industrial districts and inter-firm co-operation in Italy*, Geneva, International Institute for Labour Studies.

Regini, M.; Sabel, C.F. (eds.), 1989. *Strategie di riaggiustimento industriale*, Bologna, Il Mulino.

Regalia, I. 1987. "Non piu apprendisti stregoni? Sindacati e istituzioni in periferia", in *Stato e Mercato*, No. 19, pp. 43-71.

Ricoveri, G. et al. 1991. "Labour and social conditions in Italian industrial districts", in *Labour and Society*, Vol. 16, No. 1.

Sabel, C.F. 1989a. "Flexible specialisation and the re-emergence of regional economies," in Hirst, P.; Zeitlin, J. (eds.): *Reversing industrial decline? Industrial structure and policy in Britain and her competitors*, pp. 17-70.

---. 1989b. "Equity and efficiency in a federal welfare state", Paper presented to the Nordic Working Group on the New Welfare State, Copenhagen, 8 August.

Sabel, C.F.; Zeitlin, J. 1985. "Historical alternatives to mass production: Politics, markets and technology in nineteenth-century industrialization", in *Past and Present*, No. 108, pp. 133-76.

---. (eds.), forthcoming. *Worlds of possibility: Flexibility and mass production in western industrialization*.

Samuels, A. 1989. *The plural psyche*, London, Routledge.

Sengenberger, W. et al. (eds.) 1990. *The re-emergence of small enterprises. Industrial restructuring in industrialised countries*, Geneva, International Institute for Labour Studies.

Sforzi, F. 1989. "The geography of industrial districts in Italy," in Goodman, E. et al., (eds.): *Small firms and industrial districts in Italy*, pp. 153-65.

---. 1990. "The quantitative importance of Marshallian industrial districts in the Italian economy," in Pyke, F. et al., (eds.): *Industrial districts and inter-firm co-operation in Italy*, pp. 75-107.

Trigilia, C. 1986. *Grandi partiti e piccole imprese*, Bologna, Il Mulino.

---. 1989a. "Small-firm development and political subcultures in Italy," in Goodman, E. et al., (eds.): *Small firms and industrial districts in Italy*, pp. 174-97.

---. 1989b. "Il distretto industriale di Prato," in Regini, M.; Sabel, C.F. (eds.): *Strategie di riaggiustimento industriale*, pp. 283-334.

---. 1990. "Work and politics in the Third Italy's industrial districts," in Pyke, F. et al., (eds.): *Industrial districts and inter-firm co-operation in Italy*, pp. 160-84.

Zeitlin, J. (ed.) 1989. "Local industrial strategies," special issue of *Economy and Society*, Vol. 18, No. 4.

Imprimé en Suisse
en janvier 1992